Story & Art by
Kazune Kawahara

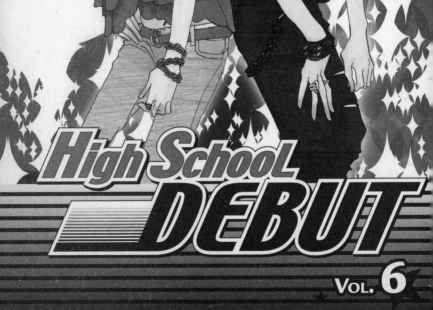

High School DEBUT

VOL. **6**

High School DEBUT

★ ★ Contents

Story Thus Far...

High school freshman Haruna used to spend all her time playing softball in junior high, but now she wants to give her all to finding true love instead! While her "love coach" Yoh is training her on how to be popular with guys, the two of them start dating.

Everything is going great until Haruna's old rival, Leona, turns up. Leona was an ace batter in middle school but could never get over the fact that she couldn't hit Haruna's pitches. Her plans to break up Yoh and Haruna's relationship backfire and only succeed in bringing the couple closer together. To make things worse, Leona discovers that it was actually Mami's skill that was making her lose.

Leona points out that Mami is the only one among Haruna's friends without a boyfriend, so Haruna plots to set Mami up with Asaoka. Haruna starts spending a lot of time with Asaoka, but Yoh misunderstands and gets jealous! They get into a real big fight, but Asaoka finds a way to bring them back together. That's not the end of the trouble for our heroine though...

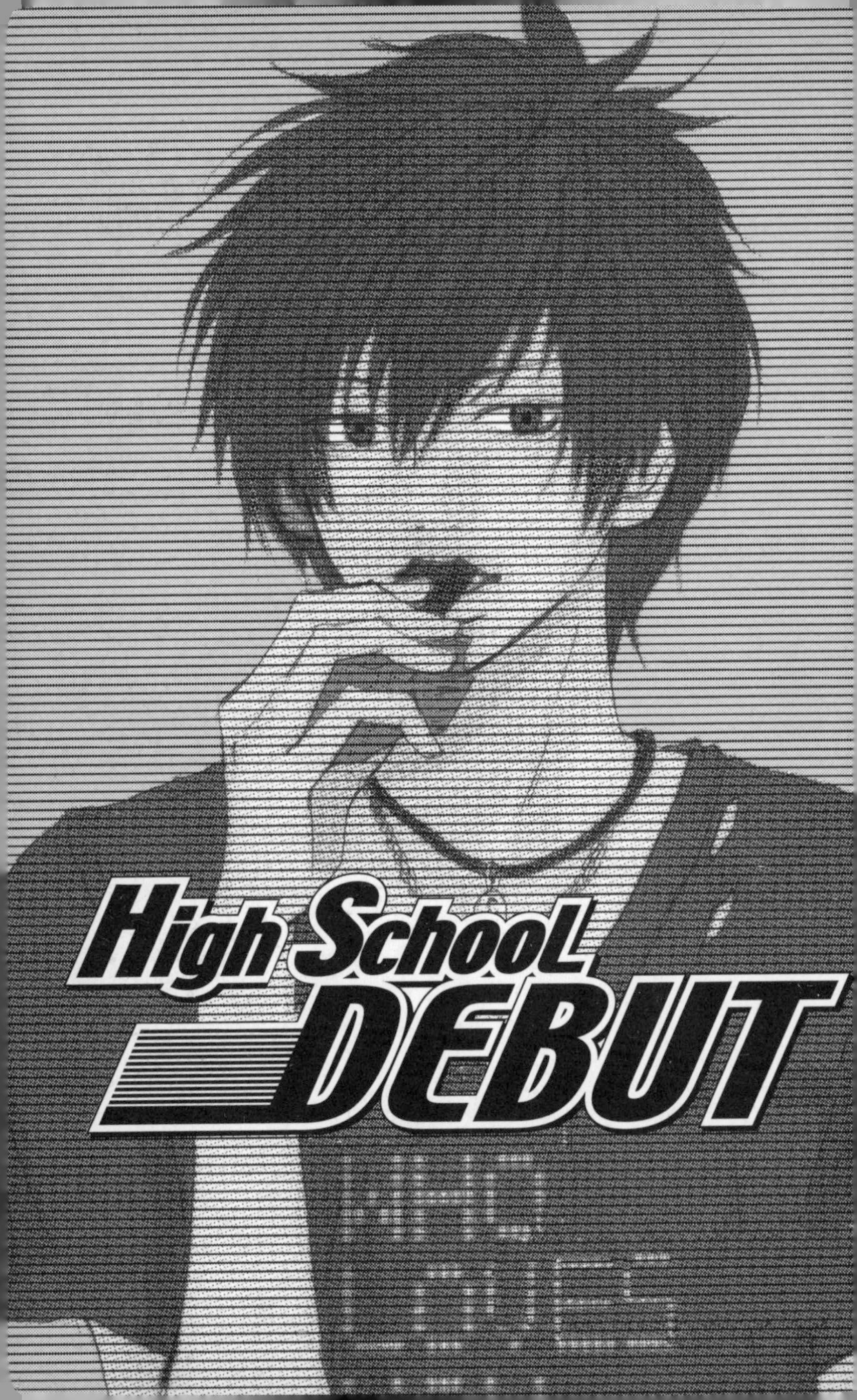
High School
DEBUT

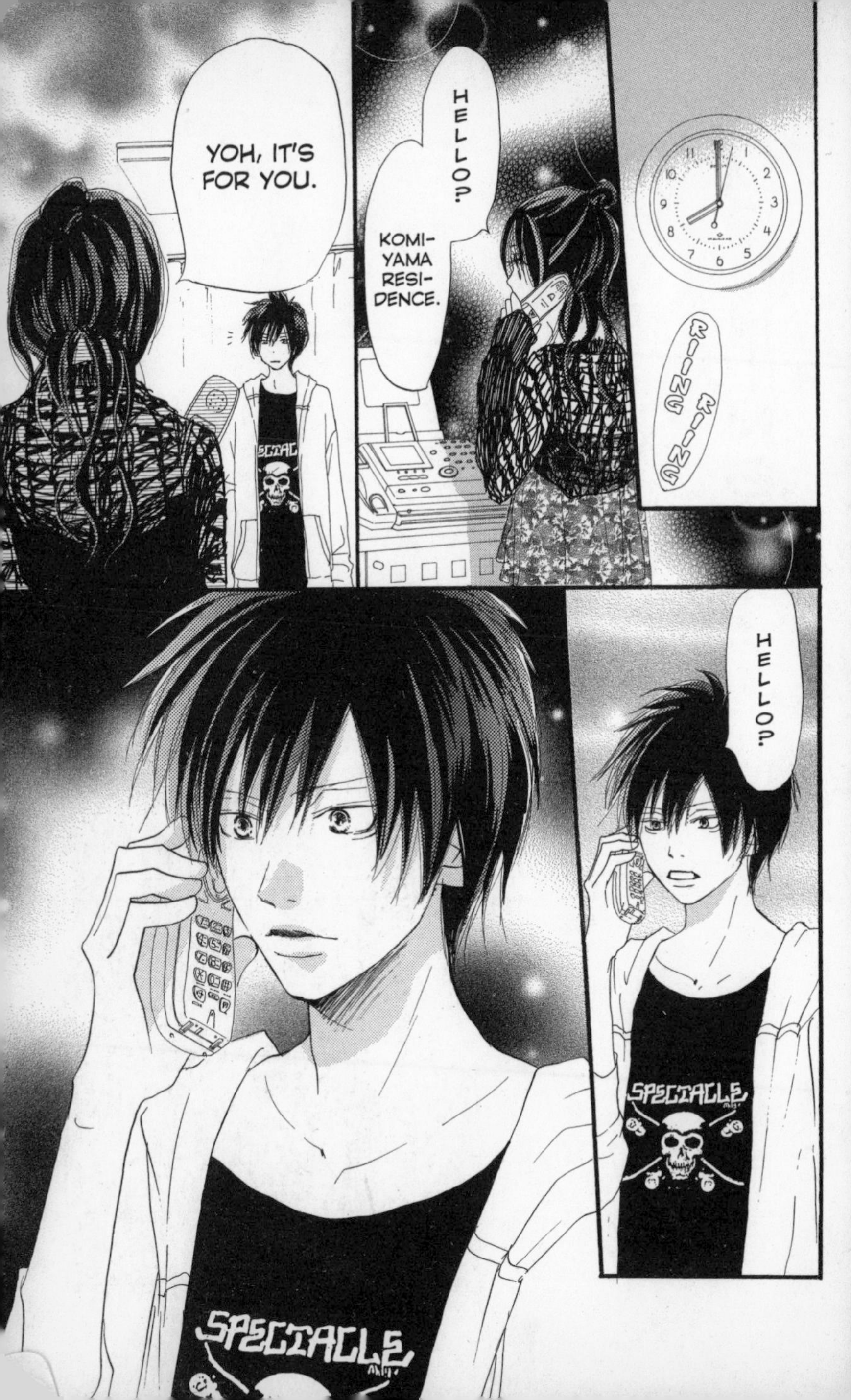
RIIING RIIING
HELLO?
KOMIYAMA RESIDENCE.
YOH, IT'S FOR YOU.
HELLO?

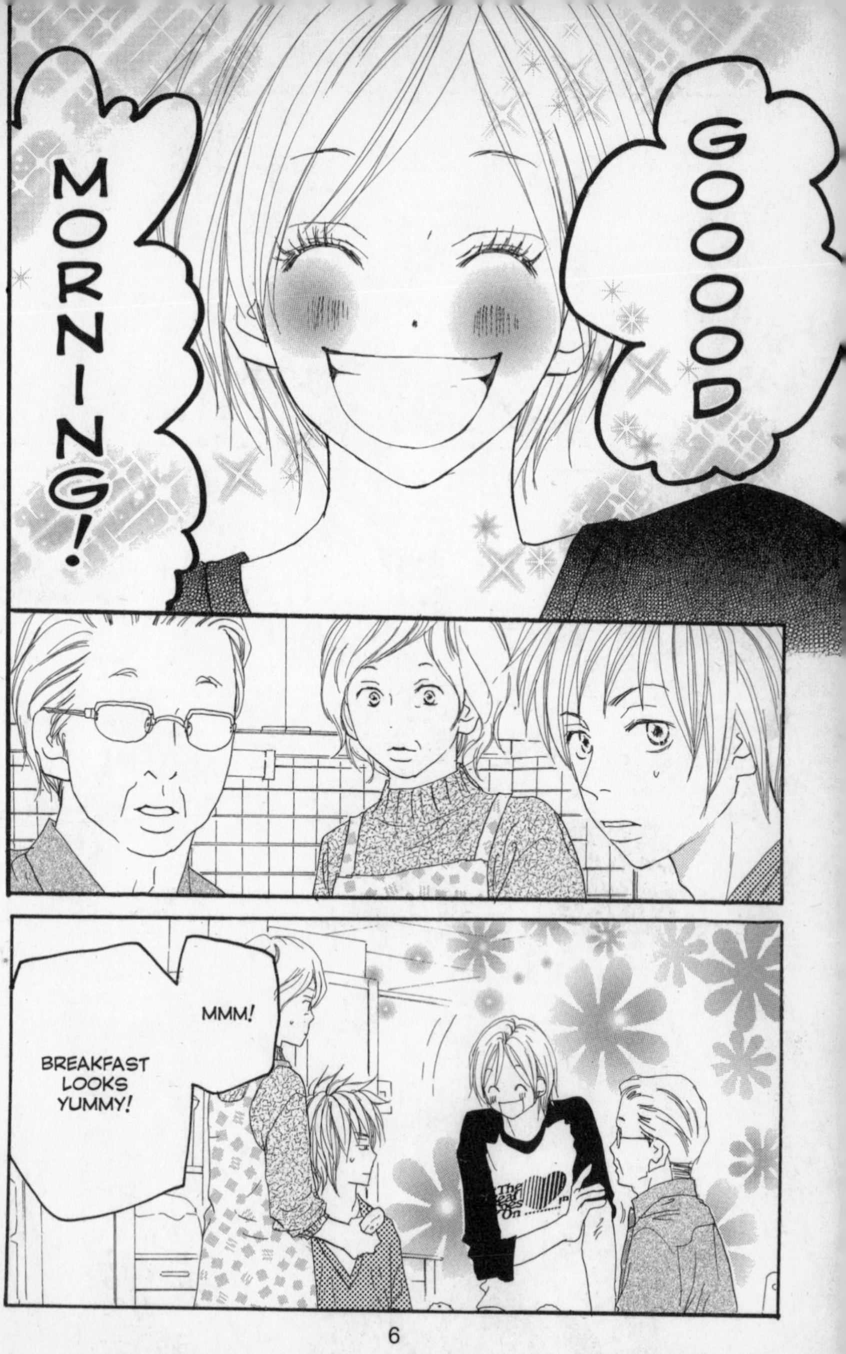
GOOOOD
MORNING!
MMM!
BREAKFAST LOOKS YUMMY!

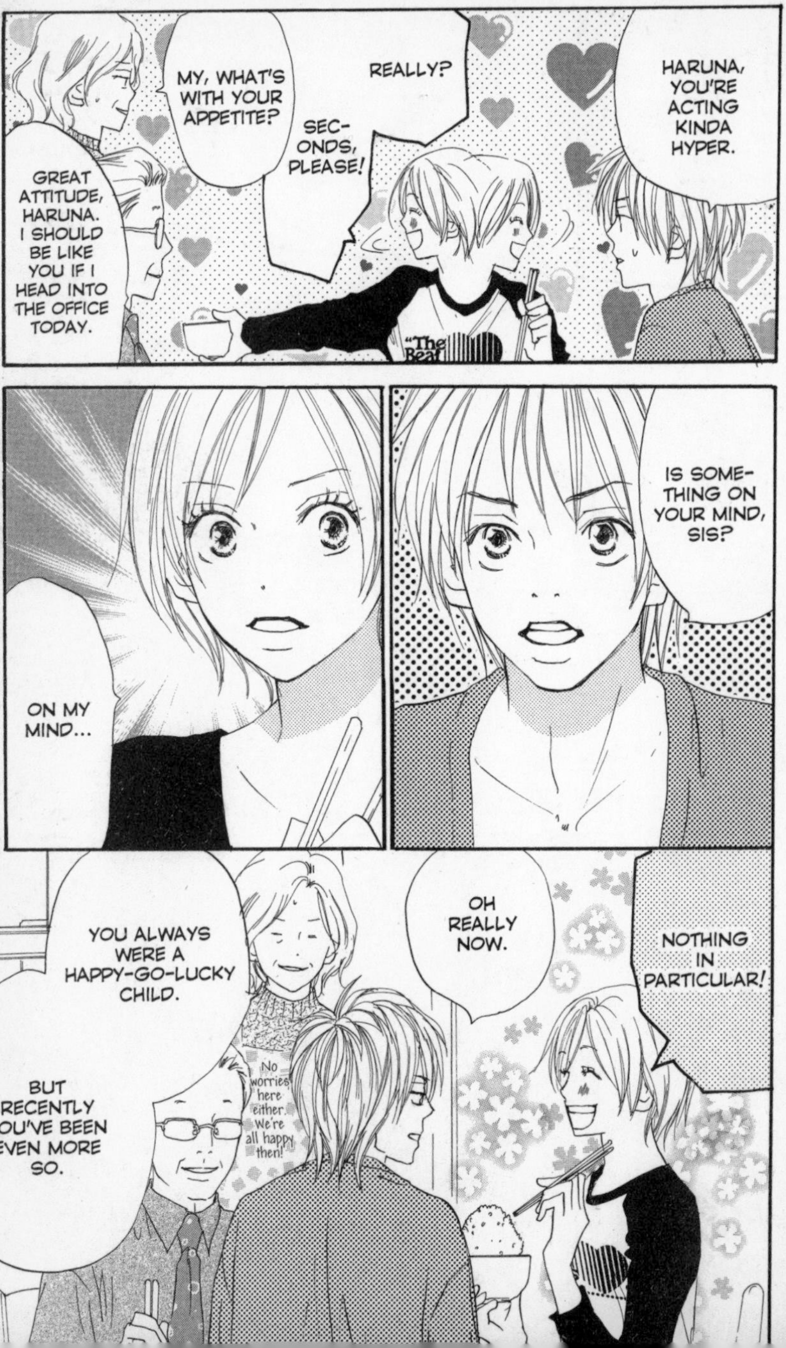
HARUNA, YOU'RE ACTING KINDA HYPER.
REALLY?
SEC-ONDS, PLEASE!
MY, WHAT'S WITH YOUR APPETITE?
GREAT ATTITUDE, HARUNA. I SHOULD BE LIKE YOU IF I HEAD INTO THE OFFICE TODAY.
IS SOME-THING ON YOUR MIND, SIS?
ON MY MIND...
NOTHING IN PARTICULAR!
OH REALLY NOW.
YOU ALWAYS WERE A HAPPY-GO-LUCKY CHILD.
No worries here either. We're all happy then!
BUT RECENTLY YOU'VE BEEN EVEN MORE SO.

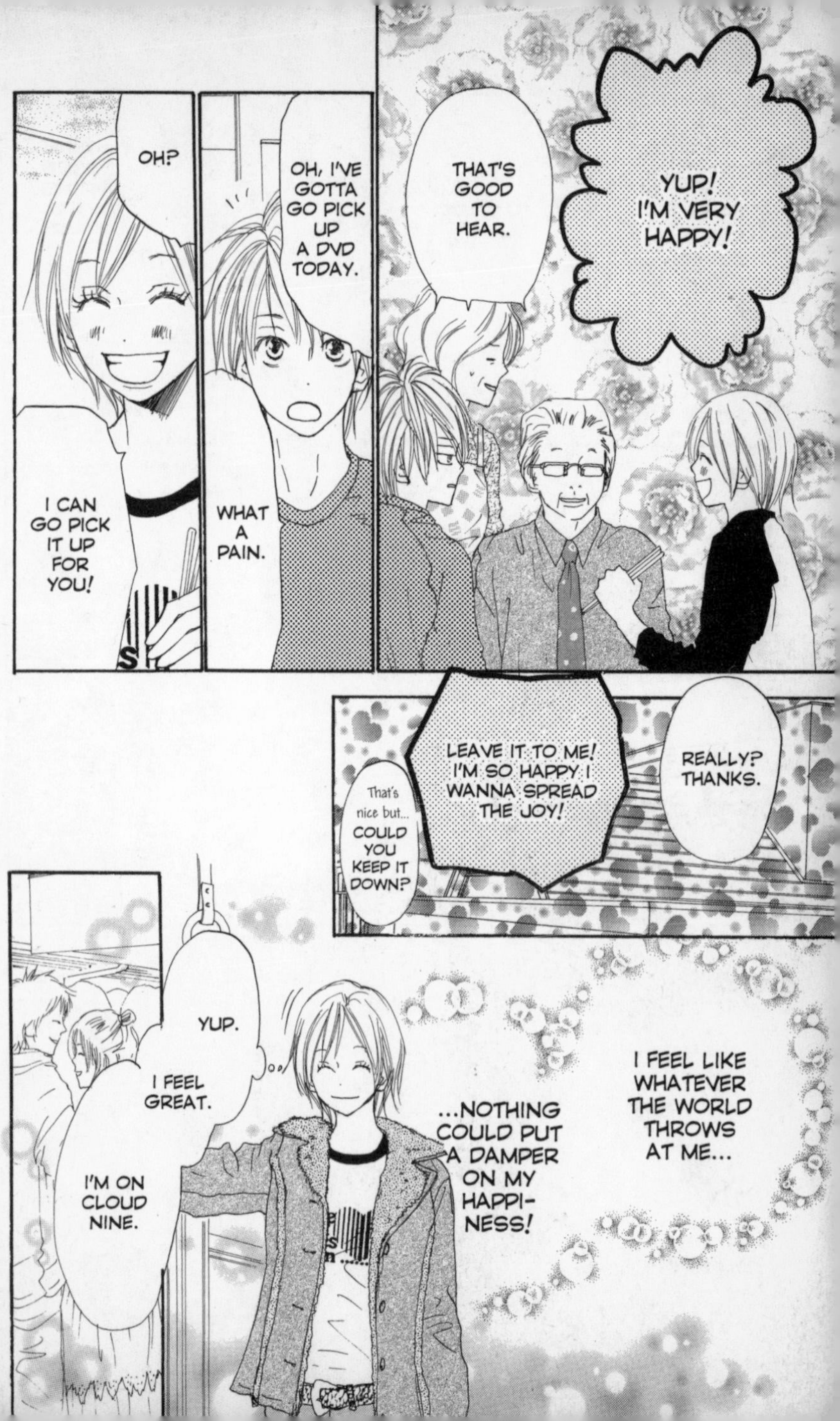
YUP! I'M VERY HAPPY!
THAT'S GOOD TO HEAR.
OH, I'VE GOTTA GO PICK UP A DVD TODAY.
WHAT A PAIN.
OH?
I CAN GO PICK IT UP FOR YOU!
REALLY? THANKS.
LEAVE IT TO ME! I'M SO HAPPY I WANNA SPREAD THE JOY!
That's nice but... COULD YOU KEEP IT DOWN?
I FEEL LIKE WHATEVER THE WORLD THROWS AT ME...
...NOTHING COULD PUT A DAMPER ON MY HAPPI-NESS!
YUP.
I FEEL GREAT.
I'M ON CLOUD NINE.

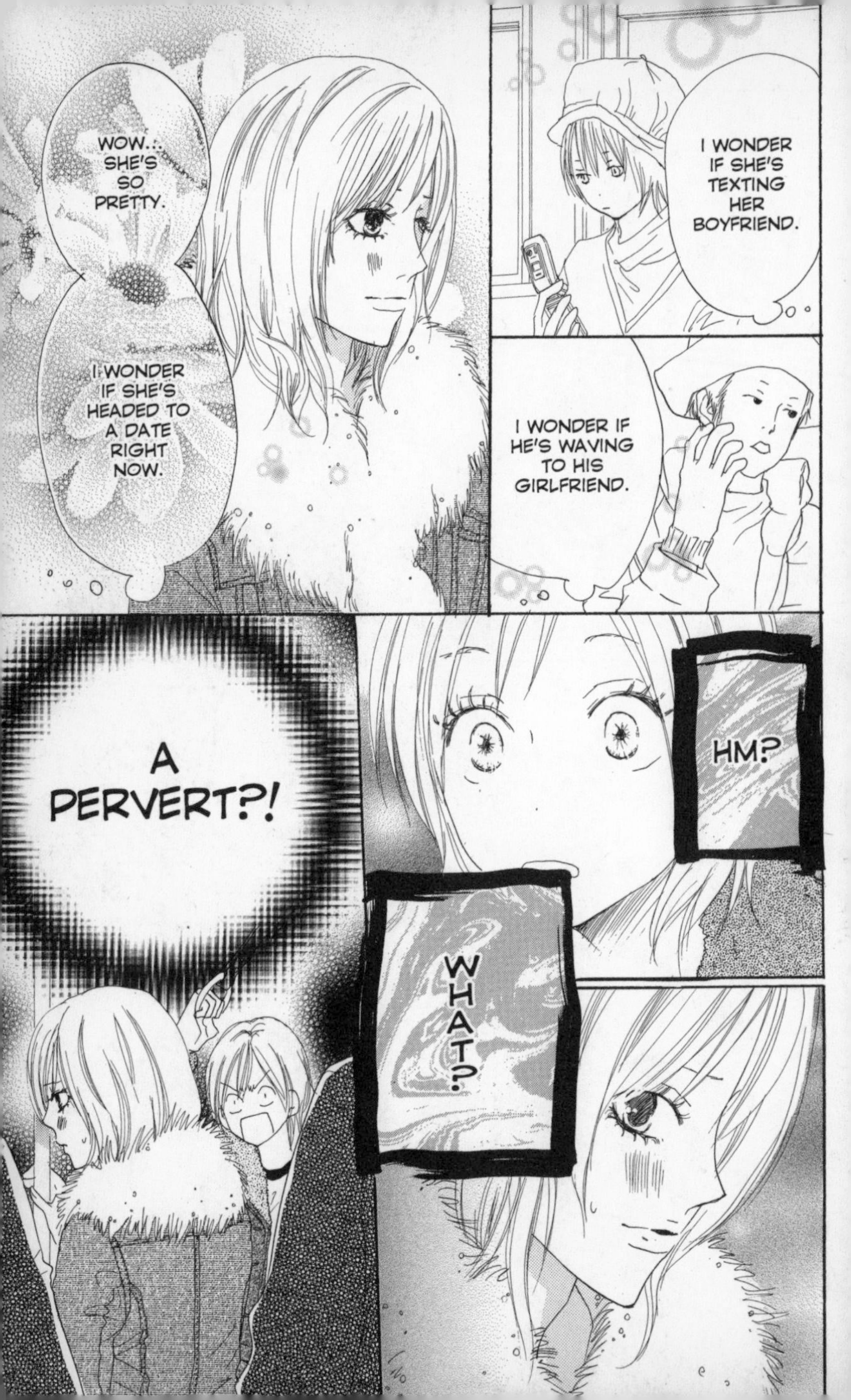
I WONDER IF SHE'S TEXTING HER BOYFRIEND.
I WONDER IF HE'S WAVING TO HIS GIRLFRIEND.
WOW... SHE'S SO PRETTY.
I WONDER IF SHE'S HEADED TO A DATE RIGHT NOW.
HM?
WHAT?
A PERVERT?!

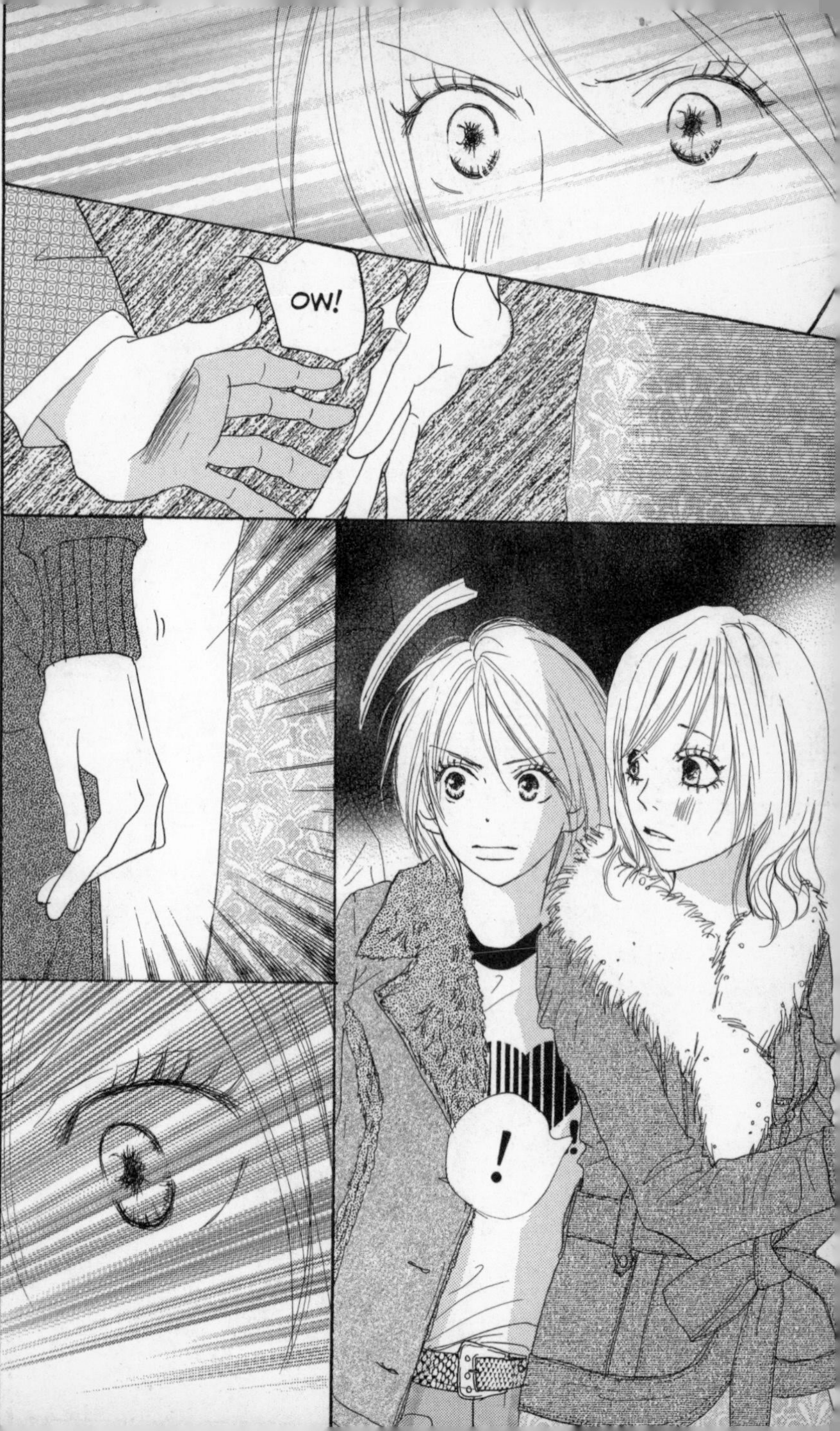
OW!
!

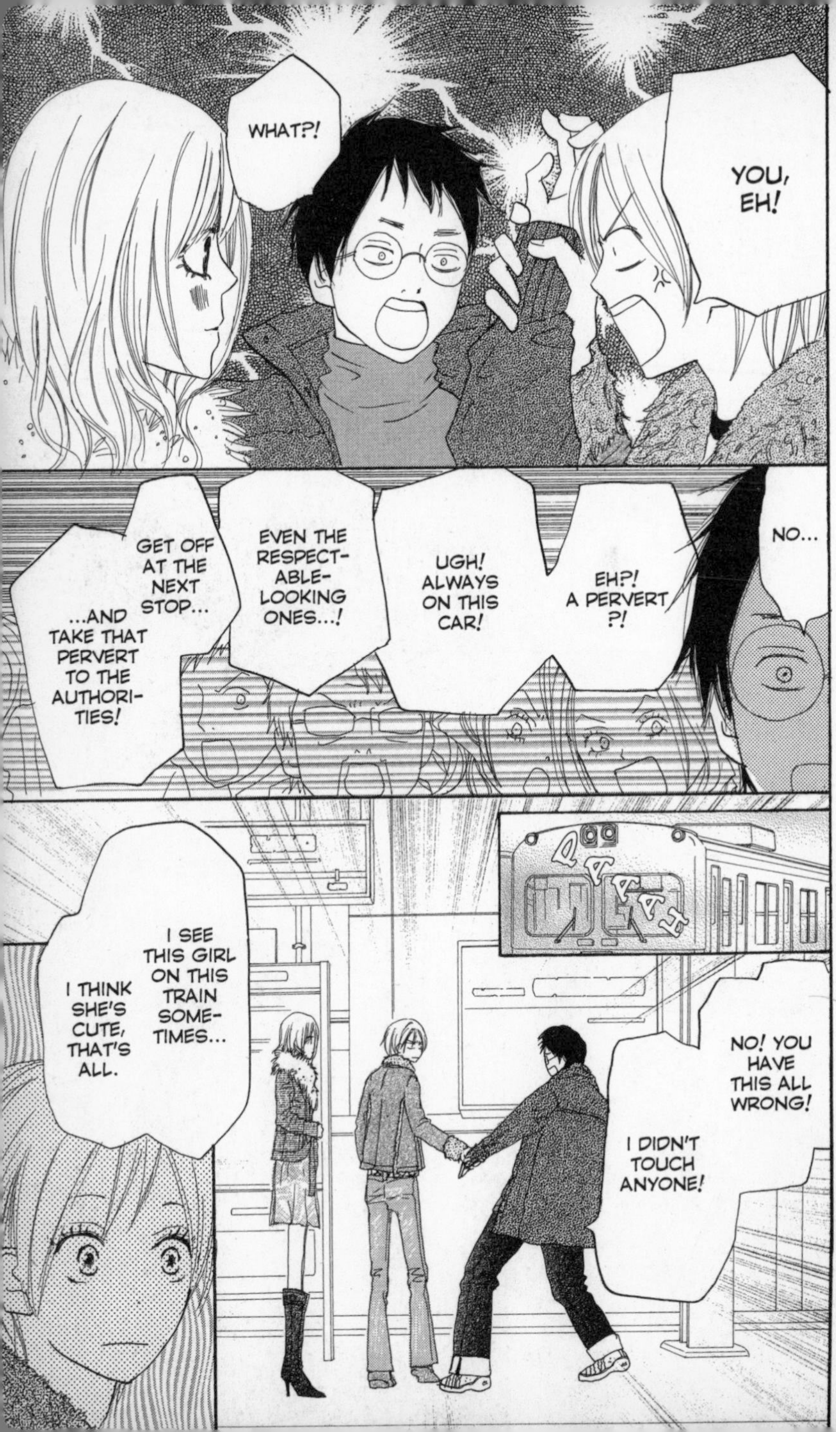
YOU, EH!
WHAT?!
NO...
EH?! A PERVERT ?!
UGH! ALWAYS ON THIS CAR!
EVEN THE RESPECT-ABLE-LOOKING ONES...!
GET OFF AT THE NEXT STOP...
...AND TAKE THAT PERVERT TO THE AUTHORITIES!
NO! YOU HAVE THIS ALL WRONG!
I DIDN'T TOUCH ANYONE!
I SEE THIS GIRL ON THIS TRAIN SOME-TIMES...
I THINK SHE'S CUTE, THAT'S ALL.

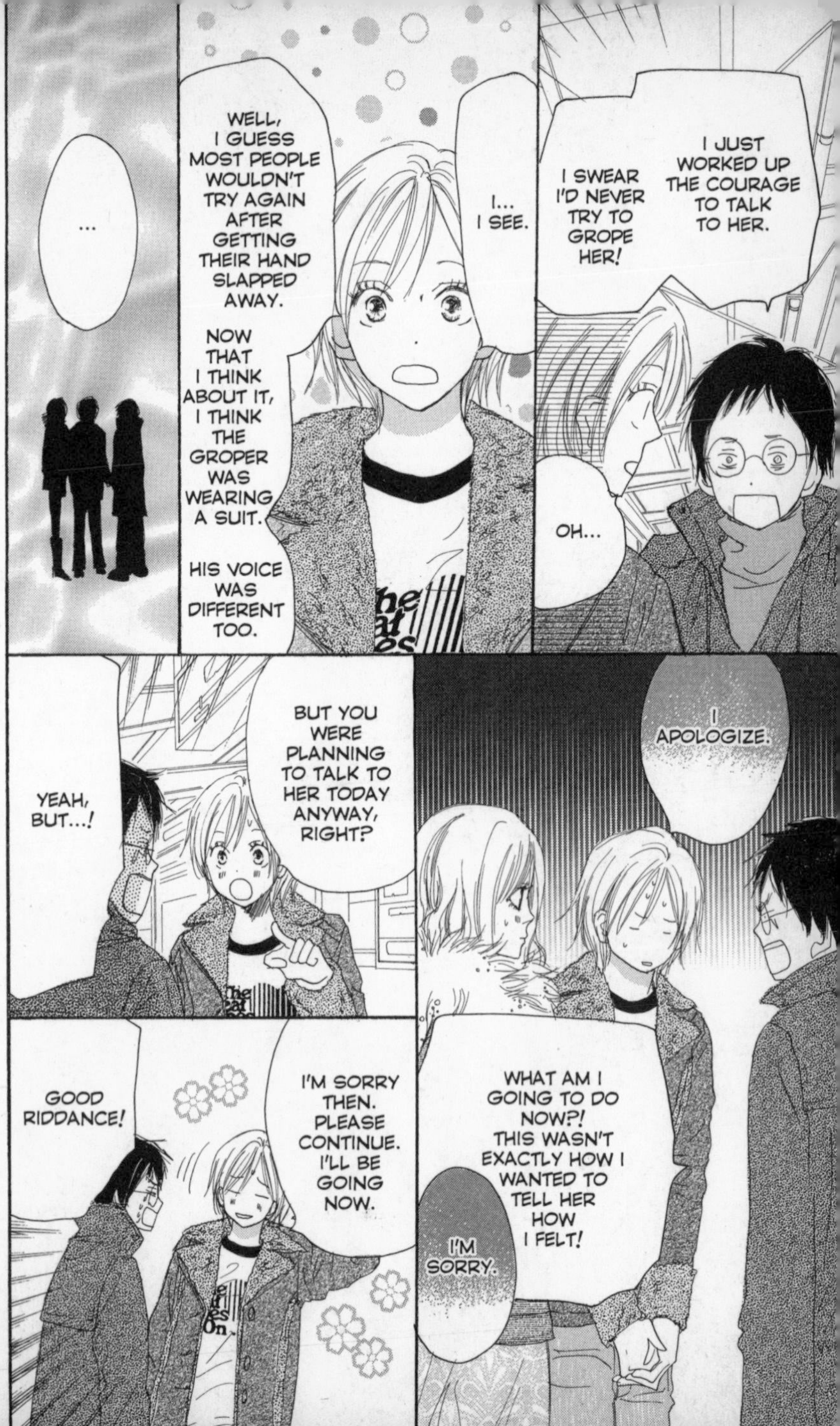
I JUST WORKED UP THE COURAGE TO TALK TO HER.
I SWEAR I'D NEVER TRY TO GROPE HER!
OH...
I... I SEE.
WELL, I GUESS MOST PEOPLE WOULDN'T TRY AGAIN AFTER GETTING THEIR HAND SLAPPED AWAY.
NOW THAT I THINK ABOUT IT, I THINK THE GROPER WAS WEARING A SUIT.
HIS VOICE WAS DIFFERENT TOO.
...
I APOLOGIZE.
BUT YOU WERE PLANNING TO TALK TO HER TODAY ANYWAY, RIGHT?
YEAH, BUT...!
WHAT AM I GOING TO DO NOW?! THIS WASN'T EXACTLY HOW I WANTED TO TELL HER HOW I FELT!
I'M SORRY.
I'M SORRY THEN. PLEASE CONTINUE. I'LL BE GOING NOW.
GOOD RIDDANCE!

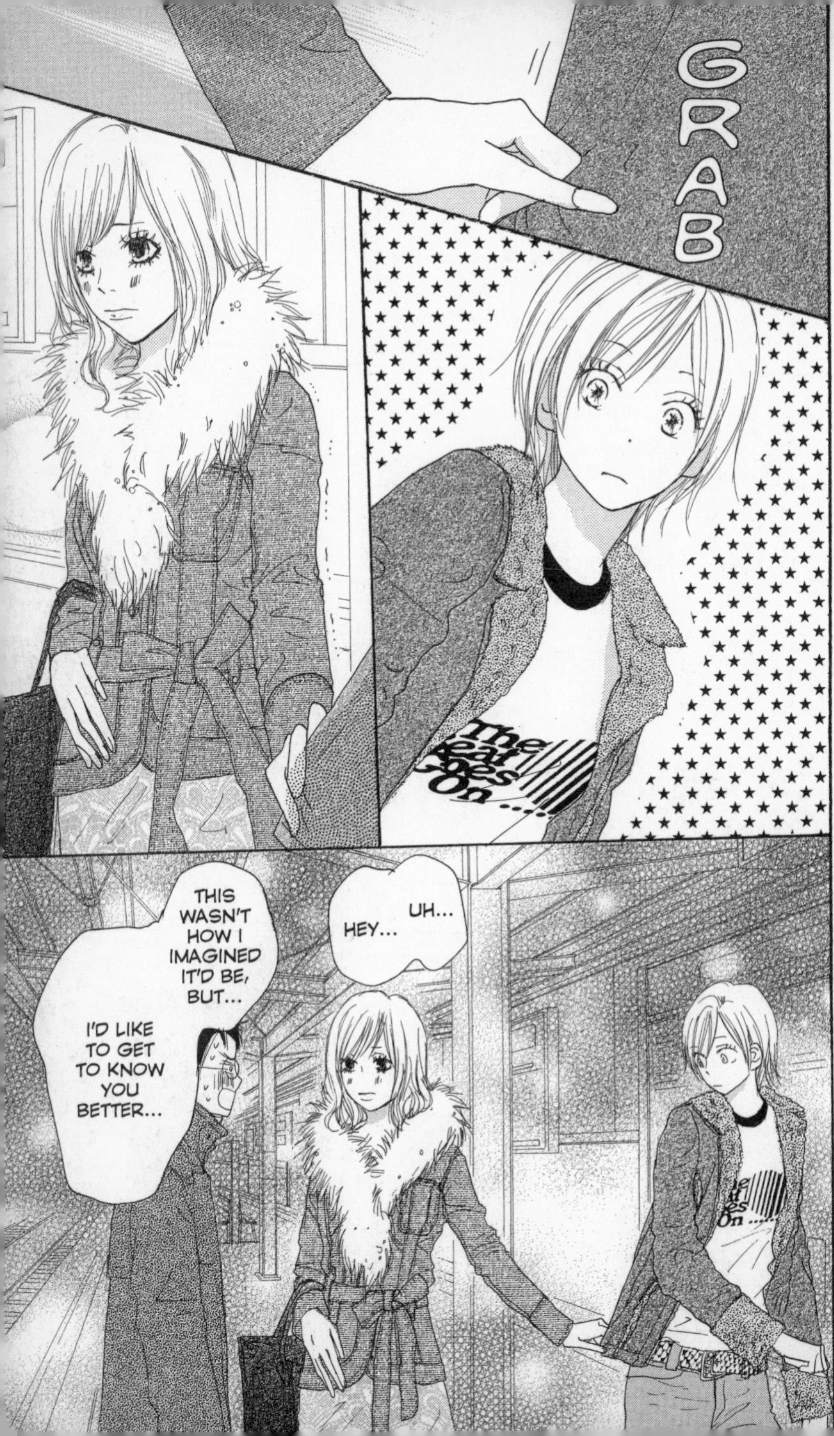
GRAB
UH... HEY...
THIS WASN'T HOW I IMAGINED IT'D BE, BUT...
I'D LIKE TO GET TO KNOW YOU BETTER...

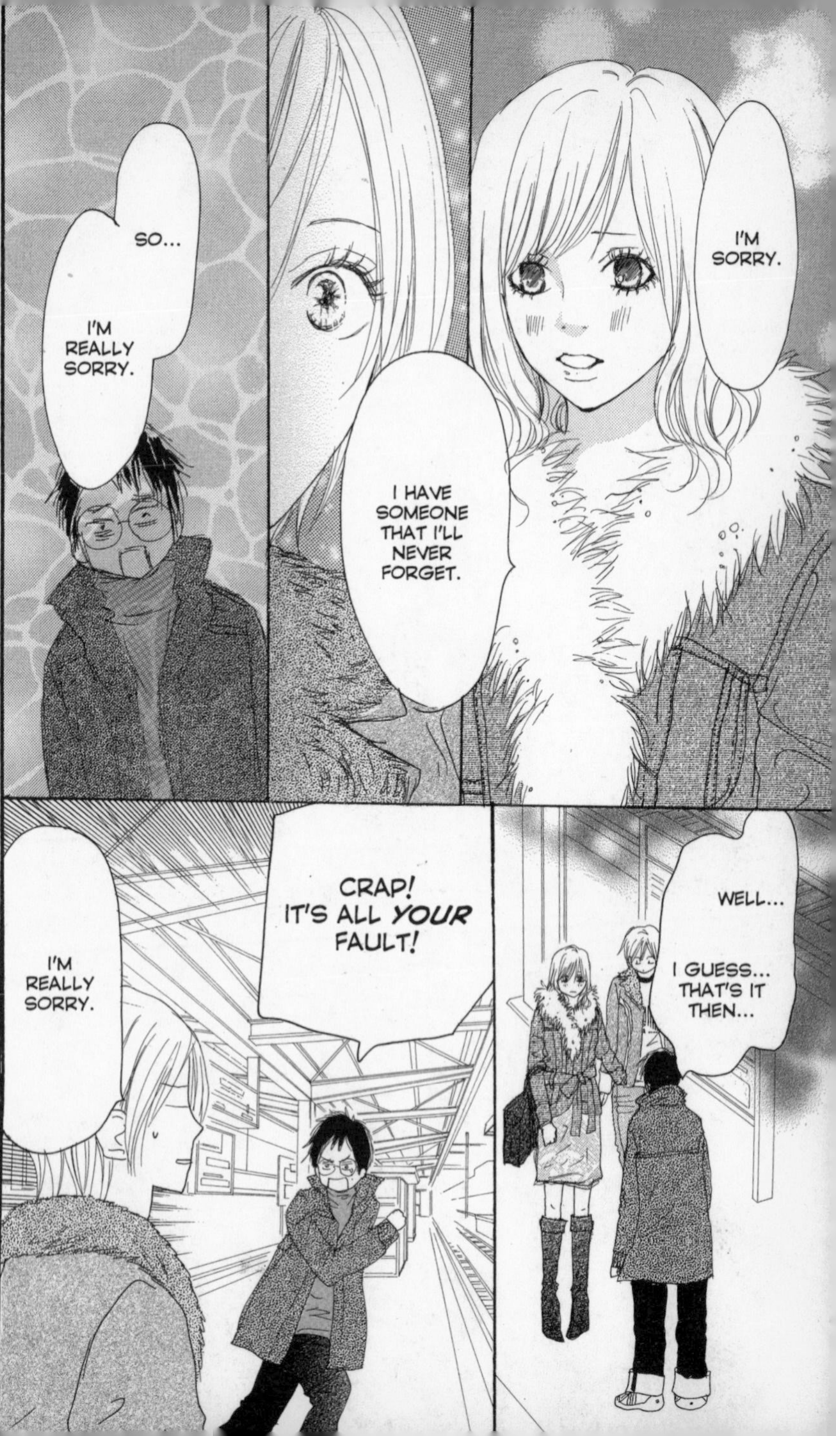
I'M SORRY.
I HAVE SOMEONE THAT I'LL NEVER FORGET.
SO...
I'M REALLY SORRY.
WELL...
I GUESS... THAT'S IT THEN...
CRAP! IT'S ALL *YOUR* FAULT!
I'M REALLY SORRY.

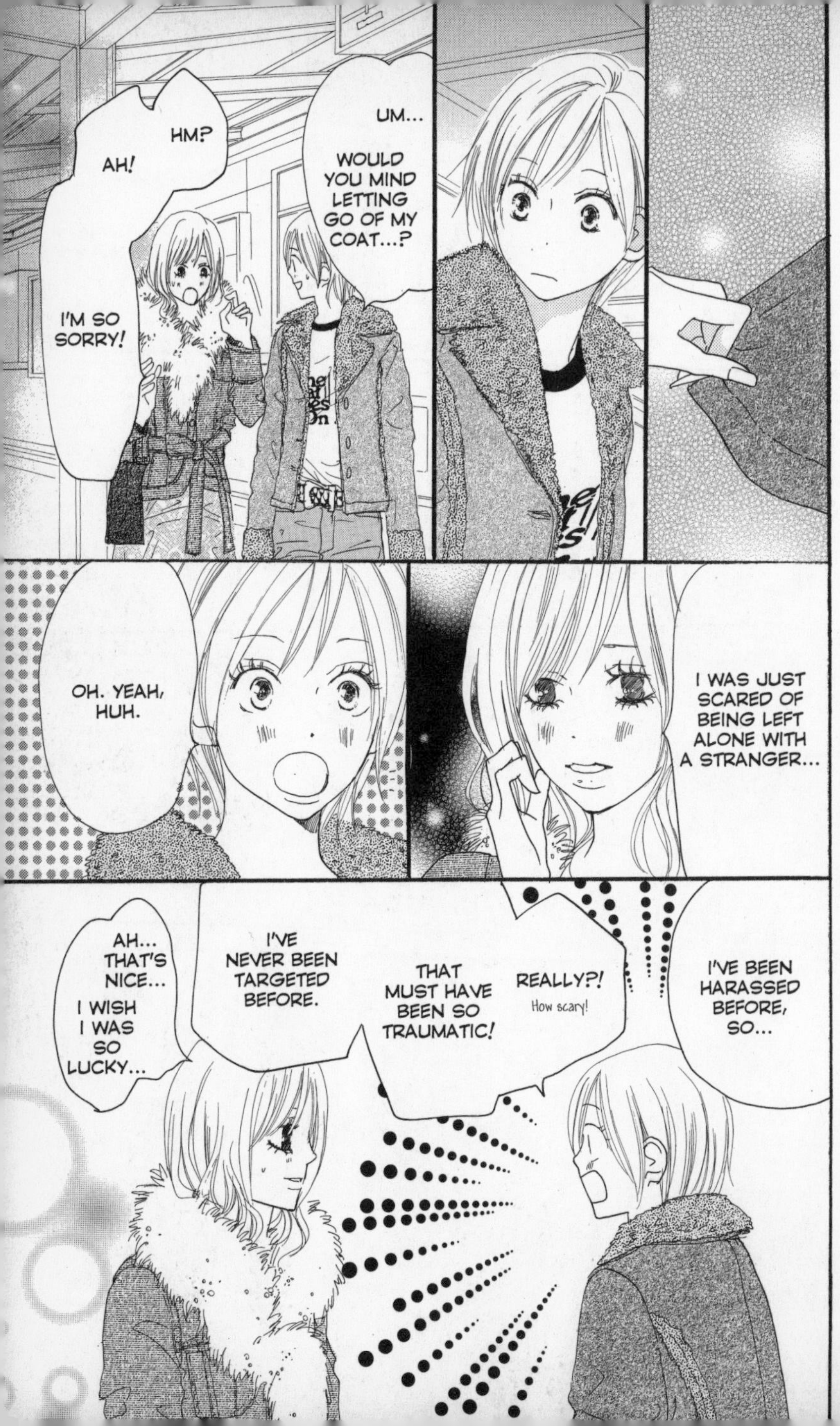
UM... WOULD YOU MIND LETTING GO OF MY COAT...?
HM? AH!
I'M SO SORRY!
I WAS JUST SCARED OF BEING LEFT ALONE WITH A STRANGER...
OH. YEAH, HUH.
I'VE BEEN HARASSED BEFORE, SO...
REALLY?!
How scary!
THAT MUST HAVE BEEN SO TRAUMATIC!
I'VE NEVER BEEN TARGETED BEFORE.
AH... THAT'S NICE... I WISH I WAS SO LUCKY...

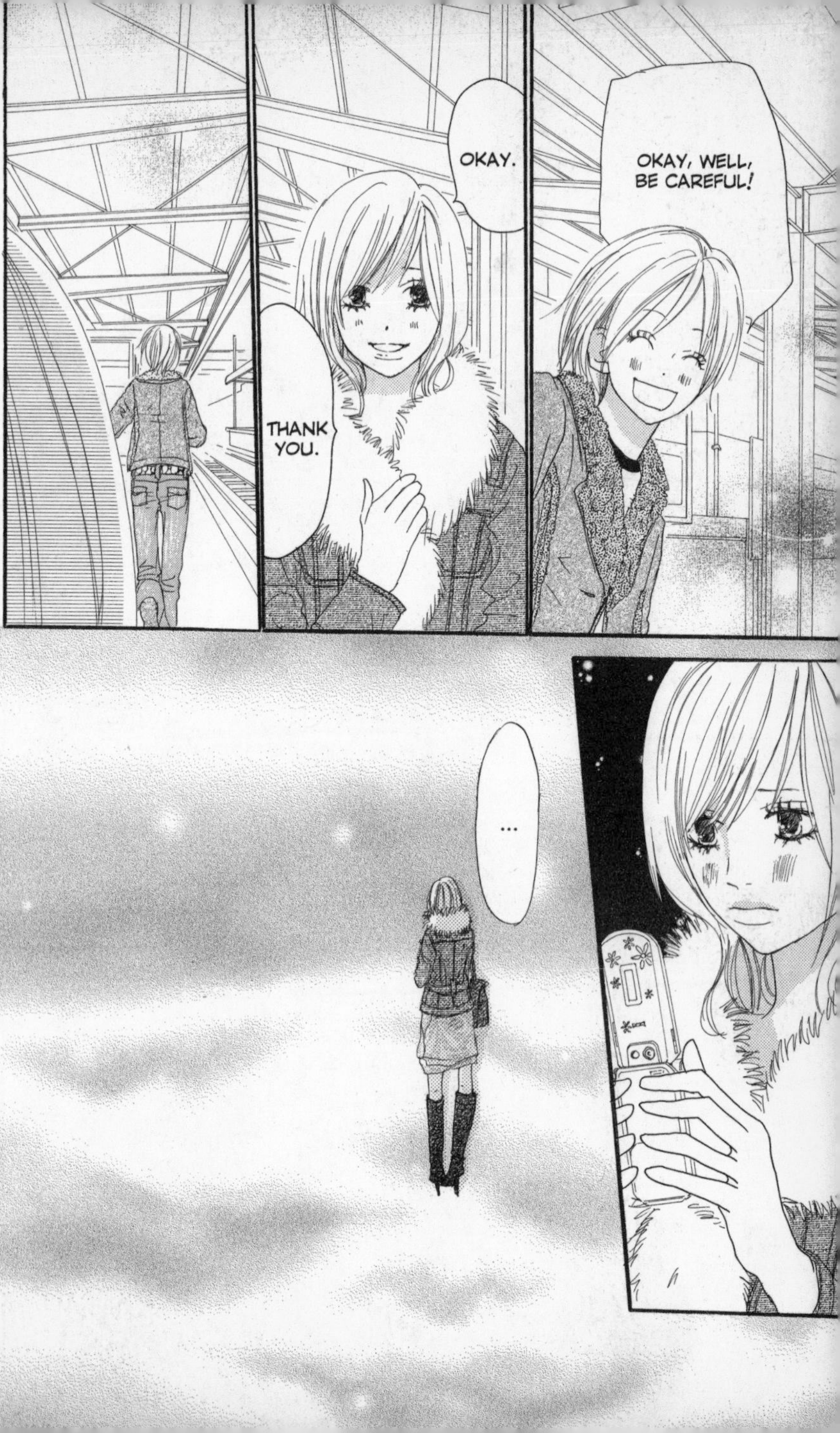
OKAY, WELL, BE CAREFUL!
OKAY.
THANK YOU.
...

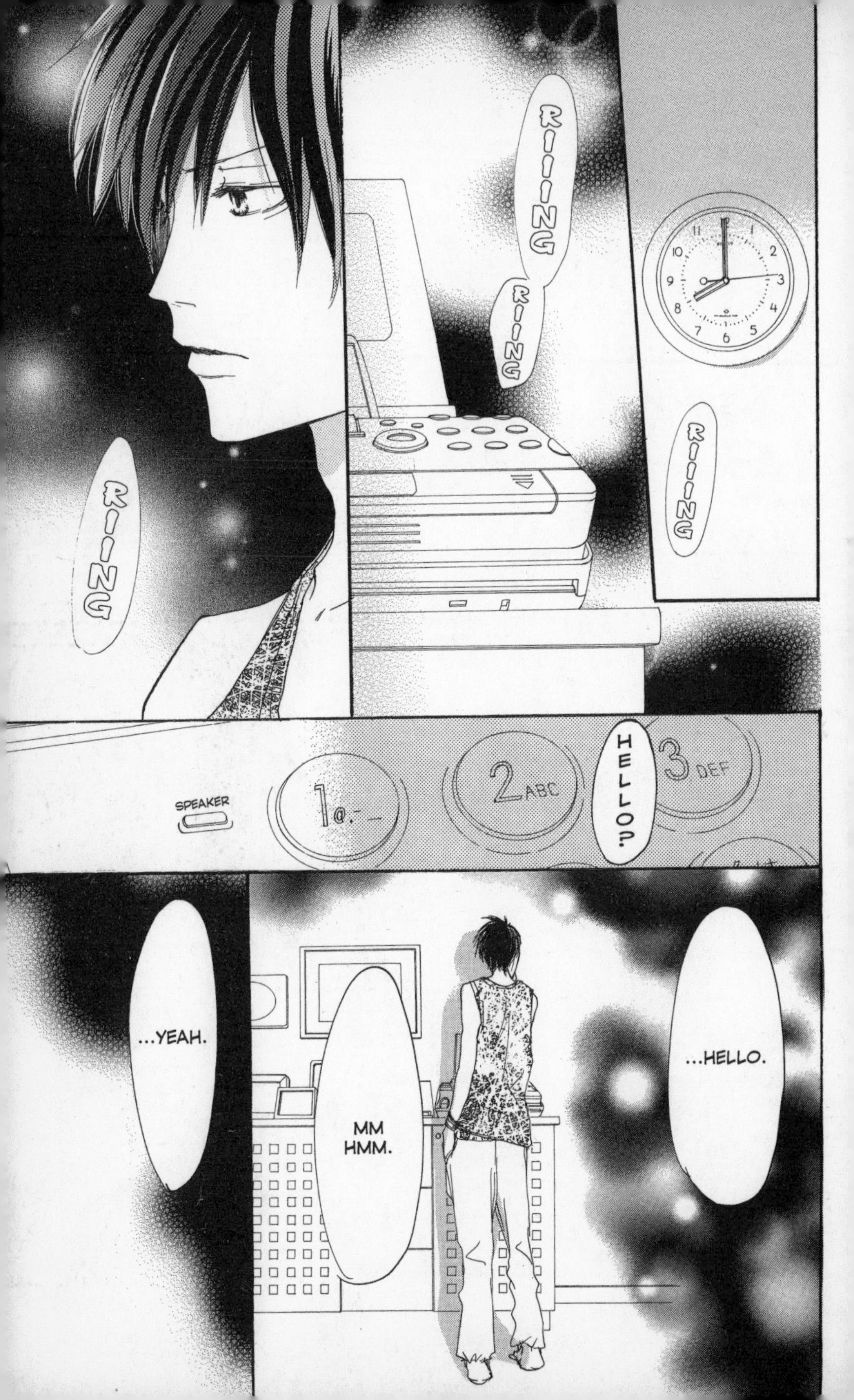
RIIING
RIIING
RIIING
RIIING
HELLO?
SPEAKER
1@.-_
2ABC
3DEF
...HELLO.
MM HMM.
...YEAH.

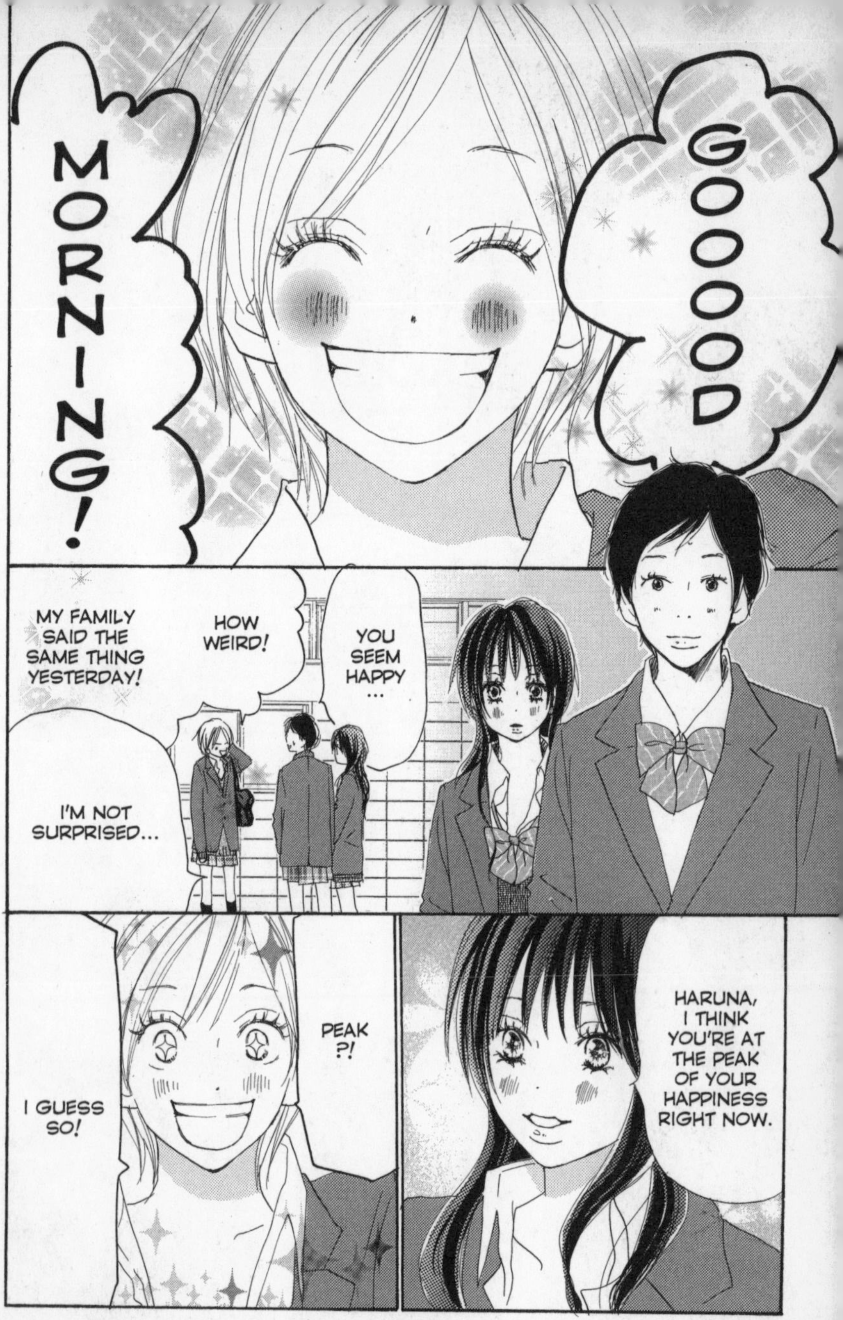
GOOOOD
MORNING!
YOU SEEM HAPPY...
HOW WEIRD!
MY FAMILY SAID THE SAME THING YESTERDAY!
I'M NOT SURPRISED...
HARUNA, I THINK YOU'RE AT THE PEAK OF YOUR HAPPINESS RIGHT NOW.
PEAK?!
I GUESS SO!

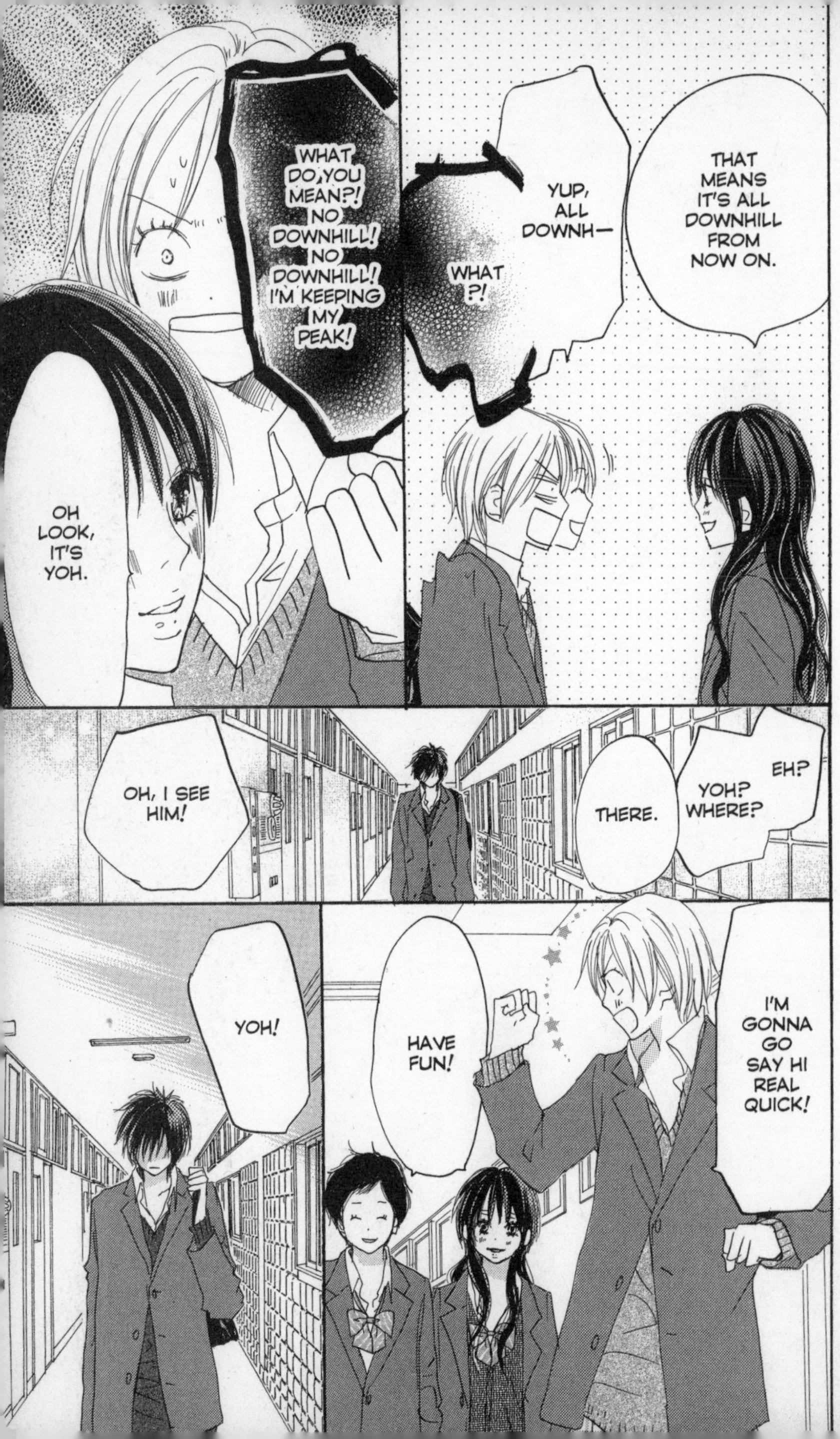
THAT MEANS IT'S ALL DOWNHILL FROM NOW ON.
YUP, ALL DOWNH—
WHAT?!
WHAT DO YOU MEAN?! NO DOWNHILL! NO DOWNHILL! I'M KEEPING MY PEAK!
OH LOOK, IT'S YOH.
EH?
YOH? WHERE?
THERE.
OH, I SEE HIM!
I'M GONNA GO SAY HI REAL QUICK!
HAVE FUN!
YOH!

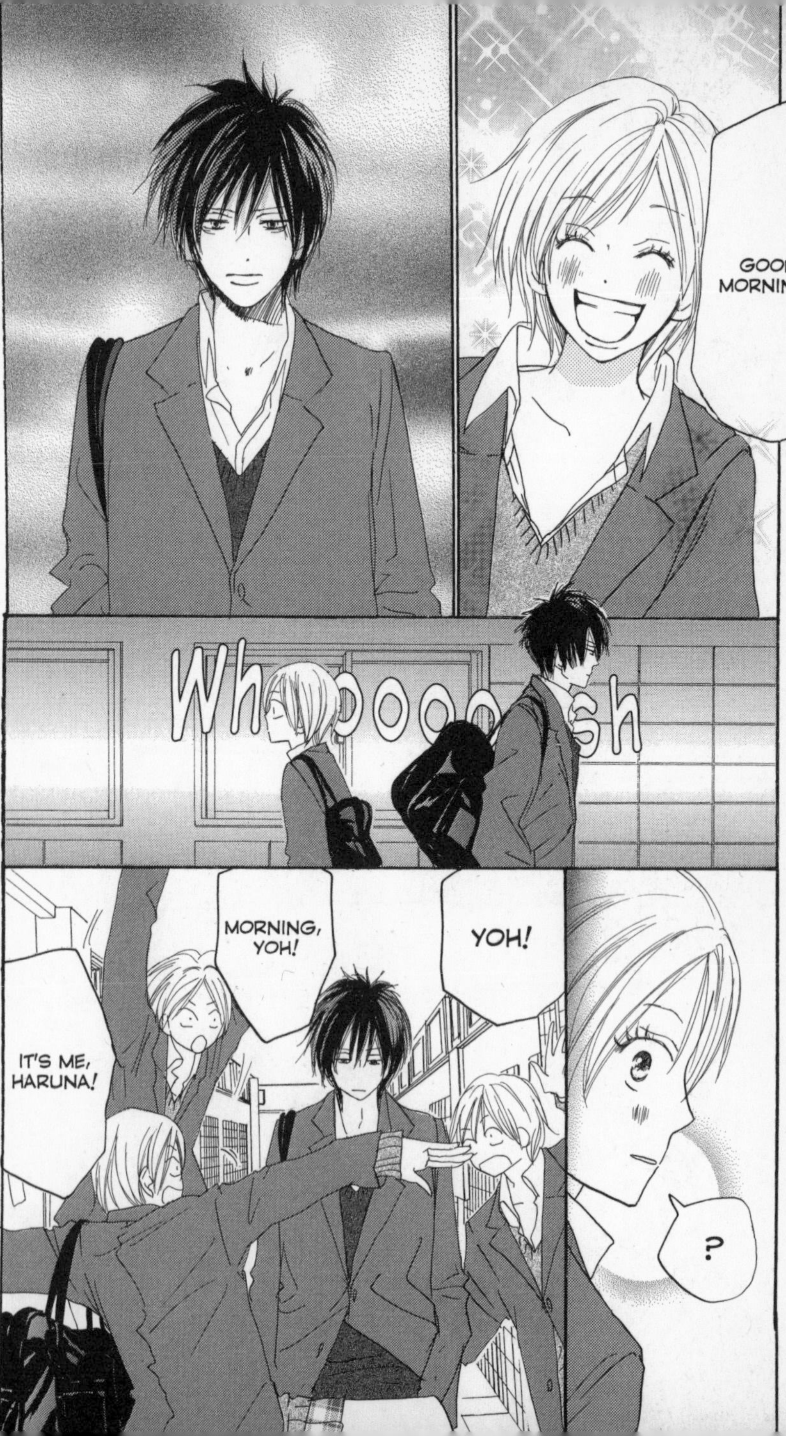
GOOD MORNING!
Wh ooo sh
?
YOH!
MORNING, YOH!
IT'S ME, HARUNA!

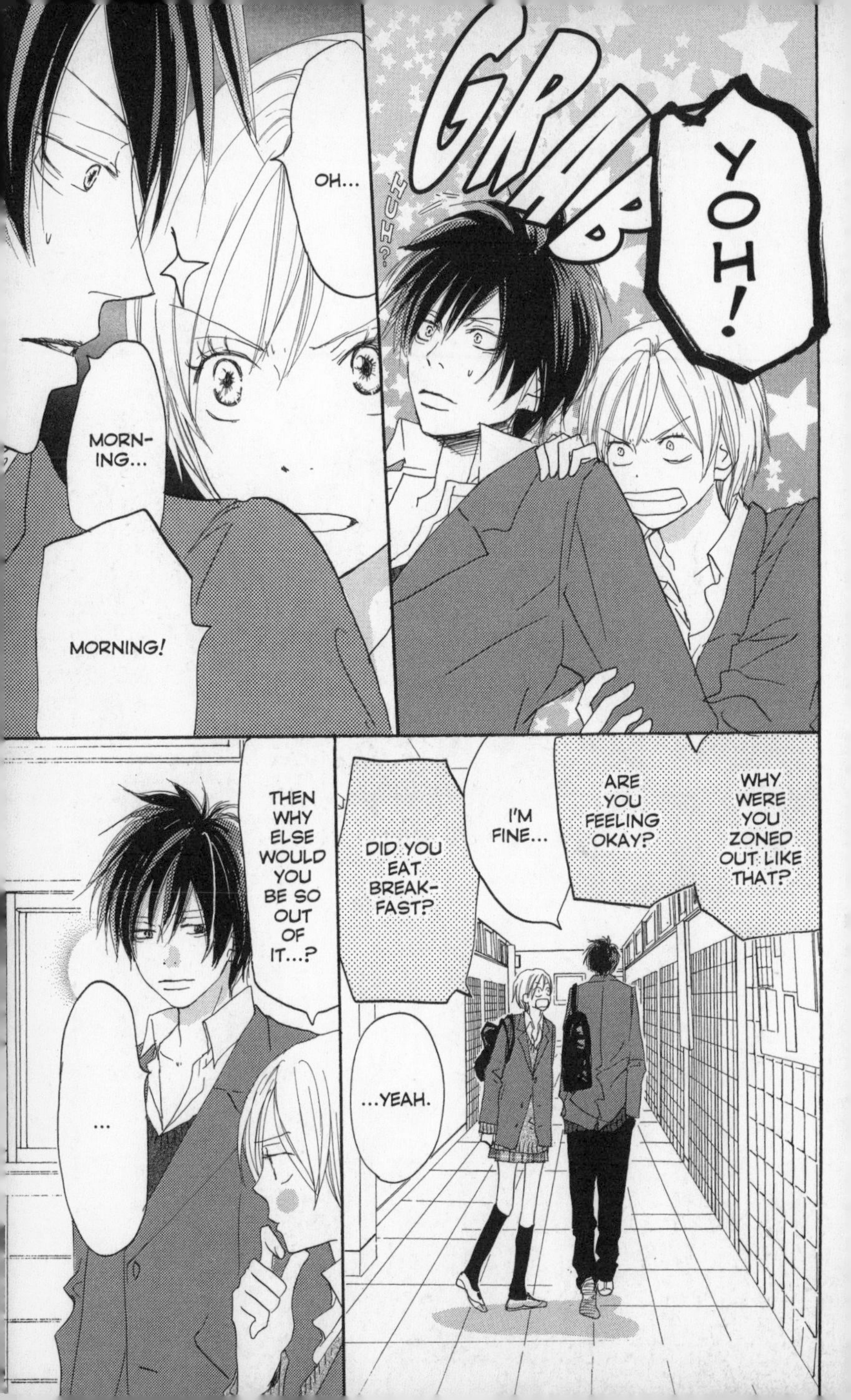
YOH!
GRAB
HUH?
OH...
MORNING...
MORNING!
WHY WERE YOU ZONED OUT LIKE THAT?
ARE YOU FEELING OKAY?
I'M FINE...
DID YOU EAT BREAKFAST?
...YEAH.
THEN WHY ELSE WOULD YOU BE SO OUT OF IT...?
...

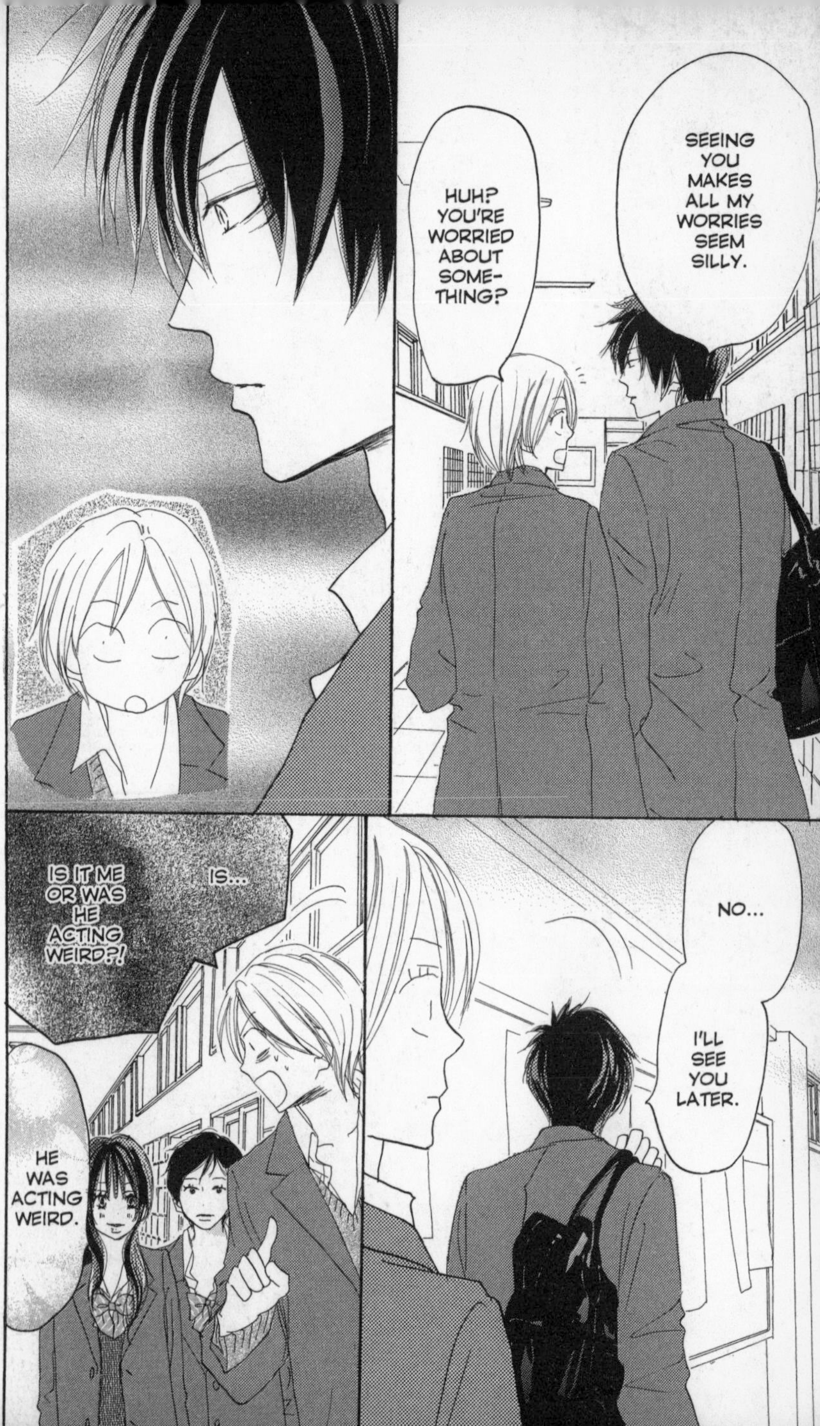
SEEING YOU MAKES ALL MY WORRIES SEEM SILLY.
HUH? YOU'RE WORRIED ABOUT SOME-THING?
NO...
I'LL SEE YOU LATER.
IS...
IS IT ME OR WAS HE ACTING WEIRD?!
HE WAS ACTING WEIRD.

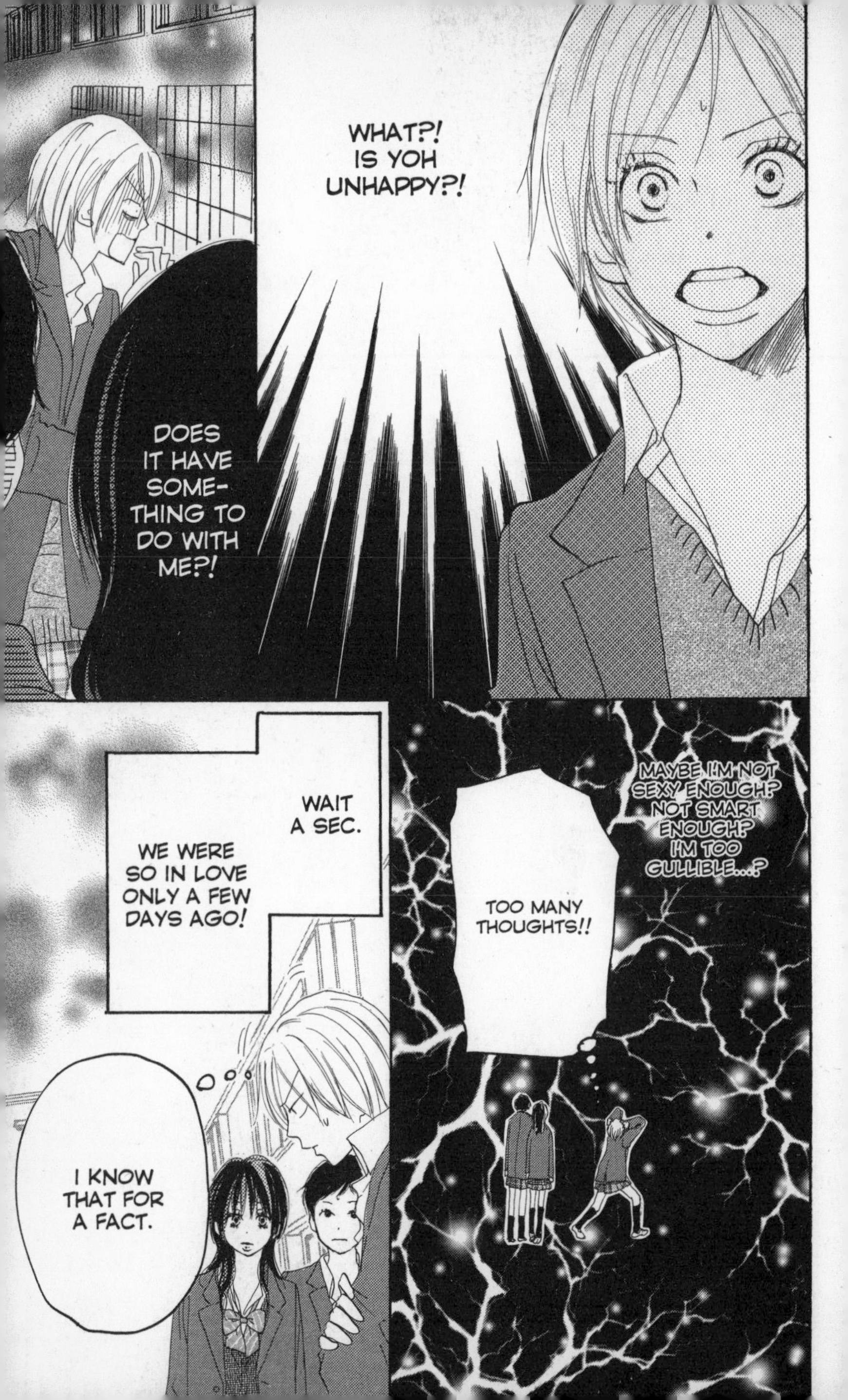
WHAT?! IS YOH UNHAPPY?!
DOES IT HAVE SOME-THING TO DO WITH ME?!
MAYBE I'M NOT SEXY ENOUGH? NOT SMART ENOUGH? I'M TOO GULLIBLE...?
TOO MANY THOUGHTS!!
WAIT A SEC.
WE WERE SO IN LOVE ONLY A FEW DAYS AGO!
I KNOW THAT FOR A FACT.

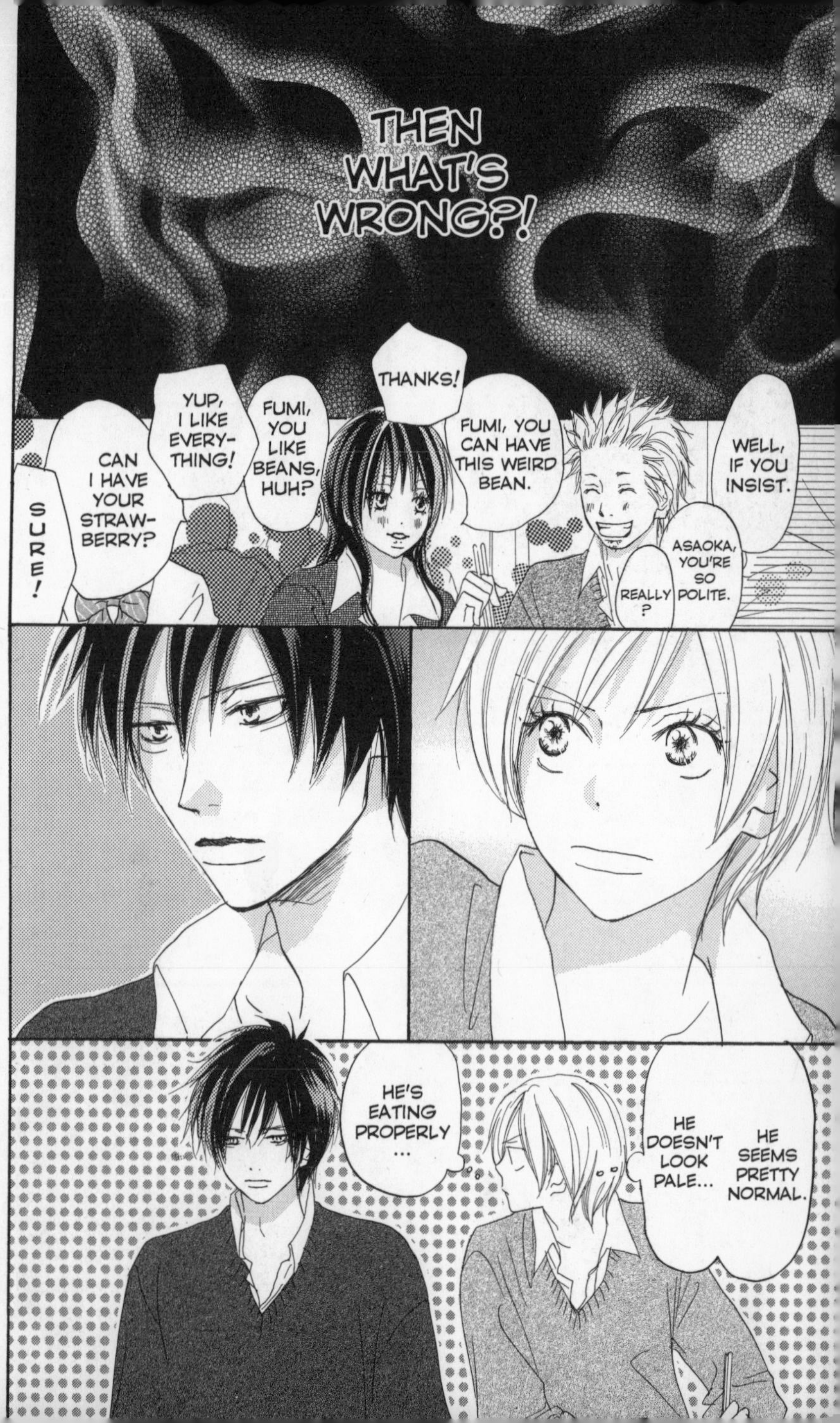
THEN WHAT'S WRONG?!
WELL, IF YOU INSIST.
ASAOKA, YOU'RE SO POLITE.
REALLY?
FUMI, YOU CAN HAVE THIS WEIRD BEAN.
THANKS!
FUMI, YOU LIKE BEANS, HUH?
YUP, I LIKE EVERY-THING!
CAN I HAVE YOUR STRAW-BERRY?
SURE!
HE SEEMS PRETTY NORMAL.
HE DOESN'T LOOK PALE...
HE'S EATING PROPERLY...

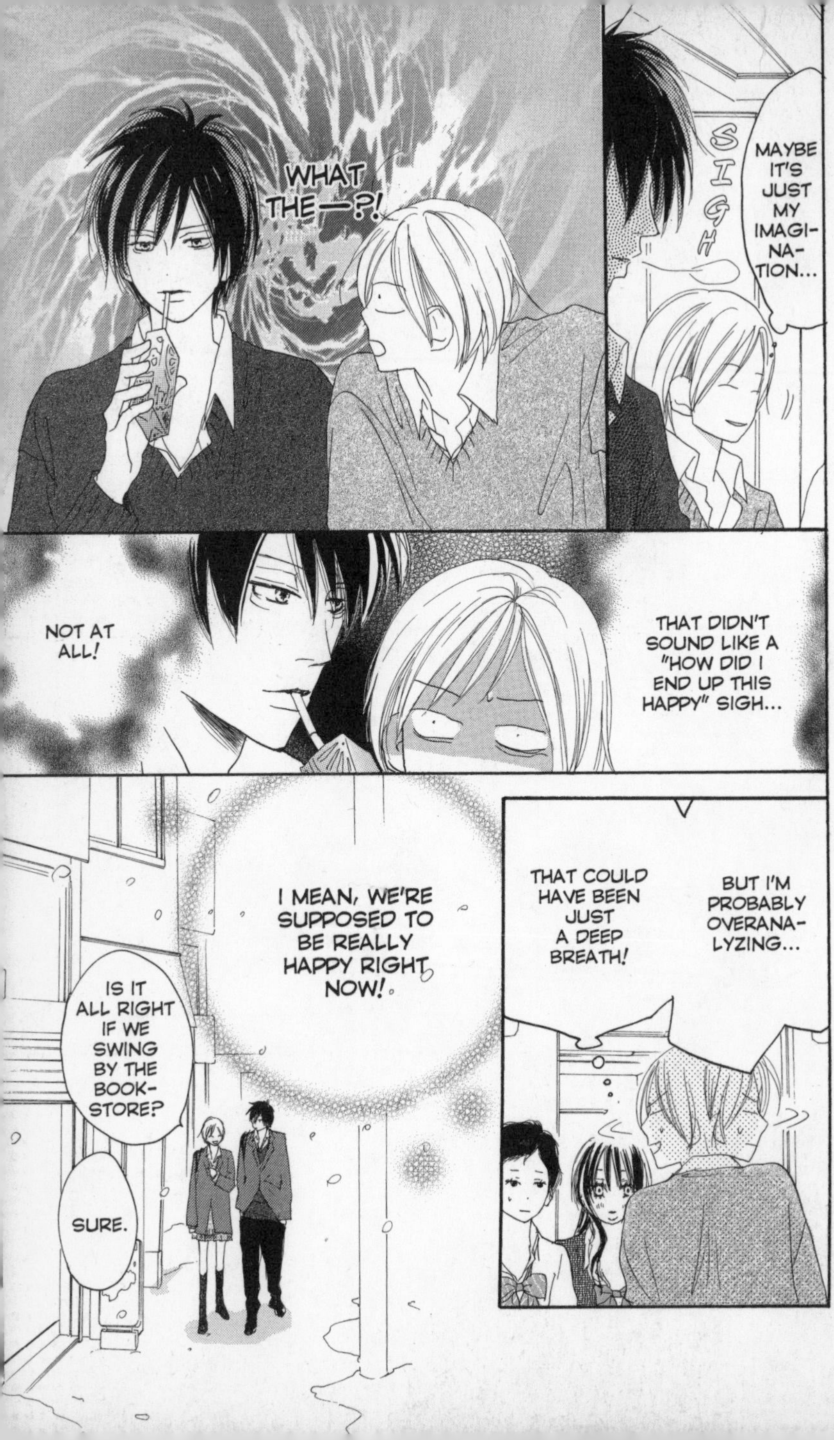
MAYBE IT'S JUST MY IMAGINATION...
SIGH
WHAT THE—?!
THAT DIDN'T SOUND LIKE A "HOW DID I END UP THIS HAPPY" SIGH...
NOT AT ALL!
BUT I'M PROBABLY OVERANALYZING...
THAT COULD HAVE BEEN JUST A DEEP BREATH!
I MEAN, WE'RE SUPPOSED TO BE REALLY HAPPY RIGHT NOW!
IS IT ALL RIGHT IF WE SWING BY THE BOOKSTORE?
SURE.

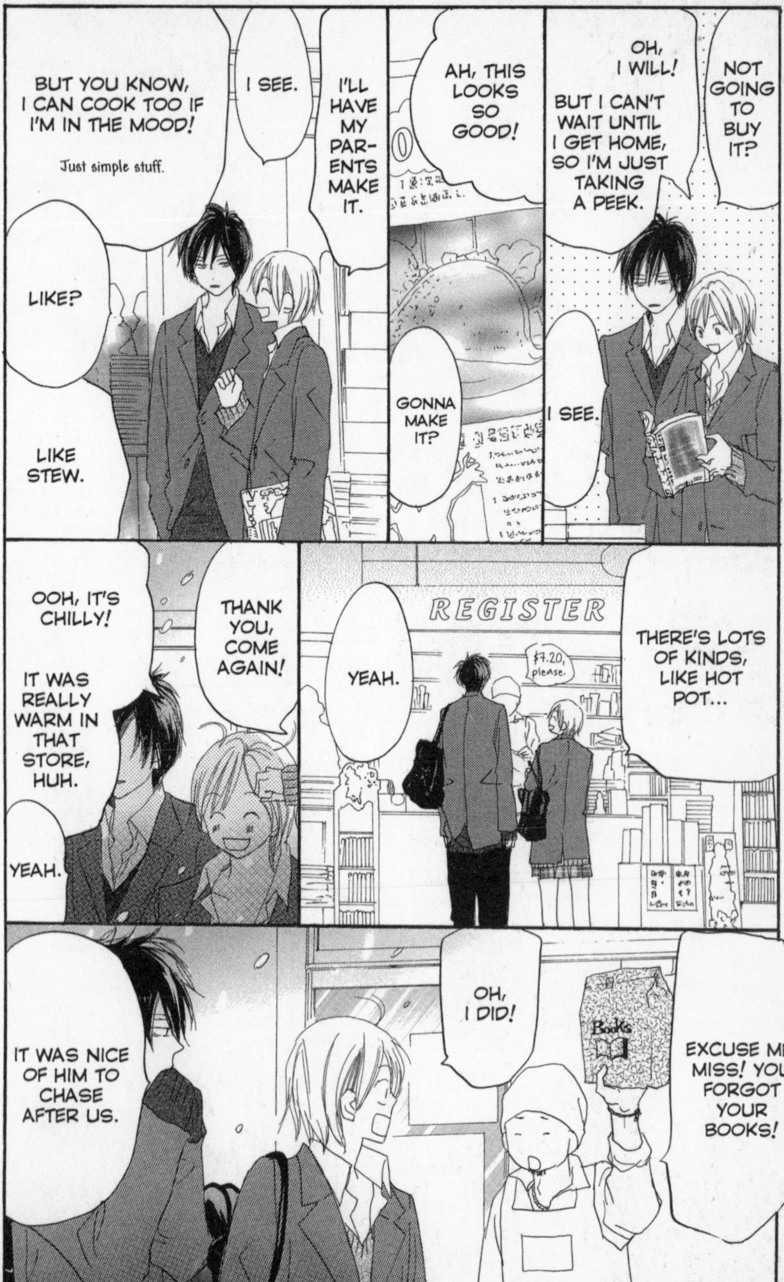
NOT GOING TO BUY IT?
OH, I WILL!
BUT I CAN'T WAIT UNTIL I GET HOME, SO I'M JUST TAKING A PEEK.
I SEE.
AH, THIS LOOKS SO GOOD!
GONNA MAKE IT?
I'LL HAVE MY PAR-ENTS MAKE IT.
I SEE.
BUT YOU KNOW, I CAN COOK TOO IF I'M IN THE MOOD!
Just simple stuff.
LIKE?
LIKE STEW.
THERE'S LOTS OF KINDS, LIKE HOT POT...
REGISTER
$7.20, please.
YEAH.
THANK YOU, COME AGAIN!
OOH, IT'S CHILLY!
IT WAS REALLY WARM IN THAT STORE, HUH.
YEAH.
EXCUSE ME, MISS! YOU FORGOT YOUR BOOKS!
Books
OH, I DID!
IT WAS NICE OF HIM TO CHASE AFTER US.

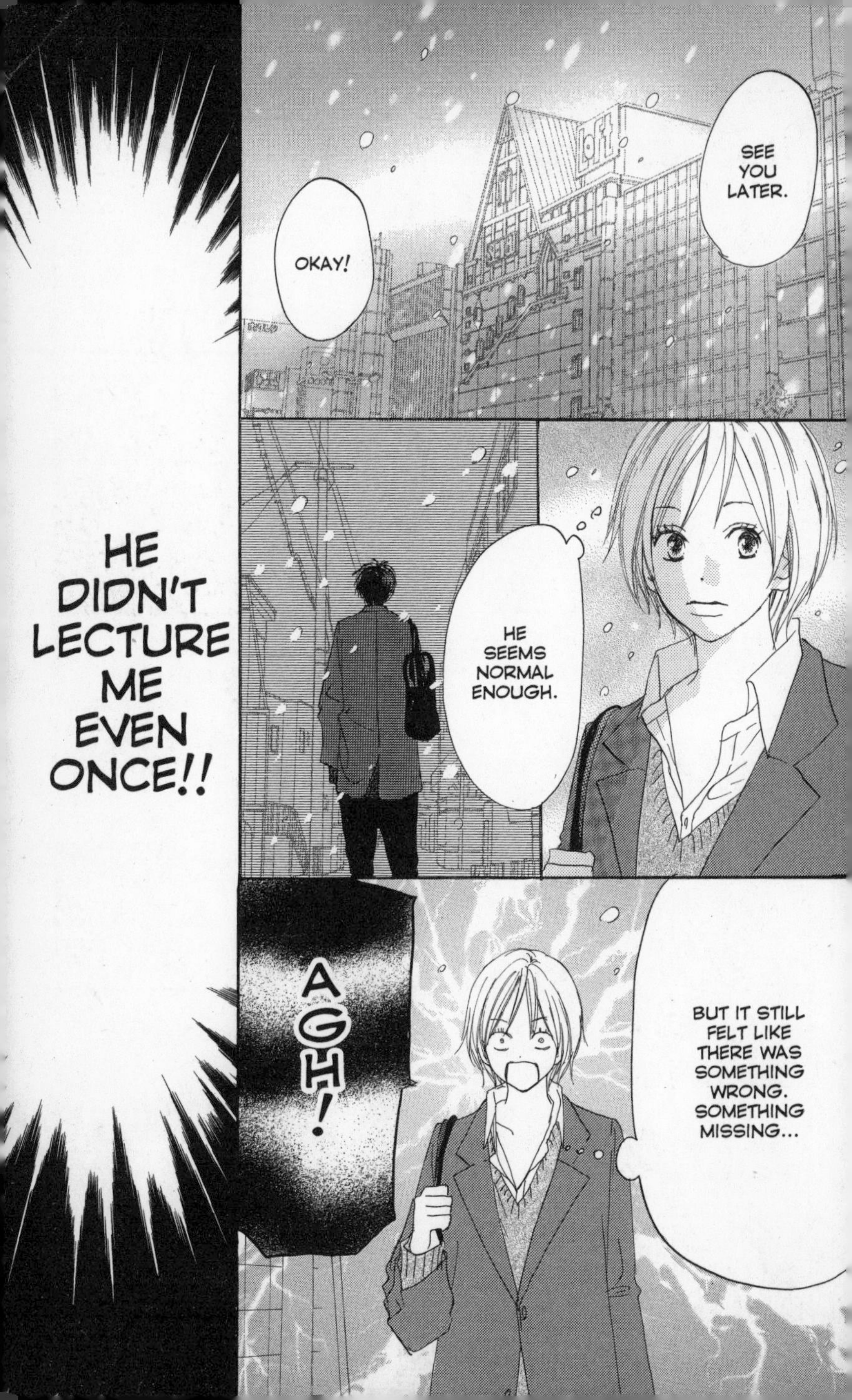
SEE YOU LATER.
OKAY!
HE SEEMS NORMAL ENOUGH.
BUT IT STILL FELT LIKE THERE WAS SOMETHING WRONG. SOMETHING MISSING...
AGH!
HE DIDN'T LECTURE ME EVEN ONCE!!

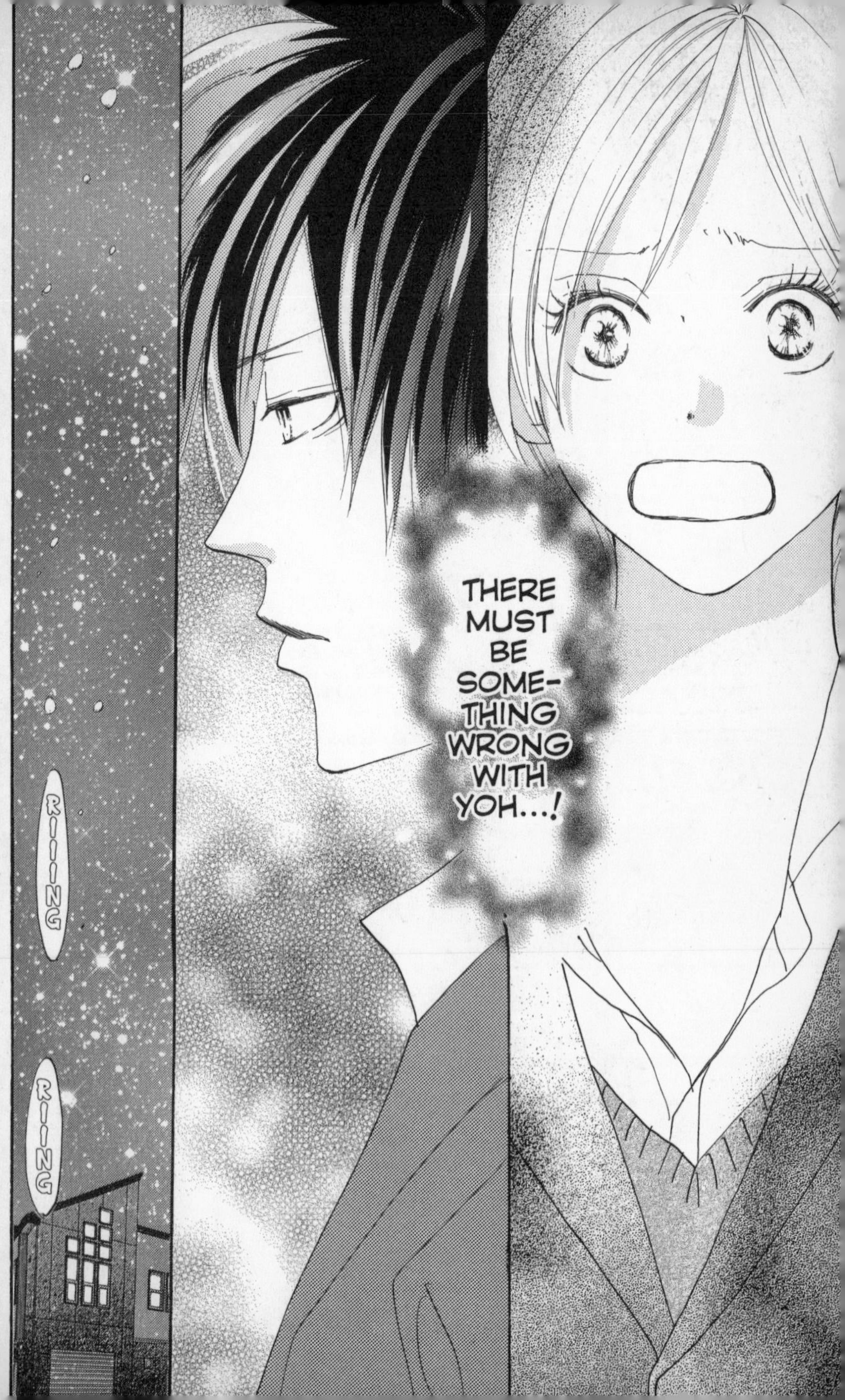
THERE MUST BE SOME-THING WRONG WITH YOH...!
RIIING
RIIING

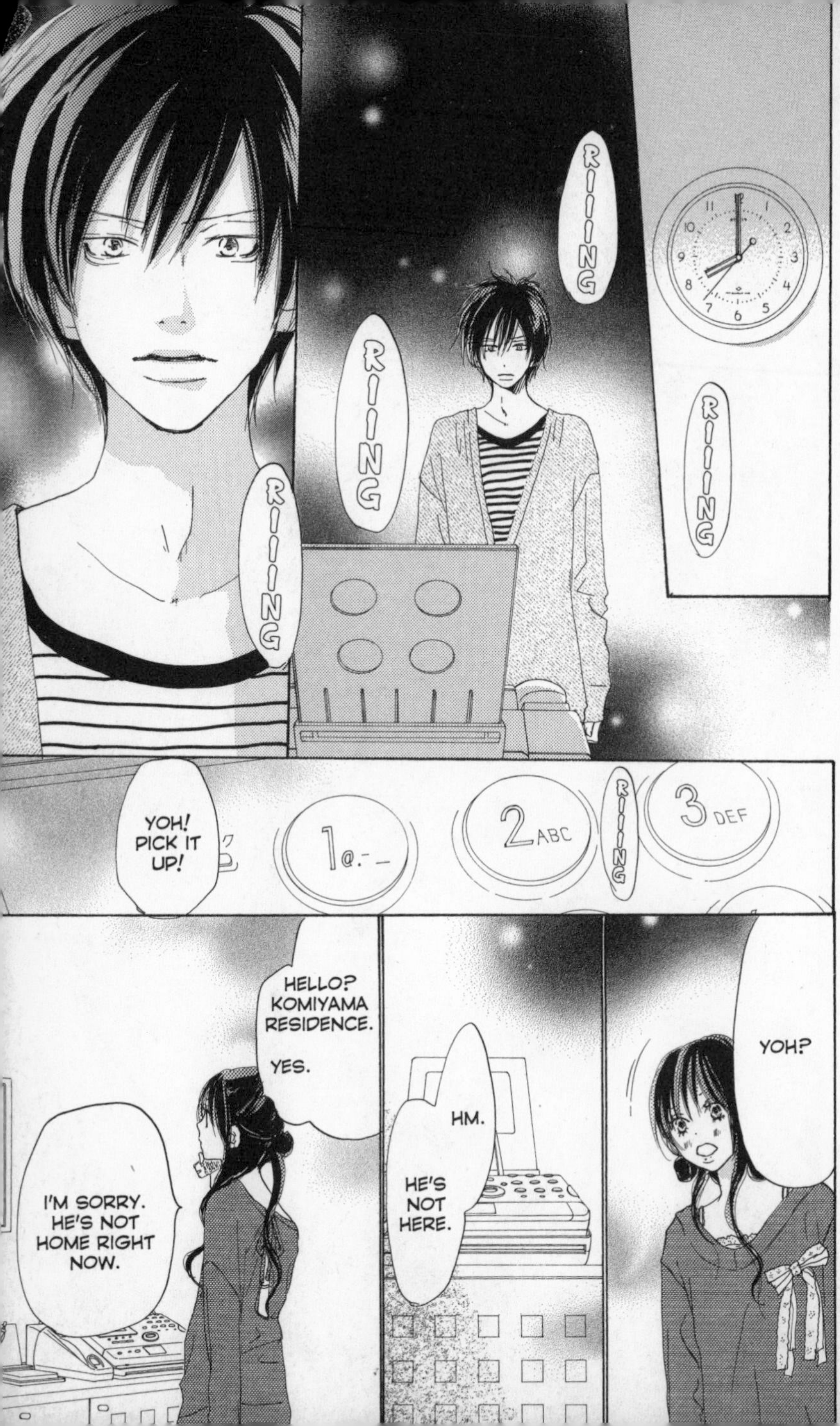
RIIIING
RIIIING
RIIIING
RIIIING
3 DEF
RIIIING
2 ABC
1 @.-_
YOH! PICK IT UP!
YOH?
HM.
HE'S NOT HERE.
HELLO? KOMIYAMA RESIDENCE.
YES.
I'M SORRY. HE'S NOT HOME RIGHT NOW.

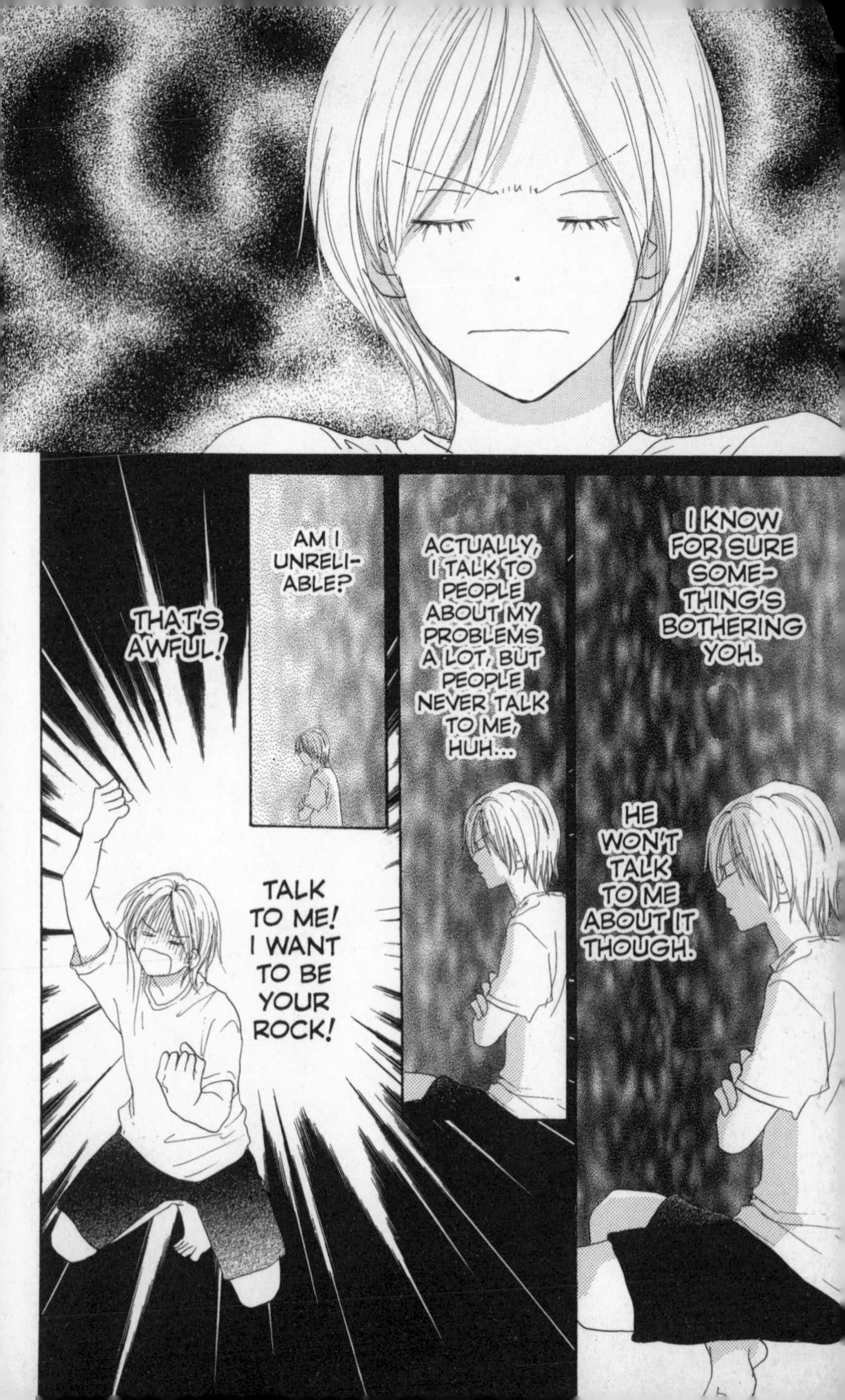
I KNOW FOR SURE SOME-THING'S BOTHERING YOH.
HE WON'T TALK TO ME ABOUT IT THOUGH.
ACTUALLY, I TALK TO PEOPLE ABOUT MY PROBLEMS A LOT, BUT PEOPLE NEVER TALK TO ME, HUH...
AM I UNRELI-ABLE?
THAT'S AWFUL!
TALK TO ME! I WANT TO BE YOUR ROCK!

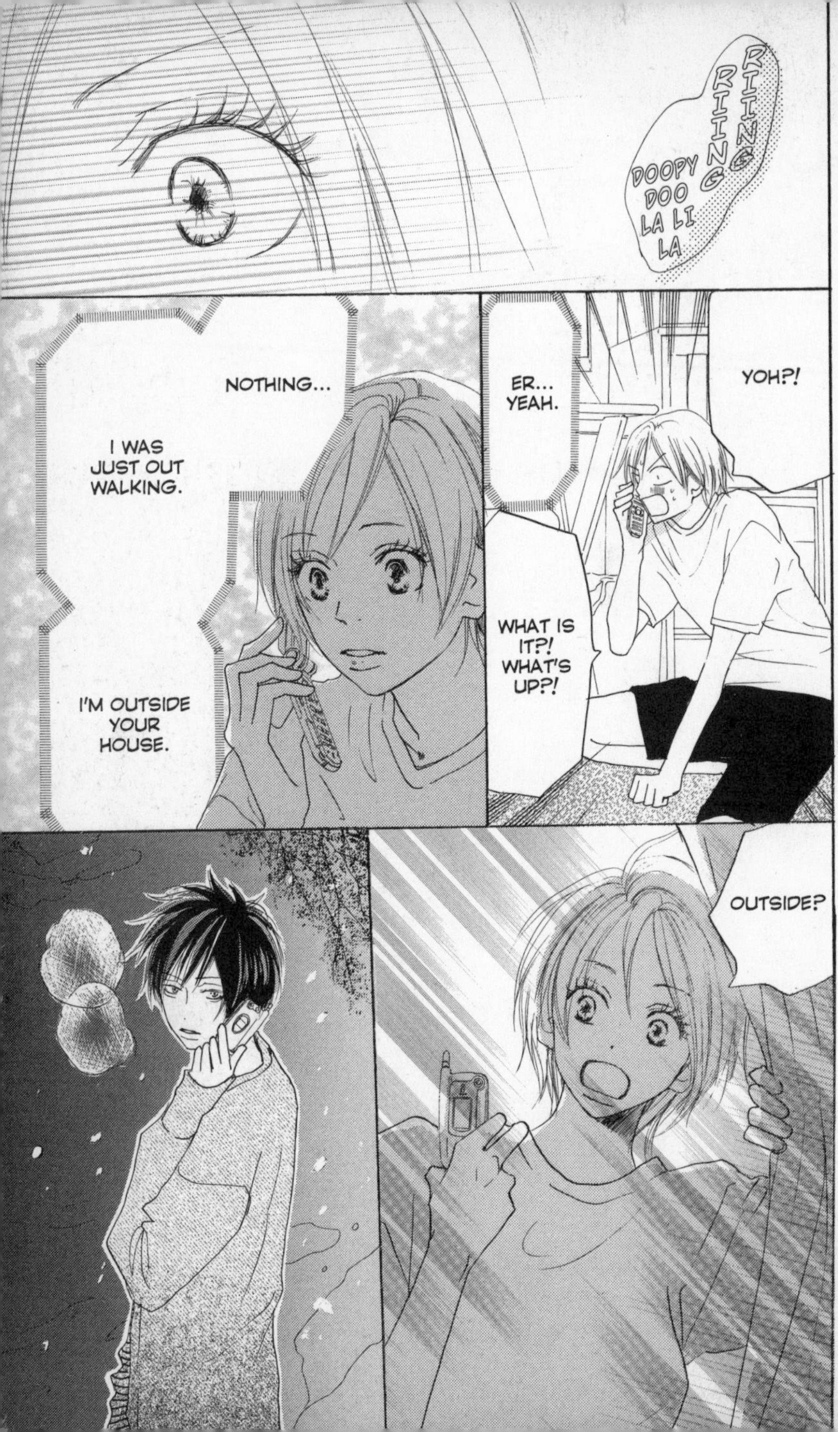
RIING RIING
DOOPY DOO LA LI LA
YOH?!
ER... YEAH.
WHAT IS IT?! WHAT'S UP?!
NOTHING...
I WAS JUST OUT WALKING.
I'M OUTSIDE YOUR HOUSE.
OUTSIDE?

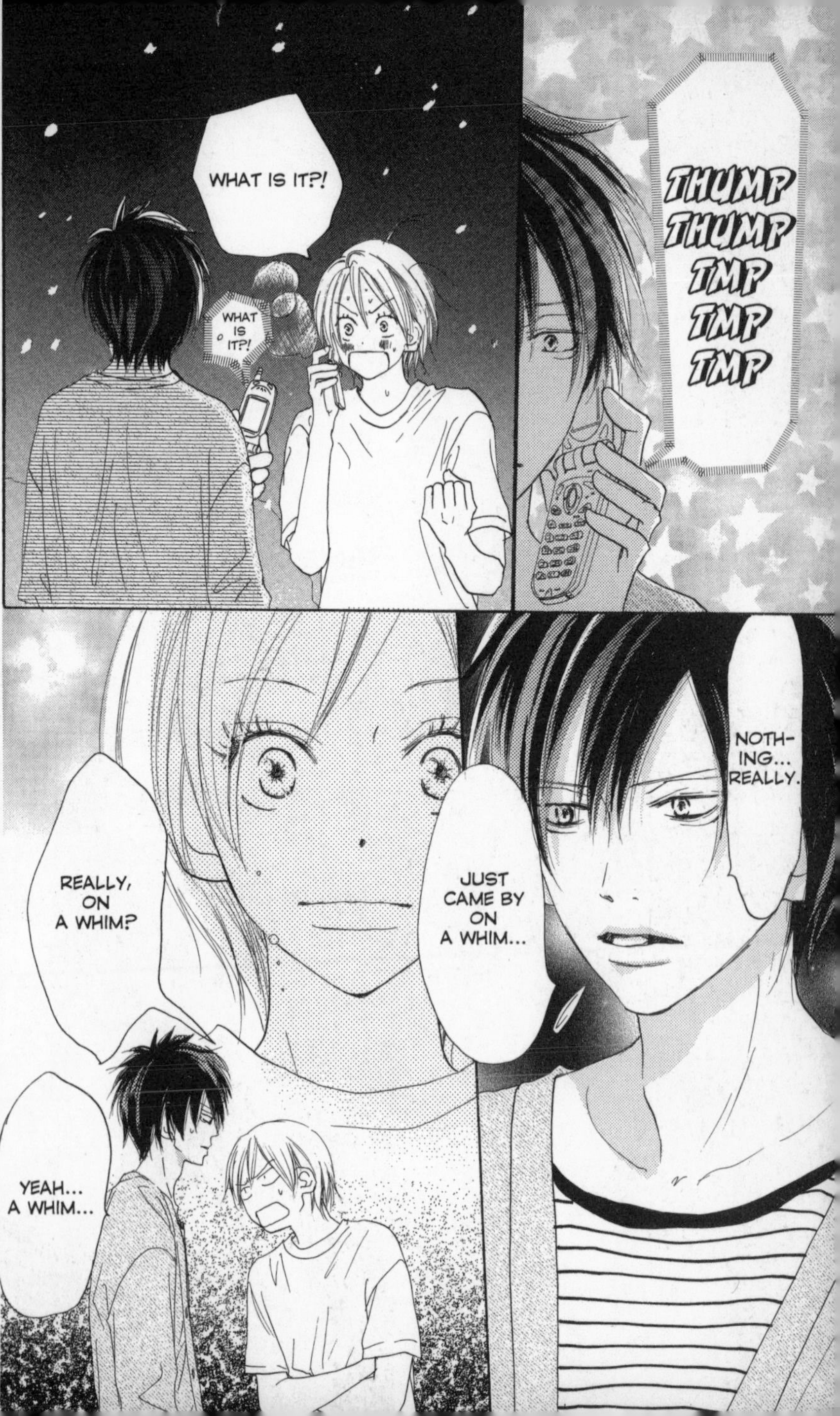
THUMP THUMP TMP TMP TMP
WHAT IS IT?!
WHAT IS IT?!
NOTHING... REALLY.
JUST CAME BY ON A WHIM...
REALLY, ON A WHIM?
YEAH... A WHIM...

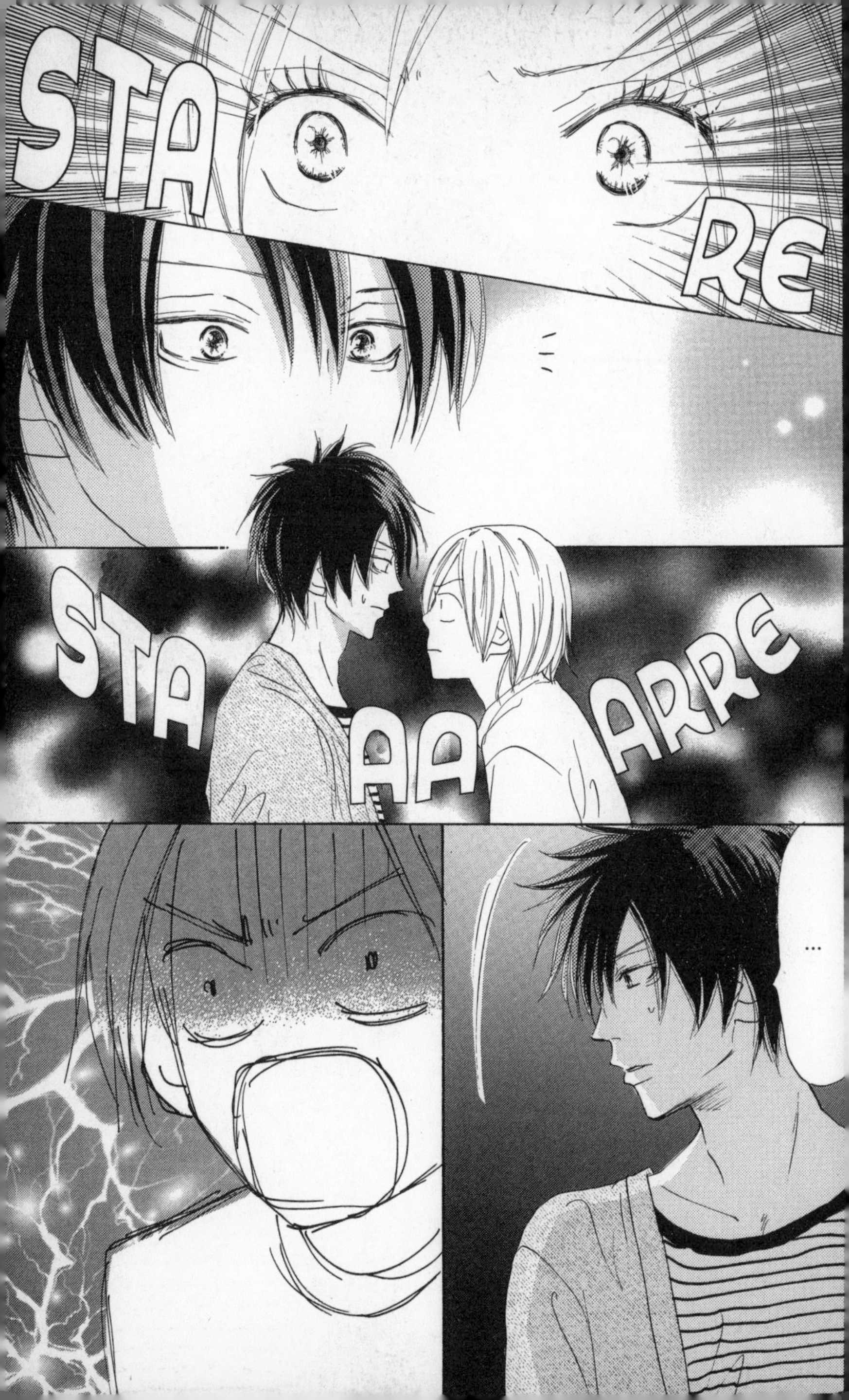
STA
RE
STA
AA
ARRE
...

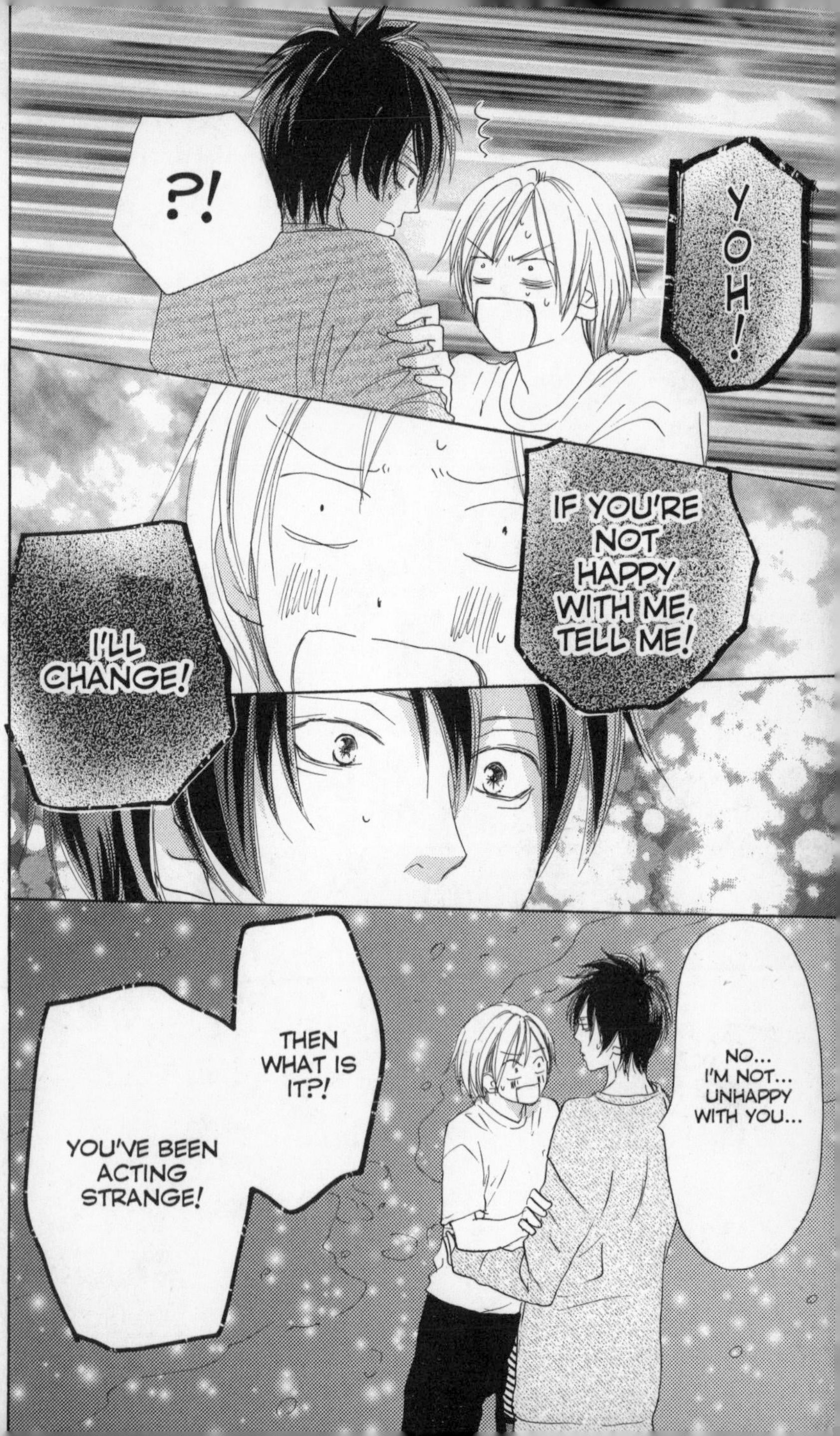
YOH!
?!
IF YOU'RE NOT HAPPY WITH ME, TELL ME!
I'LL CHANGE!
NO... I'M NOT... UNHAPPY WITH YOU...
THEN WHAT IS IT?!
YOU'VE BEEN ACTING STRANGE!

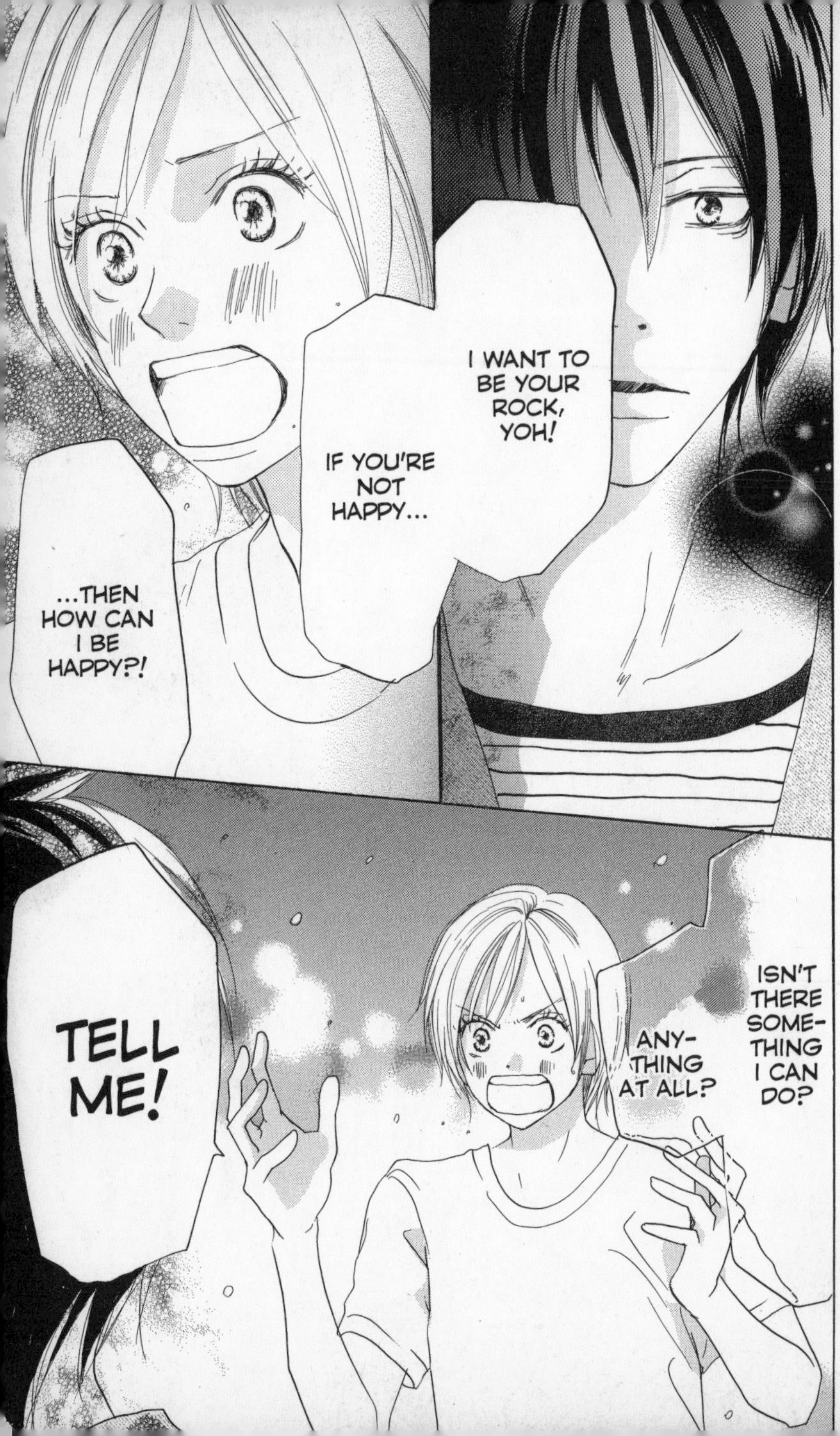
I WANT TO BE YOUR ROCK, YOH!
IF YOU'RE NOT HAPPY...
...THEN HOW CAN I BE HAPPY?!
ISN'T THERE SOME-THING I CAN DO?
ANY-THING AT ALL?
TELL ME!

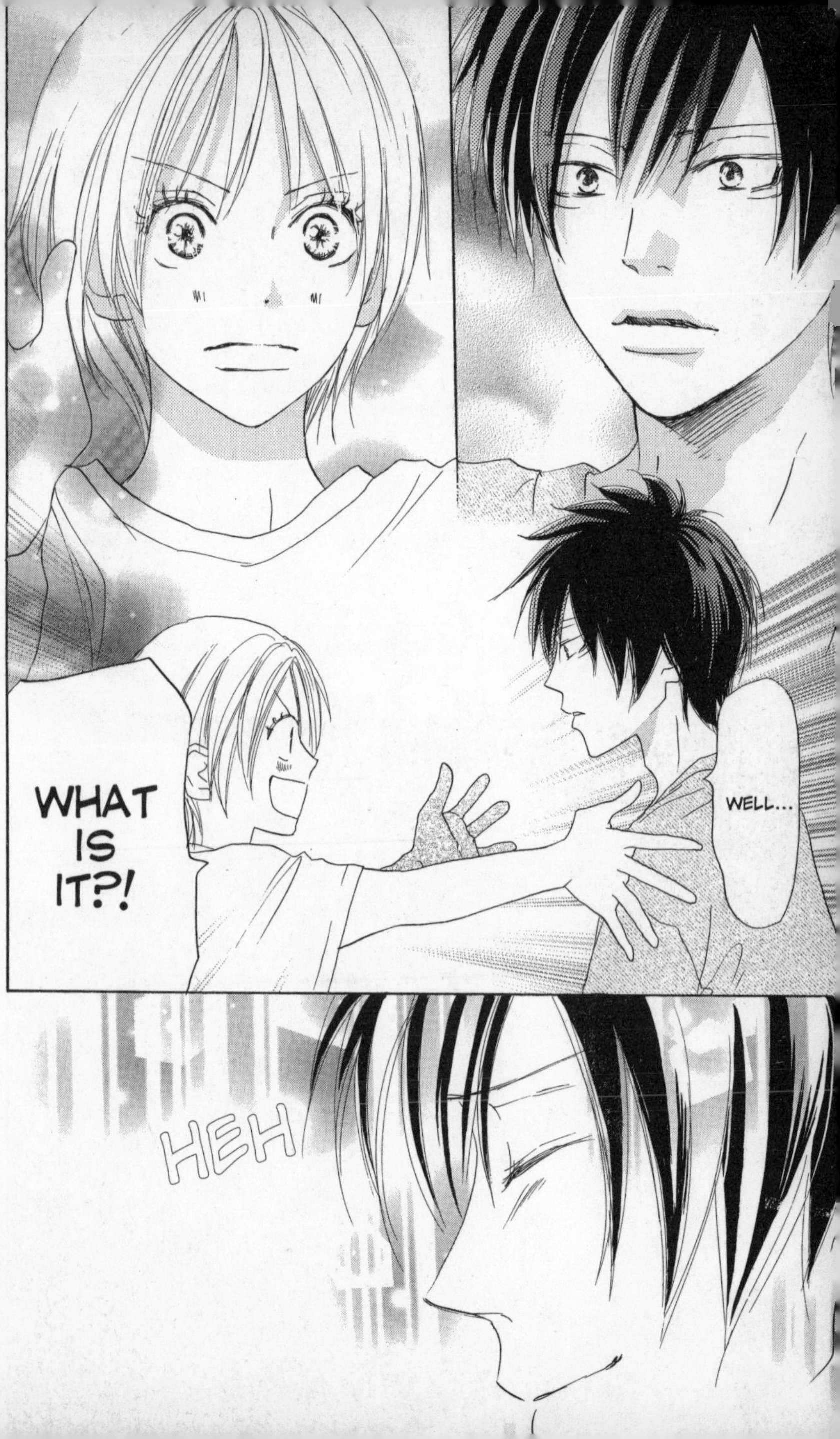
WELL...
WHAT IS IT?!
HEH

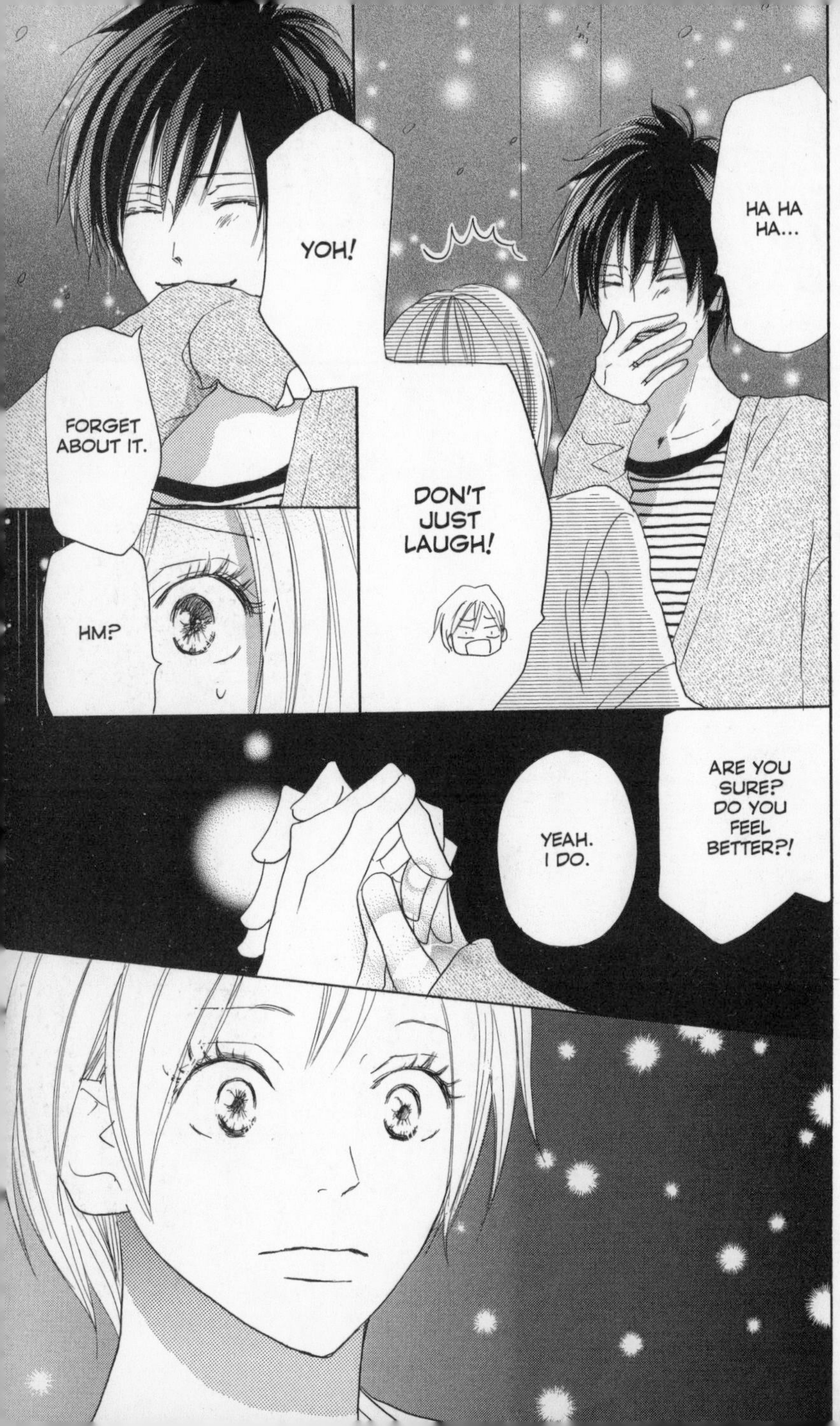
HA HA HA...
YOH!
DON'T JUST LAUGH!
FORGET ABOUT IT.
HM?
ARE YOU SURE? DO YOU FEEL BETTER?!
YEAH. I DO.

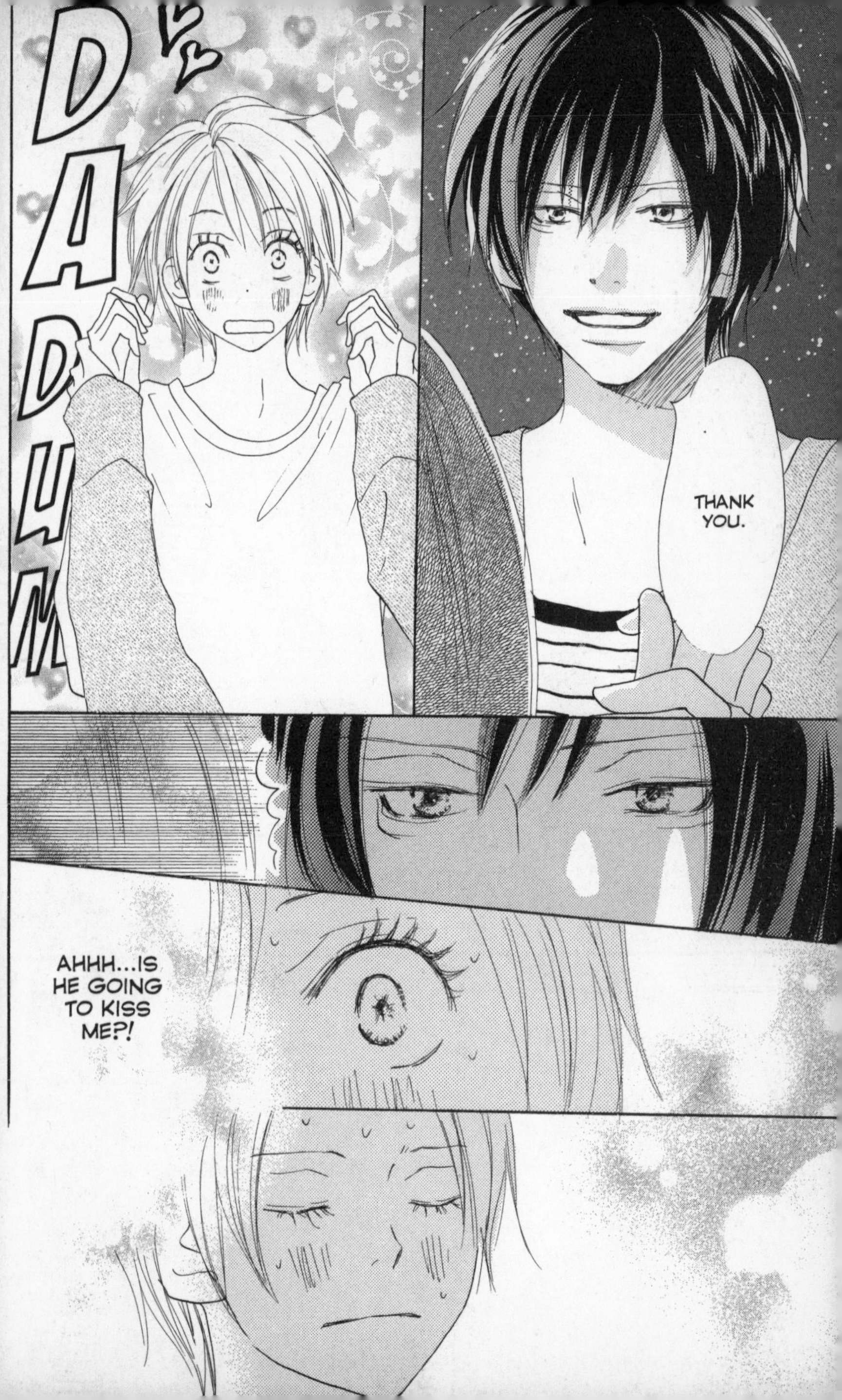
THANK YOU.
DADUM
AHHH...IS HE GOING TO KISS ME?!

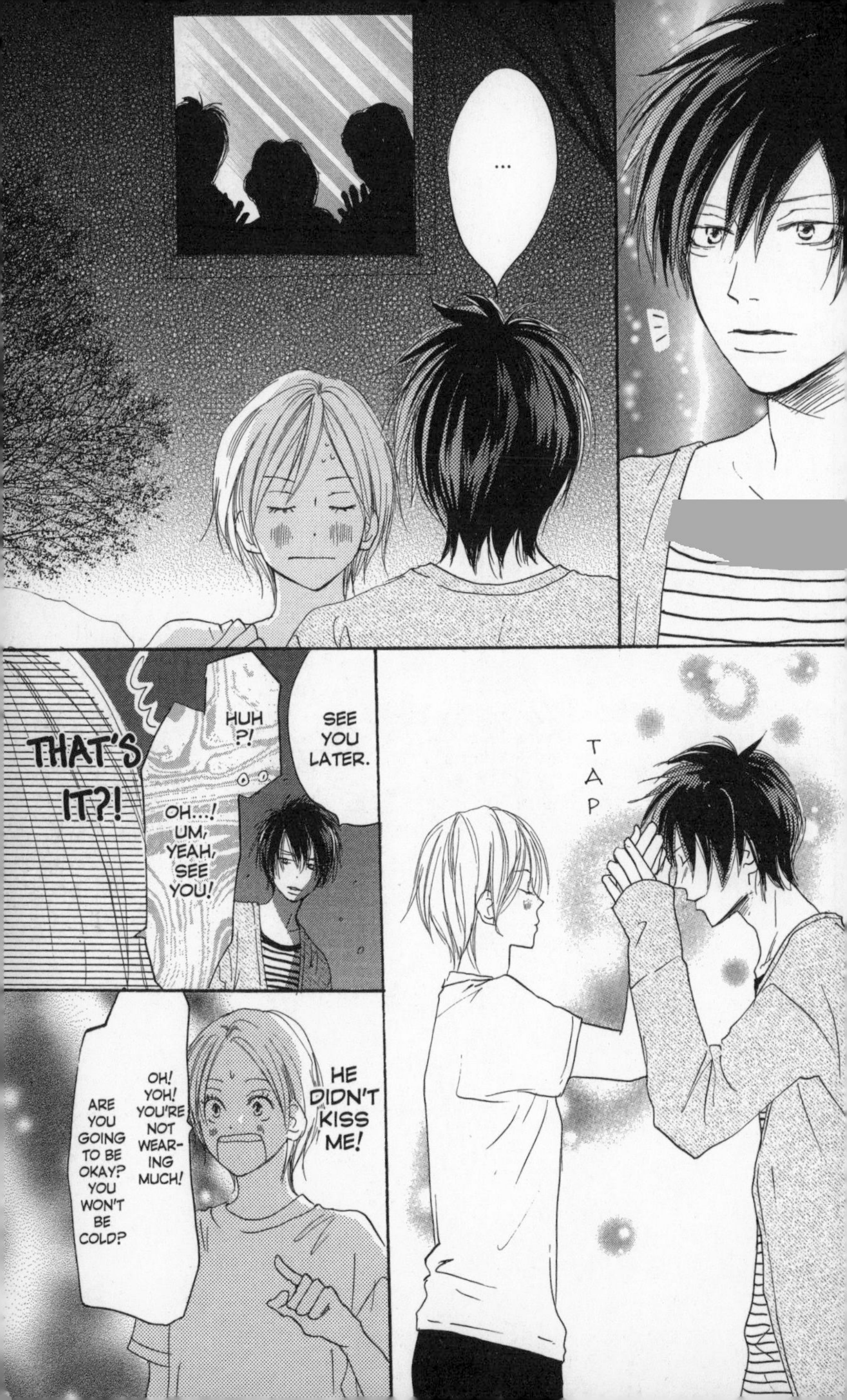
...
TAP
SEE YOU LATER.
HUH?!
OH...! UM, YEAH, SEE YOU!
THAT'S IT?!
HE DIDN'T KISS ME!
OH! YOH! YOU'RE NOT WEAR-ING MUCH!
ARE YOU GOING TO BE OKAY? YOU WON'T BE COLD?

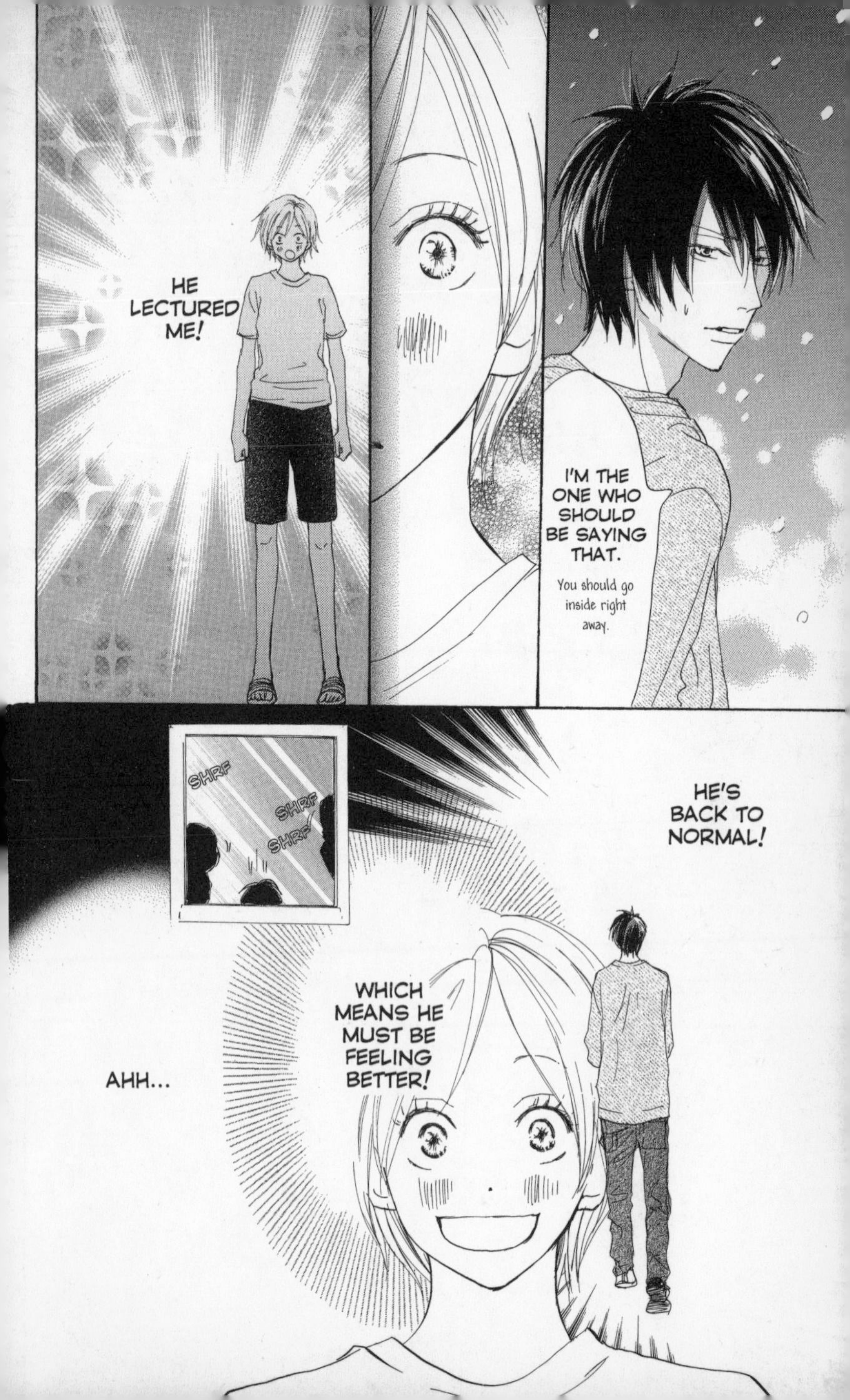
I'M THE ONE WHO SHOULD BE SAYING THAT.
You should go inside right away.
HE LECTURED ME!
HE'S BACK TO NORMAL!
SHRF
SHRF
SHRF
WHICH MEANS HE MUST BE FEELING BETTER!
AHH...

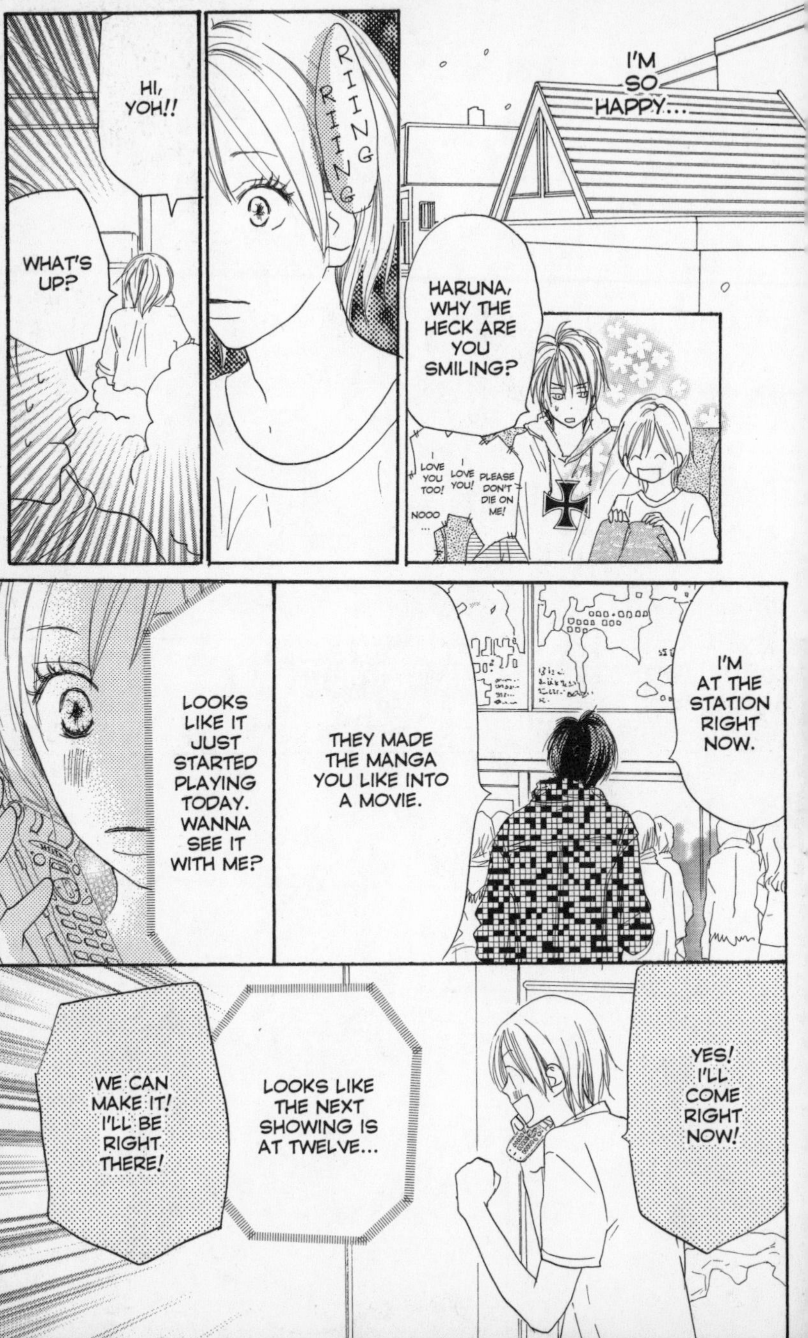
I'M SO HAPPY...
HARUNA, WHY THE HECK ARE YOU SMILING?
PLEASE DON'T DIE ON ME!
I LOVE YOU!
I LOVE YOU TOO!
NOOO...
RIIING RIIING
HI, YOH!!
WHAT'S UP?
I'M AT THE STATION RIGHT NOW.
THEY MADE THE MANGA YOU LIKE INTO A MOVIE.
LOOKS LIKE IT JUST STARTED PLAYING TODAY. WANNA SEE IT WITH ME?
YES! I'LL COME RIGHT NOW!
LOOKS LIKE THE NEXT SHOWING IS AT TWELVE...
WE CAN MAKE IT! I'LL BE RIGHT THERE!

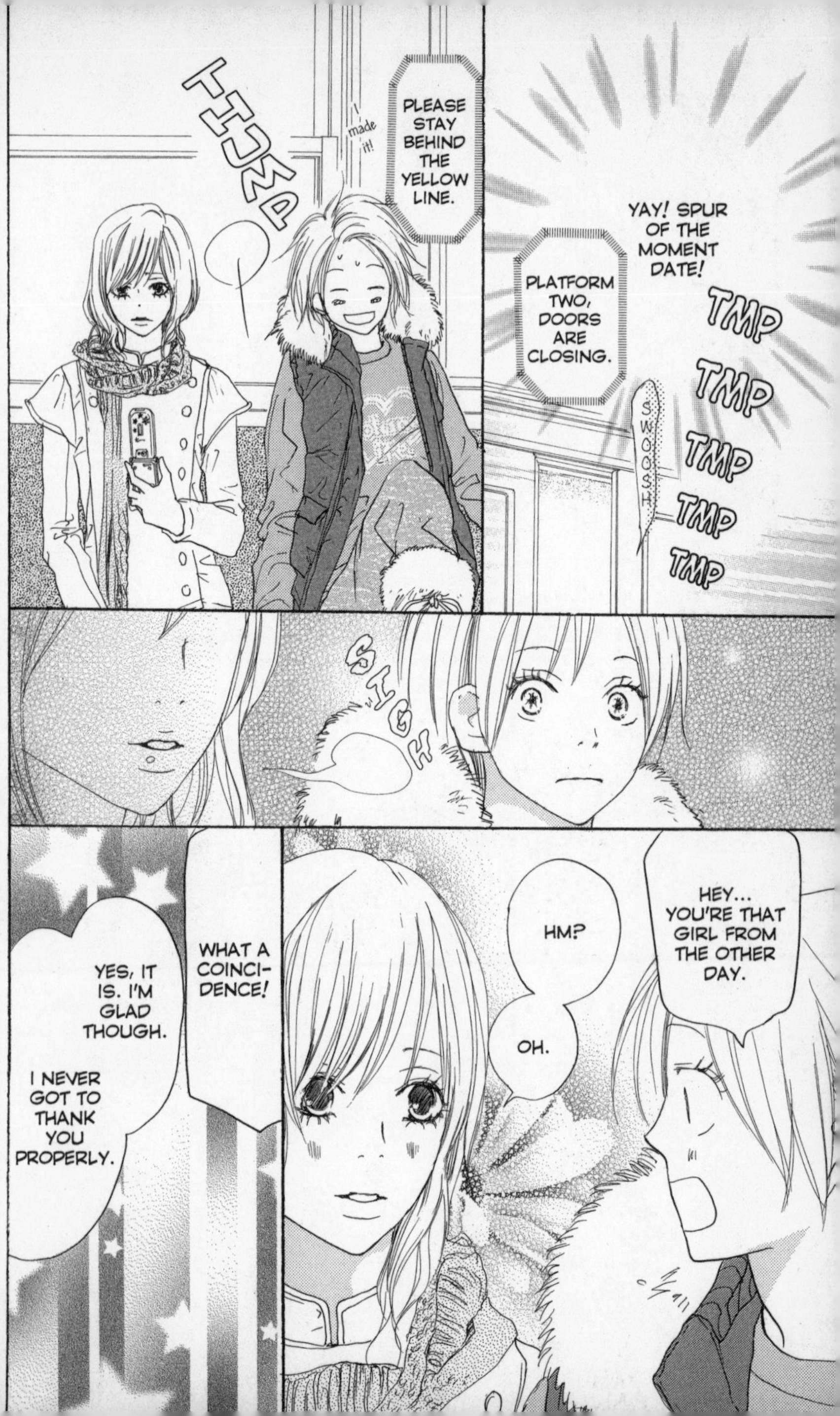
YAY! SPUR OF THE MOMENT DATE!
PLATFORM TWO, DOORS ARE CLOSING.
SWOOSH
TMP
TMP
TMP
TMP
TMP
PLEASE STAY BEHIND THE YELLOW LINE.
I made it!
THUMP
SIGH
HEY... YOU'RE THAT GIRL FROM THE OTHER DAY.
HM?
OH.
WHAT A COINCI-DENCE!
YES, IT IS. I'M GLAD THOUGH.
I NEVER GOT TO THANK YOU PROPERLY.

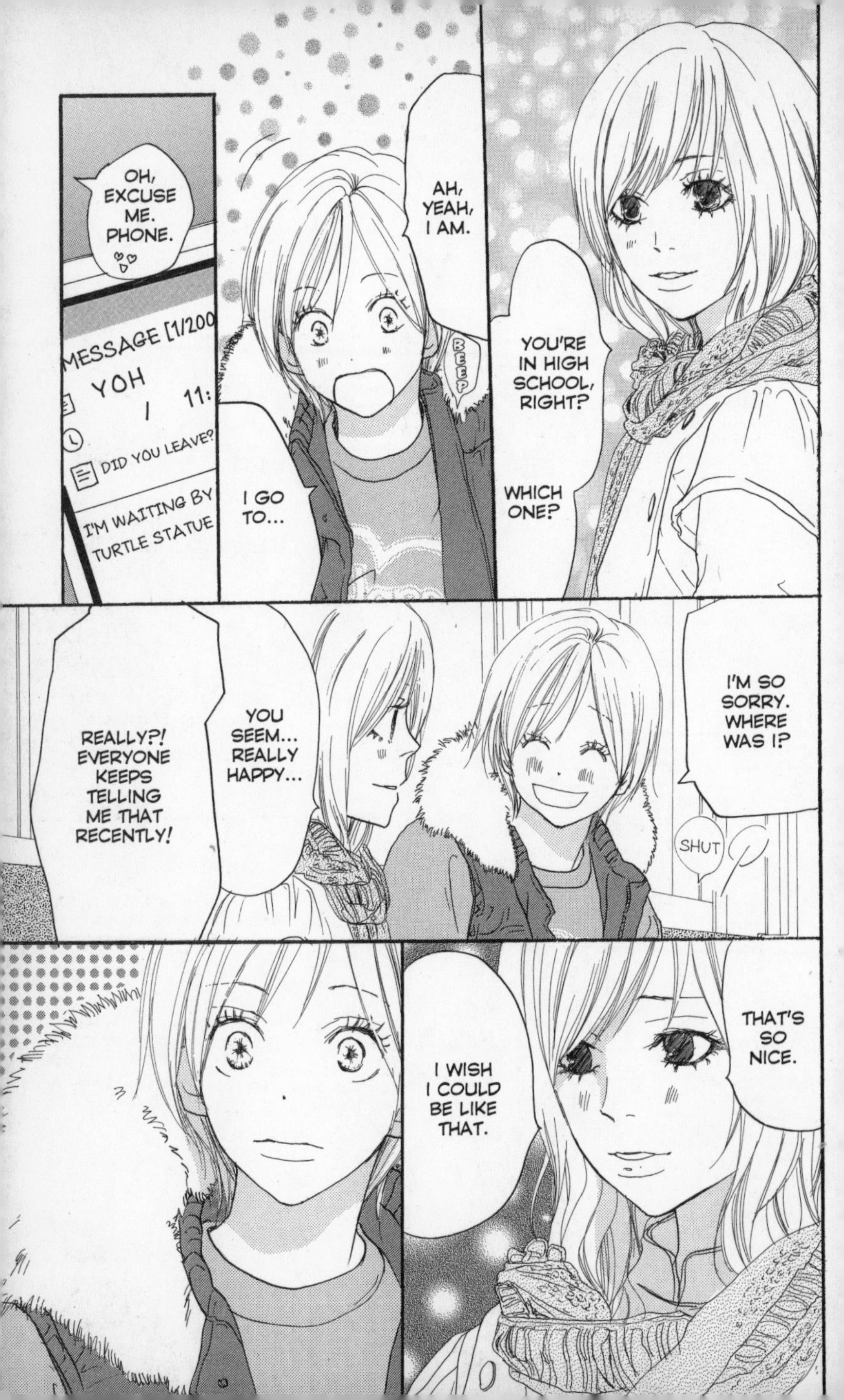
YOU'RE IN HIGH SCHOOL, RIGHT?
WHICH ONE?
AH, YEAH, I AM.
BEEP
I GO TO...
OH, EXCUSE ME. PHONE.
MESSAGE [1/200
YOH
11:
DID YOU LEAVE?
I'M WAITING BY TURTLE STATUE
I'M SO SORRY. WHERE WAS I?
SHUT
YOU SEEM... REALLY HAPPY...
REALLY?! EVERYONE KEEPS TELLING ME THAT RECENTLY!
THAT'S SO NICE.
I WISH I COULD BE LIKE THAT.

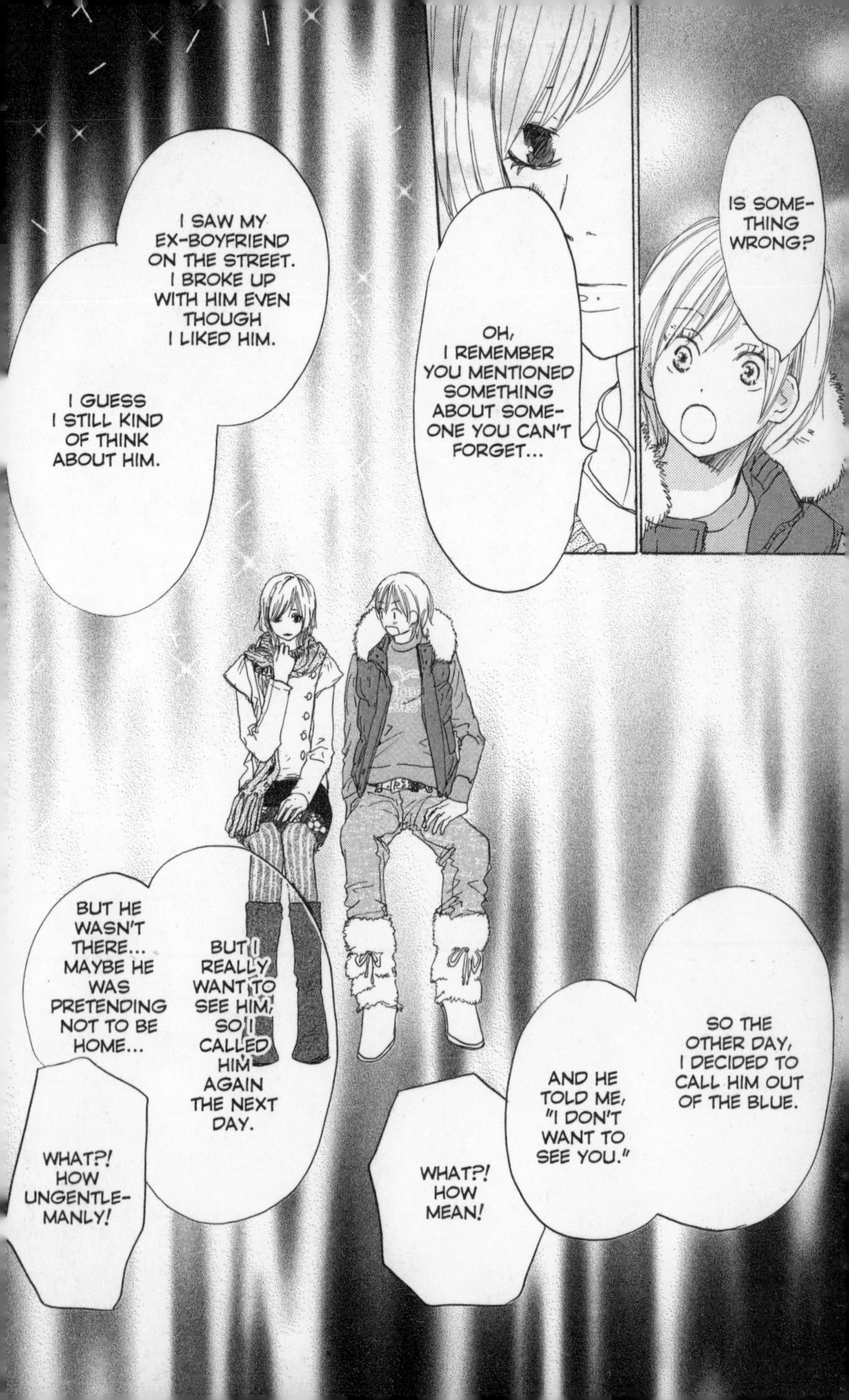

IS SOME-THING WRONG?
OH, I REMEMBER YOU MENTIONED SOMETHING ABOUT SOME-ONE YOU CAN'T FORGET...
I SAW MY EX-BOYFRIEND ON THE STREET. I BROKE UP WITH HIM EVEN THOUGH I LIKED HIM.
I GUESS I STILL KIND OF THINK ABOUT HIM.
SO THE OTHER DAY, I DECIDED TO CALL HIM OUT OF THE BLUE.
AND HE TOLD ME, "I DON'T WANT TO SEE YOU."
WHAT?! HOW MEAN!
BUT I REALLY WANT TO SEE HIM, SO I CALLED HIM AGAIN THE NEXT DAY.
BUT HE WASN'T THERE... MAYBE HE WAS PRETENDING NOT TO BE HOME...
WHAT?! HOW UNGENTLE-MANLY!

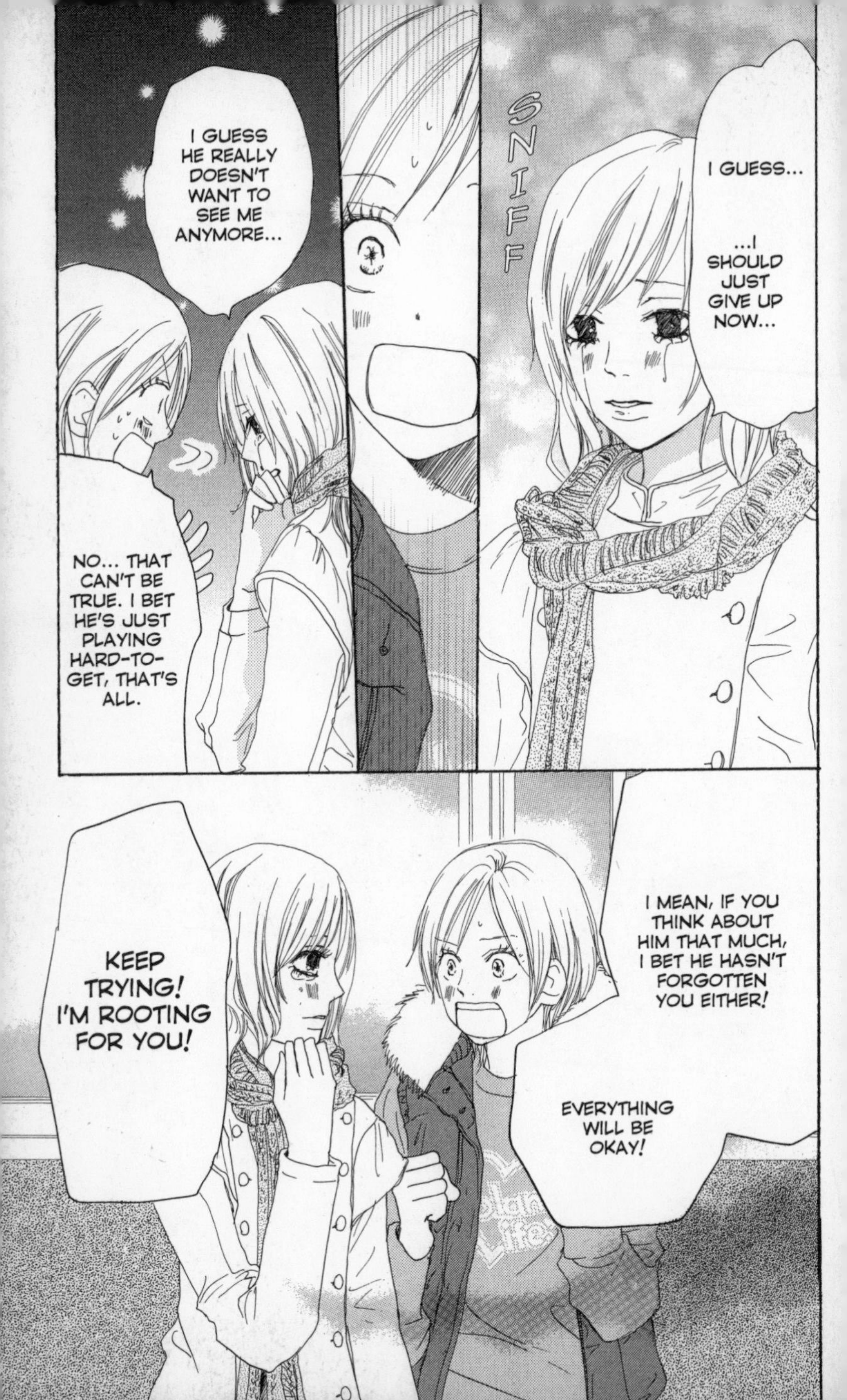
I GUESS...
...I SHOULD JUST GIVE UP NOW...
SNIFF
I GUESS HE REALLY DOESN'T WANT TO SEE ME ANYMORE...
NO... THAT CAN'T BE TRUE. I BET HE'S JUST PLAYING HARD-TO-GET, THAT'S ALL.
I MEAN, IF YOU THINK ABOUT HIM THAT MUCH, I BET HE HASN'T FORGOTTEN YOU EITHER!
EVERYTHING WILL BE OKAY!
KEEP TRYING! I'M ROOTING FOR YOU!

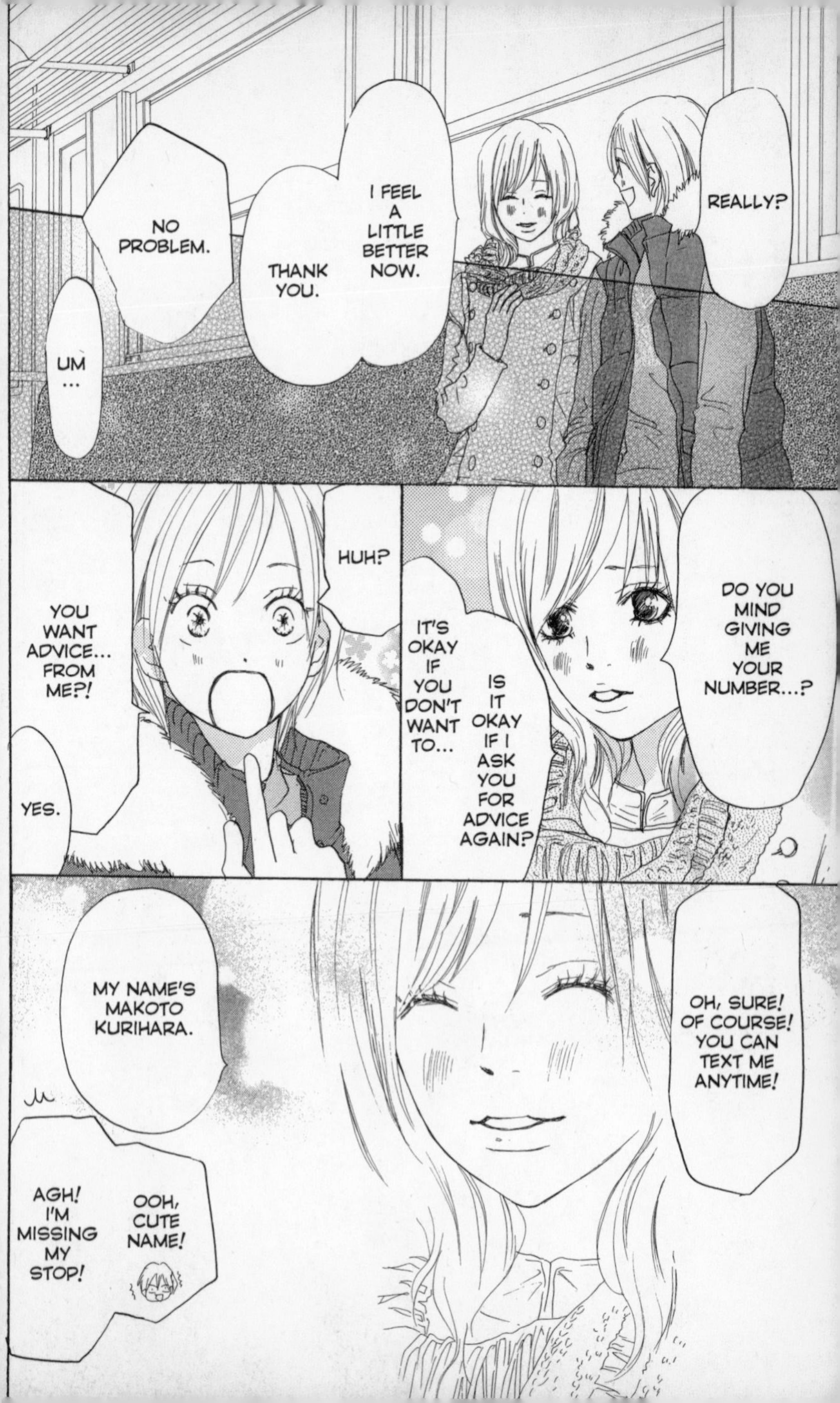
REALLY?
I FEEL A LITTLE BETTER NOW.
THANK YOU.
NO PROBLEM.
UM...
DO YOU MIND GIVING ME YOUR NUMBER...?
IS IT OKAY IF I ASK YOU FOR ADVICE AGAIN?
IT'S OKAY IF YOU DON'T WANT TO...
HUH?
YOU WANT ADVICE... FROM ME?!
YES.
OH, SURE! OF COURSE! YOU CAN TEXT ME ANYTIME!
MY NAME'S MAKOTO KURIHARA.
OOH, CUTE NAME!
AGH! I'M MISSING MY STOP!

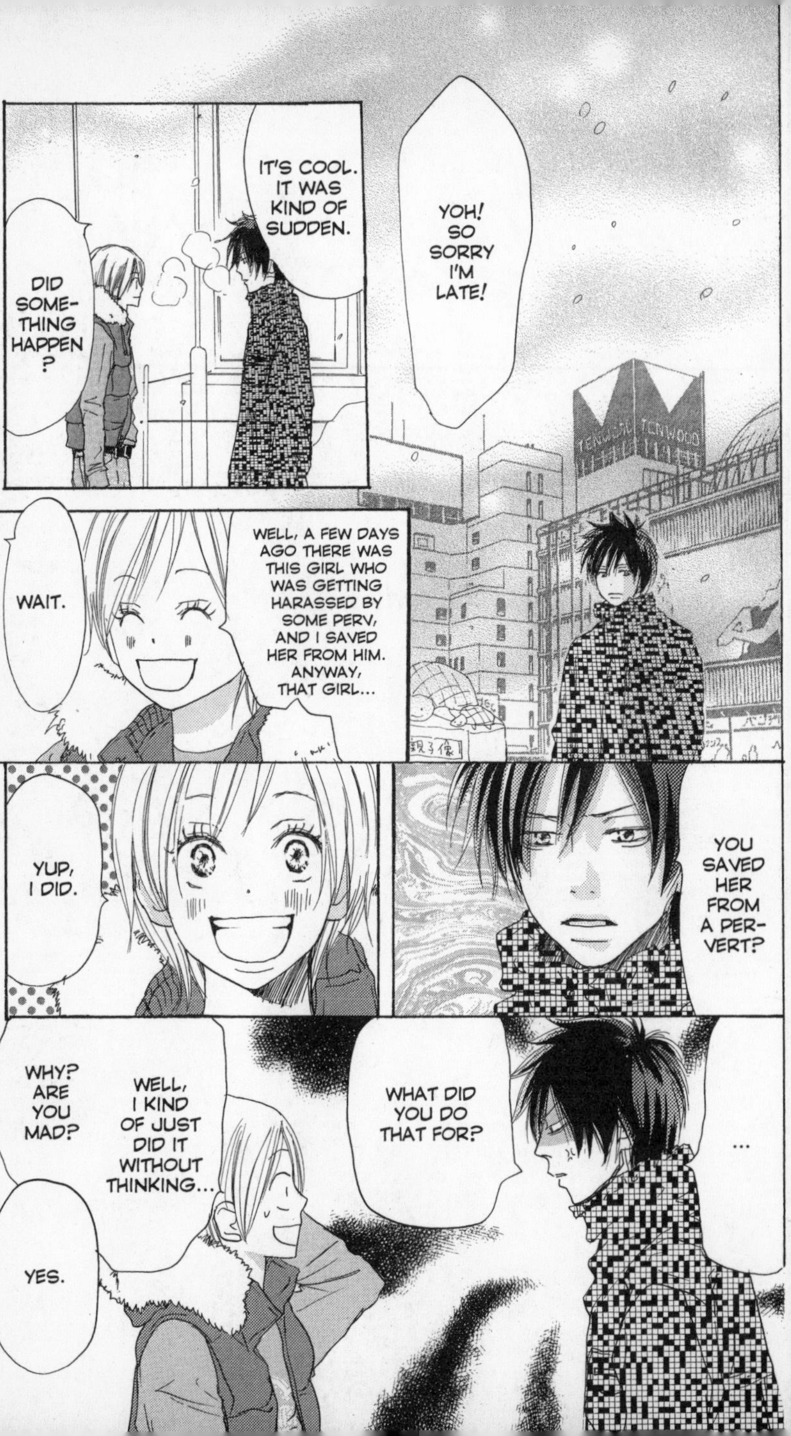
YOH! SO SORRY I'M LATE!
IT'S COOL. IT WAS KIND OF SUDDEN.
DID SOME-THING HAPPEN?
WELL, A FEW DAYS AGO THERE WAS THIS GIRL WHO WAS GETTING HARASSED BY SOME PERV, AND I SAVED HER FROM HIM. ANYWAY, THAT GIRL...
WAIT.
YOU SAVED HER FROM A PER-VERT?
YUP, I DID.
...
WHAT DID YOU DO THAT FOR?
WELL, I KIND OF JUST DID IT WITHOUT THINKING...
WHY? ARE YOU MAD?
YES.

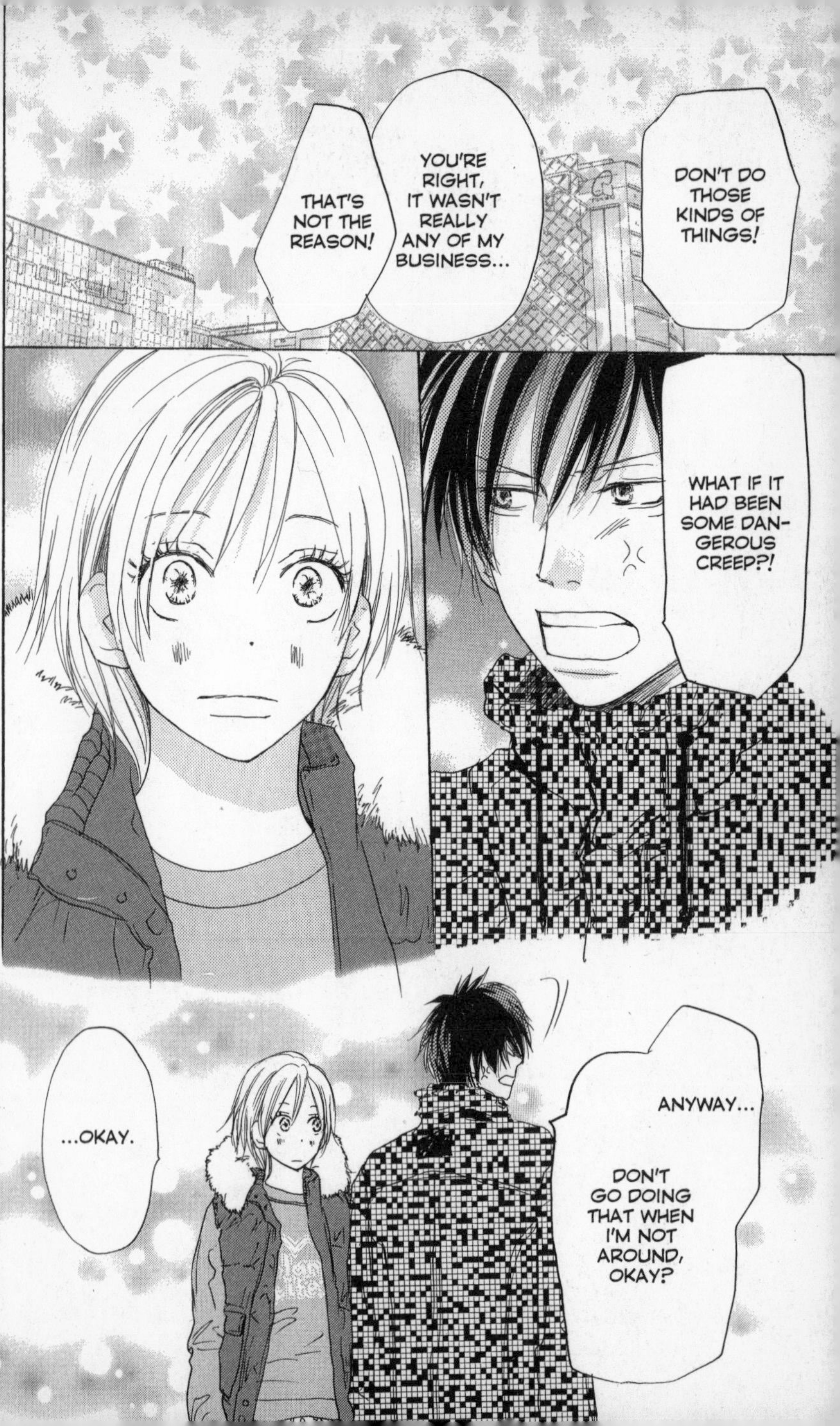
DON'T DO THOSE KINDS OF THINGS!
YOU'RE RIGHT, IT WASN'T REALLY ANY OF MY BUSINESS...
THAT'S NOT THE REASON!
WHAT IF IT HAD BEEN SOME DANGEROUS CREEP?!
ANYWAY...
DON'T GO DOING THAT WHEN I'M NOT AROUND, OKAY?
...OKAY.

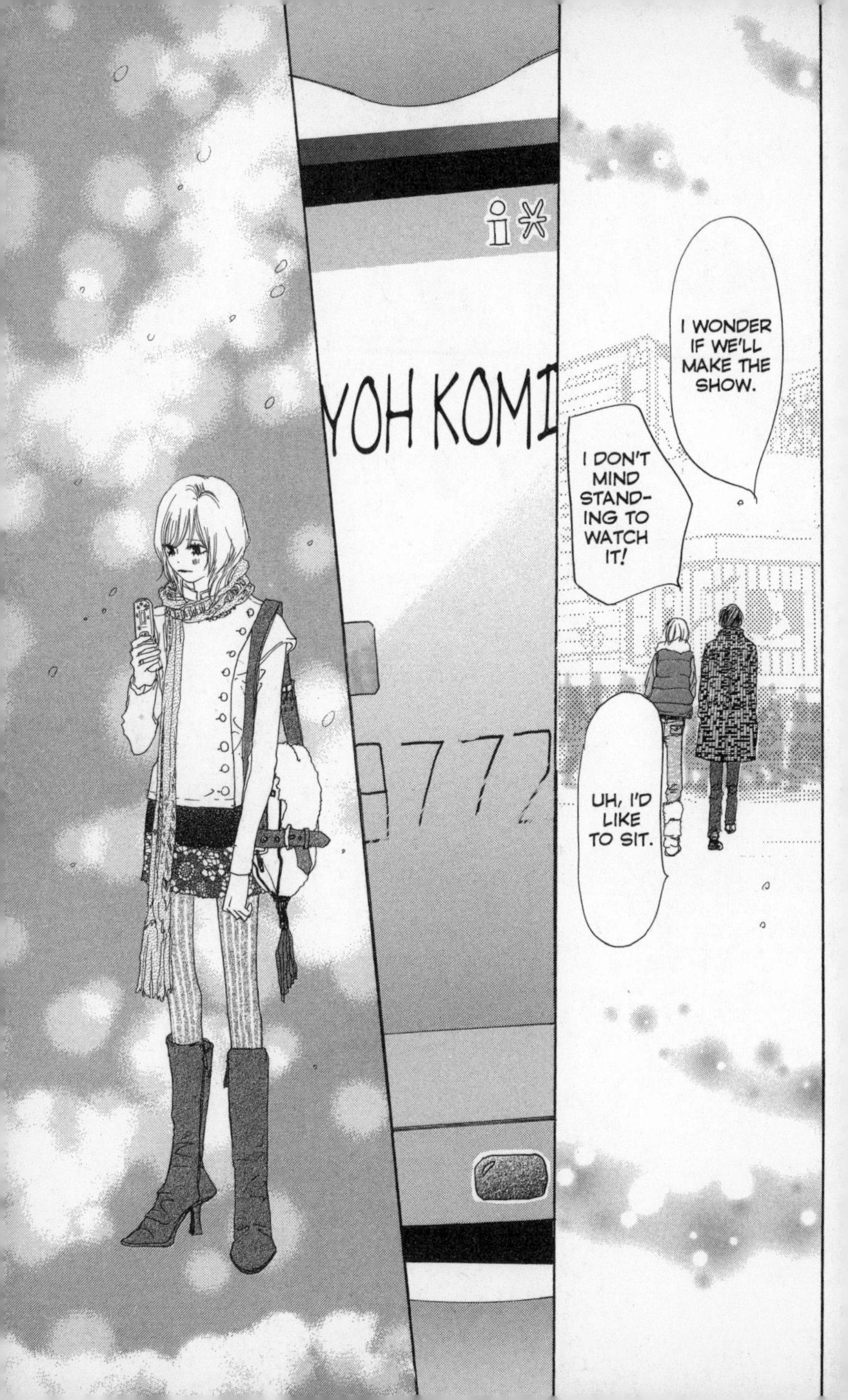
I WONDER IF WE'LL MAKE THE SHOW.
I DON'T MIND STAND-ING TO WATCH IT!
UH, I'D LIKE TO SIT.
YOH KOMI

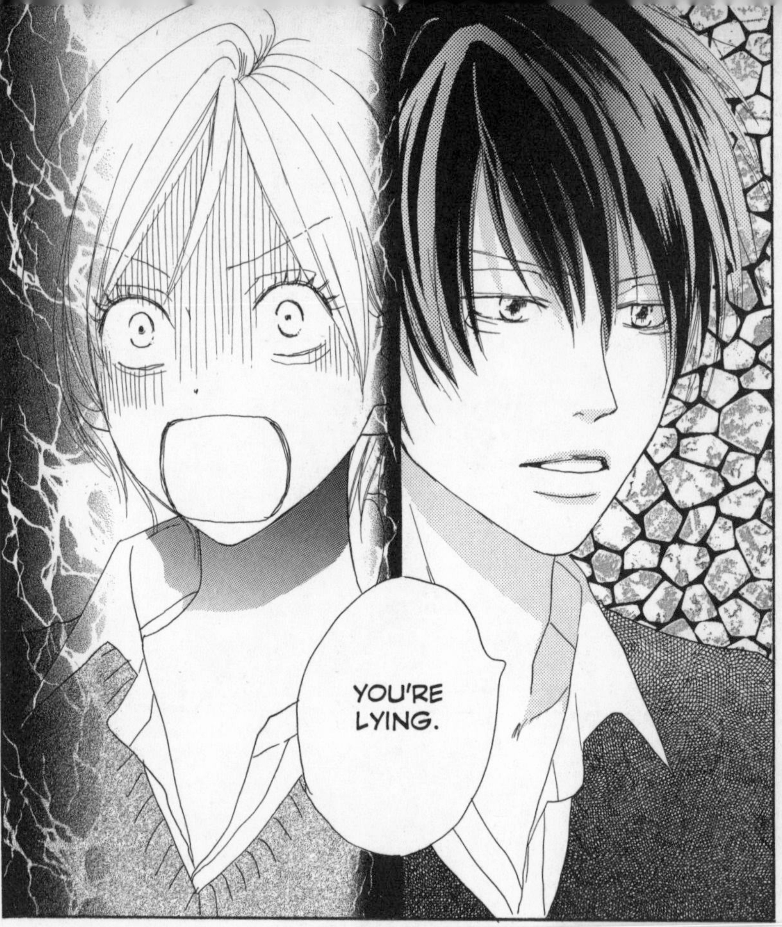
YOU'RE LYING.

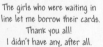

I recently took my niece to play "Oshare Majo: Love and Berry." Feeling the gaming juices (?) flowing, I told her, "Let Auntie Kazune play for a little bit." I got hooked! I mean, it's pretty dangerous when an adult can get hooked on this stuff. It made me want to collect all the cards. Collecting is fun, isn't it? Plus, you can't change clothes or win without collecting the cards... But as I was the only adult playing the game, it was a little embarrassing.

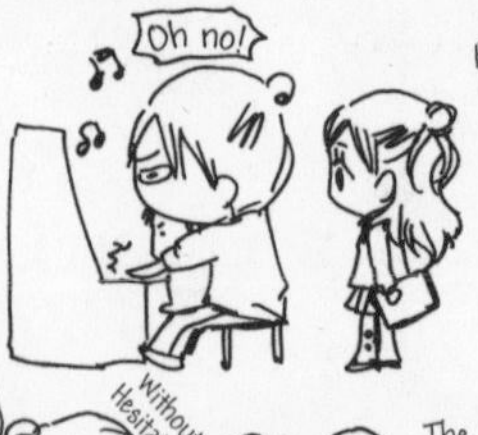
Oh no!

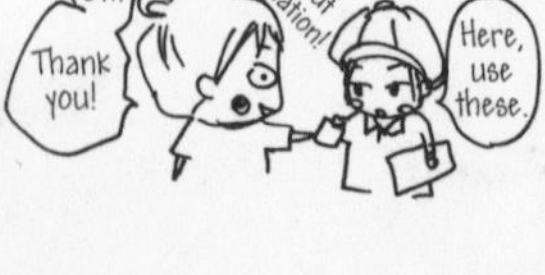
Without Hesitation!
Here, use these.
Oh!
Thank you!

The girls who were waiting in line let me borrow their cards. Thank you all! I didn't have any, after all.

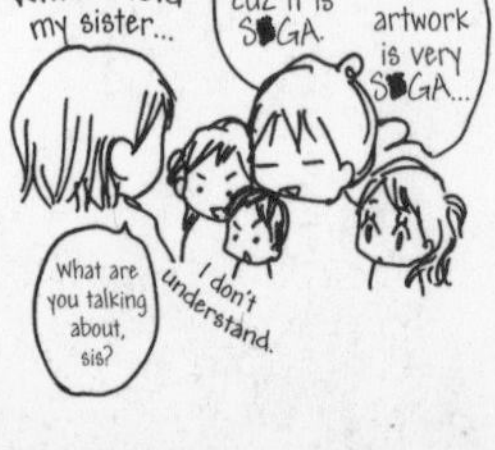
When I told my sister...
I guess cuz it is S[redacted]GA.
The artwork is very S[redacted]GA...
What are you talking about, sis?
I don't understand.

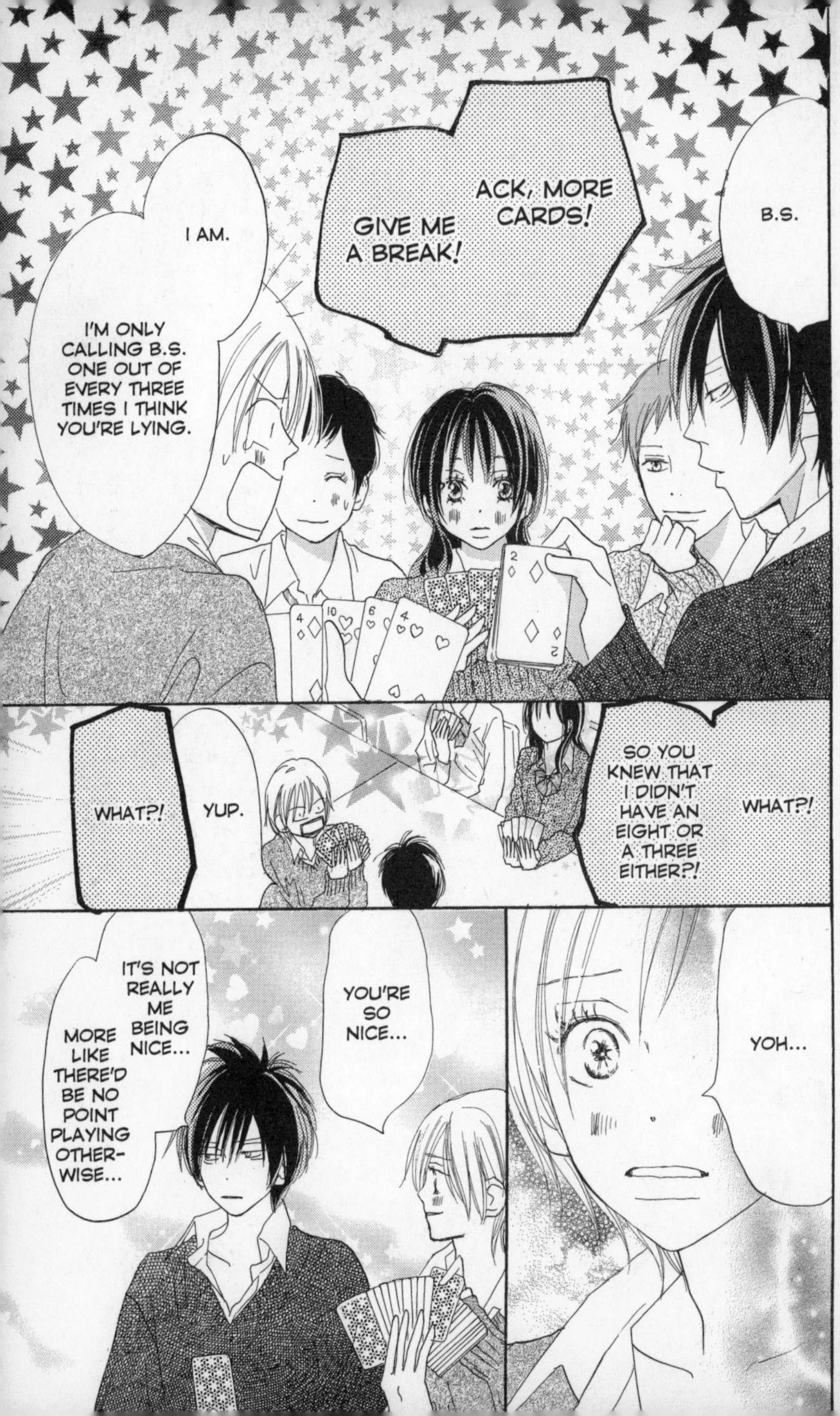
B.S.
ACK, MORE CARDS!
GIVE ME A BREAK!
I AM.
I'M ONLY CALLING B.S. ONE OUT OF EVERY THREE TIMES I THINK YOU'RE LYING.
WHAT?!
SO YOU KNEW THAT I DIDN'T HAVE AN EIGHT OR A THREE EITHER?!
YUP.
WHAT?!
YOH...
YOU'RE SO NICE...
IT'S NOT REALLY ME BEING NICE...
MORE LIKE THERE'D BE NO POINT PLAYING OTHER-WISE...

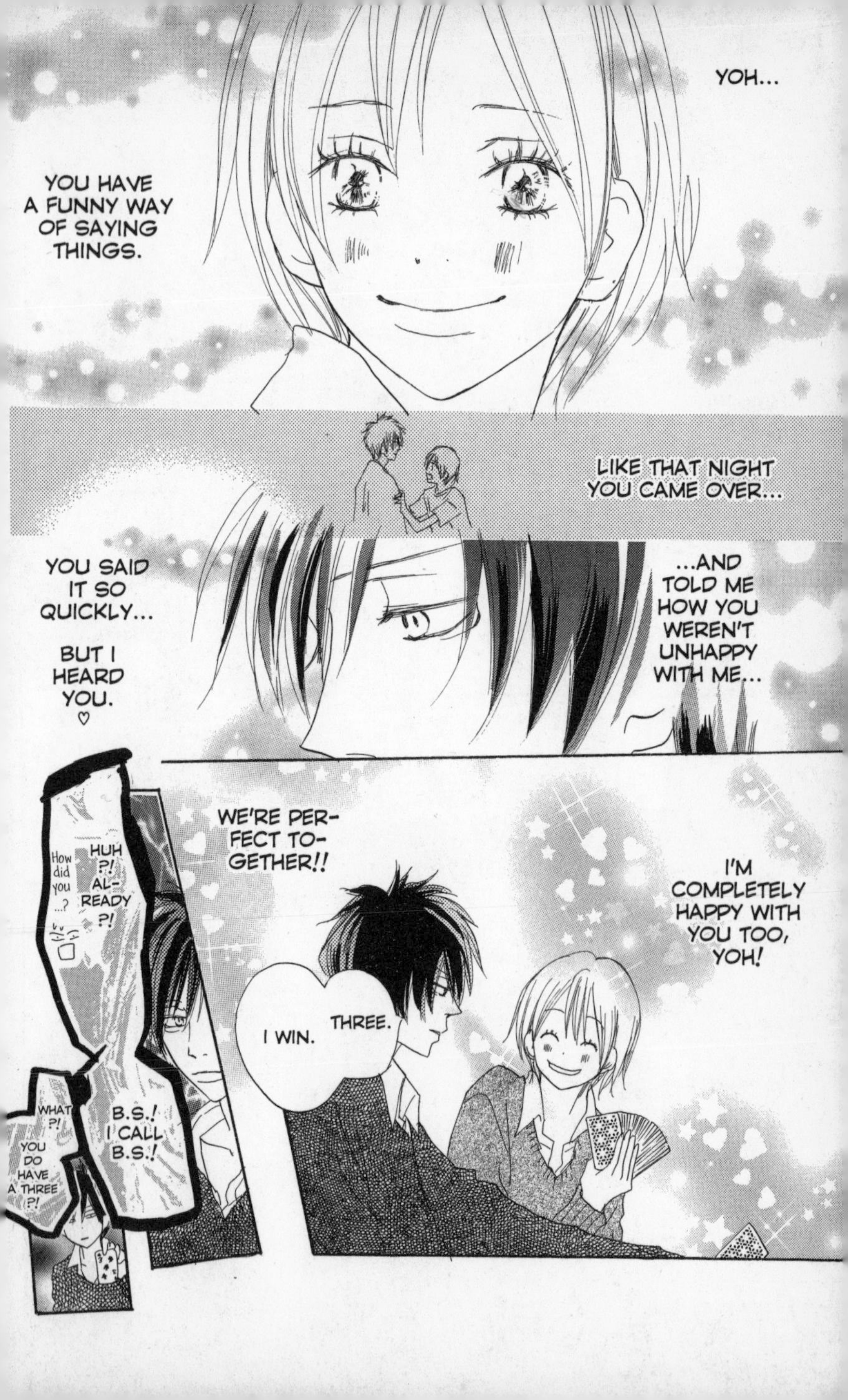
YOH...
YOU HAVE A FUNNY WAY OF SAYING THINGS.
LIKE THAT NIGHT YOU CAME OVER...
...AND TOLD ME HOW YOU WEREN'T UNHAPPY WITH ME...
YOU SAID IT SO QUICKLY...
BUT I HEARD YOU. ♡
I'M COMPLETELY HAPPY WITH YOU TOO, YOH!
WE'RE PERFECT TOGETHER!!
THREE.
I WIN.
HUH?! ALREADY?!
How did you ...?
B.S.! I CALL B.S.!
WHAT?! YOU DO HAVE A THREE?!

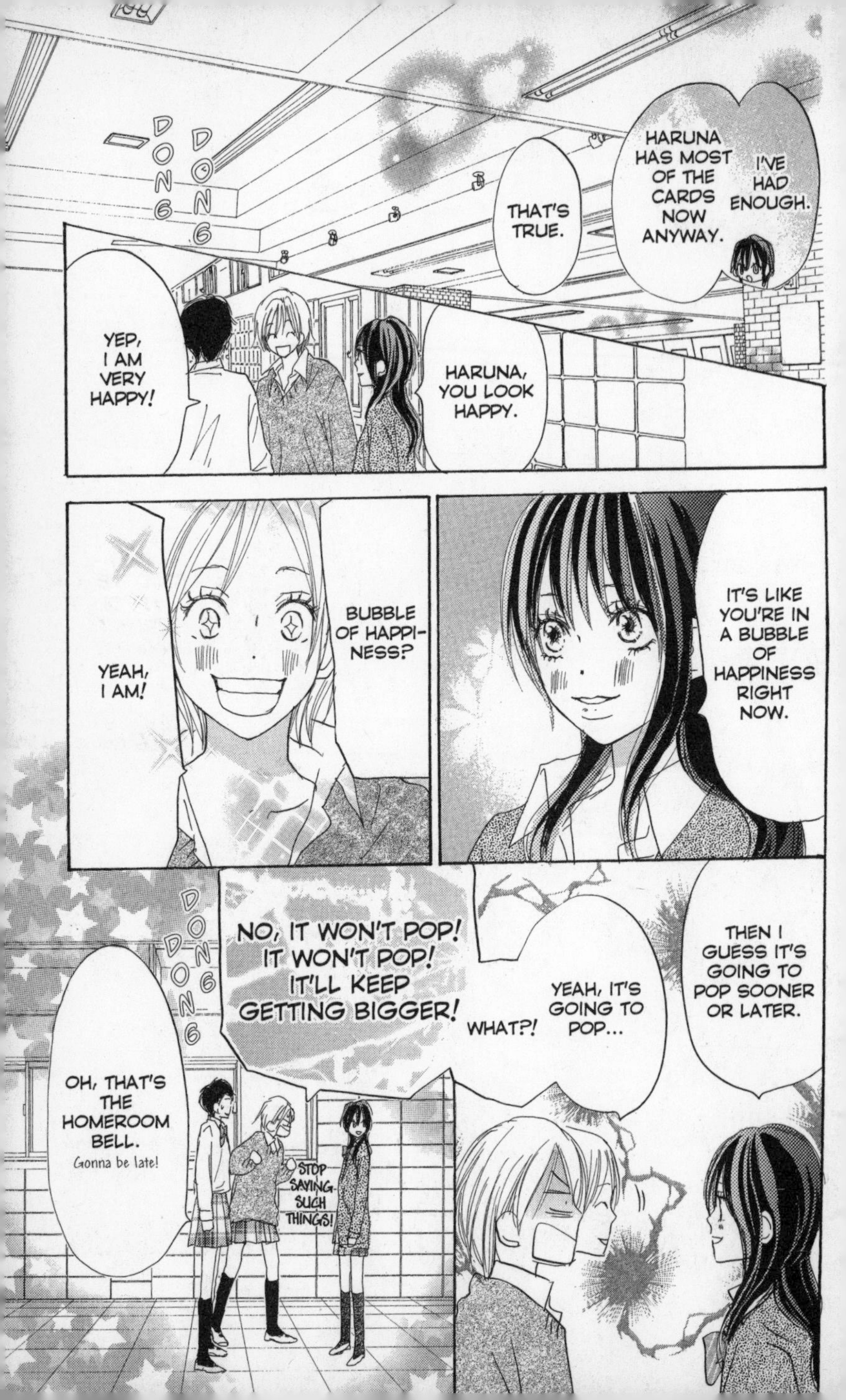
I'VE HAD ENOUGH.
HARUNA HAS MOST OF THE CARDS NOW ANYWAY.
THAT'S TRUE.
DONG DONG
HARUNA, YOU LOOK HAPPY.
YEP, I AM VERY HAPPY!
IT'S LIKE YOU'RE IN A BUBBLE OF HAPPINESS RIGHT NOW.
BUBBLE OF HAPPI-NESS?
YEAH, I AM!
THEN I GUESS IT'S GOING TO POP SOONER OR LATER.
YEAH, IT'S GOING TO POP...
WHAT?!
NO, IT WON'T POP! IT WON'T POP! IT'LL KEEP GETTING BIGGER!
DONG DONG
OH, THAT'S THE HOMEROOM BELL.
Gonna be late!
STOP SAYING SUCH THINGS!

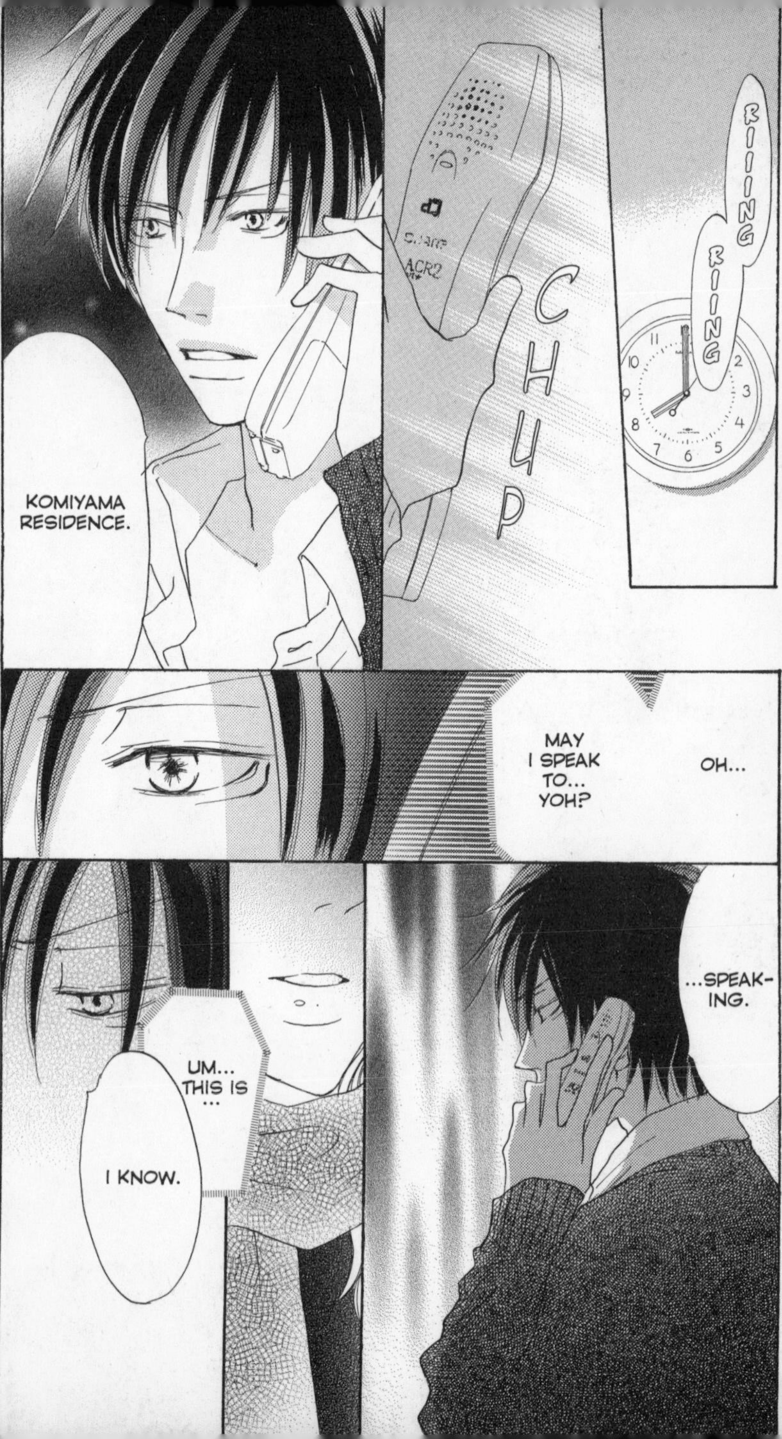
RIIIING
RING
CHUP
KOMIYAMA RESIDENCE.
OH...
MAY I SPEAK TO... YOH?
...SPEAKING.
UM... THIS IS ...
I KNOW.

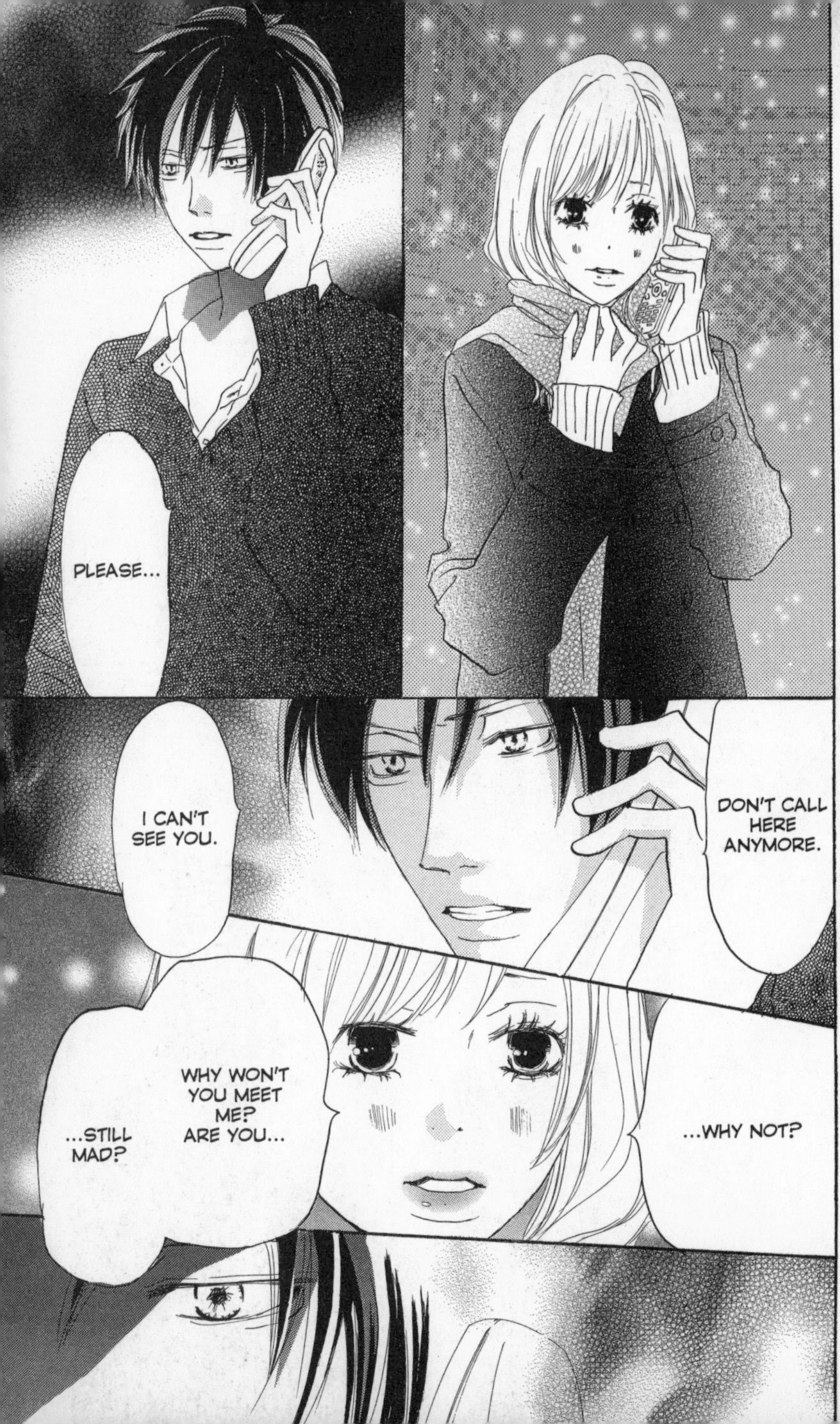
PLEASE...
DON'T CALL HERE ANYMORE.
I CAN'T SEE YOU.
...WHY NOT?
WHY WON'T YOU MEET ME? ARE YOU...
...STILL MAD?

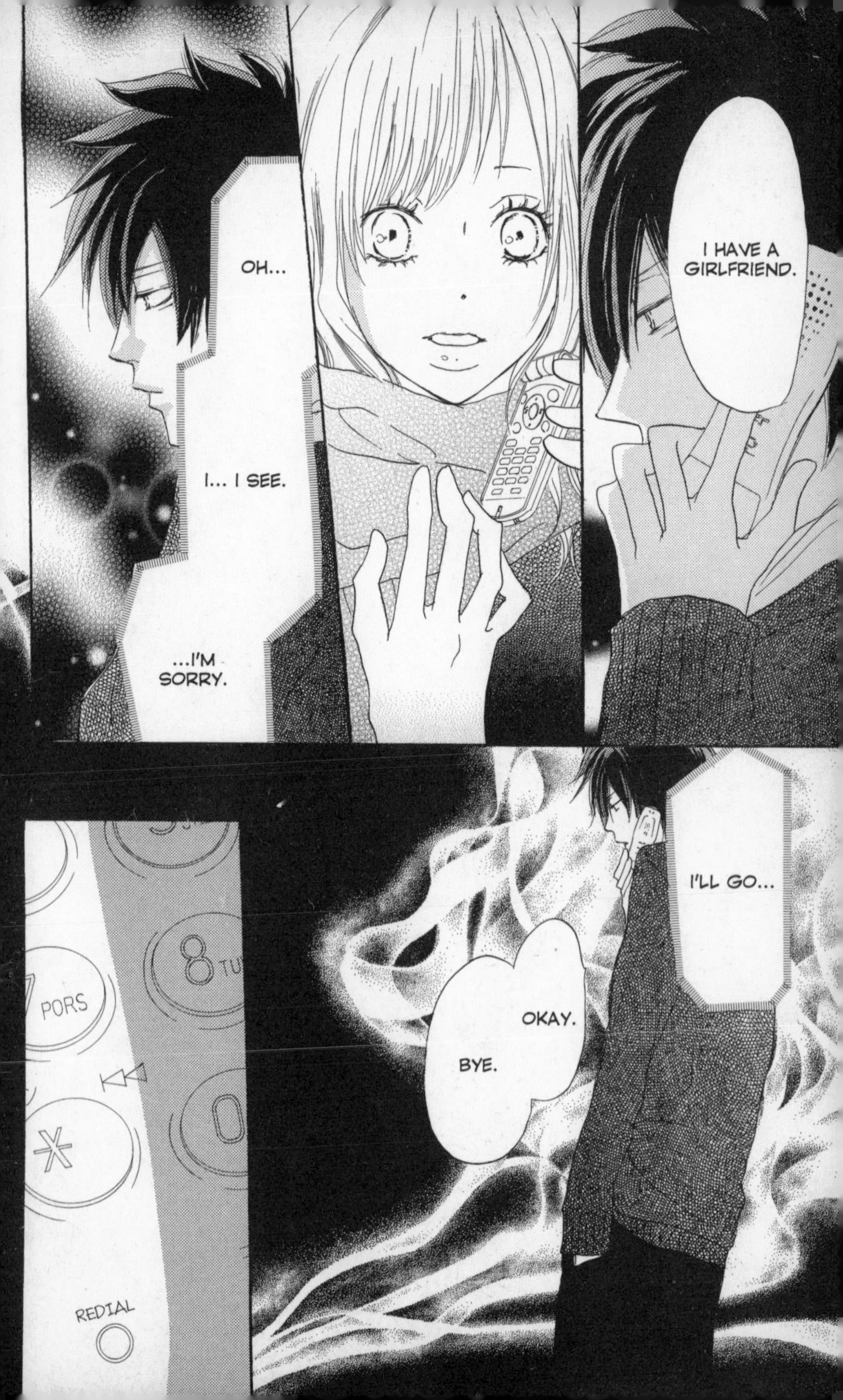
I HAVE A GIRLFRIEND.
OH...
I... I SEE.
...I'M SORRY.
I'LL GO...
OKAY.
BYE.
REDIAL

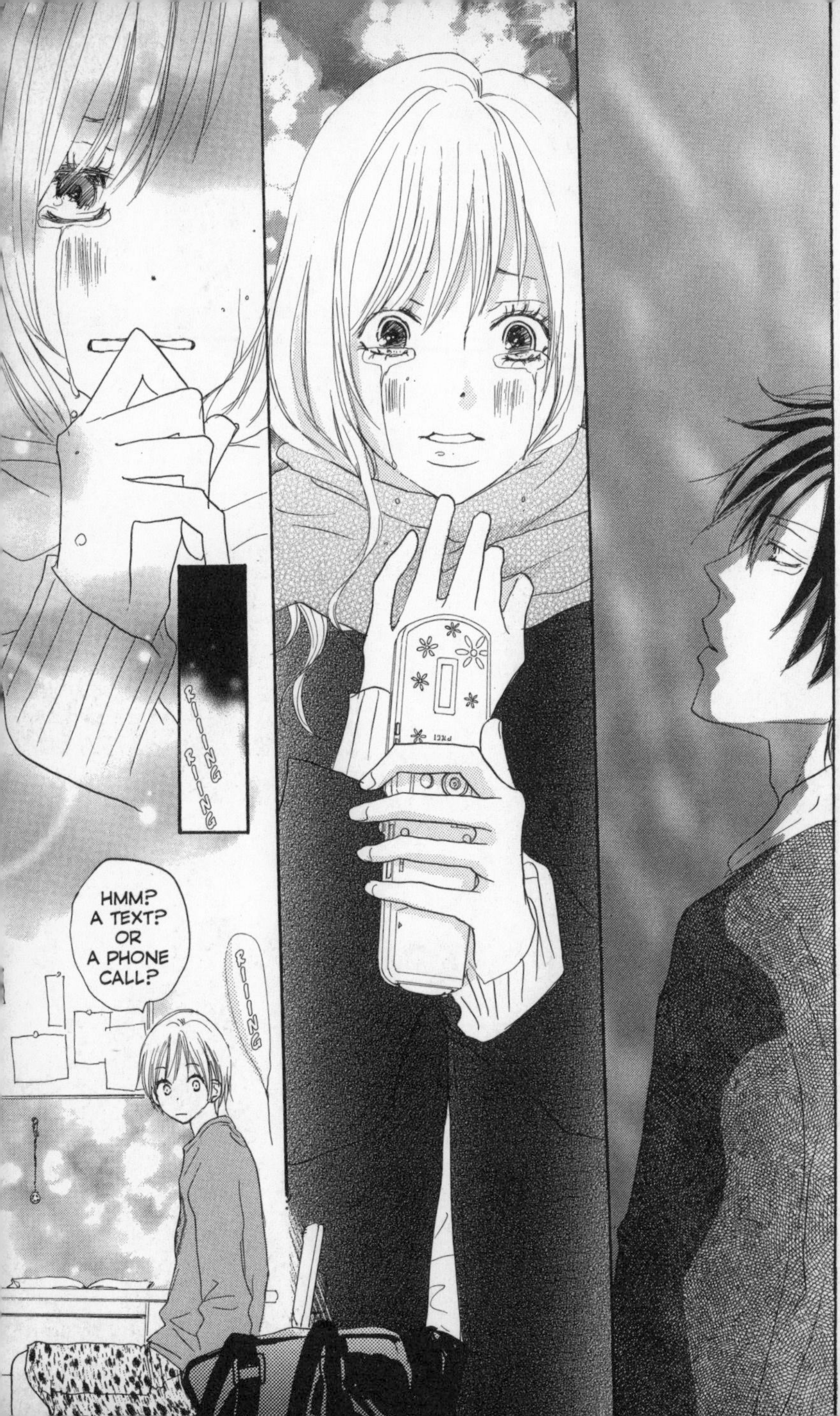
RIIING RIIING
RIIING
HMM? A TEXT? OR A PHONE CALL?

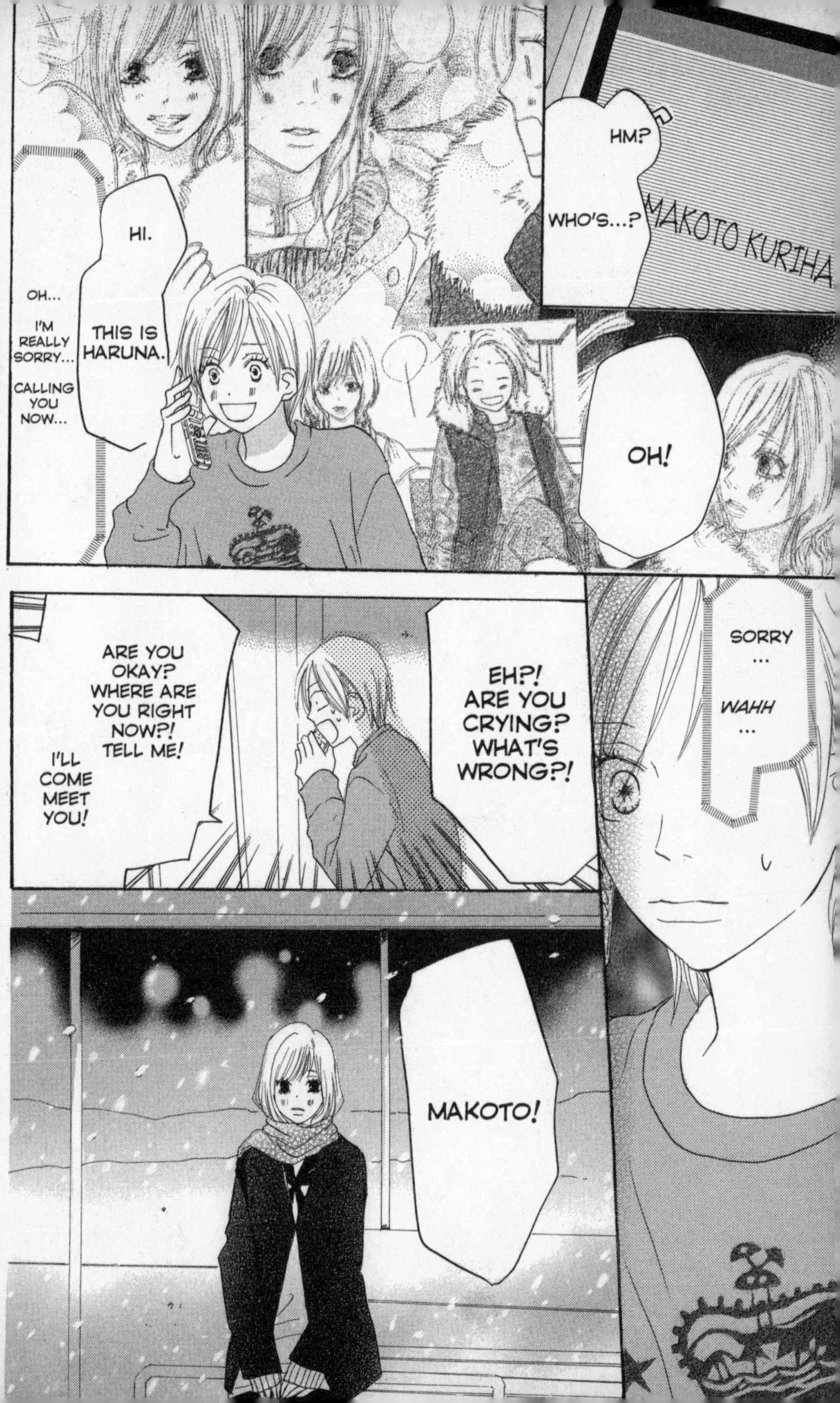

HM?
WHO'S...?
MAKOTO KURIHA
OH!
HI.
THIS IS HARUNA.
OH... I'M REALLY SORRY... CALLING YOU NOW...
SORRY... WAHH...
EH?! ARE YOU CRYING? WHAT'S WRONG?!
ARE YOU OKAY? WHERE ARE YOU RIGHT NOW?! TELL ME!
I'LL COME MEET YOU!
MAKOTO!

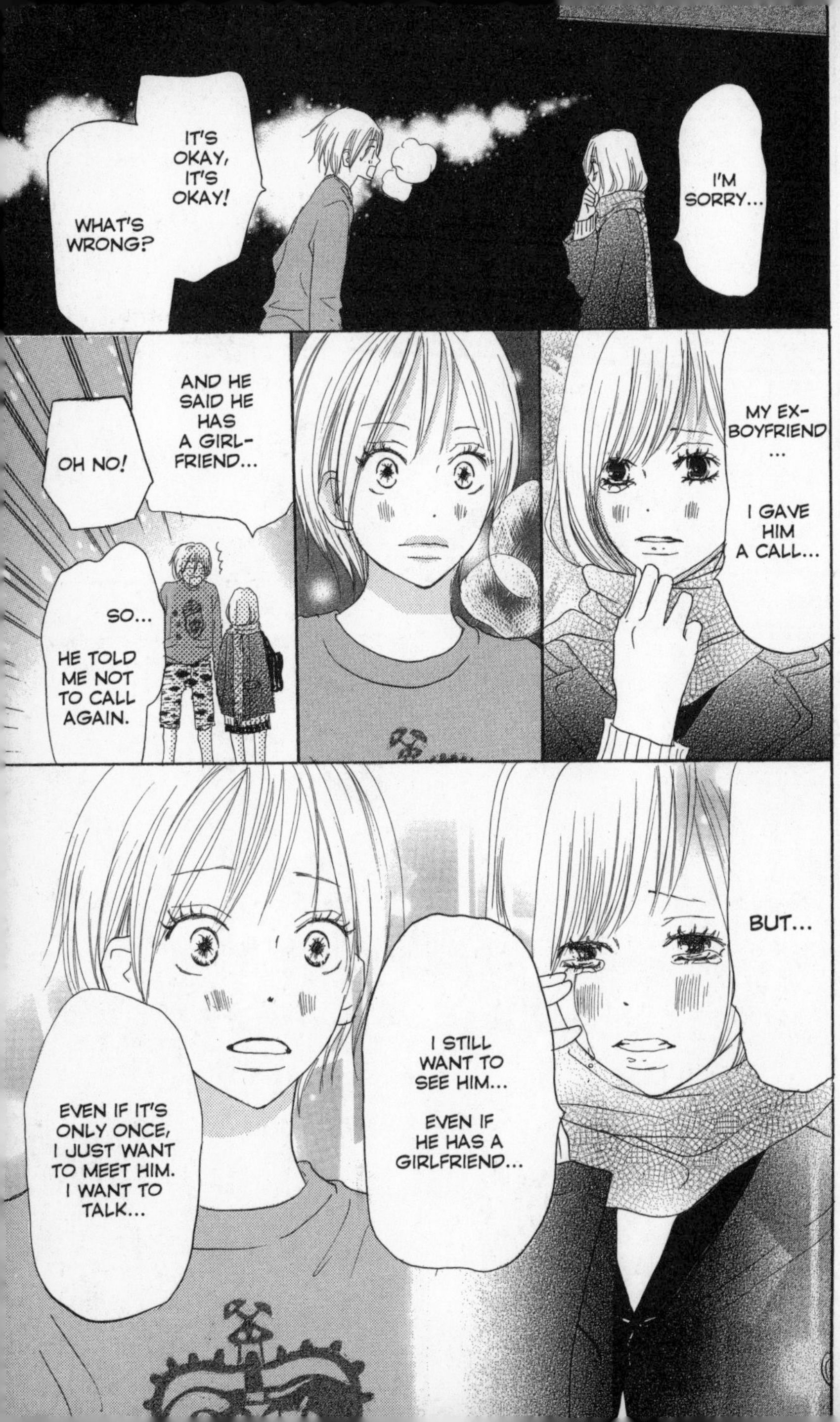
I'M SORRY...
IT'S OKAY, IT'S OKAY!
WHAT'S WRONG?
MY EX-BOYFRIEND...
I GAVE HIM A CALL...
AND HE SAID HE HAS A GIRLFRIEND...
OH NO!
SO...
HE TOLD ME NOT TO CALL AGAIN.
BUT...
I STILL WANT TO SEE HIM...
EVEN IF HE HAS A GIRLFRIEND...
EVEN IF IT'S ONLY ONCE, I JUST WANT TO MEET HIM. I WANT TO TALK...

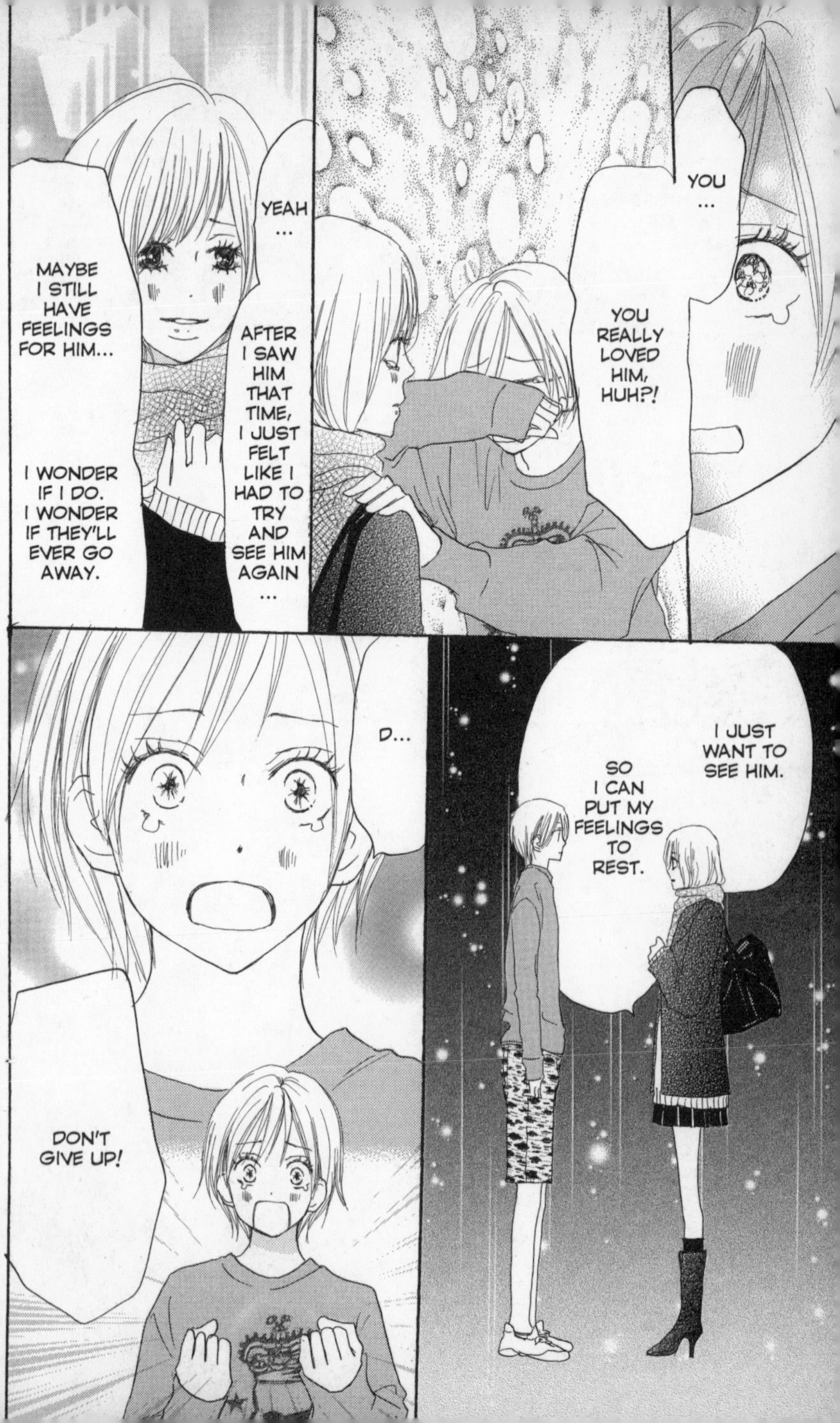
YOU ...
YOU REALLY LOVED HIM, HUH?!
YEAH ...
AFTER I SAW HIM THAT TIME, I JUST FELT LIKE I HAD TO TRY AND SEE HIM AGAIN ...
MAYBE I STILL HAVE FEELINGS FOR HIM...
I WONDER IF I DO. I WONDER IF THEY'LL EVER GO AWAY.
I JUST WANT TO SEE HIM.
SO I CAN PUT MY FEELINGS TO REST.
D...
DON'T GIVE UP!

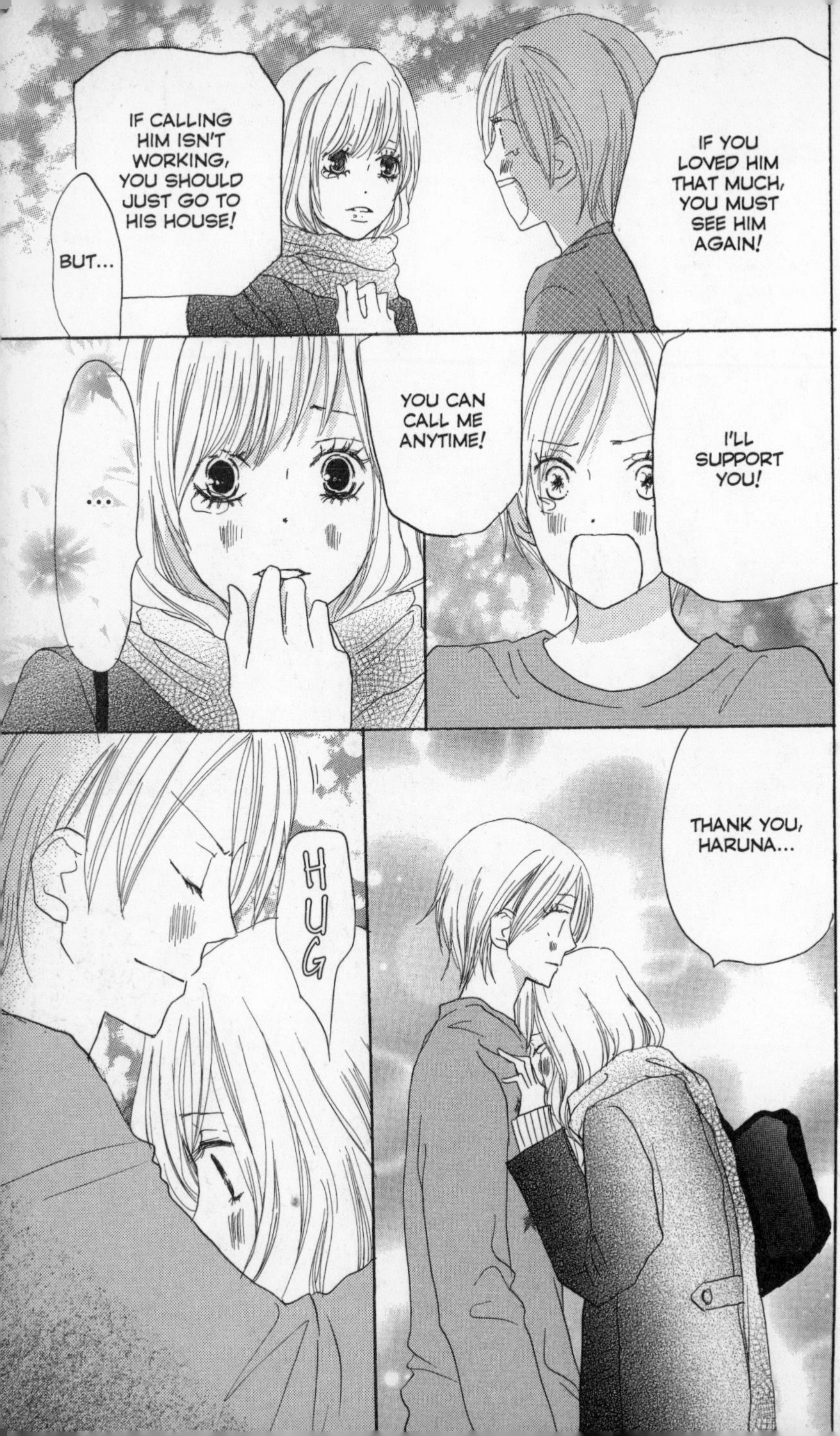
IF YOU LOVED HIM THAT MUCH, YOU MUST SEE HIM AGAIN!
IF CALLING HIM ISN'T WORKING, YOU SHOULD JUST GO TO HIS HOUSE!
BUT...
I'LL SUPPORT YOU!
YOU CAN CALL ME ANYTIME!
...
THANK YOU, HARUNA...
HUG

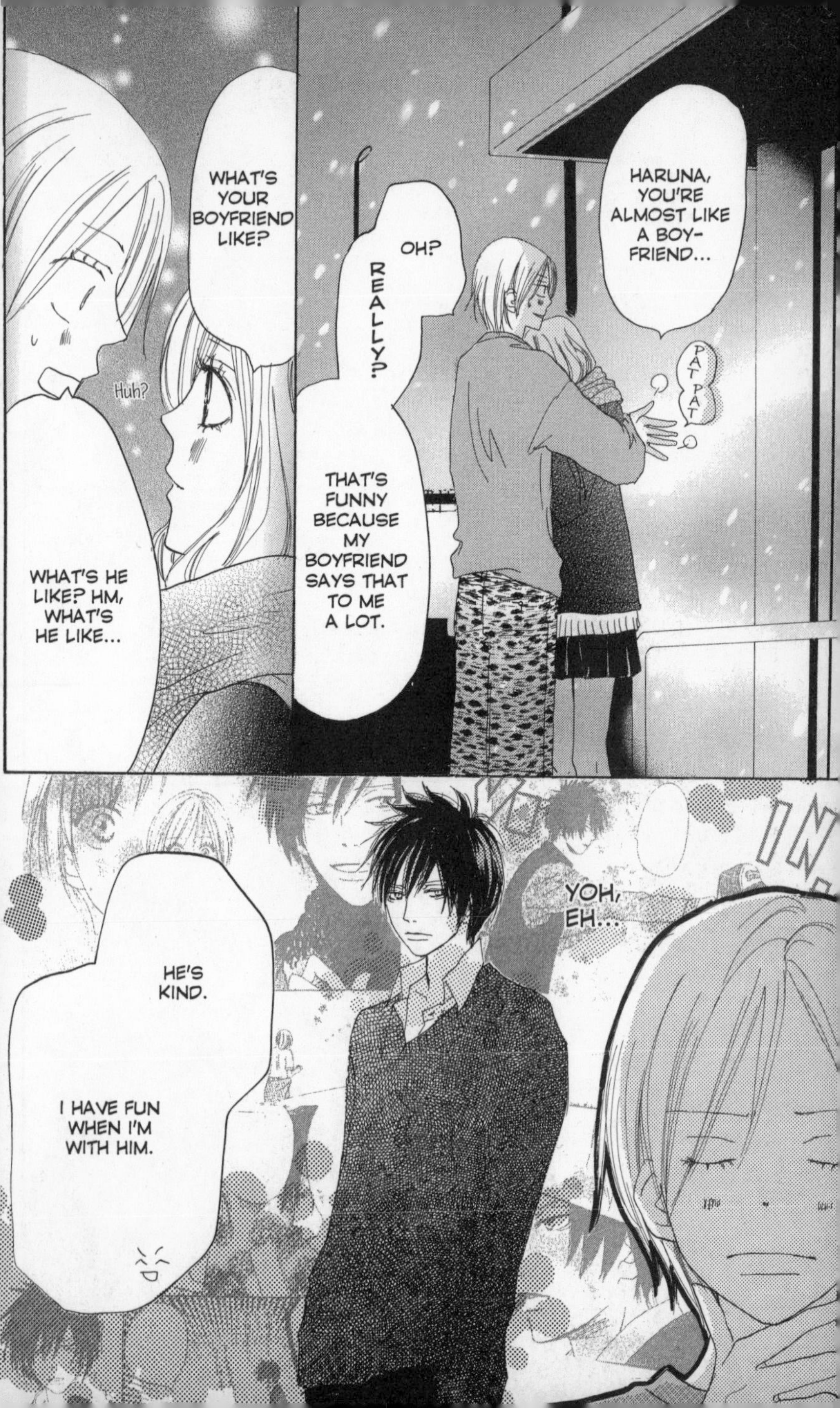
HARUNA, YOU'RE ALMOST LIKE A BOY-FRIEND...
PAT PAT
OH? REALLY?
THAT'S FUNNY BECAUSE MY BOYFRIEND SAYS THAT TO ME A LOT.
WHAT'S YOUR BOYFRIEND LIKE?
Huh?
WHAT'S HE LIKE? HM, WHAT'S HE LIKE...
YOH, EH...
HE'S KIND.
I HAVE FUN WHEN I'M WITH HIM.

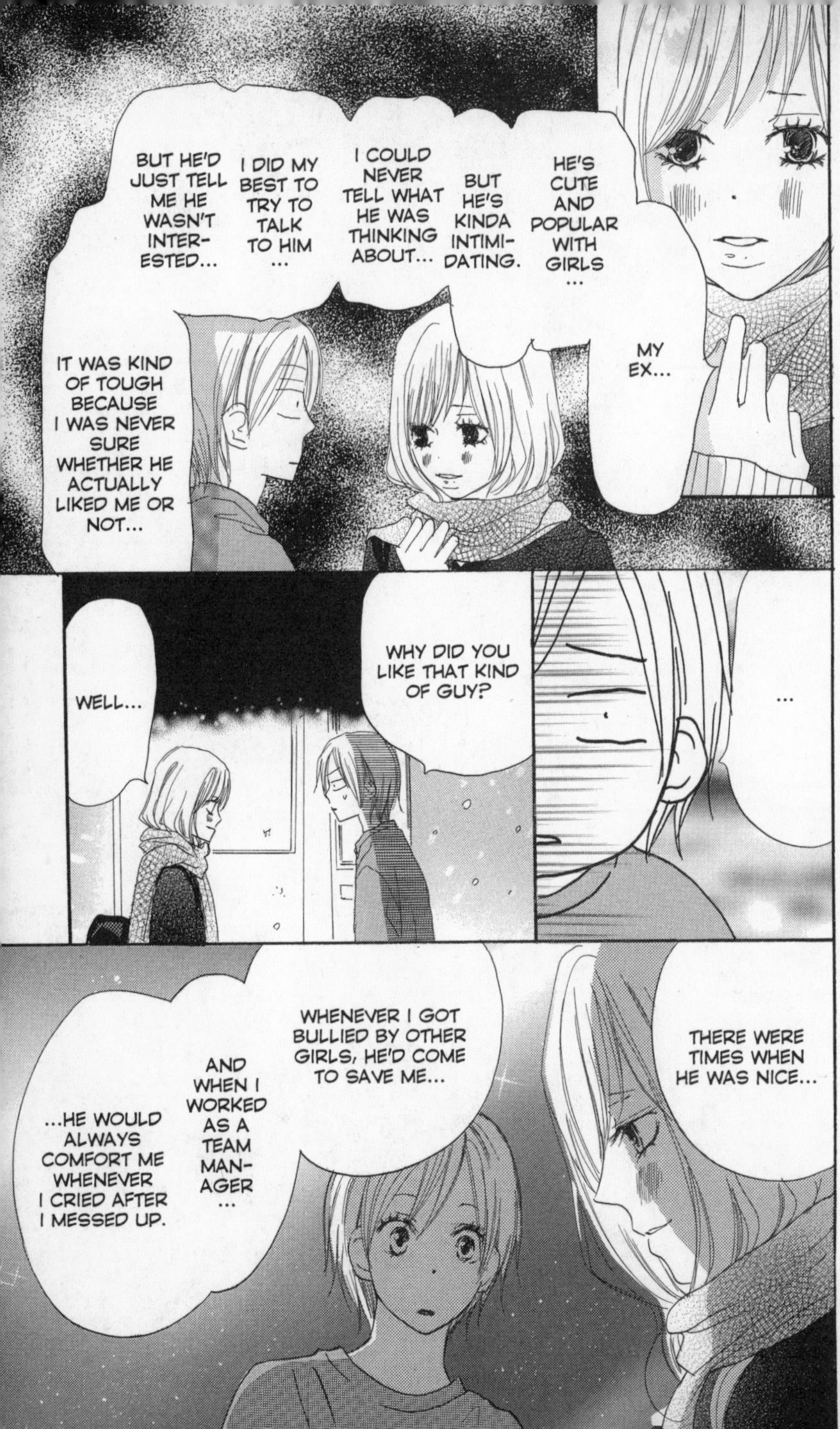
MY EX...
HE'S CUTE AND POPULAR WITH GIRLS...
BUT HE'S KINDA INTIMI-DATING.
I COULD NEVER TELL WHAT HE WAS THINKING ABOUT...
I DID MY BEST TO TRY TO TALK TO HIM...
BUT HE'D JUST TELL ME HE WASN'T INTER-ESTED...
IT WAS KIND OF TOUGH BECAUSE I WAS NEVER SURE WHETHER HE ACTUALLY LIKED ME OR NOT...
...
WHY DID YOU LIKE THAT KIND OF GUY?
WELL...
THERE WERE TIMES WHEN HE WAS NICE...
WHENEVER I GOT BULLIED BY OTHER GIRLS, HE'D COME TO SAVE ME...
AND WHEN I WORKED AS A TEAM MAN-AGER...
...HE WOULD ALWAYS COMFORT ME WHENEVER I CRIED AFTER I MESSED UP.

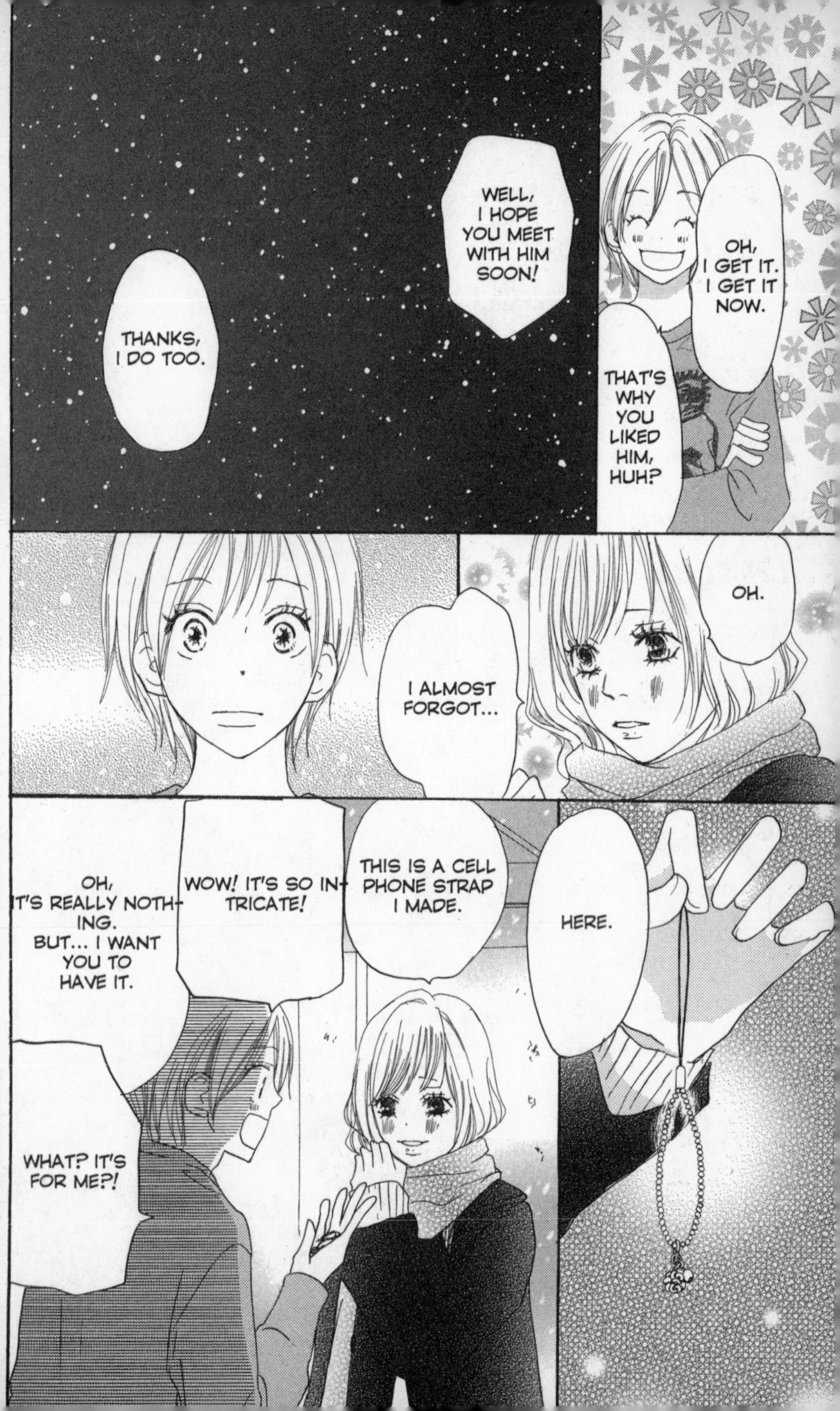
OH, I GET IT. I GET IT NOW.
THAT'S WHY YOU LIKED HIM, HUH?
WELL, I HOPE YOU MEET WITH HIM SOON!
THANKS, I DO TOO.
OH.
I ALMOST FORGOT...
HERE.
THIS IS A CELL PHONE STRAP I MADE.
WOW! IT'S SO INTRICATE!
OH, IT'S REALLY NOTHING. BUT... I WANT YOU TO HAVE IT.
WHAT? IT'S FOR ME?!

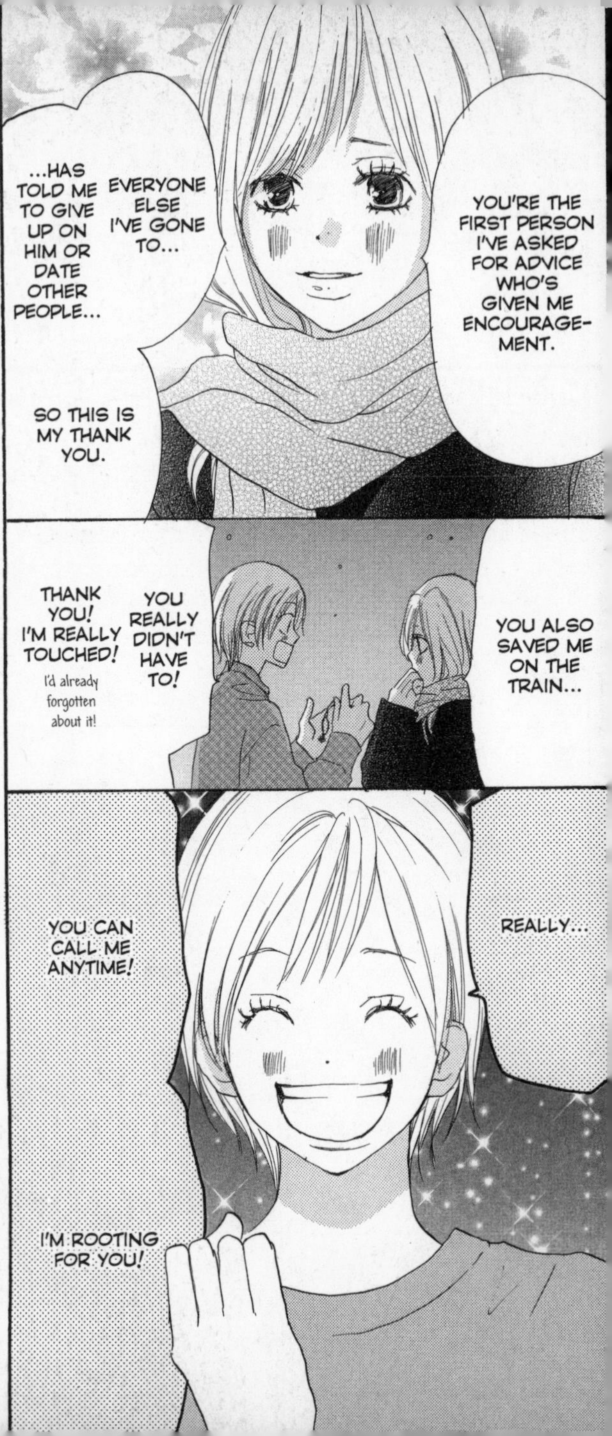
YOU'RE THE FIRST PERSON I'VE ASKED FOR ADVICE WHO'S GIVEN ME ENCOURAGE-MENT.
EVERYONE ELSE I'VE GONE TO...
...HAS TOLD ME TO GIVE UP ON HIM OR DATE OTHER PEOPLE...
SO THIS IS MY THANK YOU.
YOU ALSO SAVED ME ON THE TRAIN...
YOU REALLY DIDN'T HAVE TO!
THANK YOU! I'M REALLY TOUCHED!
I'd already forgotten about it!
REALLY...
YOU CAN CALL ME ANYTIME!
I'M ROOTING FOR YOU!

Hi, this is Kawahara. It's been three days since I started a yoga-for-dummies regime, but I haven't lost weight or gotten any more flexible.

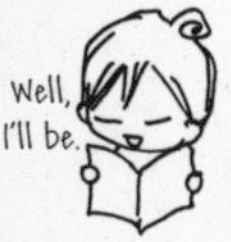
Well, I'll be.

I'll bet it's because I made it up myself! Later, I saw a book that said, "You have to do yoga properly." I think I'll pick myself up and give it another shot. In my head, I think, "I want to make myself look good," but it might be a lost cause.

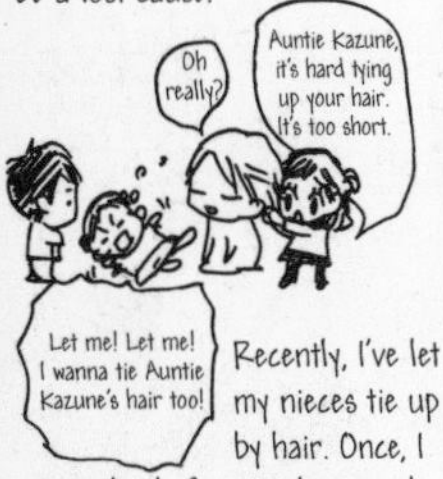
Auntie Kazune, it's hard tying up your hair. It's too short.
Oh really?
Let me! Let me! I wanna tie Auntie Kazune's hair too!

Recently, I've let my nieces tie up by hair. Once, I completely forgot it happened and walked out in public like that.

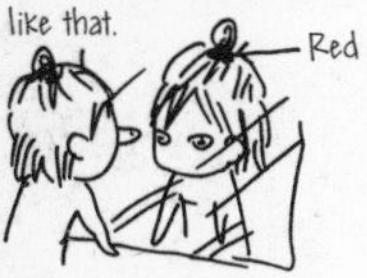
Red

There must be a limit to how bad one can look...I think. Well, starting tomorrow, I'm going to try to become good-looking! For now, I just want to lose 15 pounds. Or 22 pounds would be nice too...

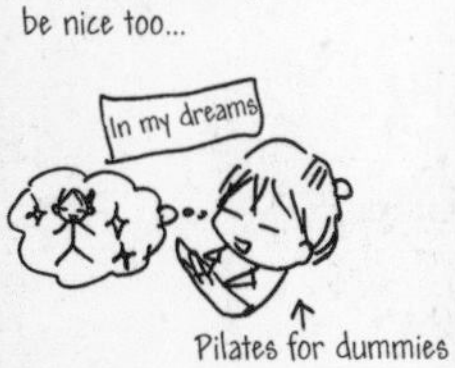
In my dreams
Pilates for dummies

If I end up writing the same thing in the next volume, feel free to laugh at me.

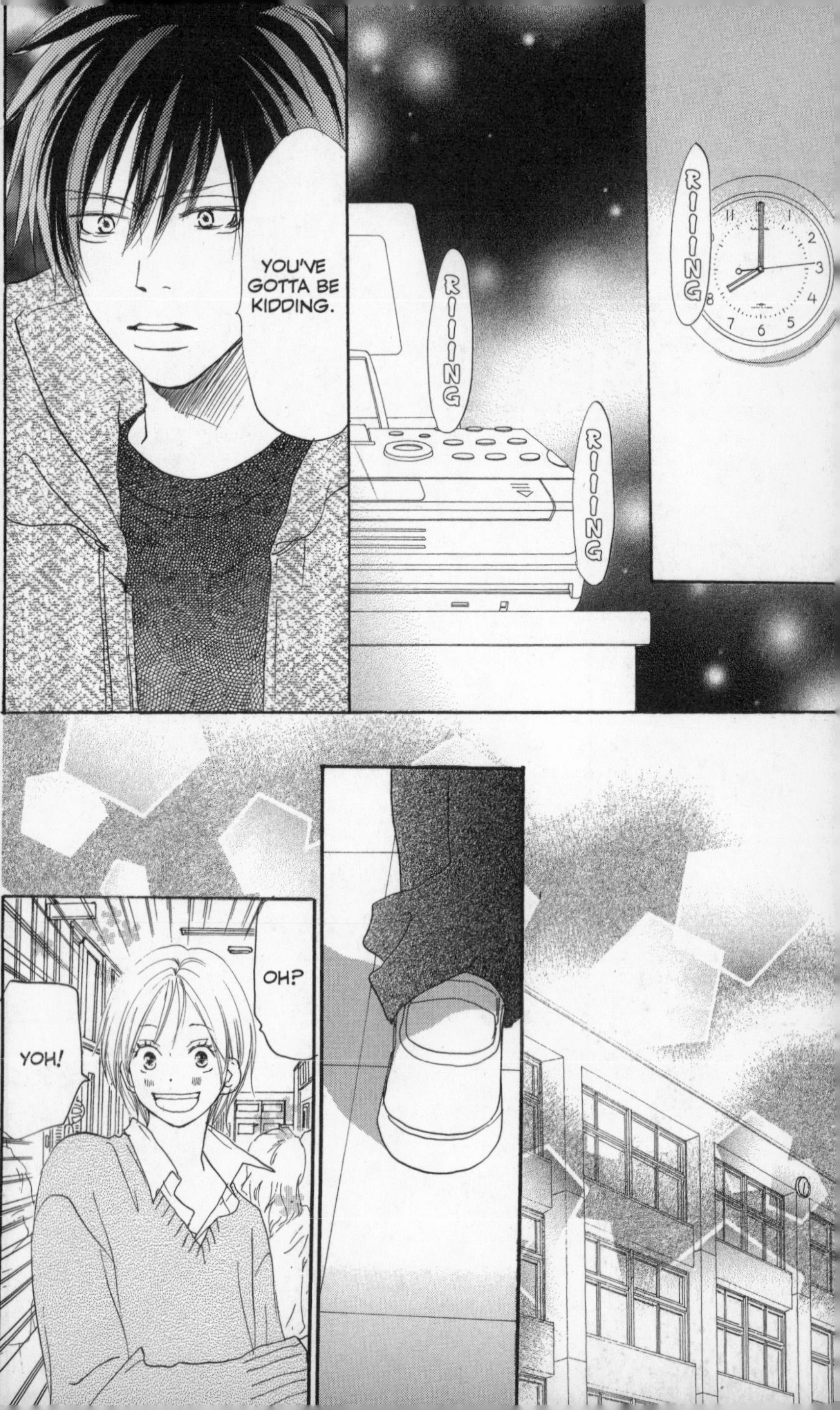
RIIING
RIIING
RIIING
YOU'VE GOTTA BE KIDDING.
OH?
YOH!

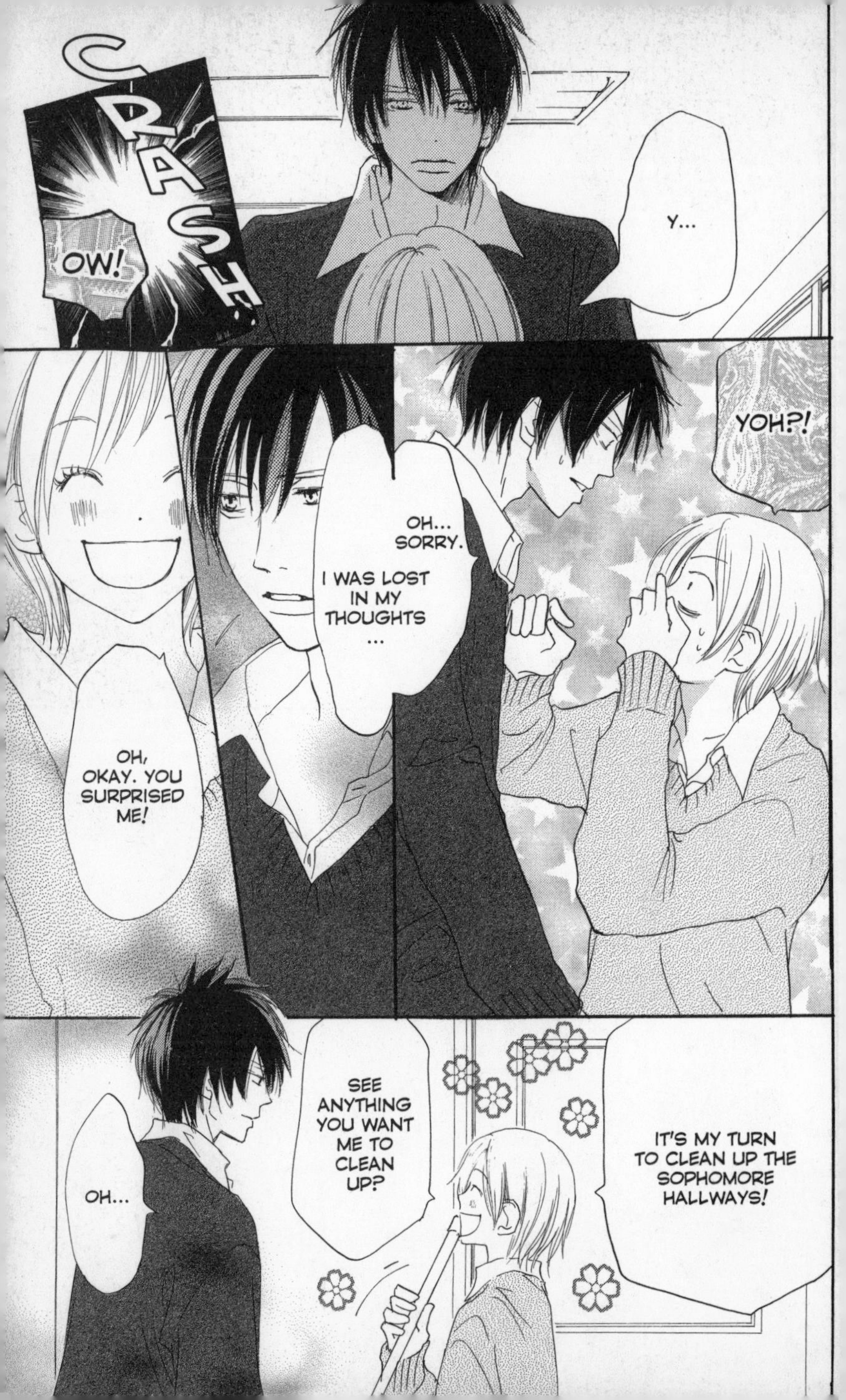
Y...
CRASH!
OW!
YOH?!
OH... SORRY.
I WAS LOST IN MY THOUGHTS...
OH, OKAY. YOU SURPRISED ME!
IT'S MY TURN TO CLEAN UP THE SOPHOMORE HALLWAYS!
SEE ANYTHING YOU WANT ME TO CLEAN UP?
OH...

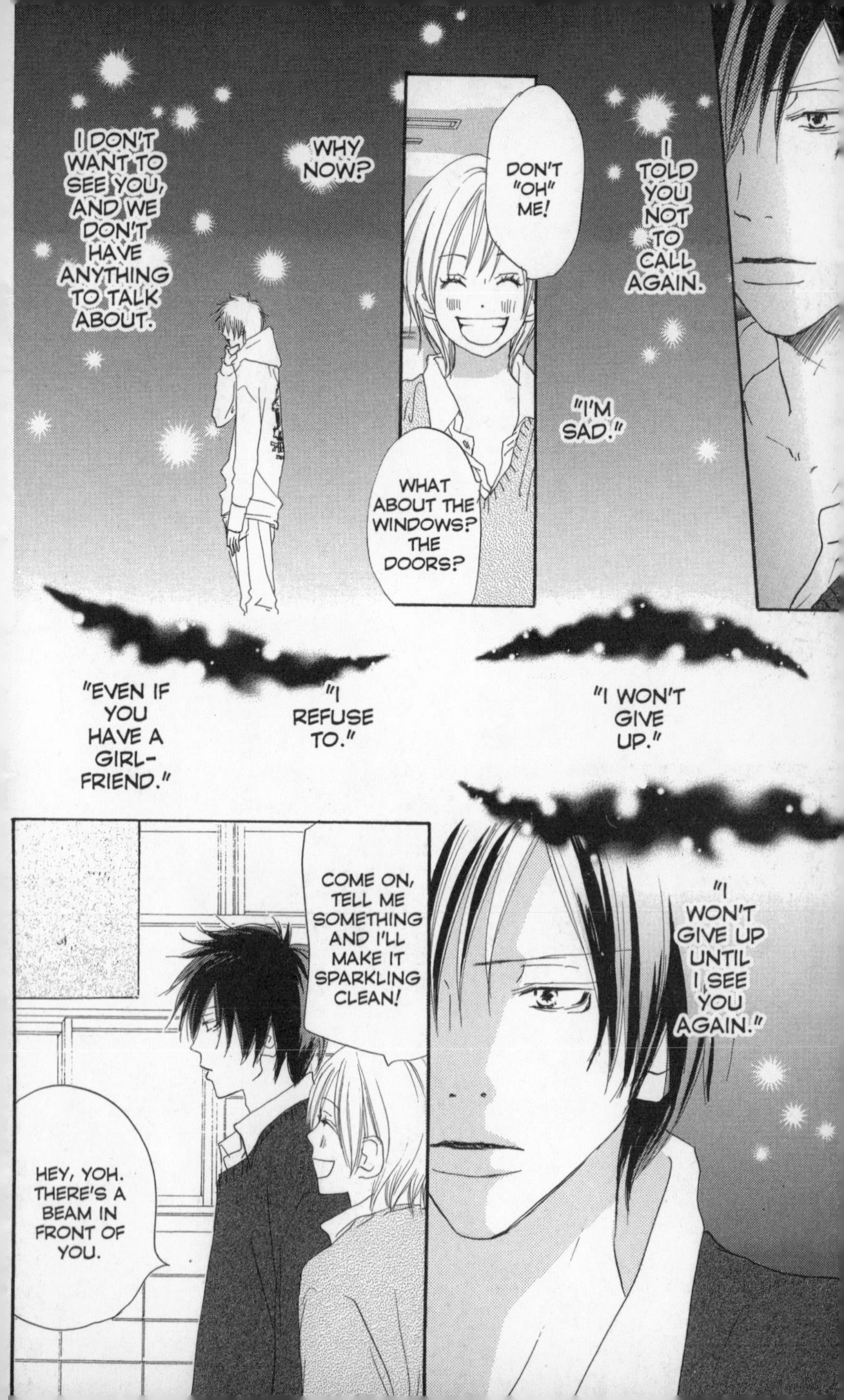
I TOLD YOU NOT TO CALL AGAIN.
"I'M SAD."
DON'T "OH" ME!
WHAT ABOUT THE WINDOWS? THE DOORS?
WHY NOW?
I DON'T WANT TO SEE YOU, AND WE DON'T HAVE ANYTHING TO TALK ABOUT.
"I WON'T GIVE UP."
"I REFUSE TO."
"EVEN IF YOU HAVE A GIRL-FRIEND."
"I WON'T GIVE UP UNTIL I SEE YOU AGAIN."
COME ON, TELL ME SOMETHING AND I'LL MAKE IT SPARKLING CLEAN!
HEY, YOH. THERE'S A BEAM IN FRONT OF YOU.

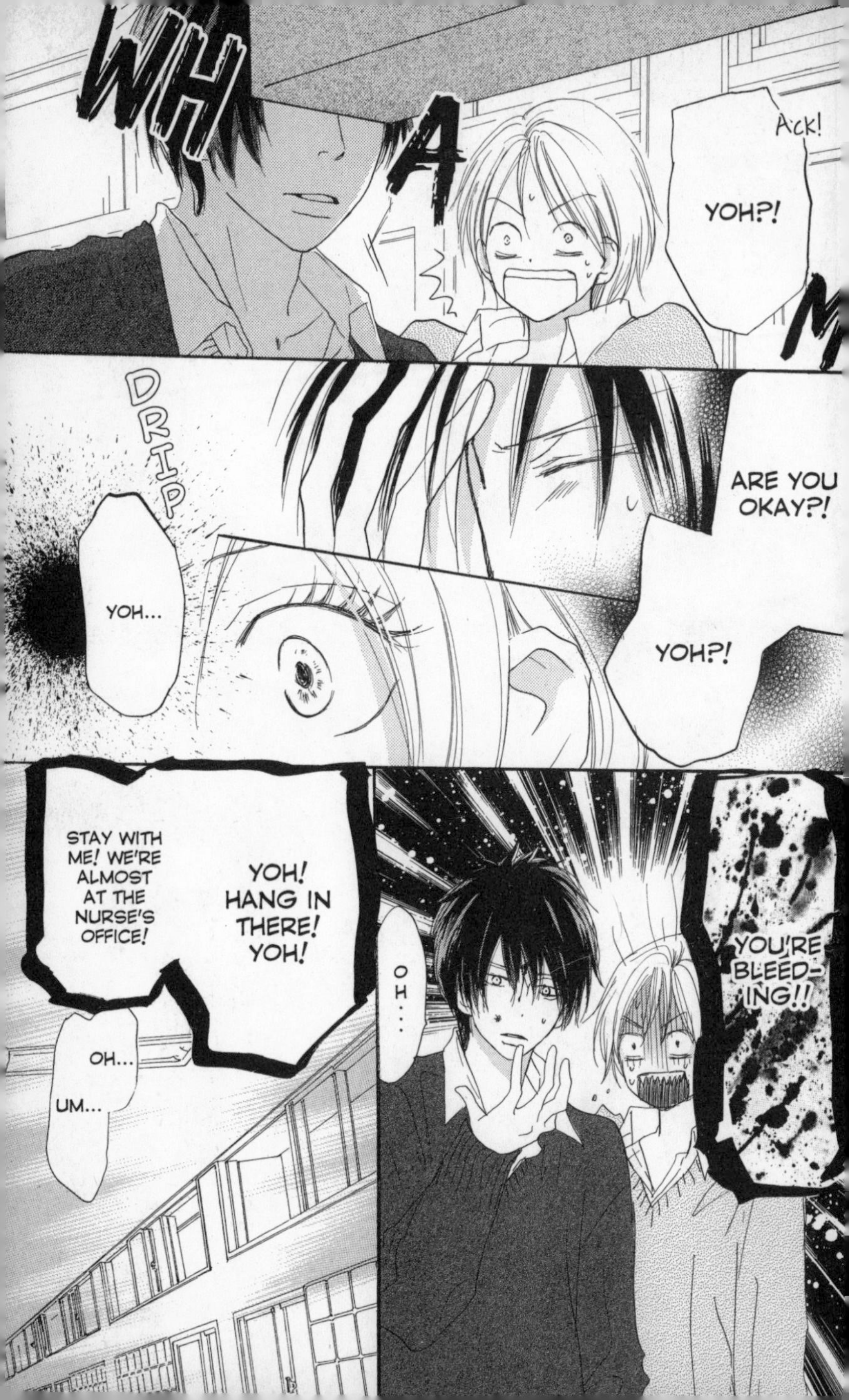
ACK! YOH?!
WHAM
ARE YOU OKAY?!
YOH?!
DRIP
YOH...
YOU'RE BLEED-ING!!
OH...
YOH! HANG IN THERE! YOH!
STAY WITH ME! WE'RE ALMOST AT THE NURSE'S OFFICE!
OH... UM...

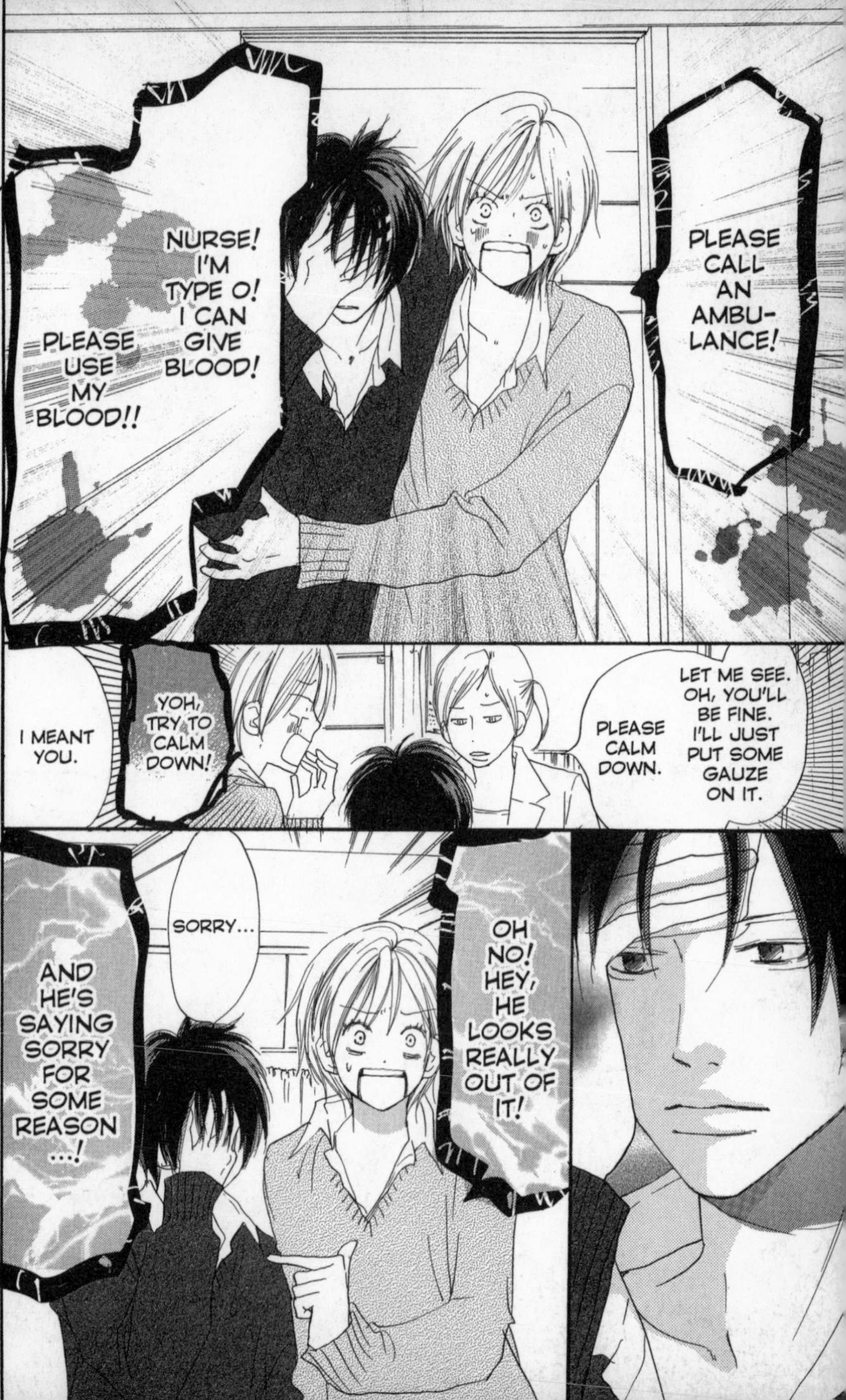
PLEASE CALL AN AMBULANCE!
NURSE! I'M TYPE O! I CAN GIVE BLOOD!
PLEASE USE MY BLOOD!!
LET ME SEE. OH, YOU'LL BE FINE. I'LL JUST PUT SOME GAUZE ON IT.
PLEASE CALM DOWN.
YOH, TRY TO CALM DOWN!
I MEANT YOU.
OH NO! HEY, HE LOOKS REALLY OUT OF IT!
SORRY...
AND HE'S SAYING SORRY FOR SOME REASON ...!

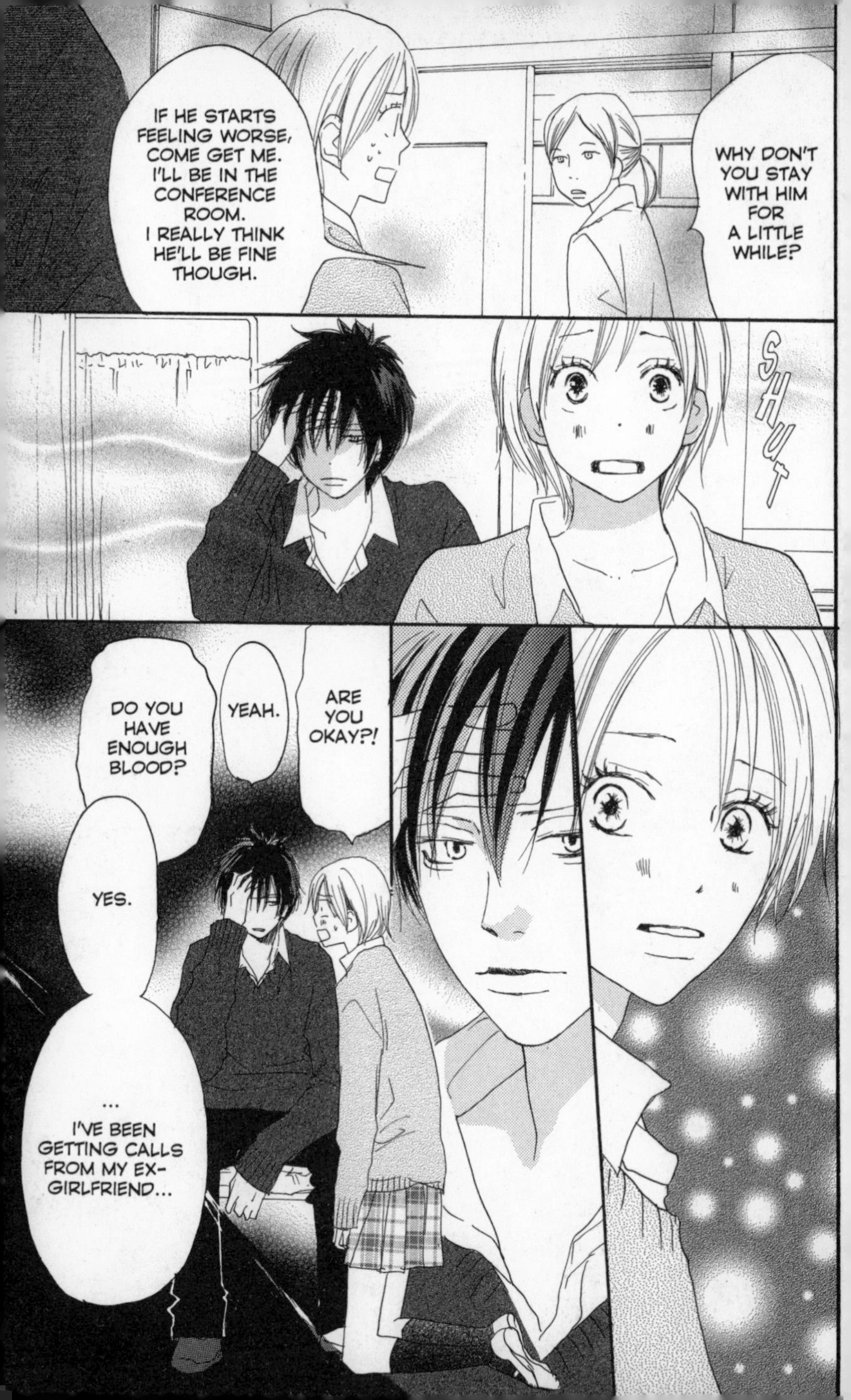
WHY DON'T YOU STAY WITH HIM FOR A LITTLE WHILE?
IF HE STARTS FEELING WORSE, COME GET ME. I'LL BE IN THE CONFERENCE ROOM. I REALLY THINK HE'LL BE FINE THOUGH.
SHUT
ARE YOU OKAY?!
YEAH.
DO YOU HAVE ENOUGH BLOOD?
YES.
... I'VE BEEN GETTING CALLS FROM MY EX-GIRLFRIEND...

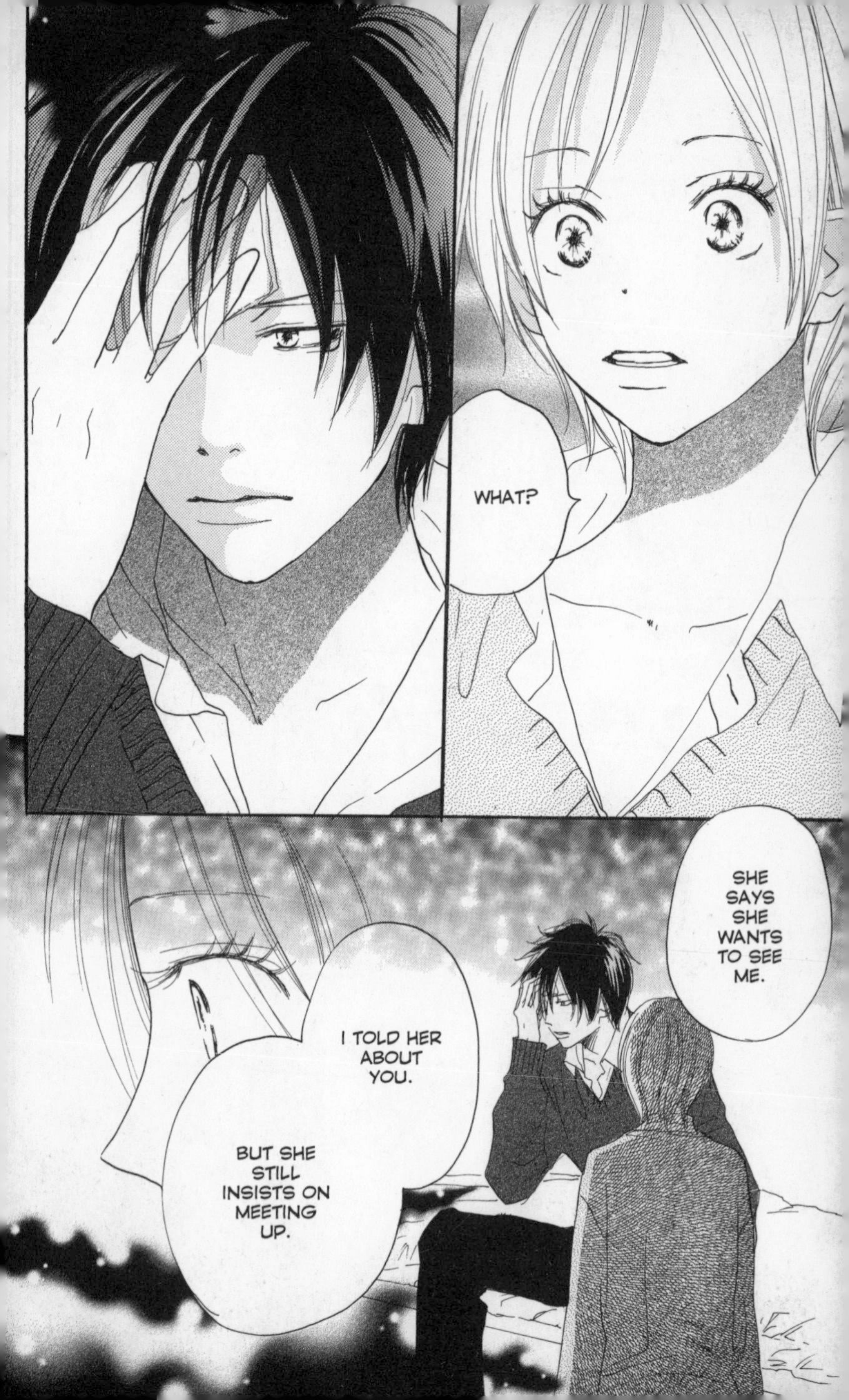
WHAT?
SHE SAYS SHE WANTS TO SEE ME.
I TOLD HER ABOUT YOU.
BUT SHE STILL INSISTS ON MEETING UP.

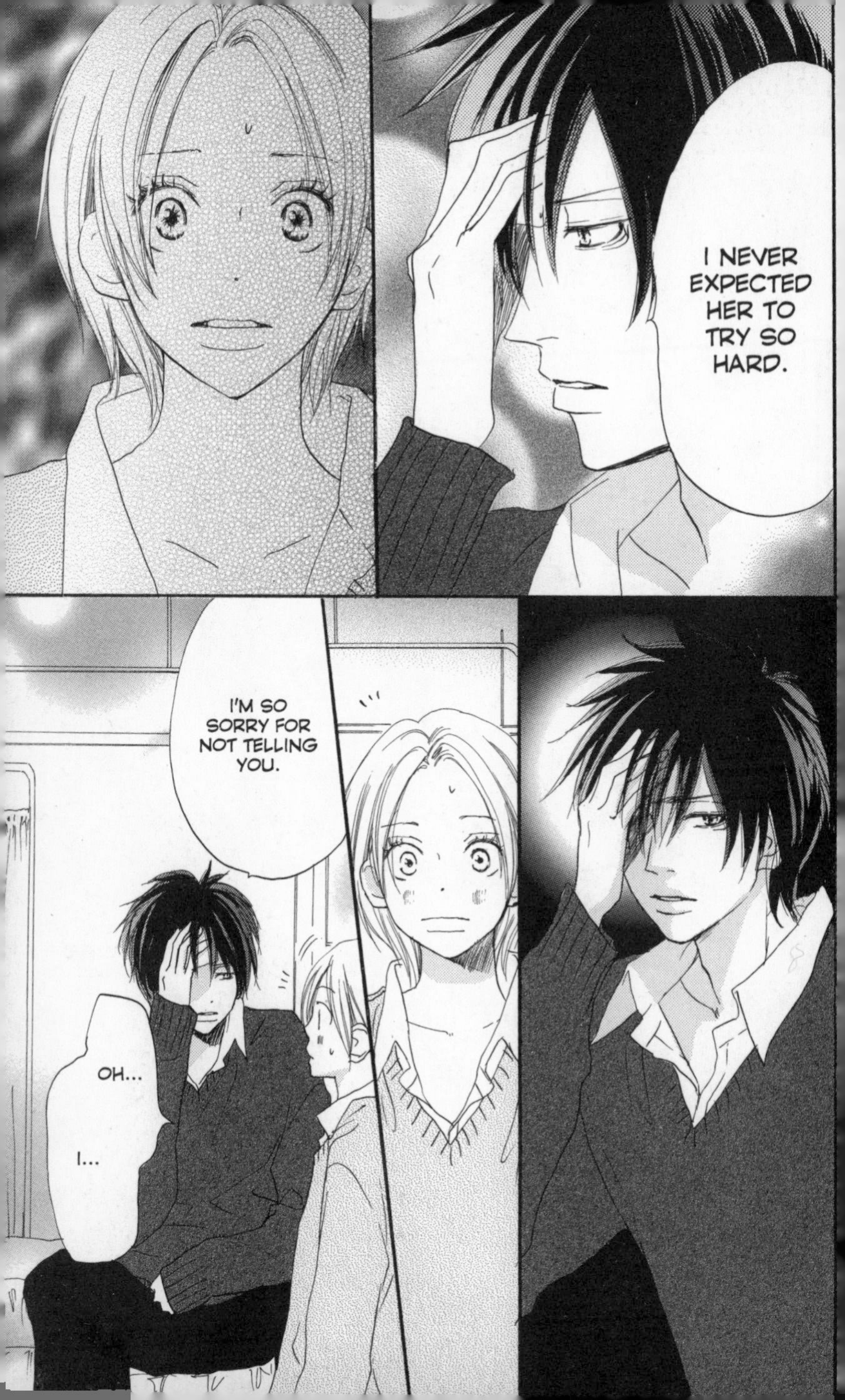
I NEVER EXPECTED HER TO TRY SO HARD.
I'M SO SORRY FOR NOT TELLING YOU.
OH...
I...

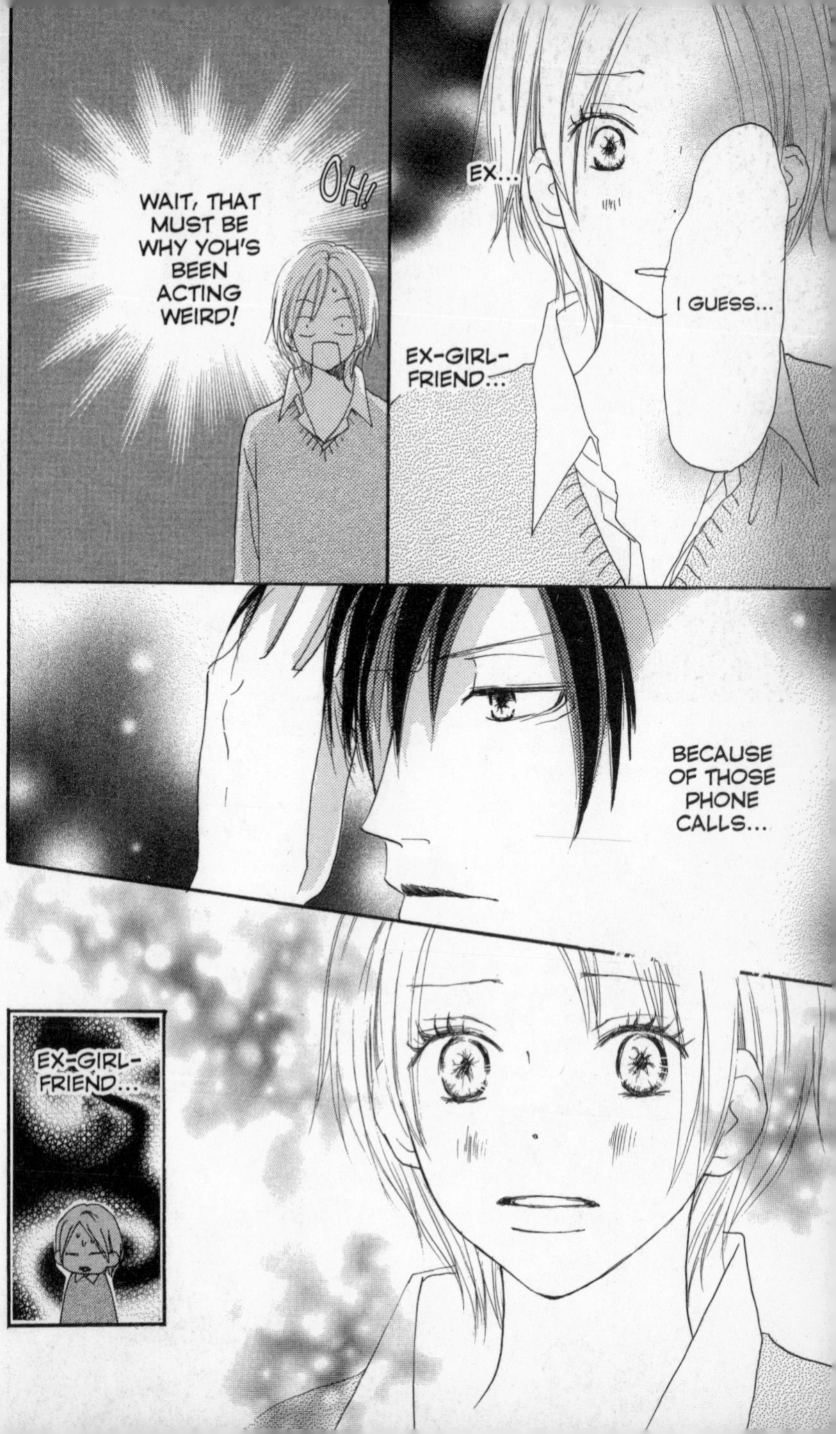
EX...
I GUESS...
EX-GIRL-FRIEND...
OH!
WAIT, THAT MUST BE WHY YOH'S BEEN ACTING WEIRD!
BECAUSE OF THOSE PHONE CALLS...
EX-GIRL-FRIEND...

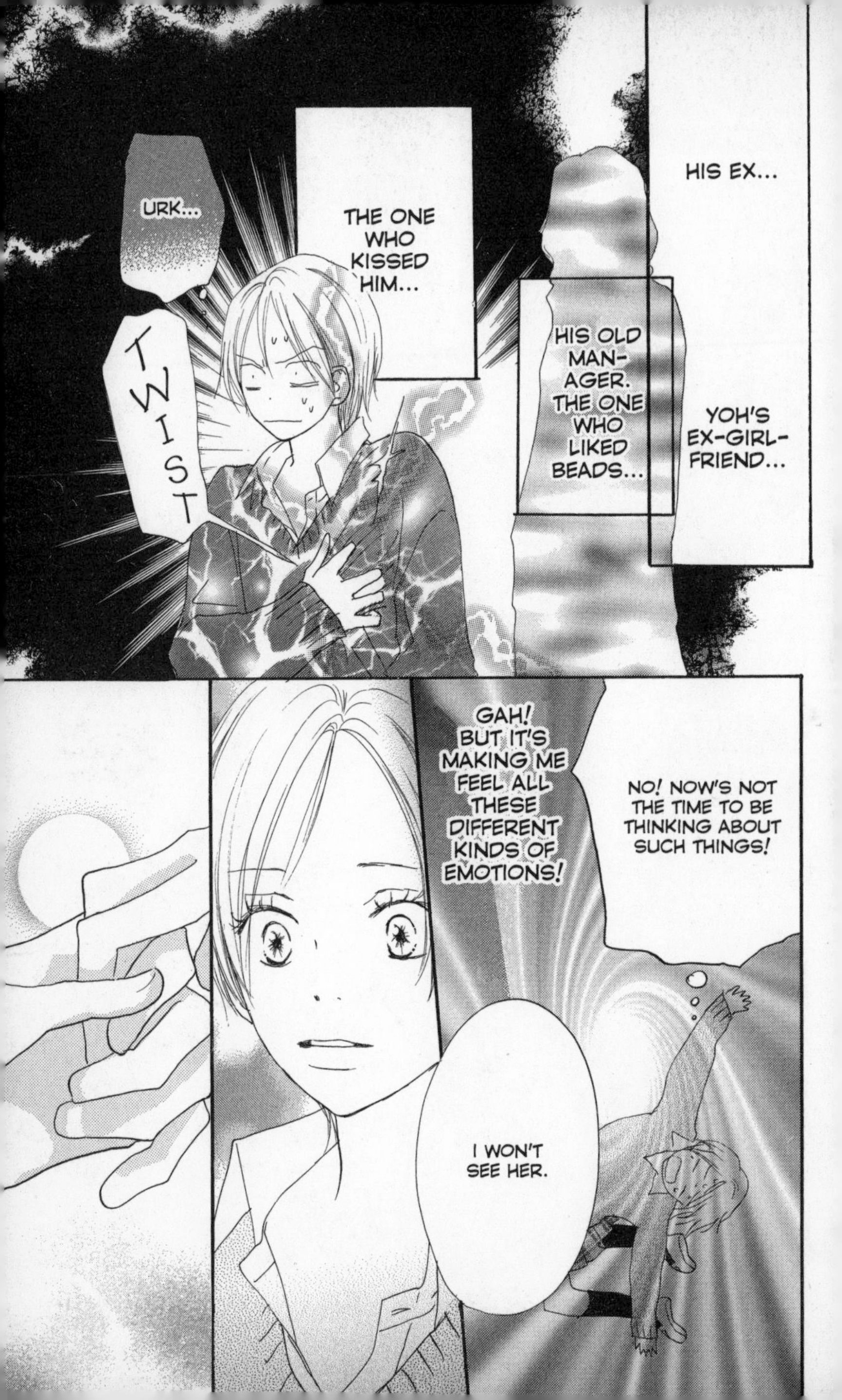
HIS EX...
YOH'S EX-GIRL-FRIEND...
HIS OLD MAN-AGER. THE ONE WHO LIKED BEADS...
THE ONE WHO KISSED HIM...
URK...
TWIST
NO! NOW'S NOT THE TIME TO BE THINKING ABOUT SUCH THINGS!
GAH! BUT IT'S MAKING ME FEEL ALL THESE DIFFERENT KINDS OF EMOTIONS!
I WON'T SEE HER.

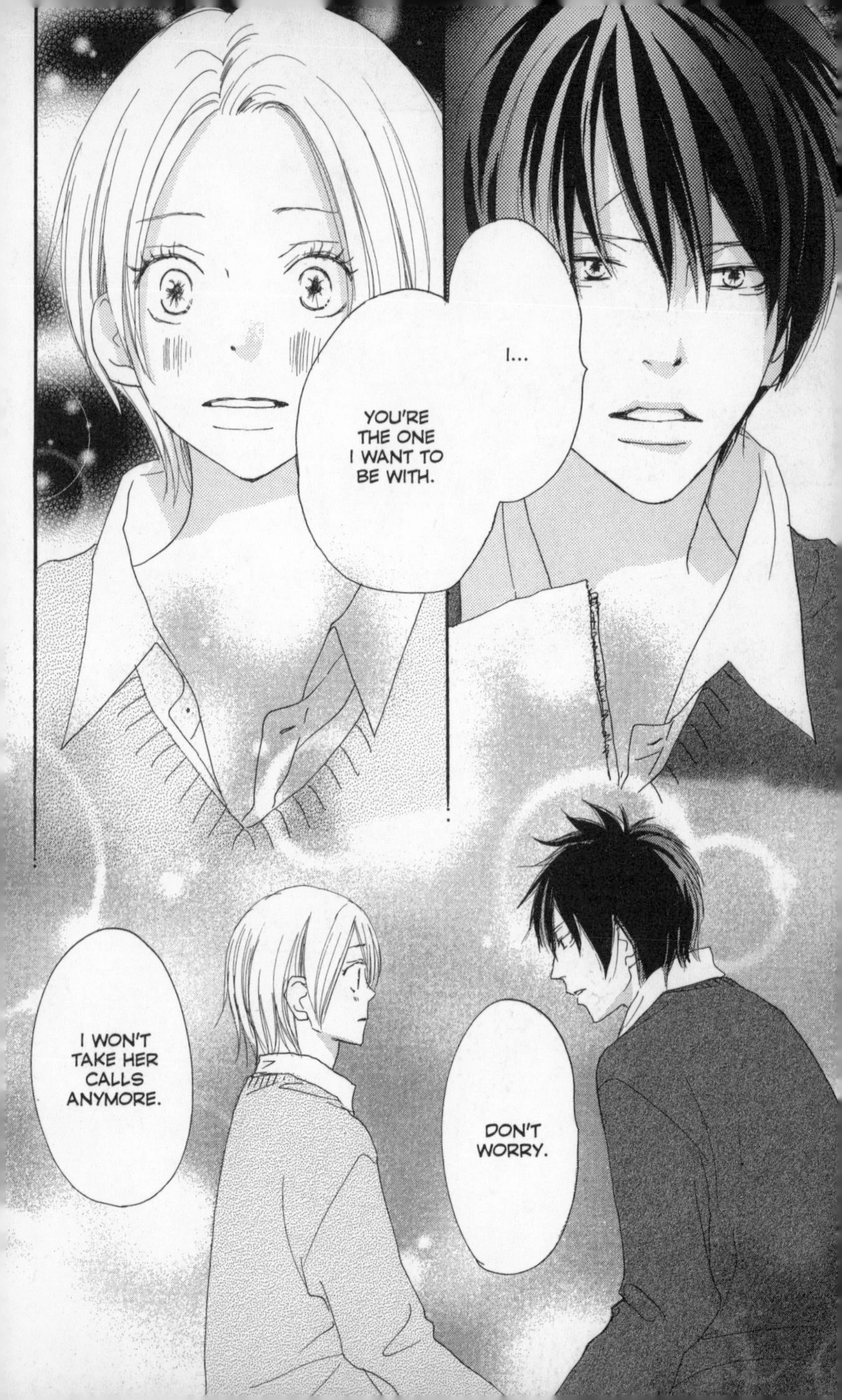
I...
YOU'RE THE ONE I WANT TO BE WITH.
DON'T WORRY.
I WON'T TAKE HER CALLS ANYMORE.

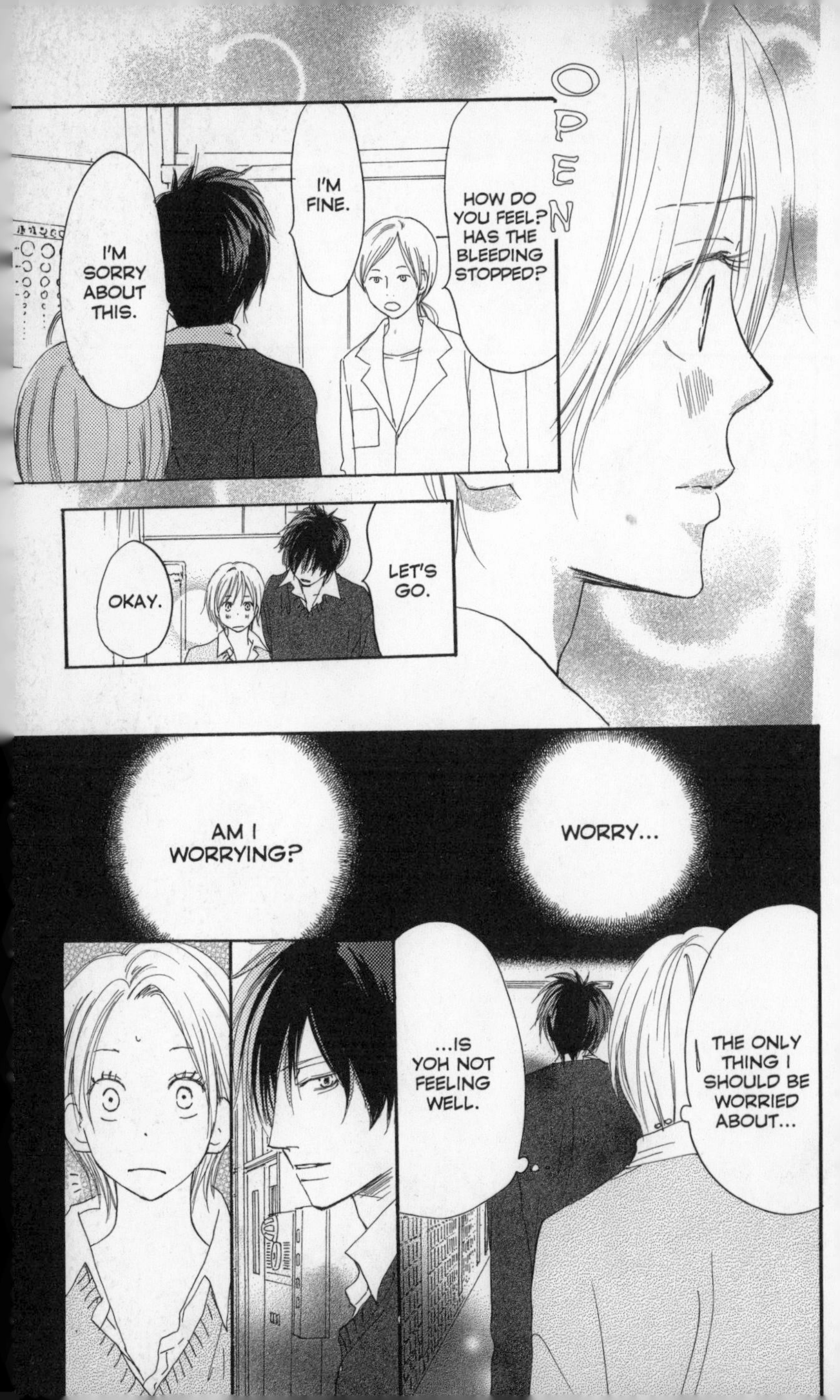
OPEN
HOW DO YOU FEEL? HAS THE BLEEDING STOPPED?
I'M FINE.
I'M SORRY ABOUT THIS.
LET'S GO.
OKAY.
WORRY...
AM I WORRYING?
THE ONLY THING I SHOULD BE WORRIED ABOUT...
...IS YOH NOT FEELING WELL.

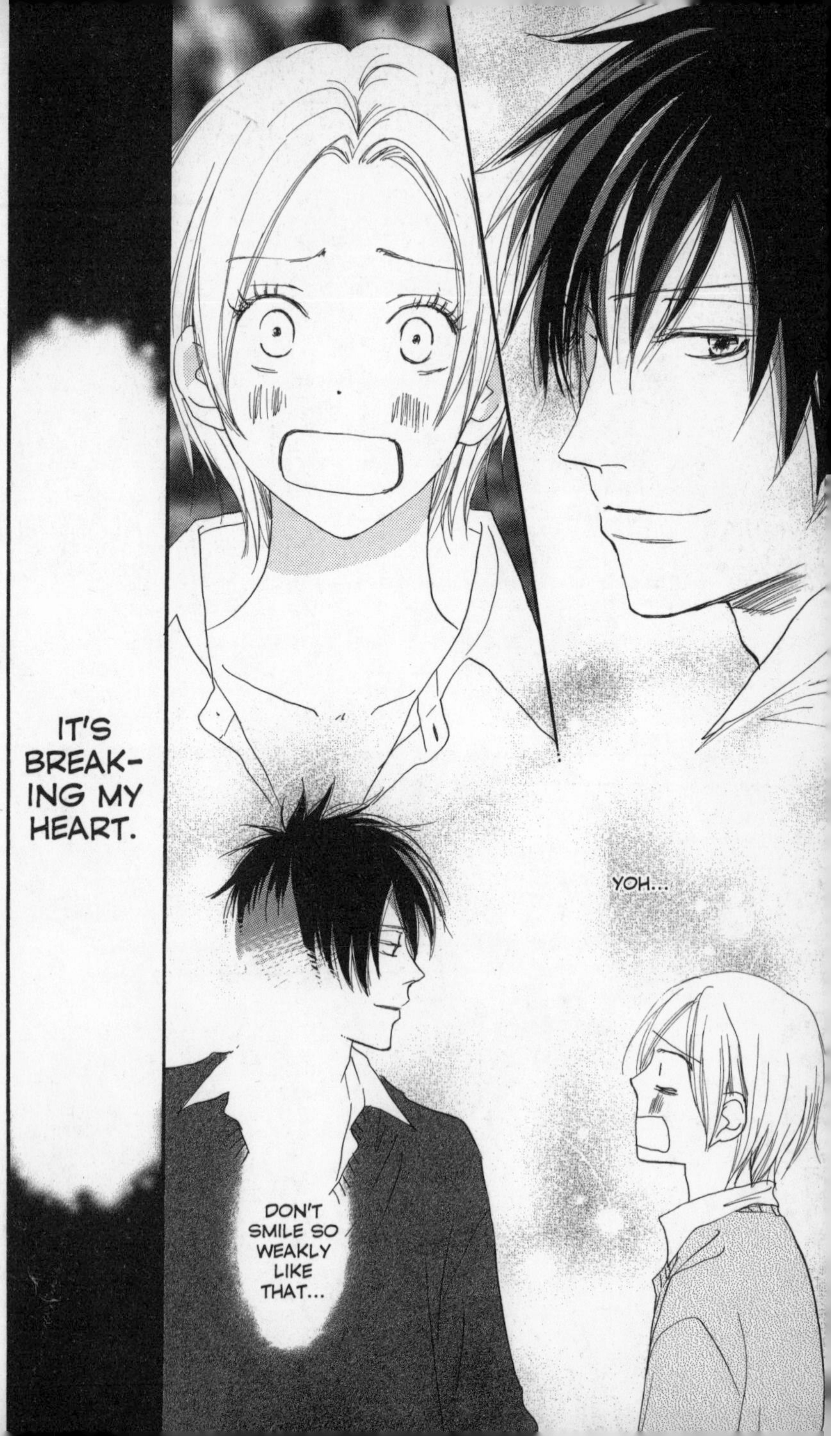
YOH...
DON'T SMILE SO WEAKLY LIKE THAT...
IT'S BREAKING MY HEART.

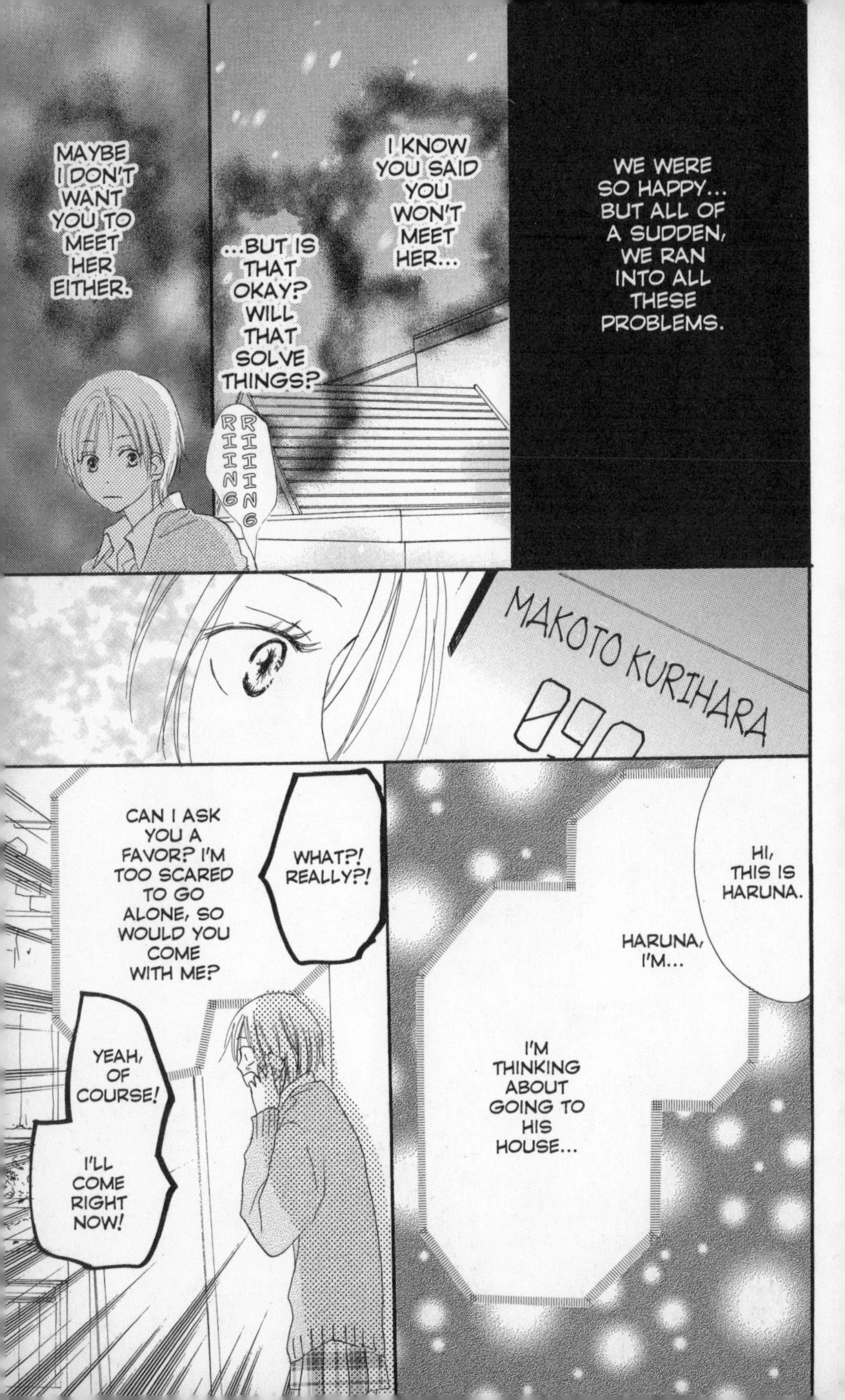

WE WERE SO HAPPY... BUT ALL OF A SUDDEN, WE RAN INTO ALL THESE PROBLEMS.
I KNOW YOU SAID YOU WON'T MEET HER...
...BUT IS THAT OKAY? WILL THAT SOLVE THINGS?
RIIING RIIING
MAYBE I DON'T WANT YOU TO MEET HER EITHER.
MAKOTO KURIHARA
090
HI, THIS IS HARUNA.
HARUNA, I'M...
I'M THINKING ABOUT GOING TO HIS HOUSE...
WHAT?! REALLY?!
CAN I ASK YOU A FAVOR? I'M TOO SCARED TO GO ALONE, SO WOULD YOU COME WITH ME?
YEAH, OF COURSE!
I'LL COME RIGHT NOW!

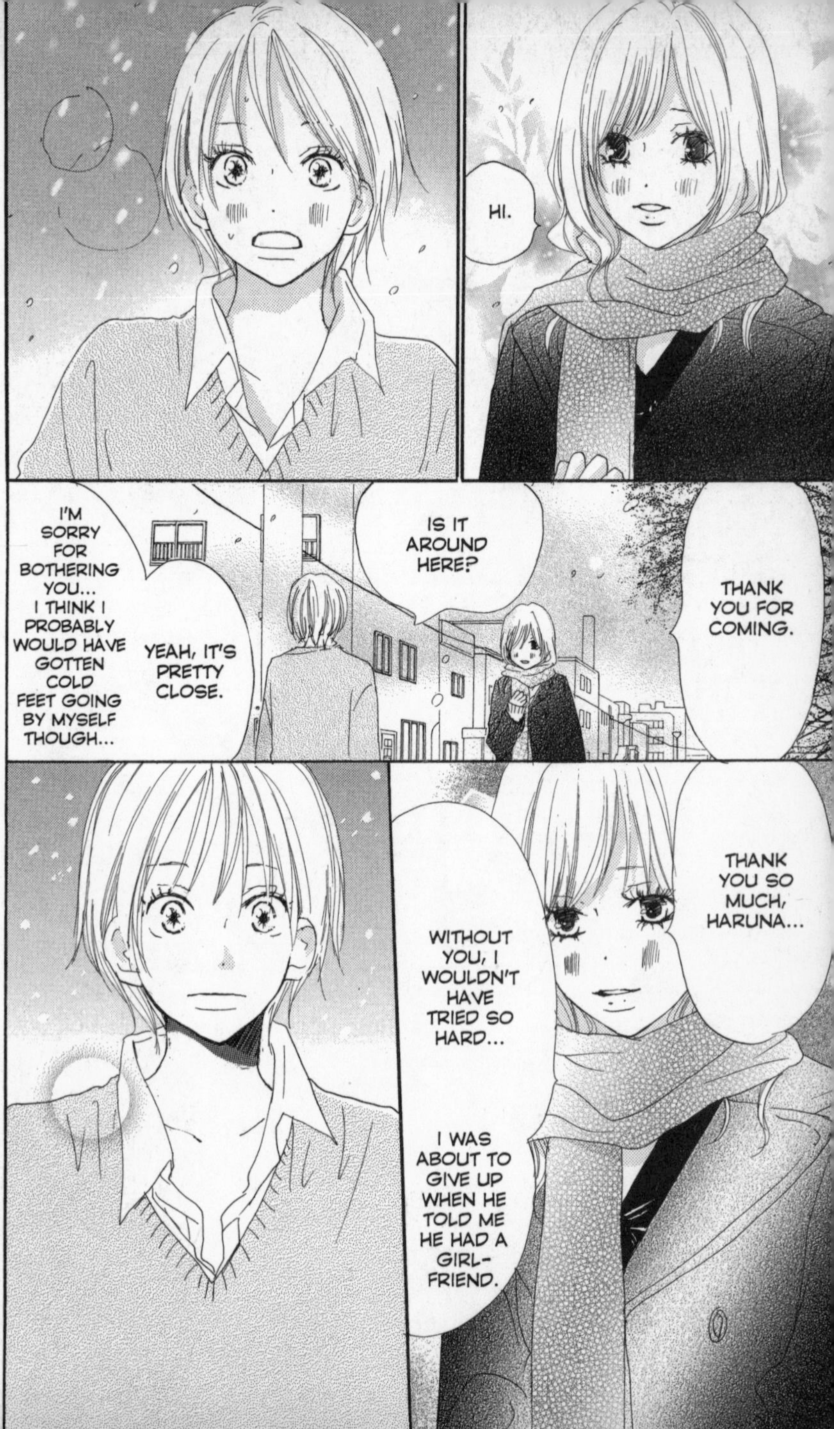
HI.
THANK YOU FOR COMING.
IS IT AROUND HERE?
YEAH, IT'S PRETTY CLOSE.
I'M SORRY FOR BOTHERING YOU... I THINK I PROBABLY WOULD HAVE GOTTEN COLD FEET GOING BY MYSELF THOUGH...
THANK YOU SO MUCH, HARUNA...
WITHOUT YOU, I WOULDN'T HAVE TRIED SO HARD...
I WAS ABOUT TO GIVE UP WHEN HE TOLD ME HE HAD A GIRL-FRIEND.

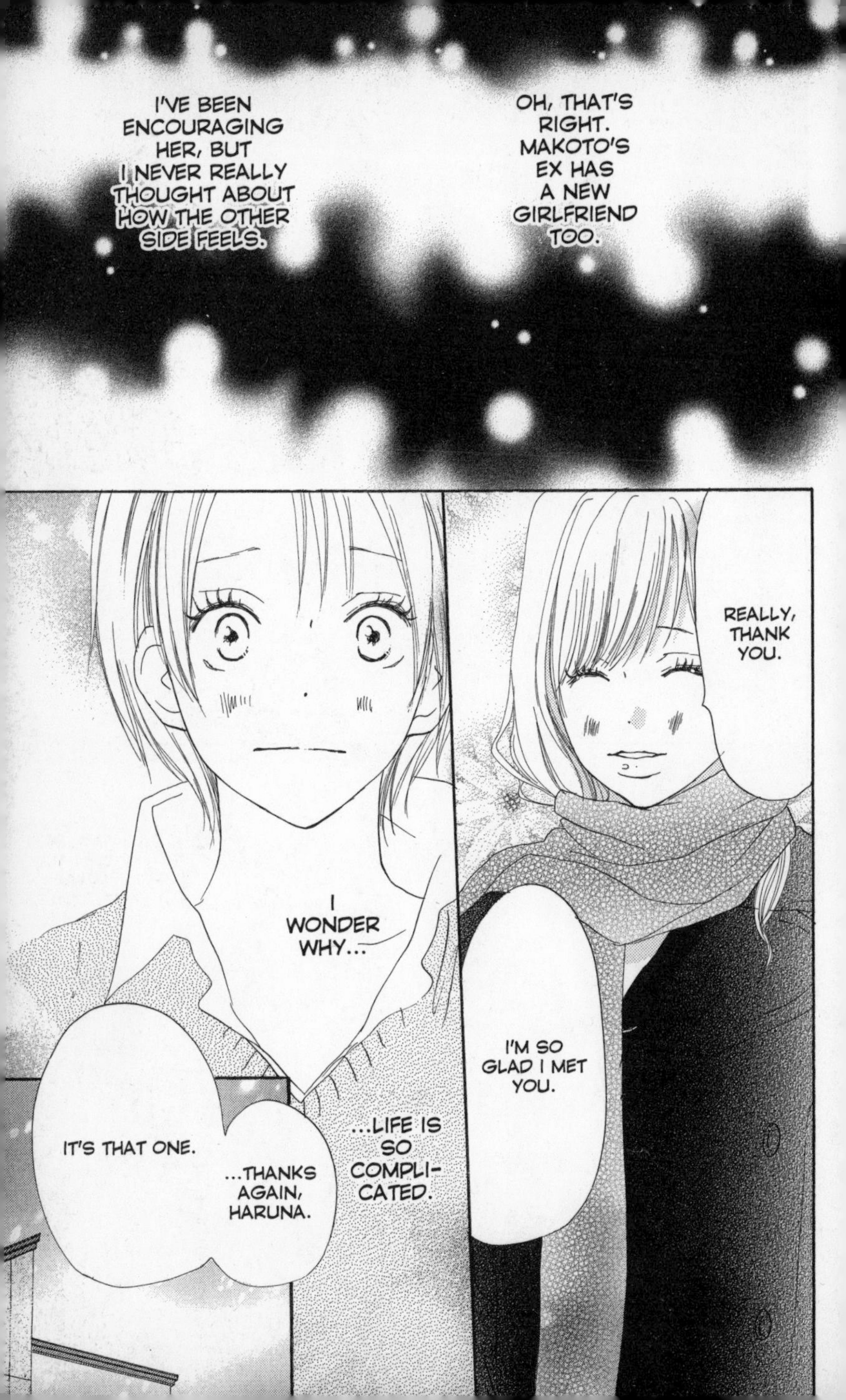
OH, THAT'S RIGHT. MAKOTO'S EX HAS A NEW GIRLFRIEND TOO.
I'VE BEEN ENCOURAGING HER, BUT I NEVER REALLY THOUGHT ABOUT HOW THE OTHER SIDE FEELS.
REALLY, THANK YOU.
I'M SO GLAD I MET YOU.
I WONDER WHY...
...LIFE IS SO COMPLI-CATED.
...THANKS AGAIN, HARUNA.
IT'S THAT ONE.

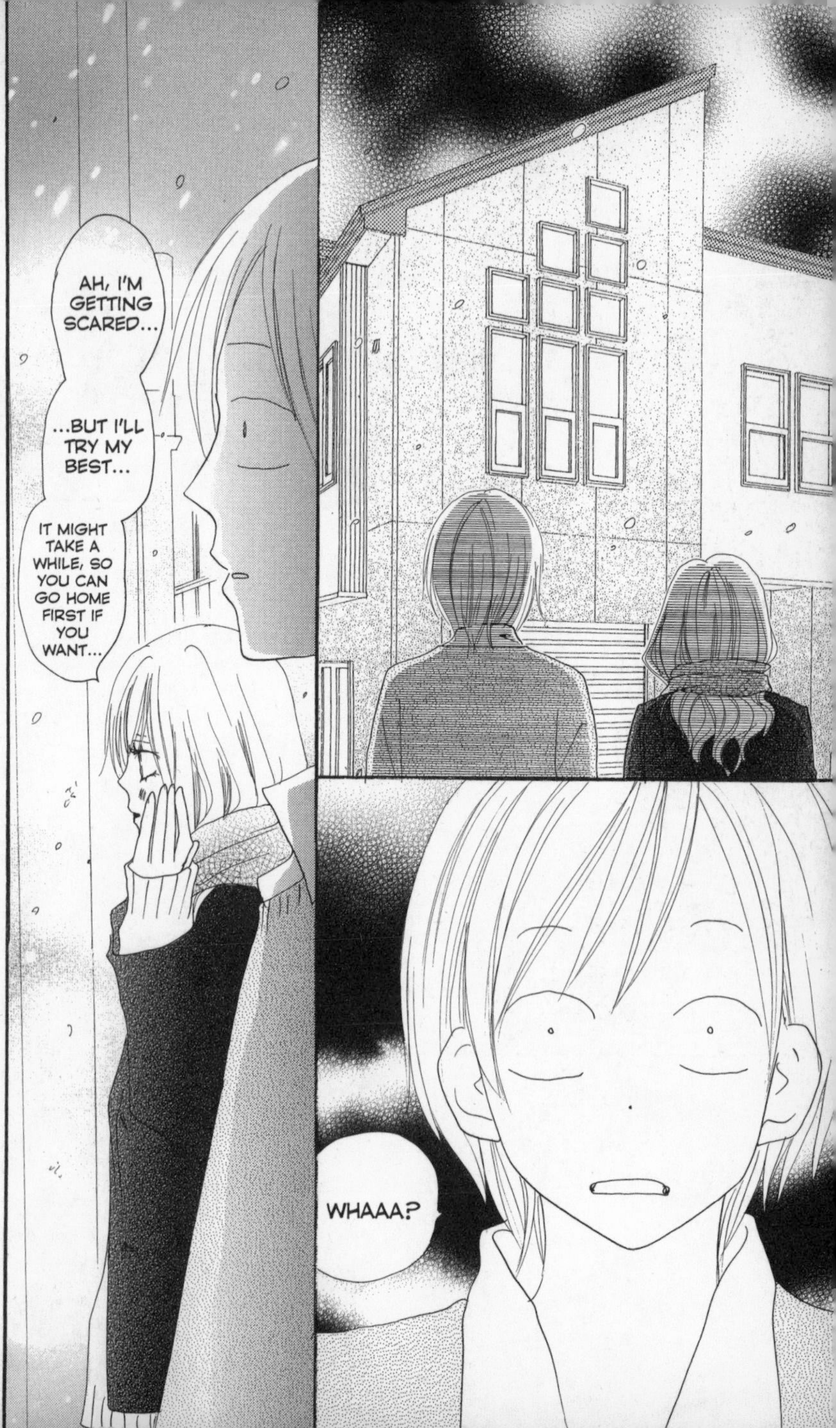
WHAAA?
AH, I'M GETTING SCARED...
...BUT I'LL TRY MY BEST...
IT MIGHT TAKE A WHILE, SO YOU CAN GO HOME FIRST IF YOU WANT...

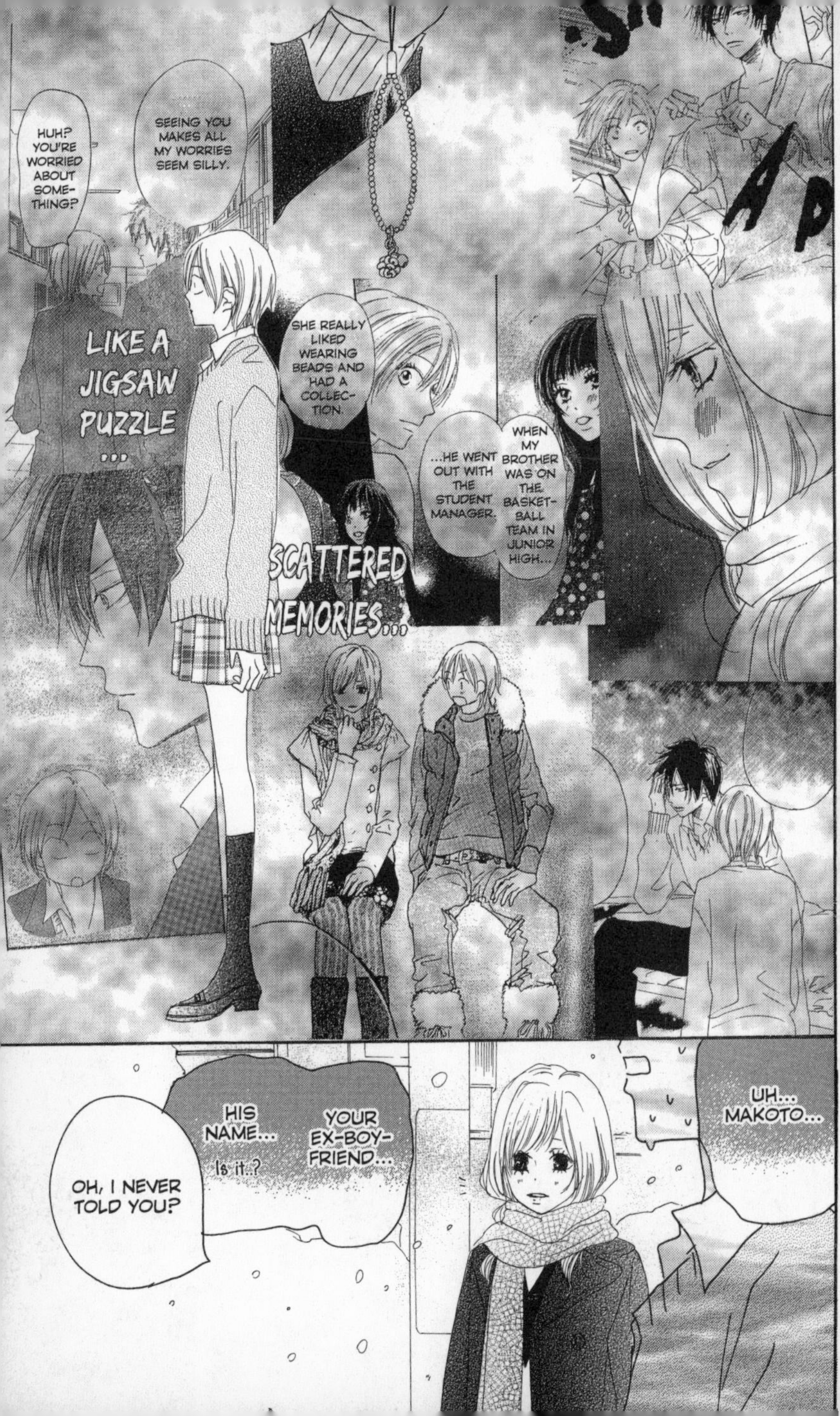
WHEN MY BROTHER WAS ON THE BASKETBALL TEAM IN JUNIOR HIGH...
...HE WENT OUT WITH THE STUDENT MANAGER.
SHE REALLY LIKED WEARING BEADS AND HAD A COLLECTION.
SCATTERED MEMORIES...
SEEING YOU MAKES ALL MY WORRIES SEEM SILLY.
HUH? YOU'RE WORRIED ABOUT SOMETHING?
LIKE A JIGSAW PUZZLE...
UH... MAKOTO...
YOUR EX-BOYFRIEND...
HIS NAME... Is it..?
OH, I NEVER TOLD YOU?

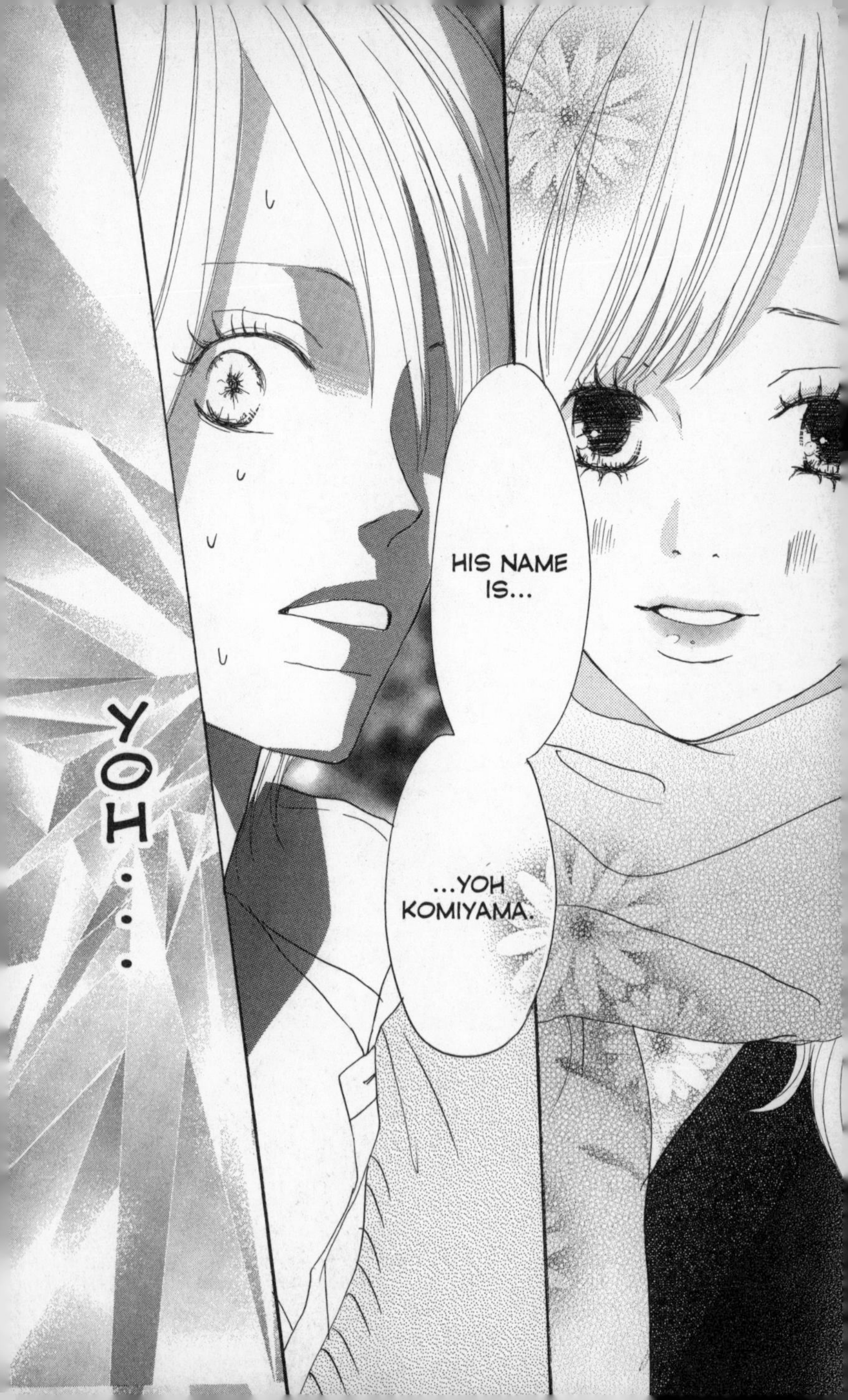
HIS NAME IS...
...YOH KOMIYAMA.
YOH...

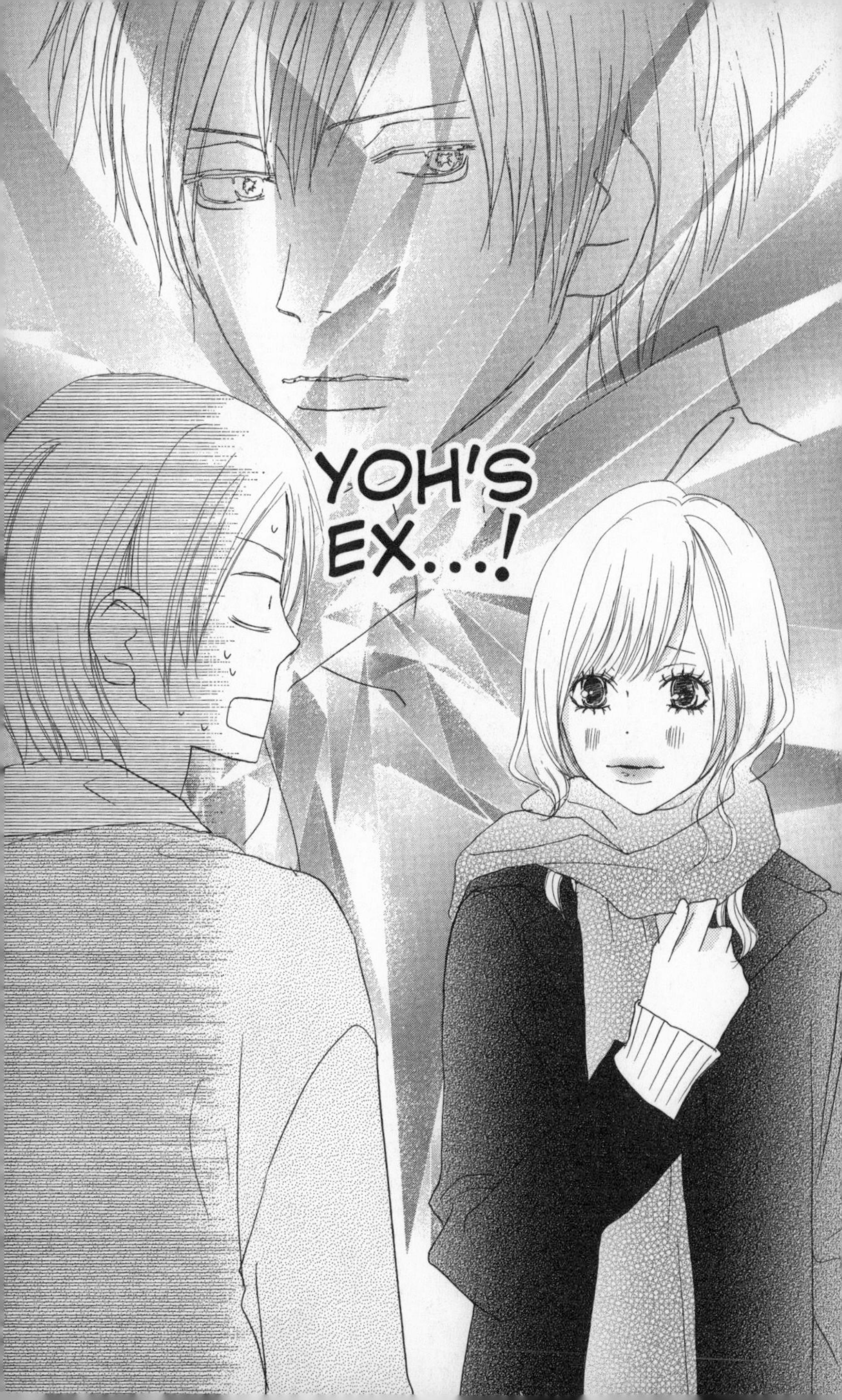
YOH'S EX...!

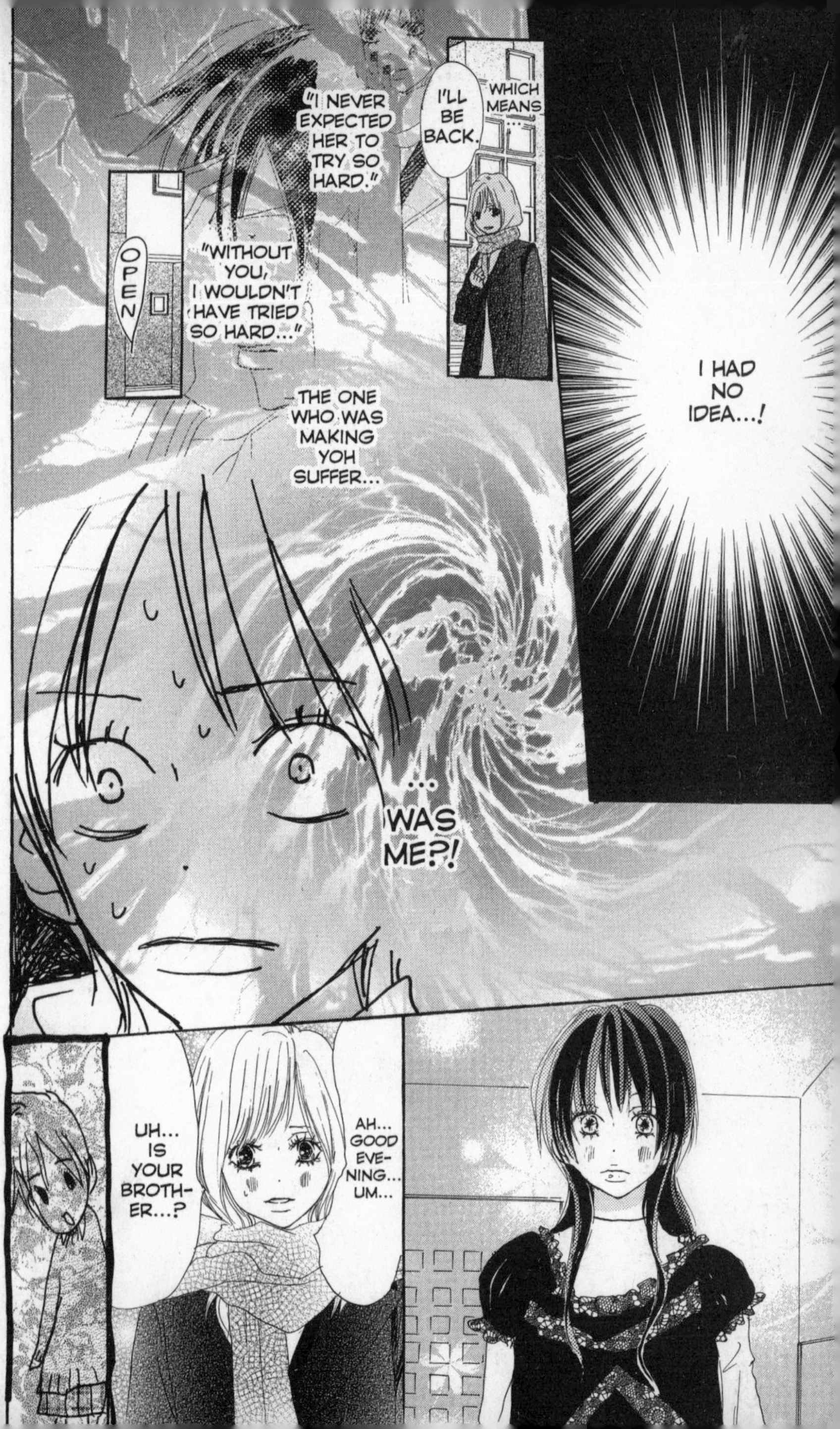
I HAD NO IDEA...!
WHICH MEANS...
I'LL BE BACK.
"I NEVER EXPECTED HER TO TRY SO HARD."
OPEN
"WITHOUT YOU, I WOULDN'T HAVE TRIED SO HARD..."
THE ONE WHO WAS MAKING YOH SUFFER...
...WAS ME?!
AH... GOOD EVE-NING... UM...
UH... IS YOUR BROTH-ER...?

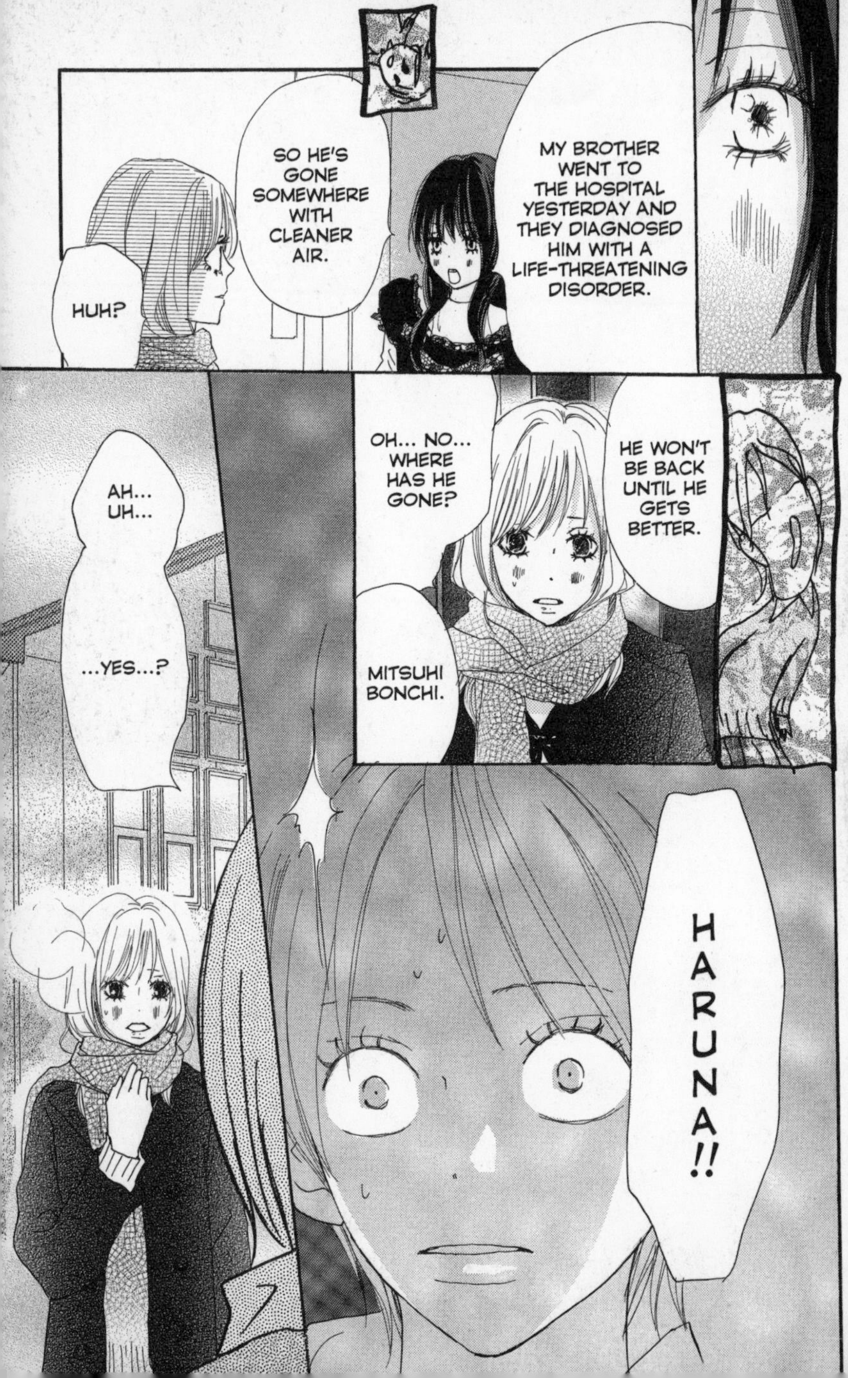
MY BROTHER WENT TO THE HOSPITAL YESTERDAY AND THEY DIAGNOSED HIM WITH A LIFE-THREATENING DISORDER.
SO HE'S GONE SOMEWHERE WITH CLEANER AIR.
HUH?
HE WON'T BE BACK UNTIL HE GETS BETTER.
OH... NO... WHERE HAS HE GONE?
MITSUHI BONCHI.
HARUNA!!
AH... UH...
...YES...?

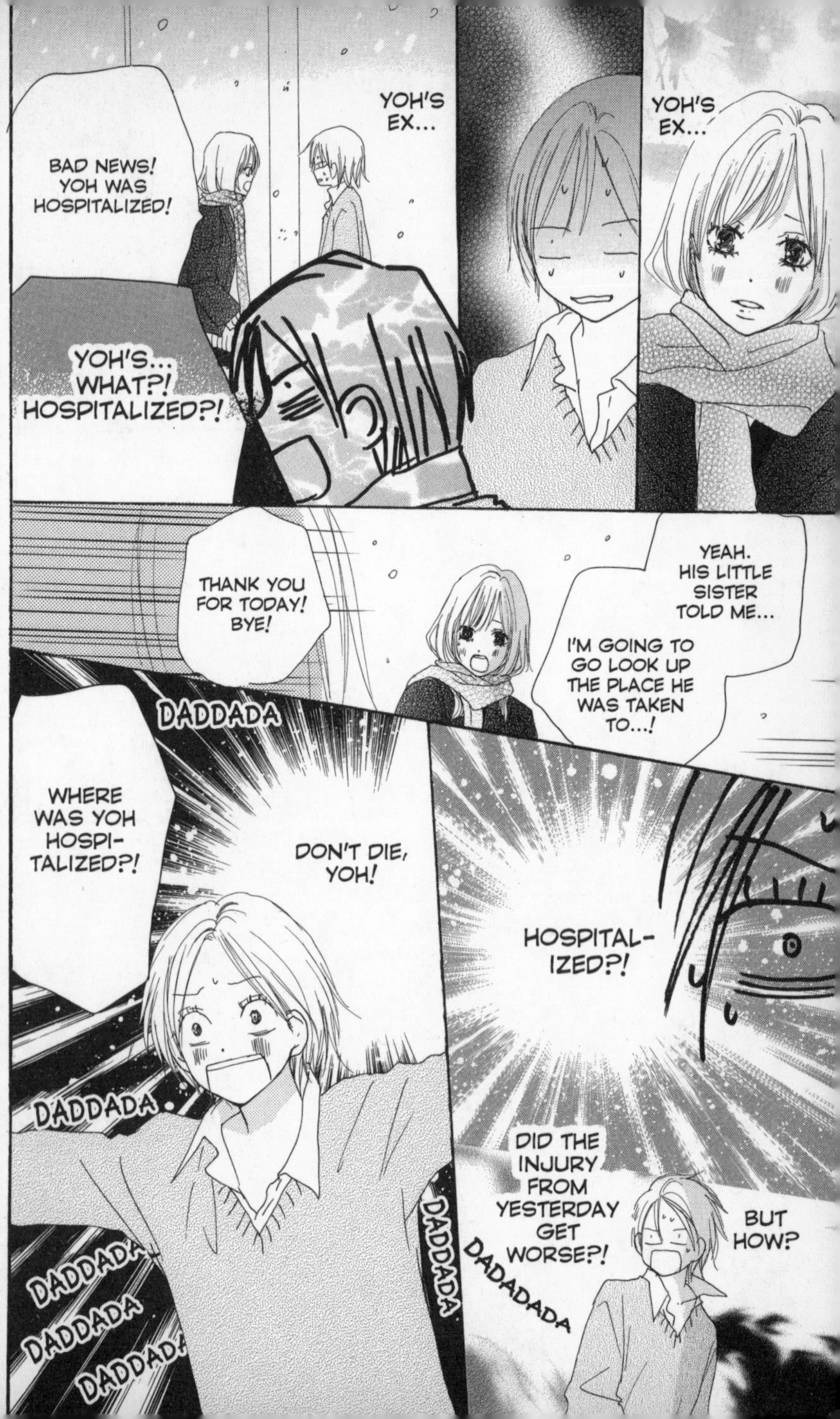
YOH'S EX...
YOH'S EX...
BAD NEWS! YOH WAS HOSPITALIZED!
YOH'S... WHAT?! HOSPITALIZED?!
YEAH. HIS LITTLE SISTER TOLD ME...
I'M GOING TO GO LOOK UP THE PLACE HE WAS TAKEN TO...!
THANK YOU FOR TODAY! BYE!
HOSPITAL-IZED?!
BUT HOW?
DID THE INJURY FROM YESTERDAY GET WORSE?!
DADADADA
DADDADA
DON'T DIE, YOH!
WHERE WAS YOH HOSPI-TALIZED?!
DADDADA
DADDADA
DADDADA
DADDADA
DADDADA
DADDADA

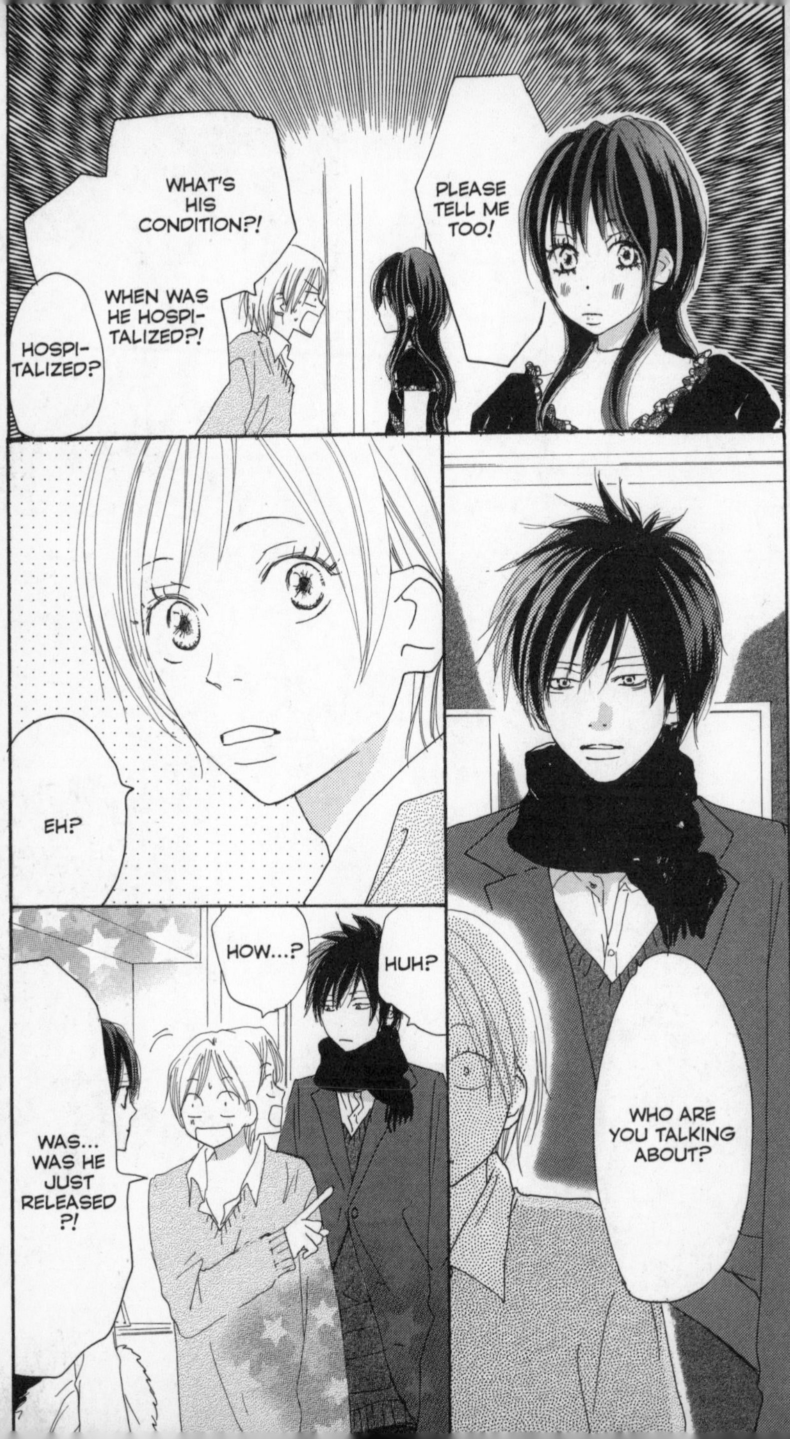
PLEASE TELL ME TOO!
WHAT'S HIS CONDITION?!
WHEN WAS HE HOSPI-TALIZED?!
HOSPI-TALIZED?
WHO ARE YOU TALKING ABOUT?
EH?
HUH?
HOW...?
WAS... WAS HE JUST RELEASED ?!

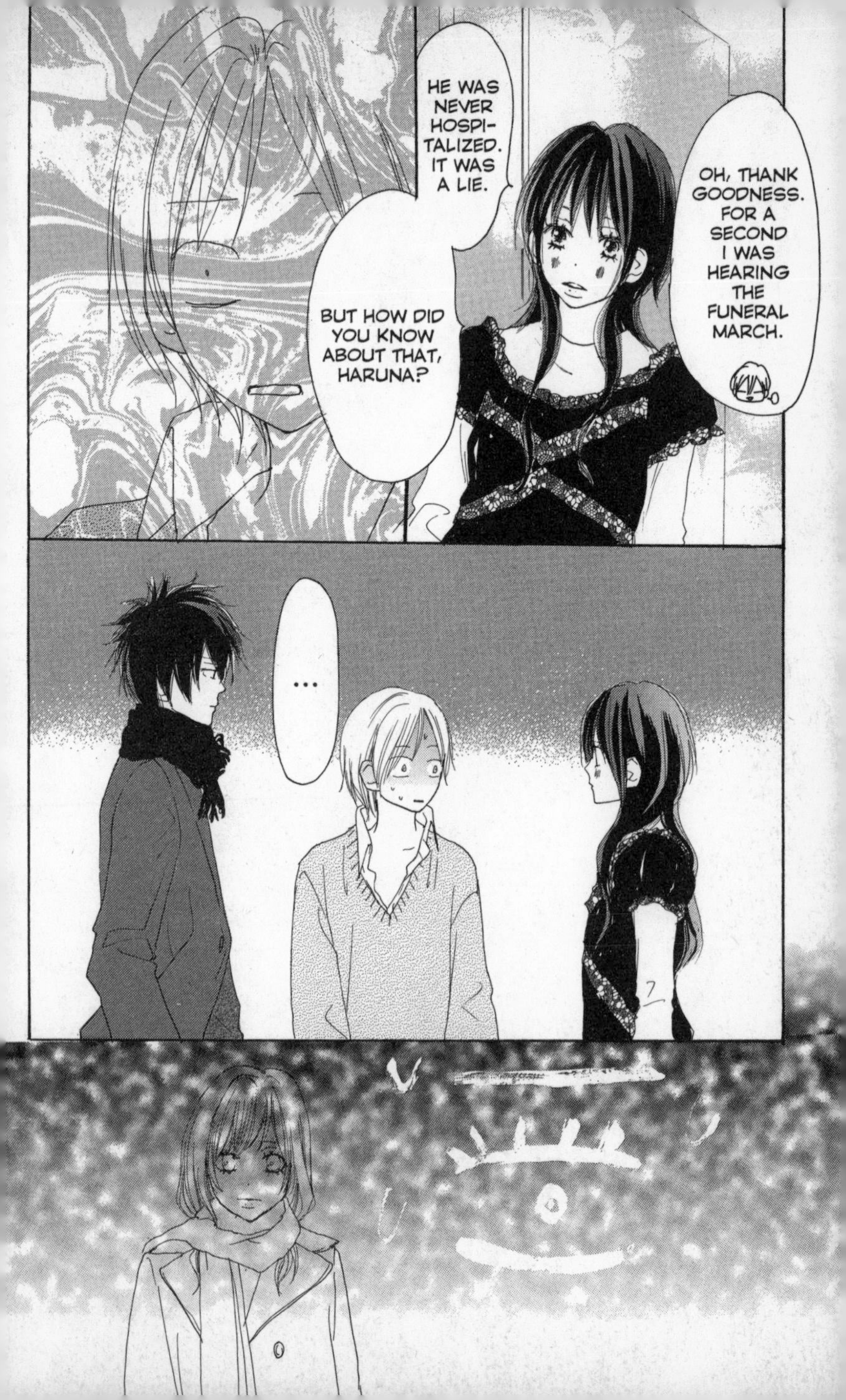
OH, THANK GOODNESS. FOR A SECOND I WAS HEARING THE FUNERAL MARCH.
HE WAS NEVER HOSPITALIZED. IT WAS A LIE.
BUT HOW DID YOU KNOW ABOUT THAT, HARUNA?
...

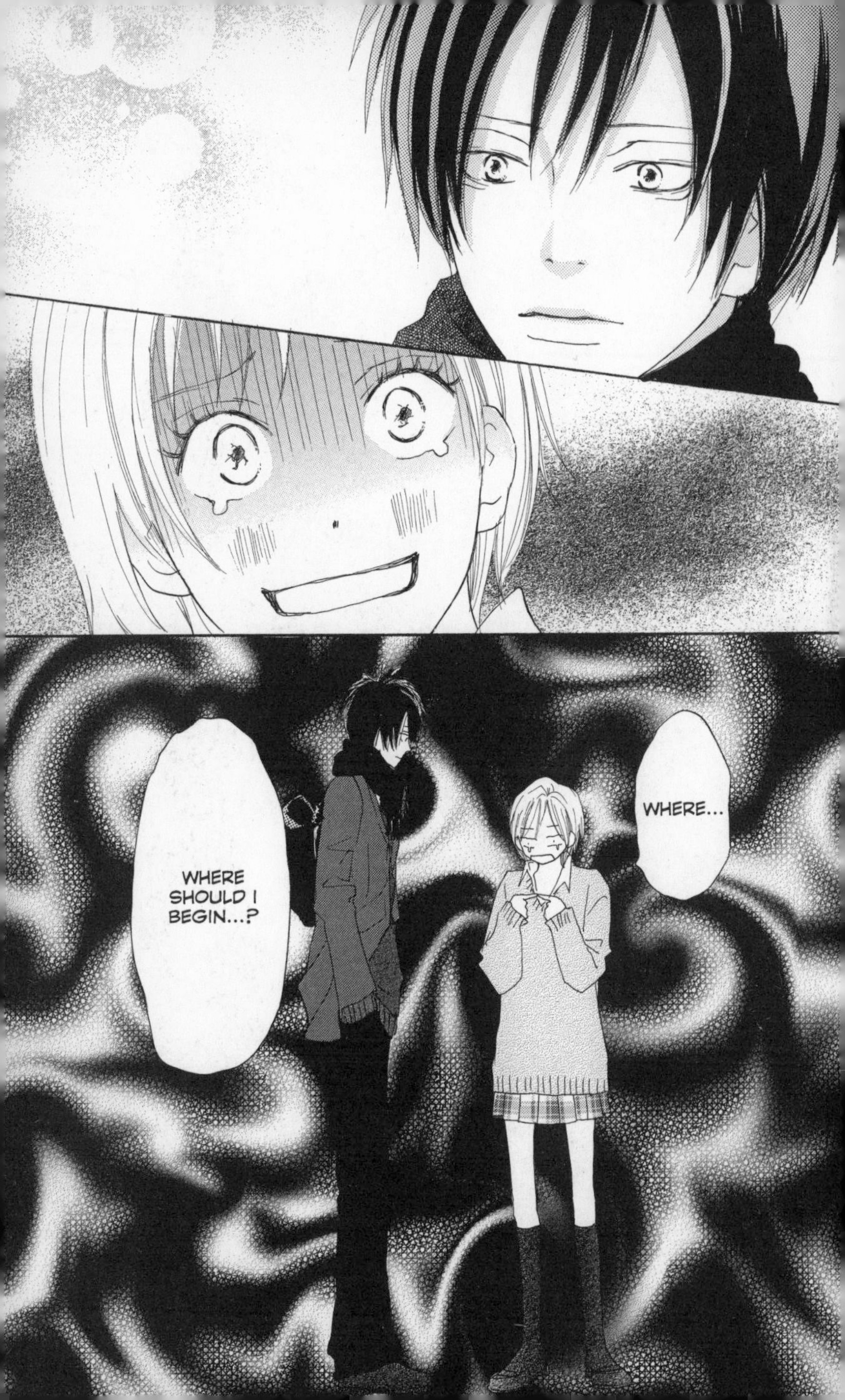
WHERE...
WHERE SHOULD I BEGIN...?

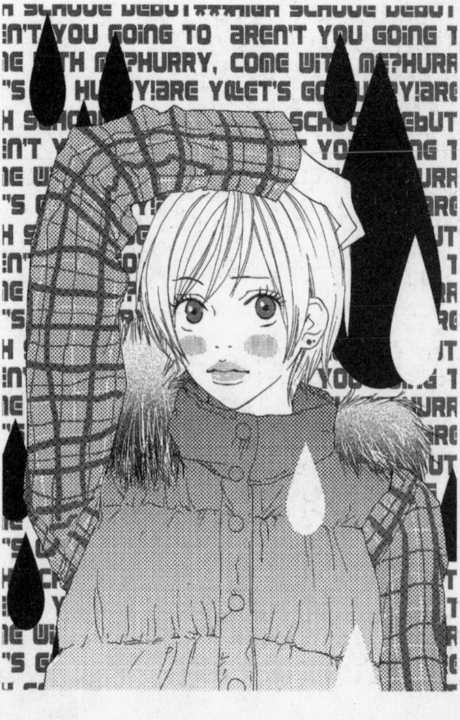

AREN'T YOU GOING TO
HURRY, COME WITH

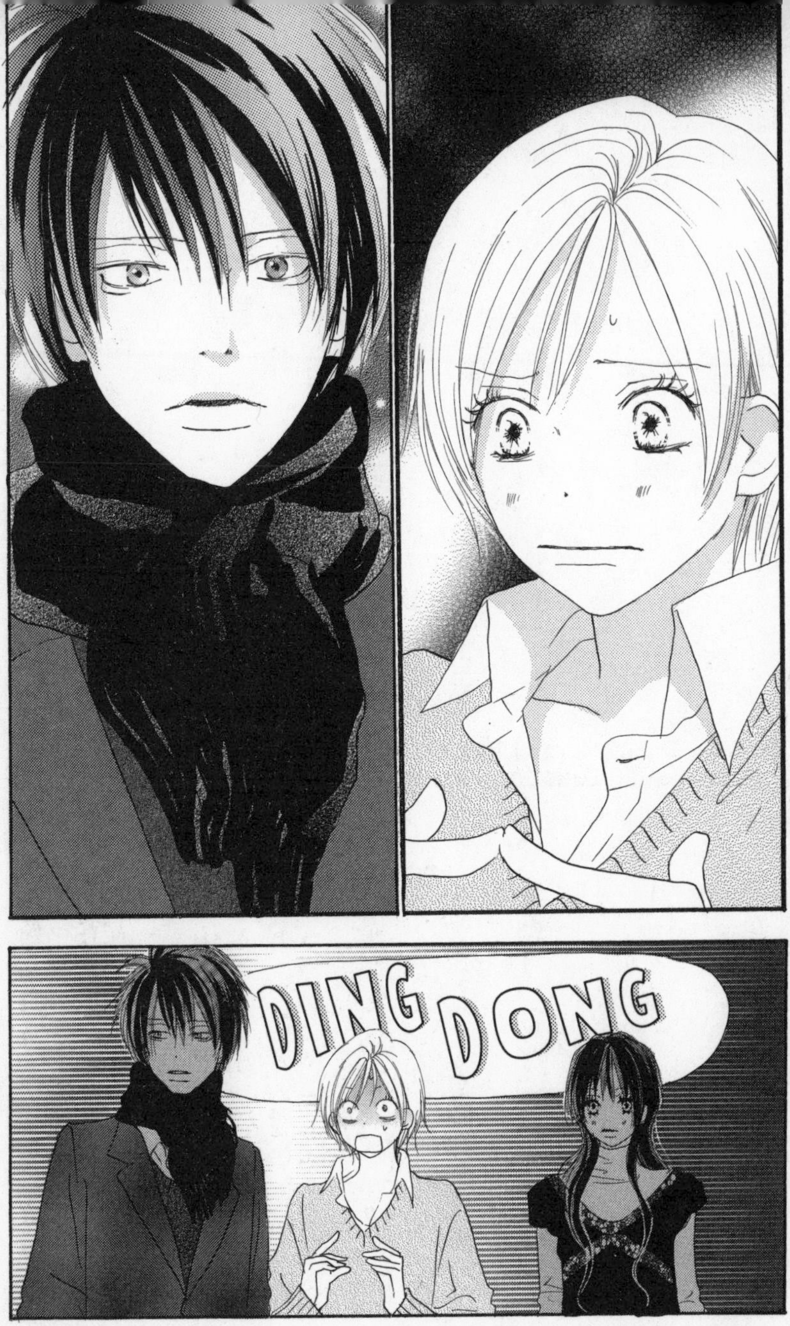
DING DONG

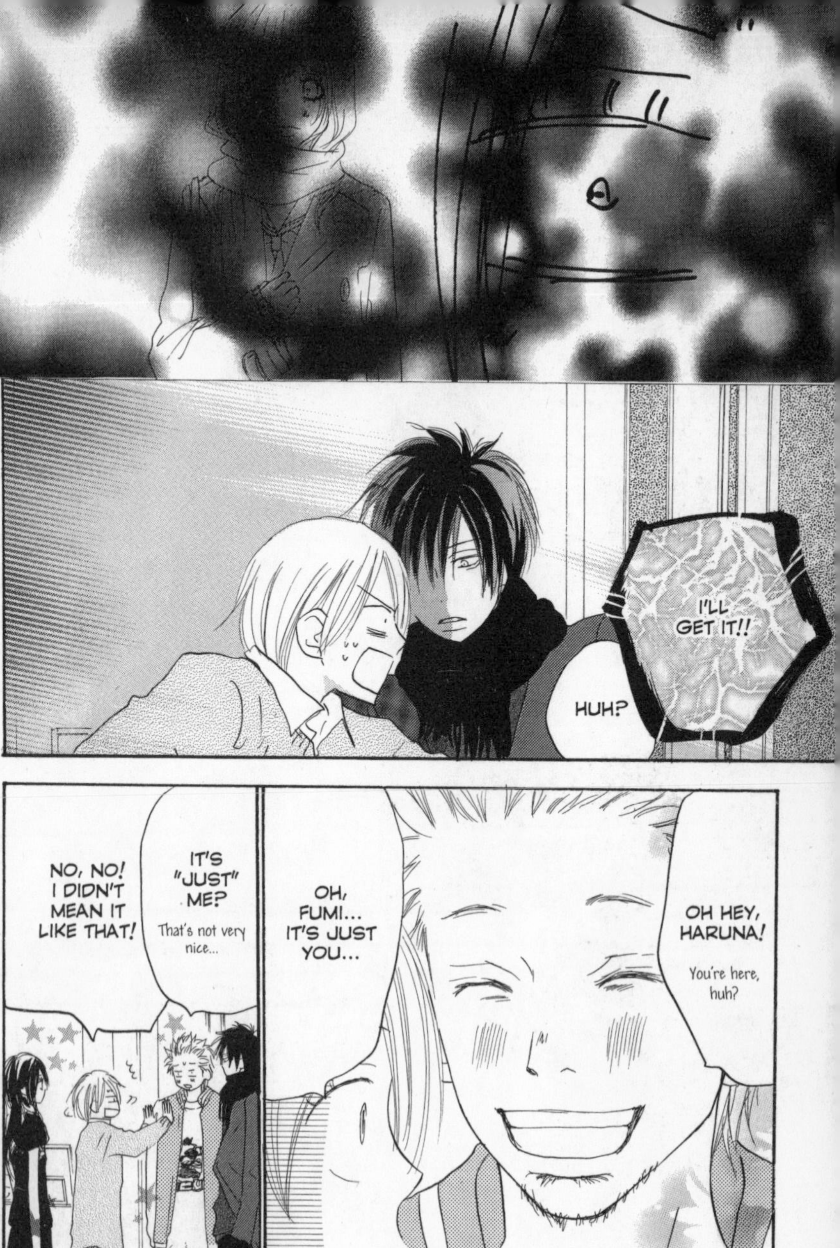

I'LL GET IT!!
HUH?
OH HEY, HARUNA! You're here, huh?
OH, FUMI... IT'S JUST YOU...
IT'S "JUST" ME? That's not very nice...
NO, NO! I DIDN'T MEAN IT LIKE THAT!

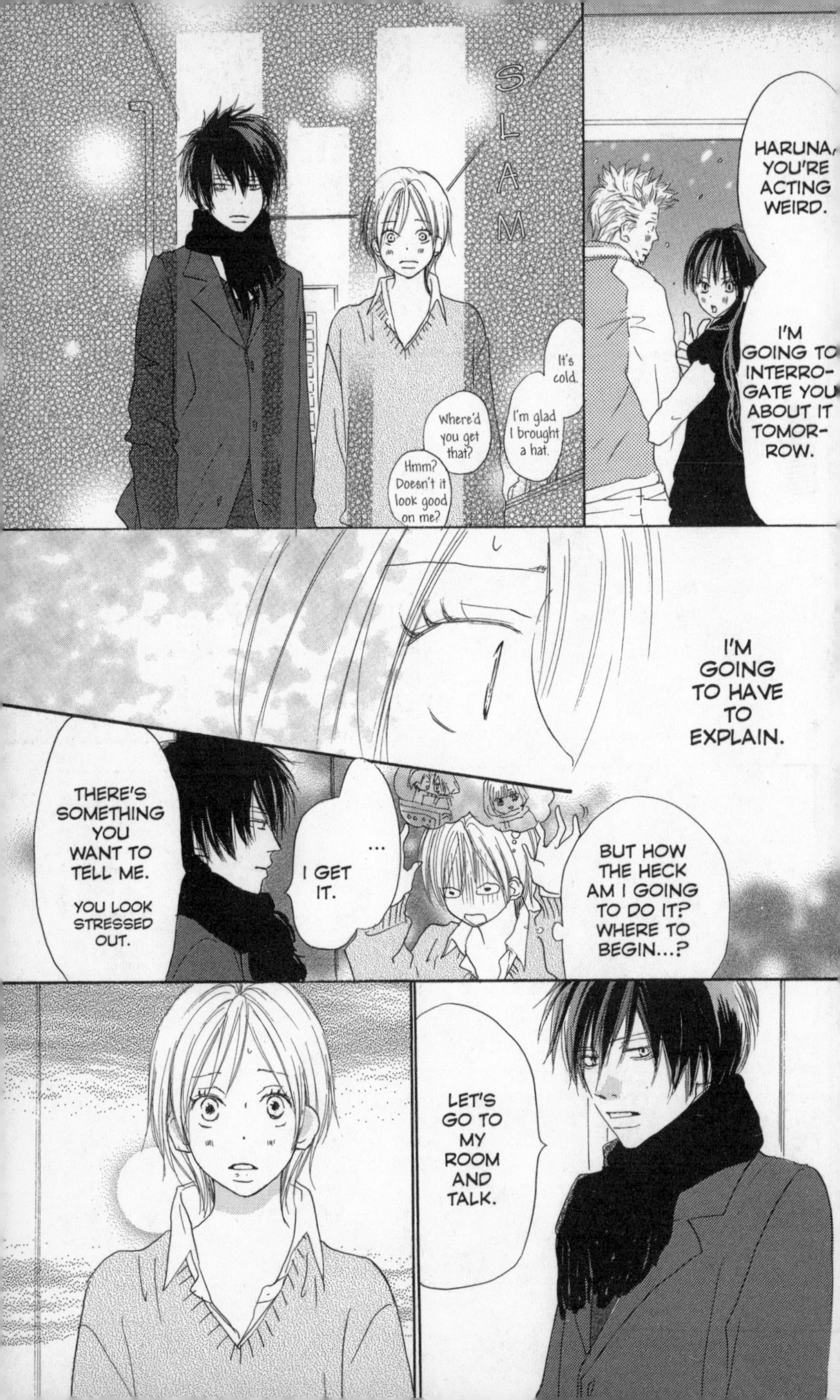
HARUNA, YOU'RE ACTING WEIRD.
I'M GOING TO INTERROGATE YOU ABOUT IT TOMORROW.
SLAM
It's cold.
I'm glad I brought a hat.
Where'd you get that?
Hmm? Doesn't it look good on me?
I'M GOING TO HAVE TO EXPLAIN.
BUT HOW THE HECK AM I GOING TO DO IT? WHERE TO BEGIN...?
... I GET IT.
THERE'S SOMETHING YOU WANT TO TELL ME.
YOU LOOK STRESSED OUT.
LET'S GO TO MY ROOM AND TALK.

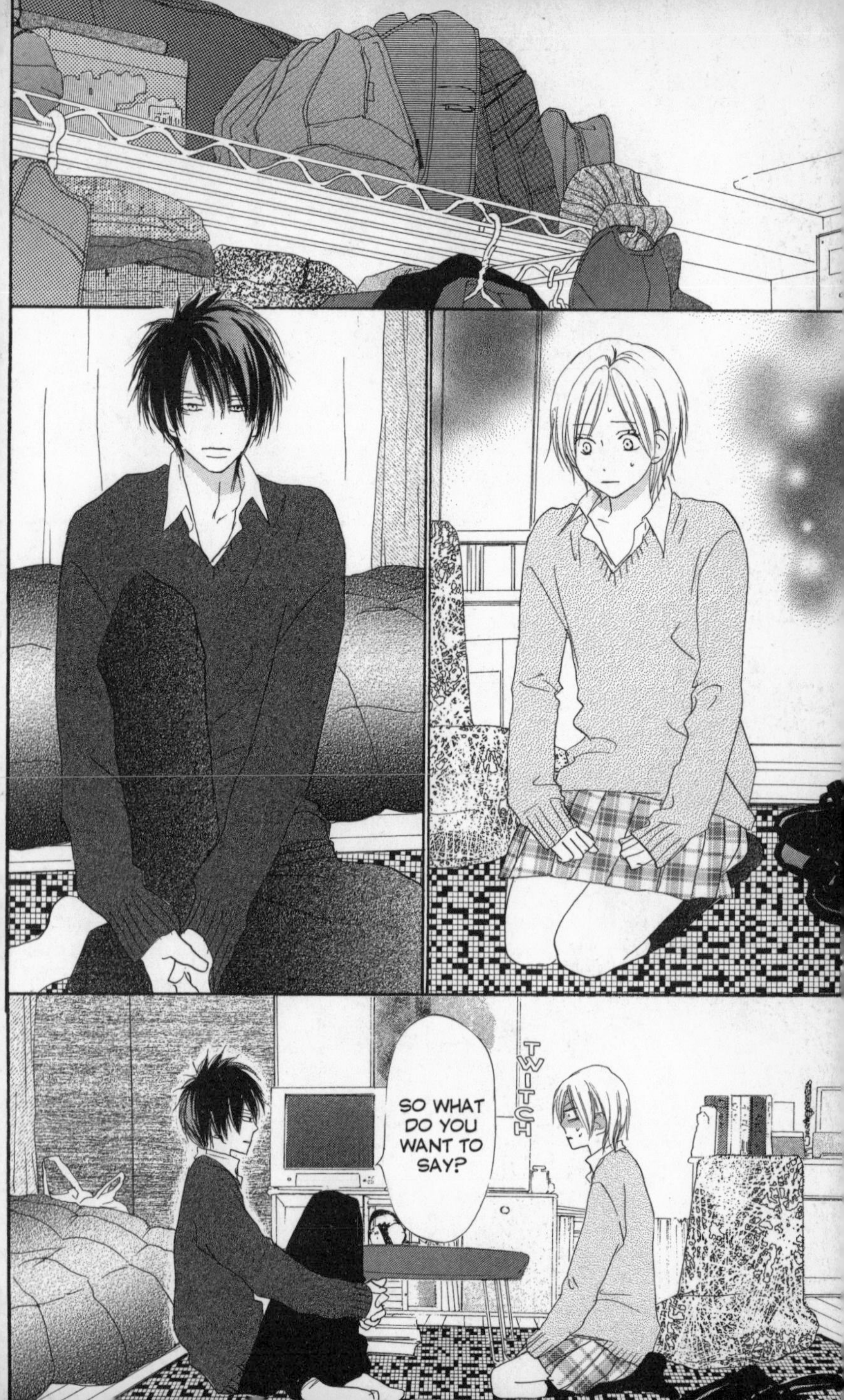
TWITCH
SO WHAT DO YOU WANT TO SAY?

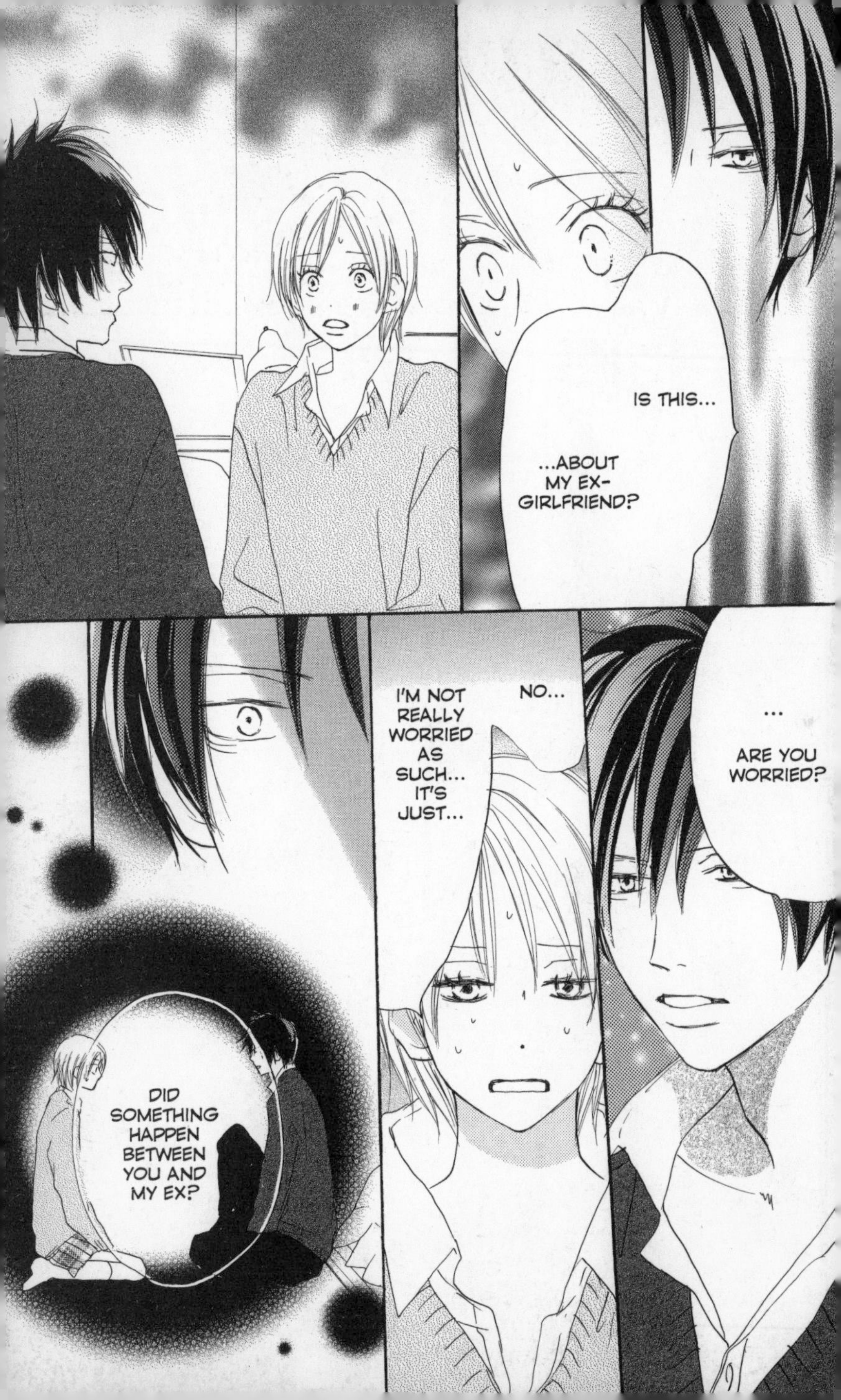
IS THIS...
...ABOUT MY EX-GIRLFRIEND?
...
ARE YOU WORRIED?
NO...
I'M NOT REALLY WORRIED AS SUCH... IT'S JUST...
DID SOMETHING HAPPEN BETWEEN YOU AND MY EX?

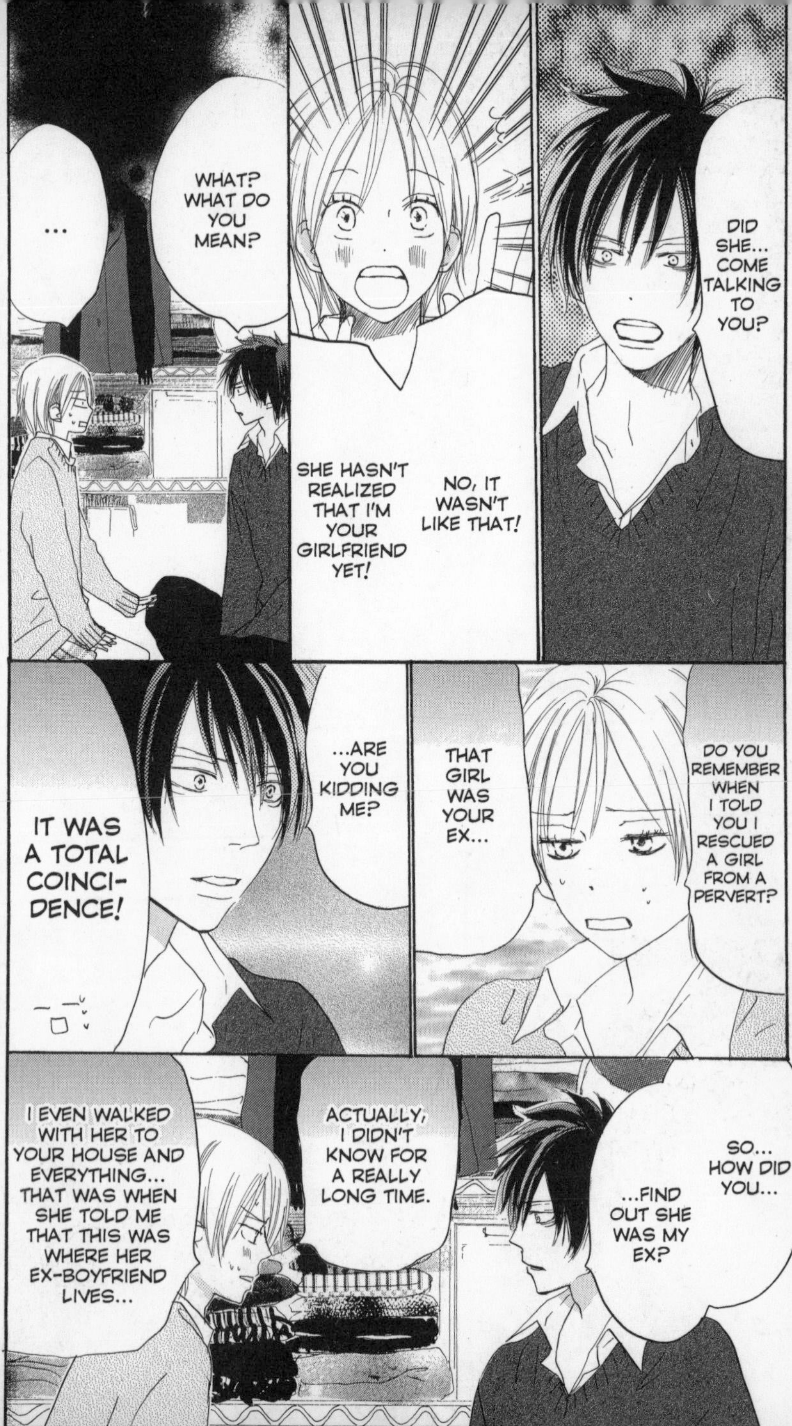
DID SHE... COME TALKING TO YOU?
NO, IT WASN'T LIKE THAT!
SHE HASN'T REALIZED THAT I'M YOUR GIRLFRIEND YET!
WHAT? WHAT DO YOU MEAN?
...
DO YOU REMEMBER WHEN I TOLD YOU I RESCUED A GIRL FROM A PERVERT?
THAT GIRL WAS YOUR EX...
...ARE YOU KIDDING ME?
IT WAS A TOTAL COINCI-DENCE!
SO... HOW DID YOU...
...FIND OUT SHE WAS MY EX?
ACTUALLY, I DIDN'T KNOW FOR A REALLY LONG TIME.
I EVEN WALKED WITH HER TO YOUR HOUSE AND EVERYTHING... THAT WAS WHEN SHE TOLD ME THAT THIS WAS WHERE HER EX-BOYFRIEND LIVES...

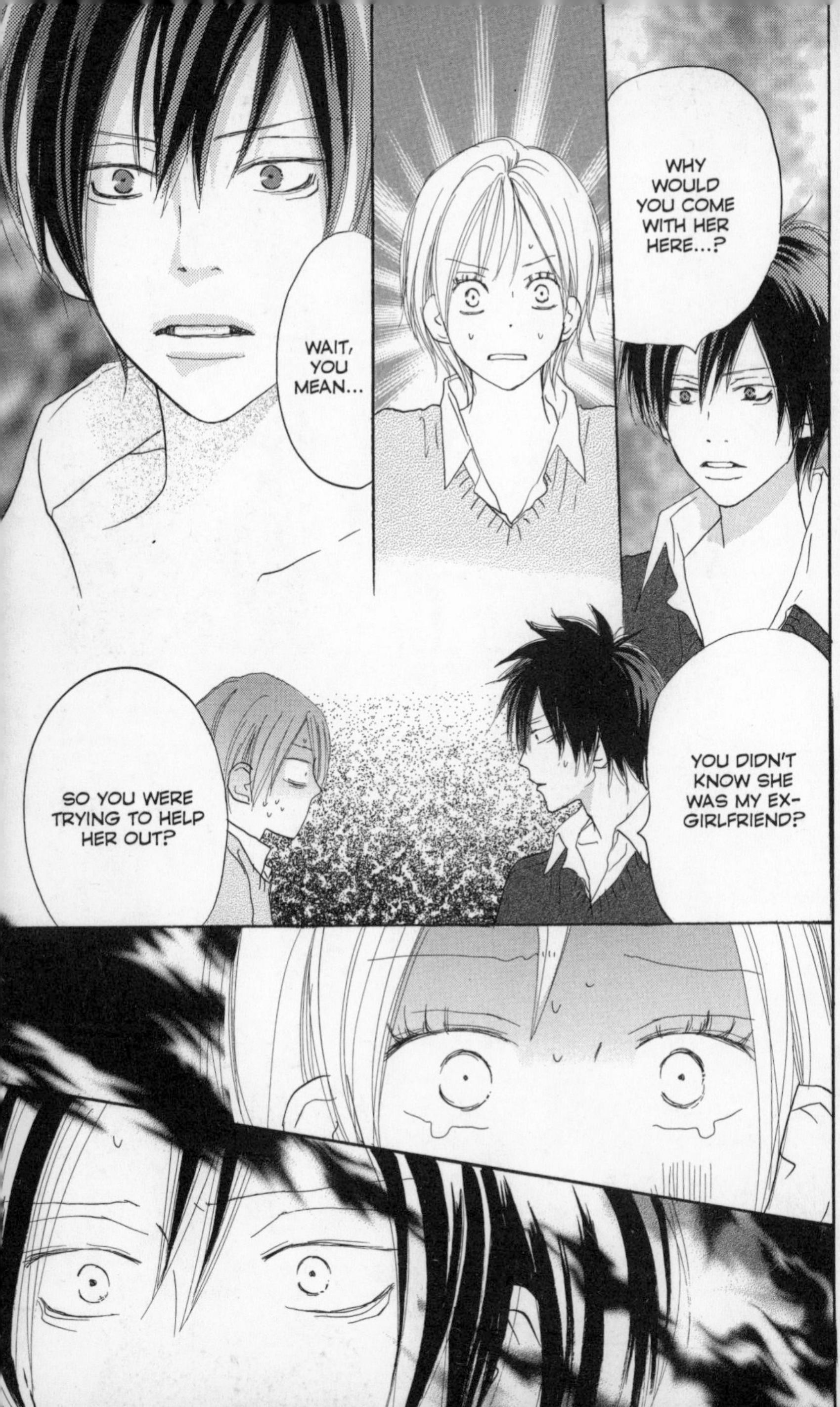
WHY WOULD YOU COME WITH HER HERE...?
WAIT, YOU MEAN...
YOU DIDN'T KNOW SHE WAS MY EX-GIRLFRIEND?
SO YOU WERE TRYING TO HELP HER OUT?

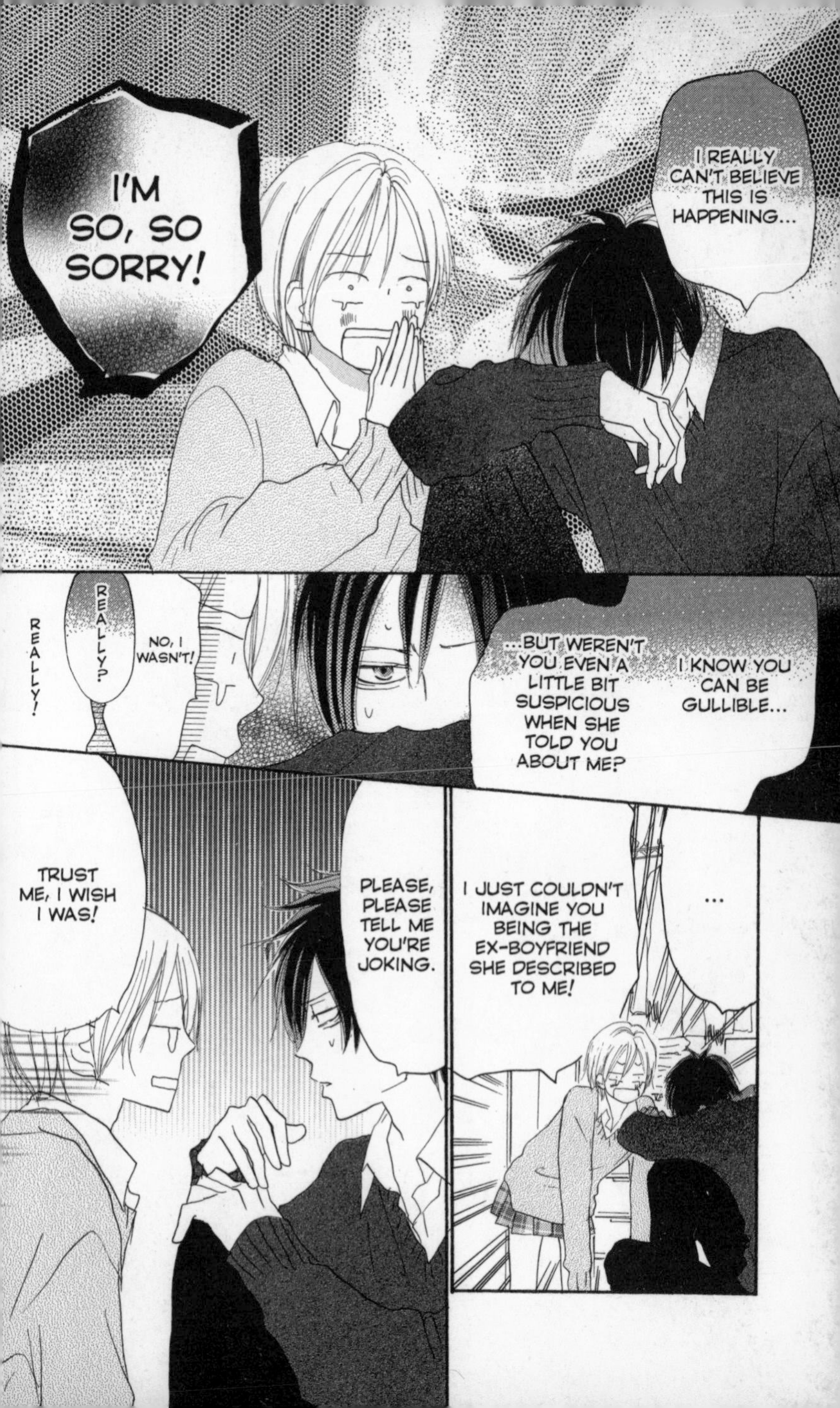
I REALLY CAN'T BELIEVE THIS IS HAPPENING...
I'M SO, SO SORRY!
I KNOW YOU CAN BE GULLIBLE...
...BUT WEREN'T YOU EVEN A LITTLE BIT SUSPICIOUS WHEN SHE TOLD YOU ABOUT ME?
NO, I WASN'T!
REALLY?
REALLY!
...
I JUST COULDN'T IMAGINE YOU BEING THE EX-BOYFRIEND SHE DESCRIBED TO ME!
PLEASE, PLEASE TELL ME YOU'RE JOKING.
TRUST ME, I WISH I WAS!

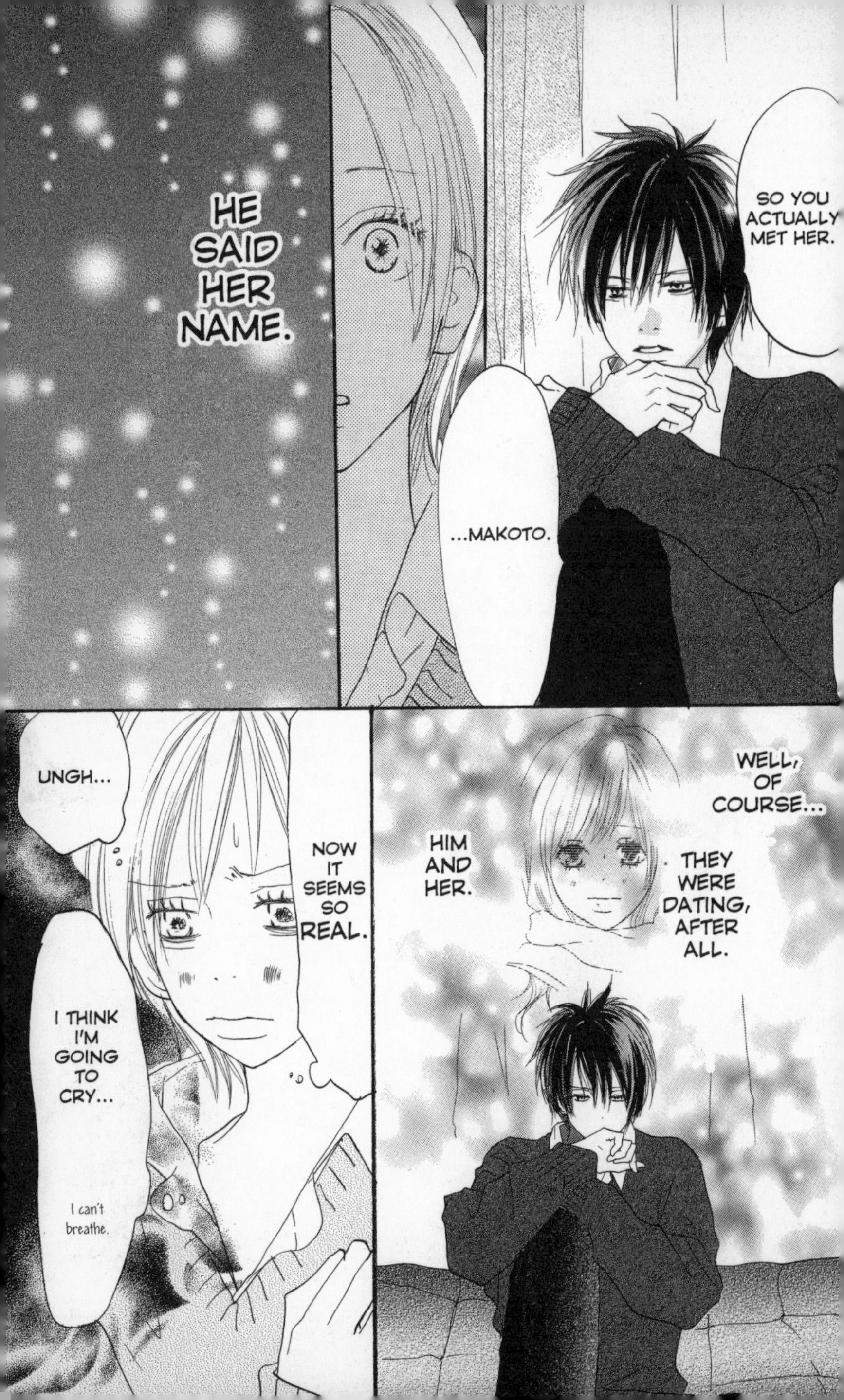
SO YOU ACTUALLY MET HER.
...MAKOTO.
HE SAID HER NAME.
WELL, OF COURSE...
THEY WERE DATING, AFTER ALL.
HIM AND HER.
NOW IT SEEMS SO REAL.
UNGH...
I THINK I'M GOING TO CRY...
I can't breathe.

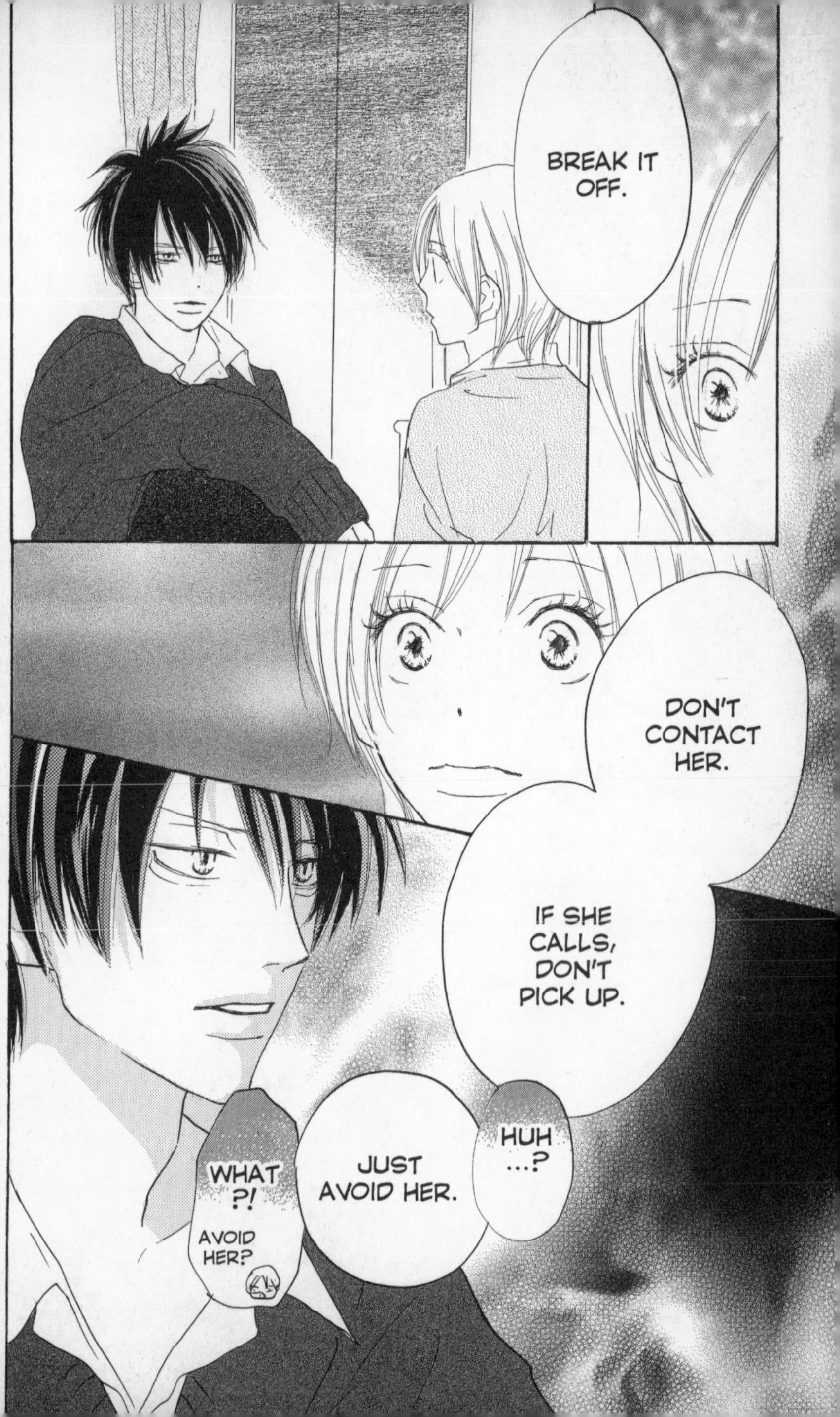
BREAK IT OFF.
DON'T CONTACT HER.
IF SHE CALLS, DON'T PICK UP.
HUH ...?
JUST AVOID HER.
WHAT ?!
AVOID HER?

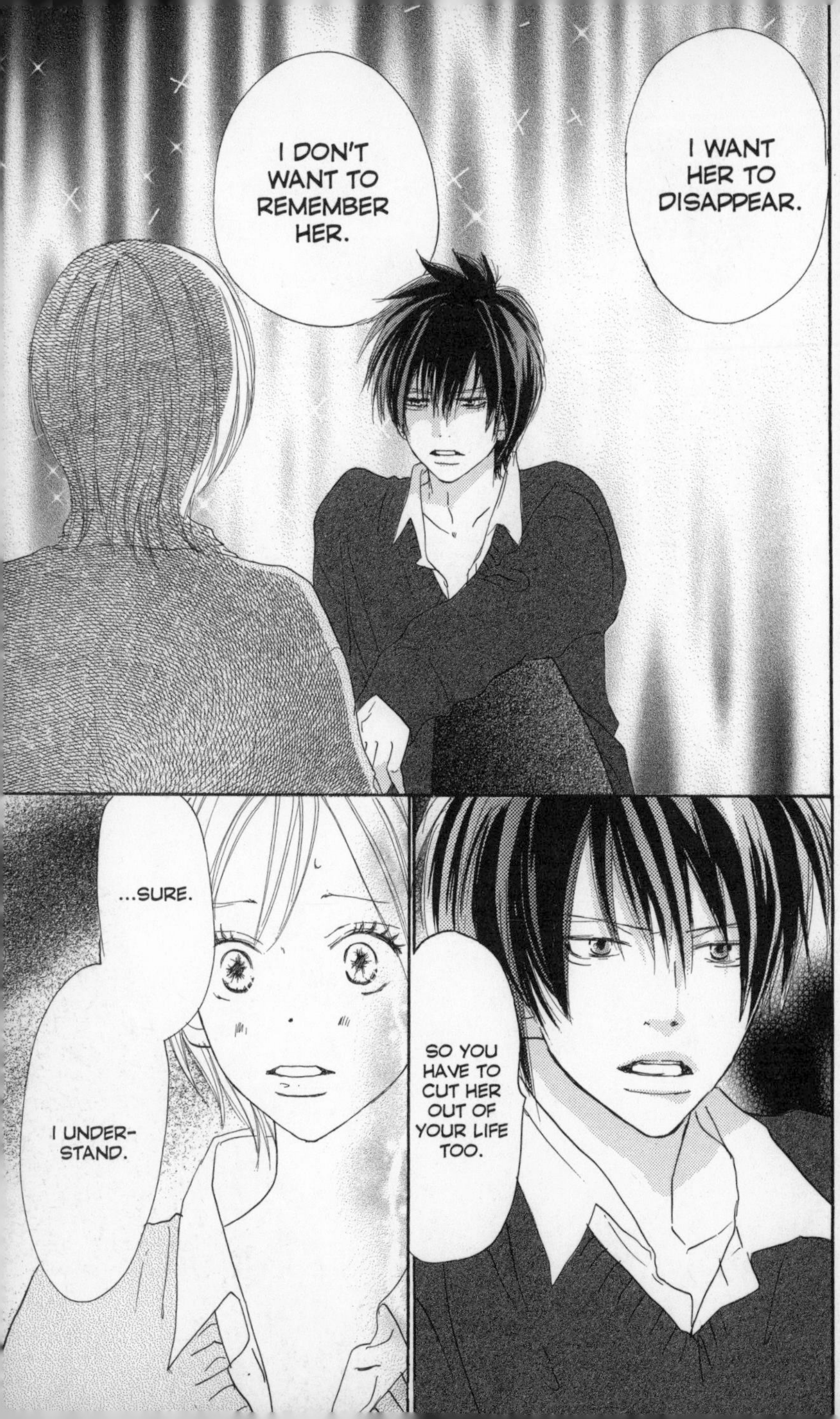
I WANT HER TO DISAPPEAR.
I DON'T WANT TO REMEMBER HER.
SO YOU HAVE TO CUT HER OUT OF YOUR LIFE TOO.
...SURE.
I UNDER-STAND.

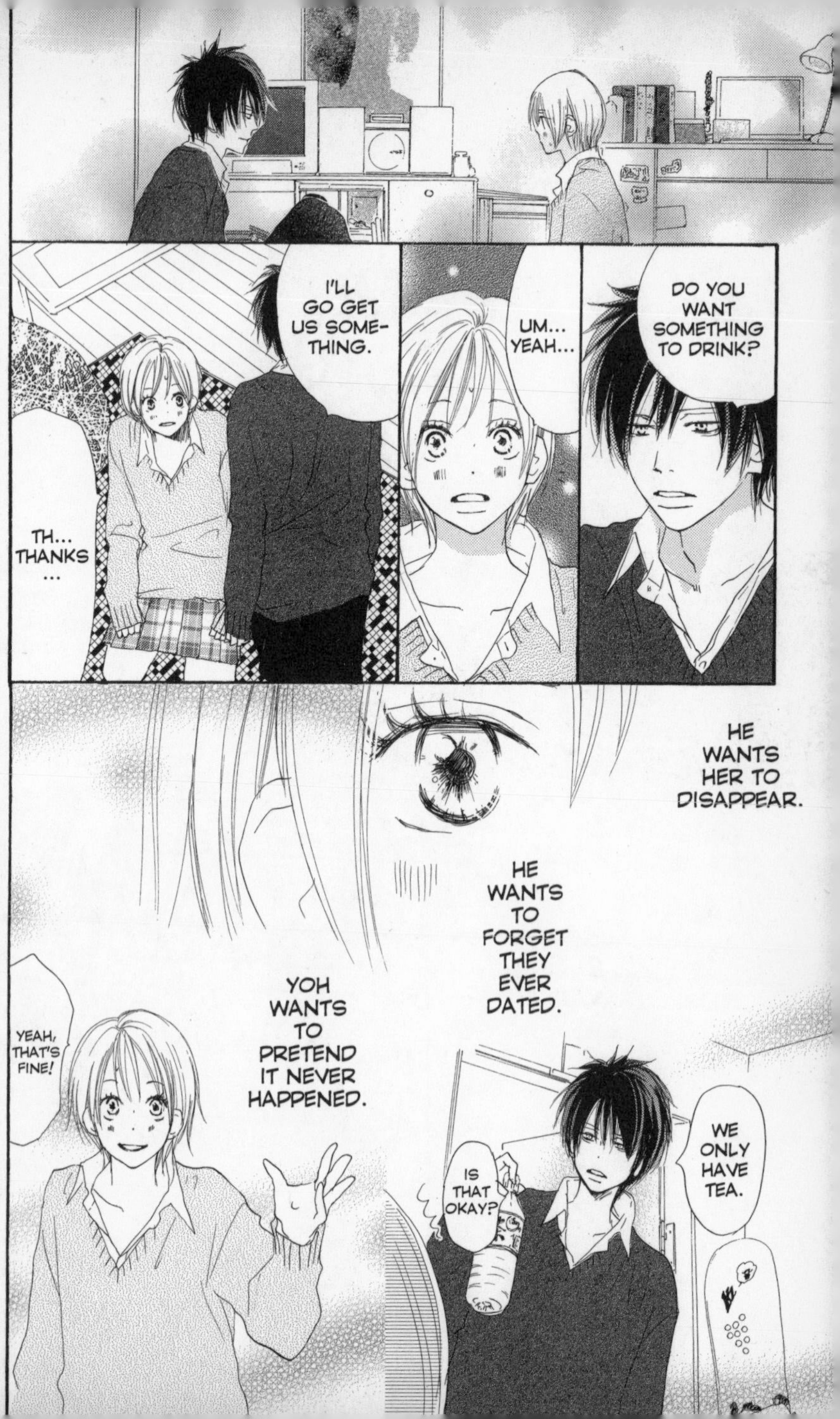
DO YOU WANT SOMETHING TO DRINK?
UM... YEAH...
I'LL GO GET US SOME-THING.
TH... THANKS ...
HE WANTS HER TO DISAPPEAR.
HE WANTS TO FORGET THEY EVER DATED.
YOH WANTS TO PRETEND IT NEVER HAPPENED.
WE ONLY HAVE TEA.
IS THAT OKAY?
YEAH, THAT'S FINE!

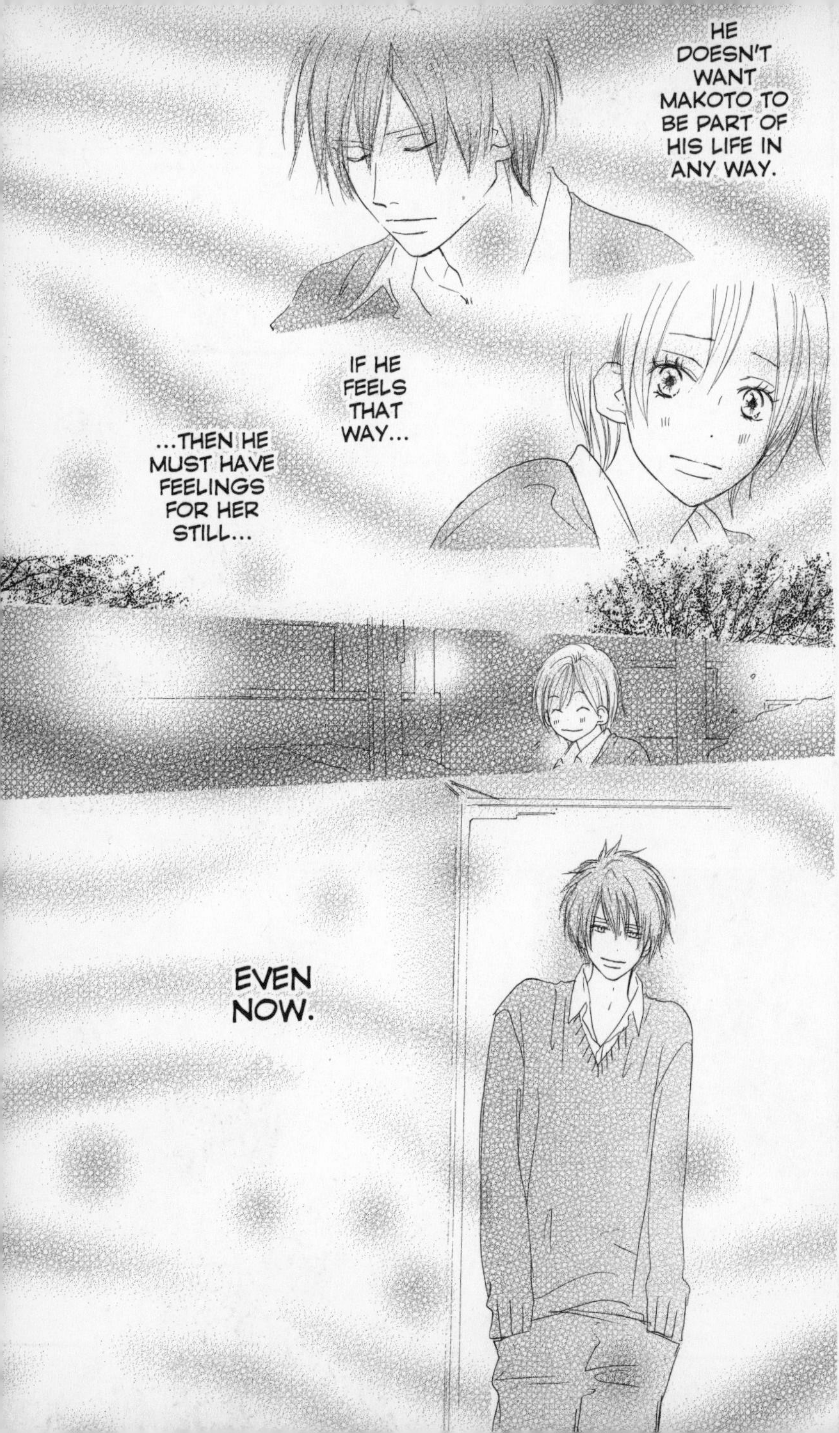
HE DOESN'T WANT MAKOTO TO BE PART OF HIS LIFE IN ANY WAY.
IF HE FEELS THAT WAY...
...THEN HE MUST HAVE FEELINGS FOR HER STILL...
EVEN NOW.

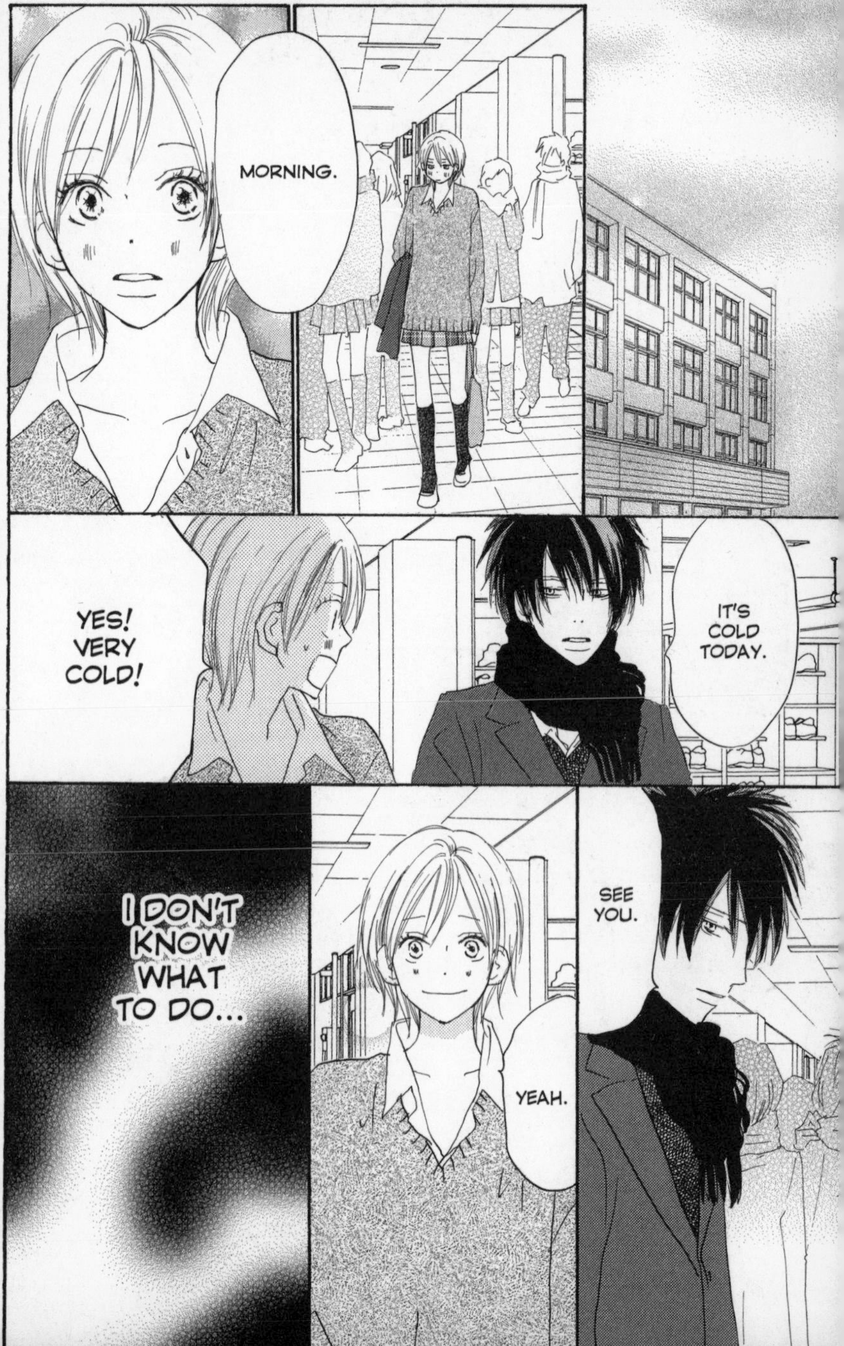
MORNING.
IT'S COLD TODAY.
YES! VERY COLD!
SEE YOU.
YEAH.
I DON'T KNOW WHAT TO DO...

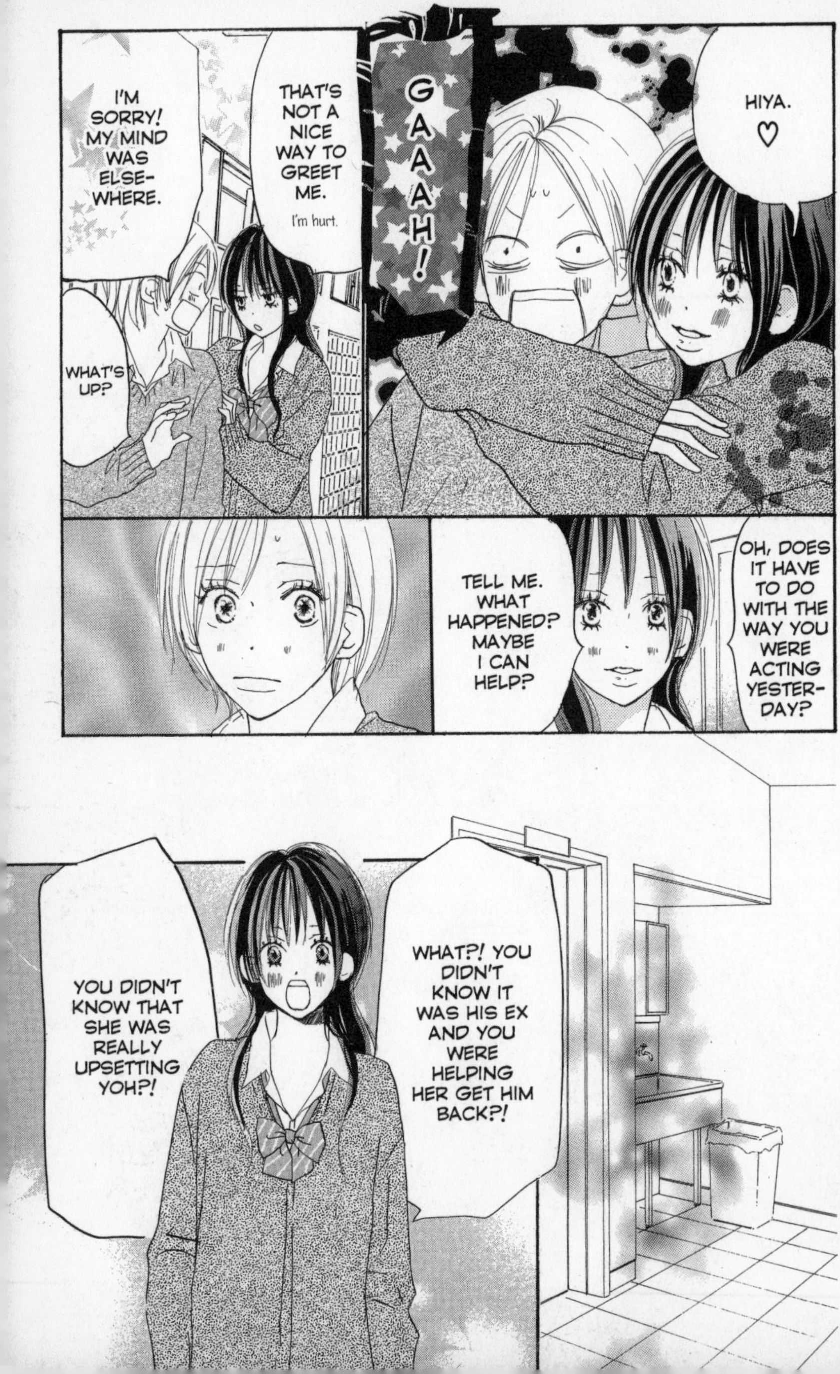
HIYA. ♡
GAAAH!
THAT'S NOT A NICE WAY TO GREET ME.
I'm hurt.
I'M SORRY! MY MIND WAS ELSEWHERE.
WHAT'S UP?
OH, DOES IT HAVE TO DO WITH THE WAY YOU WERE ACTING YESTERDAY?
TELL ME. WHAT HAPPENED? MAYBE I CAN HELP?
WHAT?! YOU DIDN'T KNOW IT WAS HIS EX AND YOU WERE HELPING HER GET HIM BACK?!
YOU DIDN'T KNOW THAT SHE WAS REALLY UPSETTING YOH?!

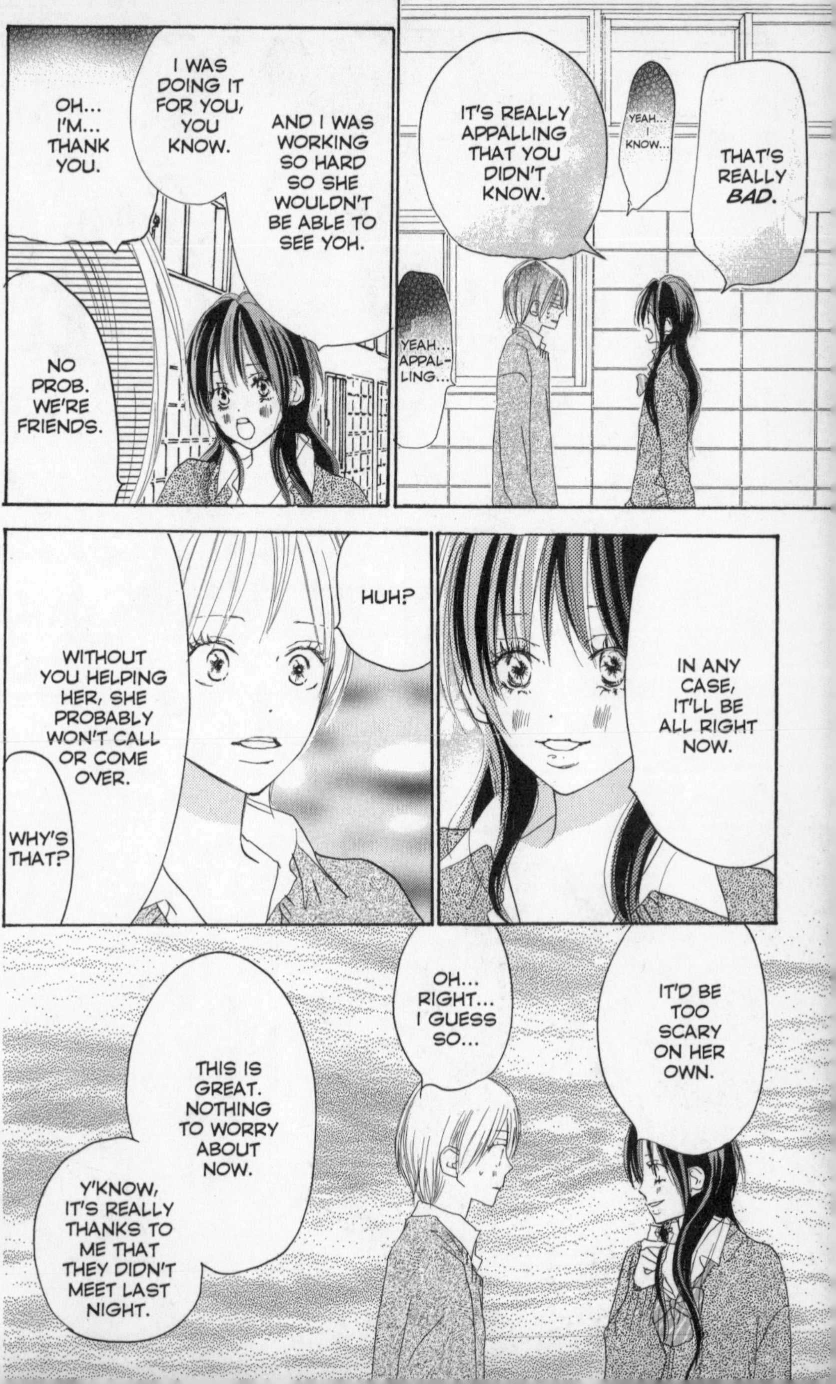
THAT'S REALLY *BAD.*
YEAH... I KNOW...
IT'S REALLY APPALLING THAT YOU DIDN'T KNOW.
YEAH... APPALLING...
AND I WAS WORKING SO HARD SO SHE WOULDN'T BE ABLE TO SEE YOH.
I WAS DOING IT FOR YOU, YOU KNOW.
OH... I'M... THANK YOU.
NO PROB. WE'RE FRIENDS.
IN ANY CASE, IT'LL BE ALL RIGHT NOW.
HUH?
WITHOUT YOU HELPING HER, SHE PROBABLY WON'T CALL OR COME OVER.
WHY'S THAT?
IT'D BE TOO SCARY ON HER OWN.
OH... RIGHT... I GUESS SO...
THIS IS GREAT. NOTHING TO WORRY ABOUT NOW.
Y'KNOW, IT'S REALLY THANKS TO ME THAT THEY DIDN'T MEET LAST NIGHT.

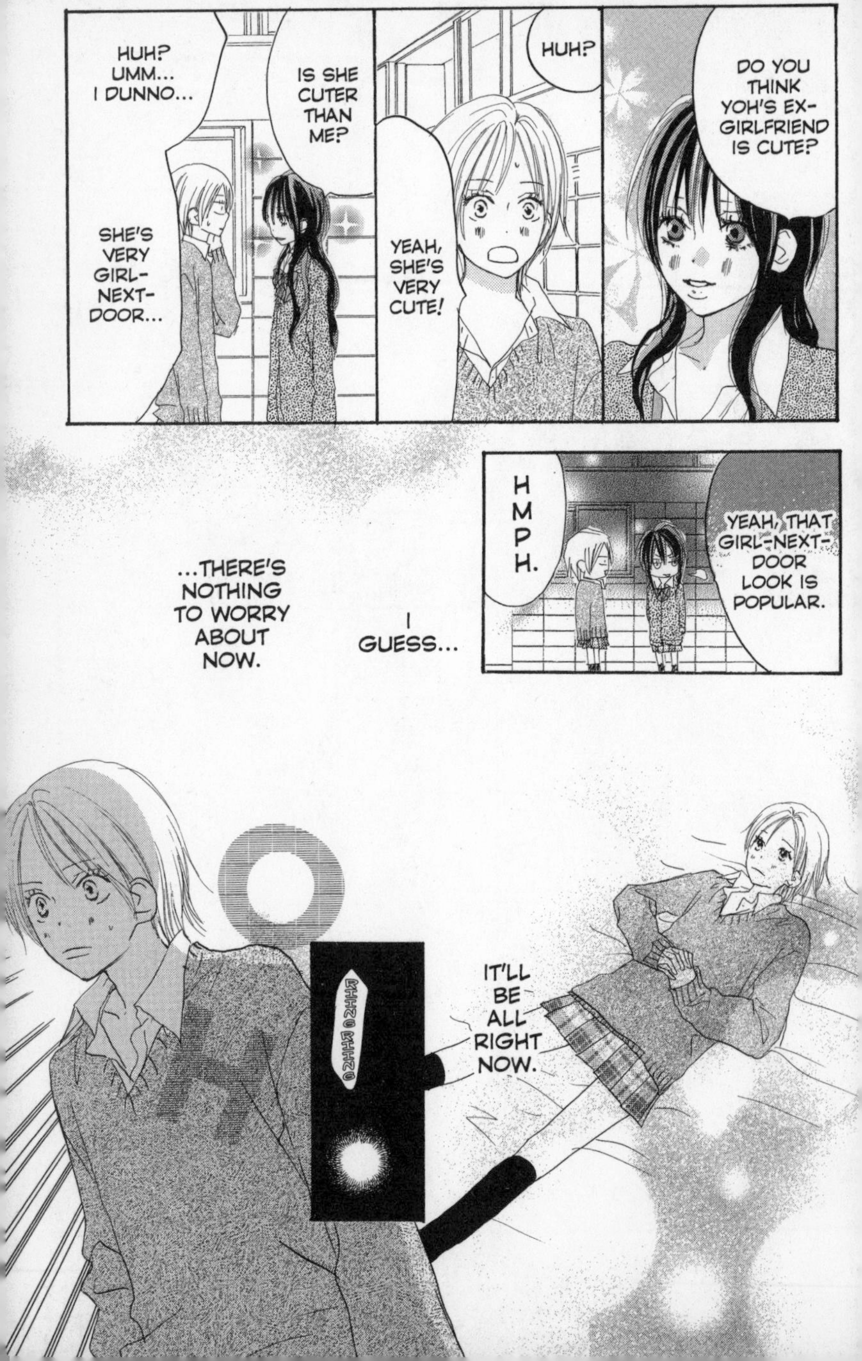
DO YOU THINK YOH'S EX-GIRLFRIEND IS CUTE?
HUH?
YEAH, SHE'S VERY CUTE!
IS SHE CUTER THAN ME?
HUH? UMM... I DUNNO...
SHE'S VERY GIRL-NEXT-DOOR...
YEAH, THAT GIRL-NEXT-DOOR LOOK IS POPULAR.
HMPH.
I GUESS...
...THERE'S NOTHING TO WORRY ABOUT NOW.
IT'LL BE ALL RIGHT NOW.
RING RING

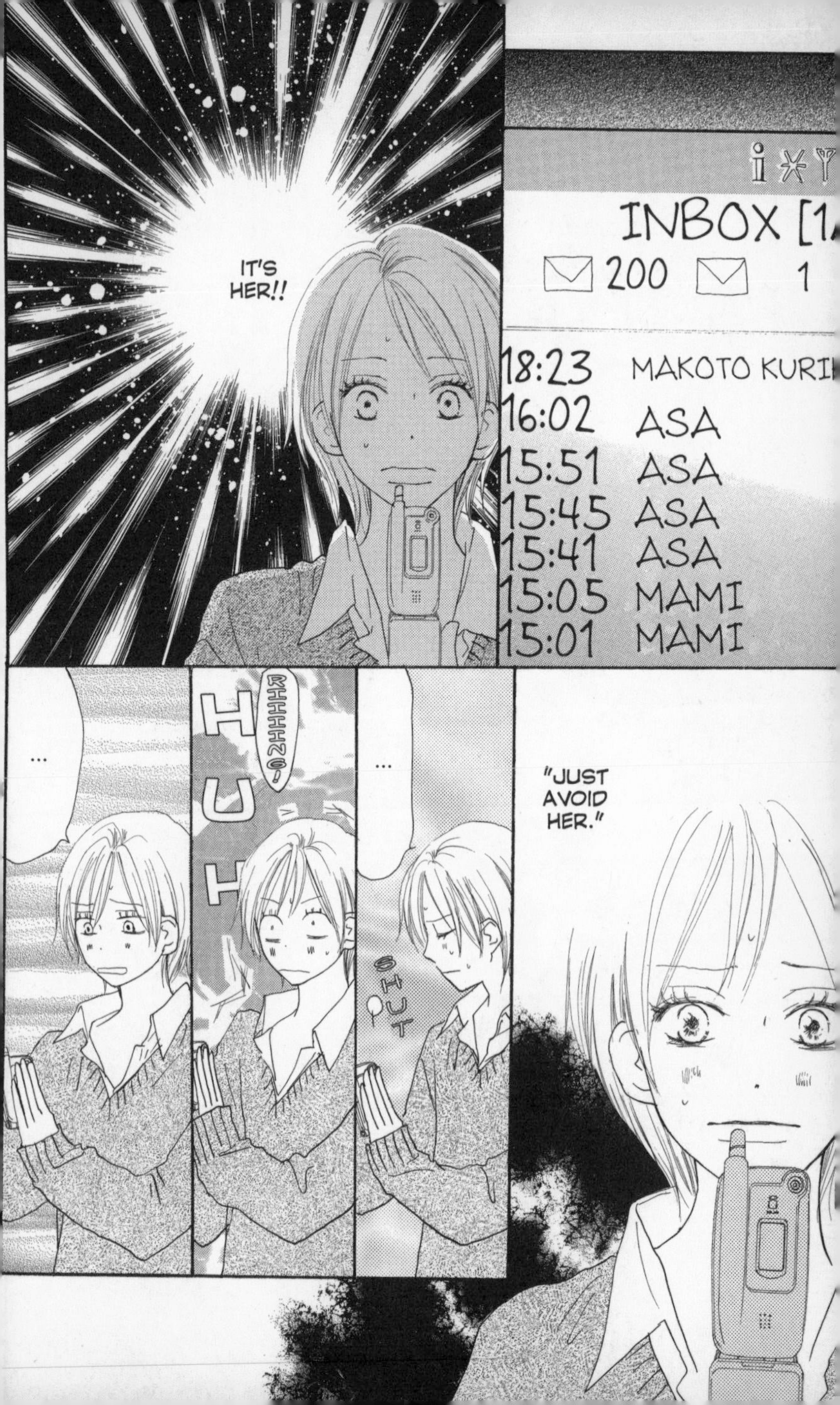
INBOX [1
200
1
18:23 MAKOTO KURI
16:02 ASA
15:51 ASA
15:45 ASA
15:41 ASA
15:05 MAMI
15:01 MAMI
IT'S HER!!
"JUST AVOID HER."
...
SHUT
RIIIIING!
HUH
...

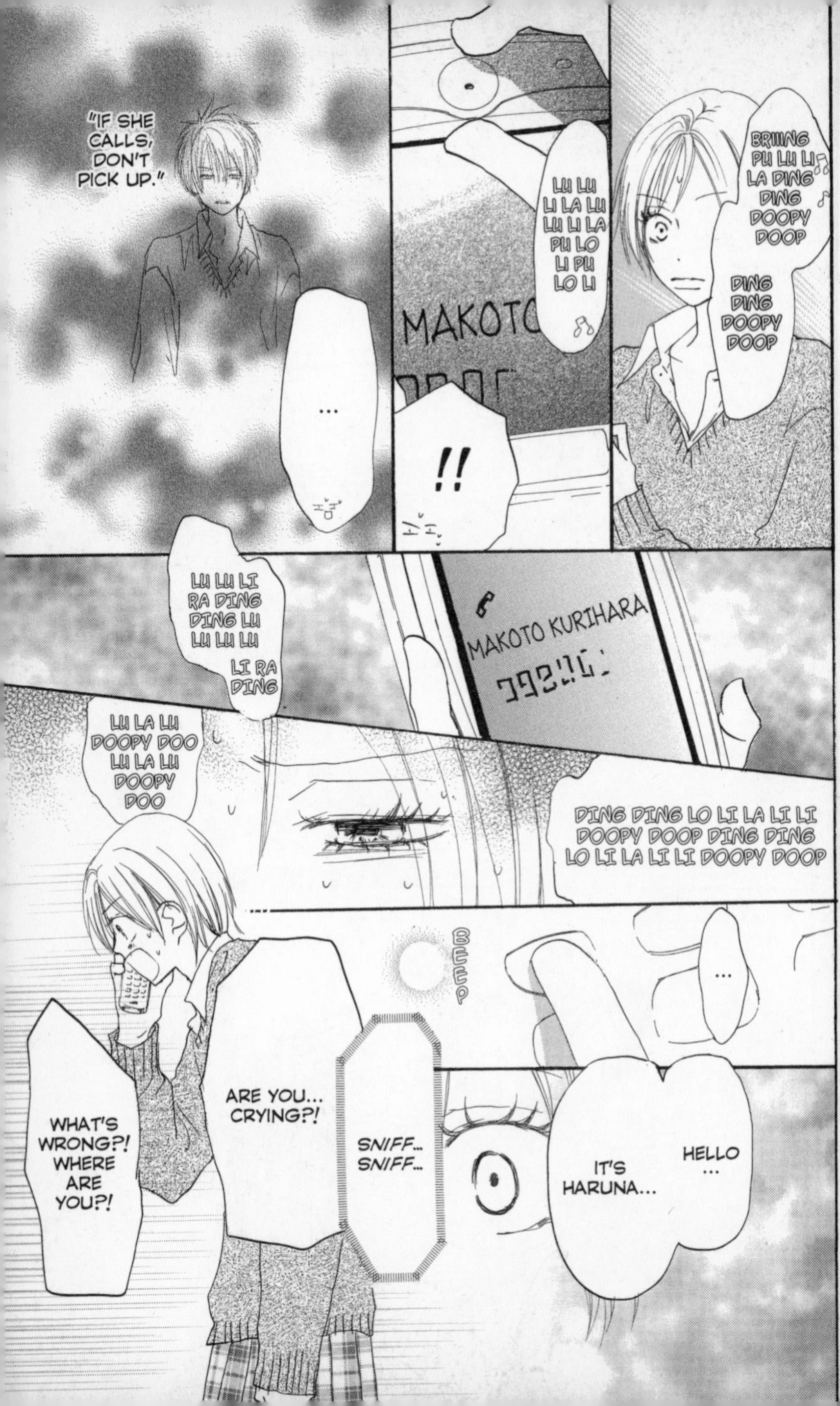
BRIIING PU LU LI LA DING DING DOOPY DOOP
DING DING DOOPY DOOP
LU LU LI LA LU LU LI LA PU LO LI PU LO LI
MAKOTO
!!
...
"IF SHE CALLS, DON'T PICK UP."
MAKOTO KURIHARA
LU LU LI RA DING DING LU LU LU LU
LI RA DING
DING DING LO LI LA LI LI DOOPY DOOP DING DING LO LI LA LI LI DOOPY DOOP
LU LA LU DOOPY DOO LU LA LU DOOPY DOO
...
BEEEP
HELLO...
IT'S HARUNA...
SNIFF... SNIFF...
ARE YOU... CRYING?!
WHAT'S WRONG?! WHERE ARE YOU?!

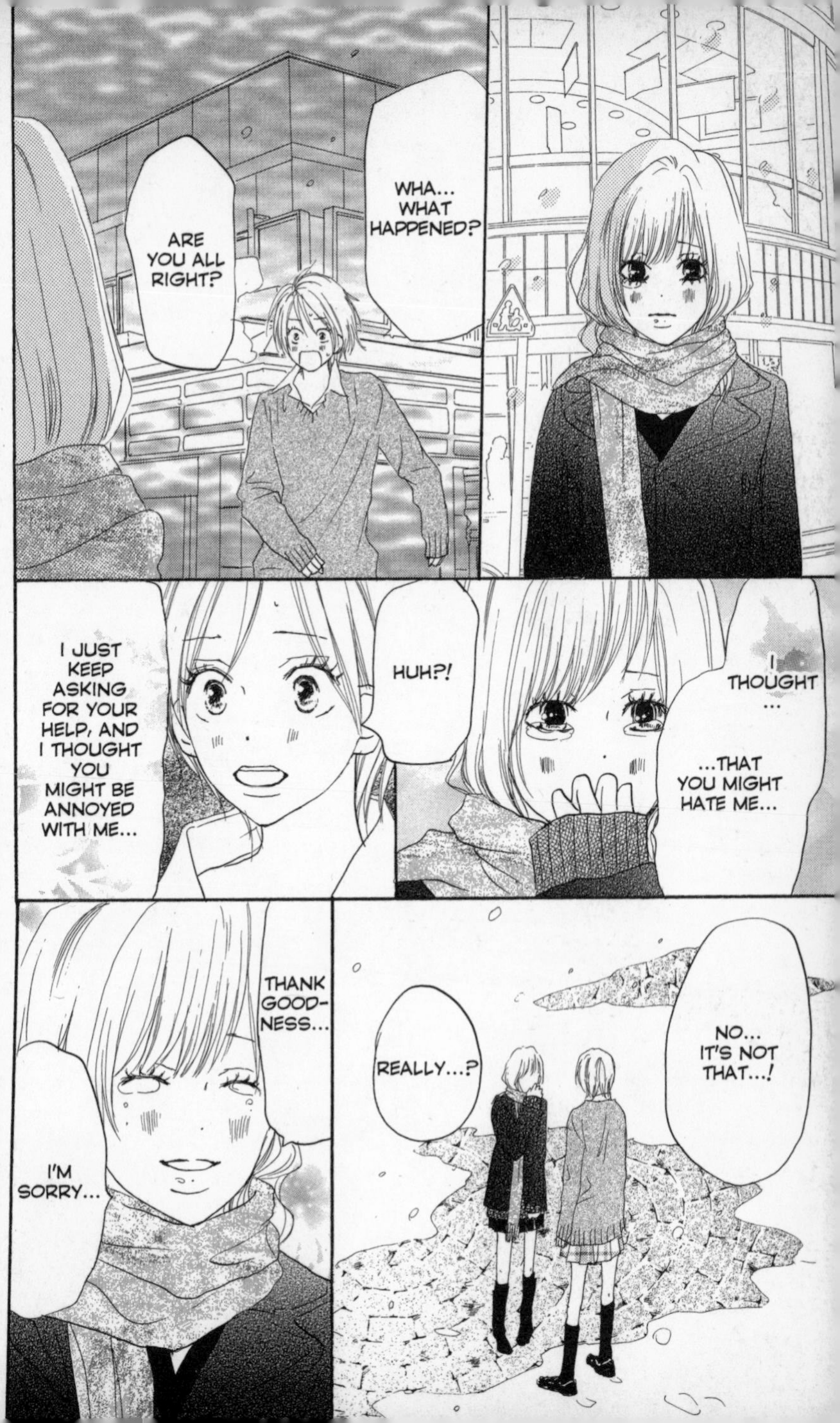
WHA... WHAT HAPPENED?
ARE YOU ALL RIGHT?
I THOUGHT ...
...THAT YOU MIGHT HATE ME...
HUH?!
I JUST KEEP ASKING FOR YOUR HELP, AND I THOUGHT YOU MIGHT BE ANNOYED WITH ME...
NO... IT'S NOT THAT...!
REALLY...?
THANK GOOD-NESS...
I'M SORRY...

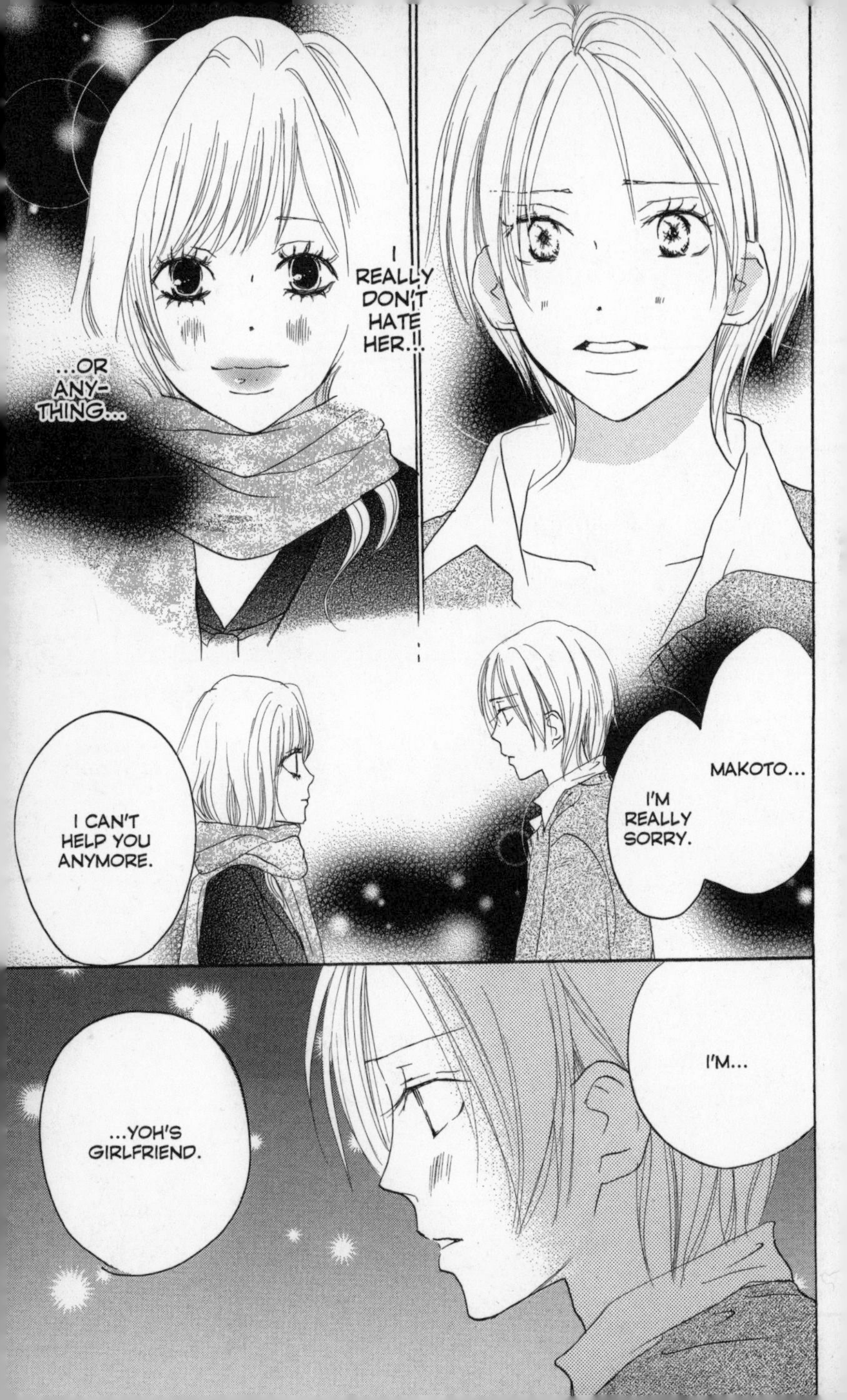
I REALLY DON'T HATE HER.!!
...OR ANY-THING...
MAKOTO... I'M REALLY SORRY.
I CAN'T HELP YOU ANYMORE.
I'M...
...YOH'S GIRLFRIEND.

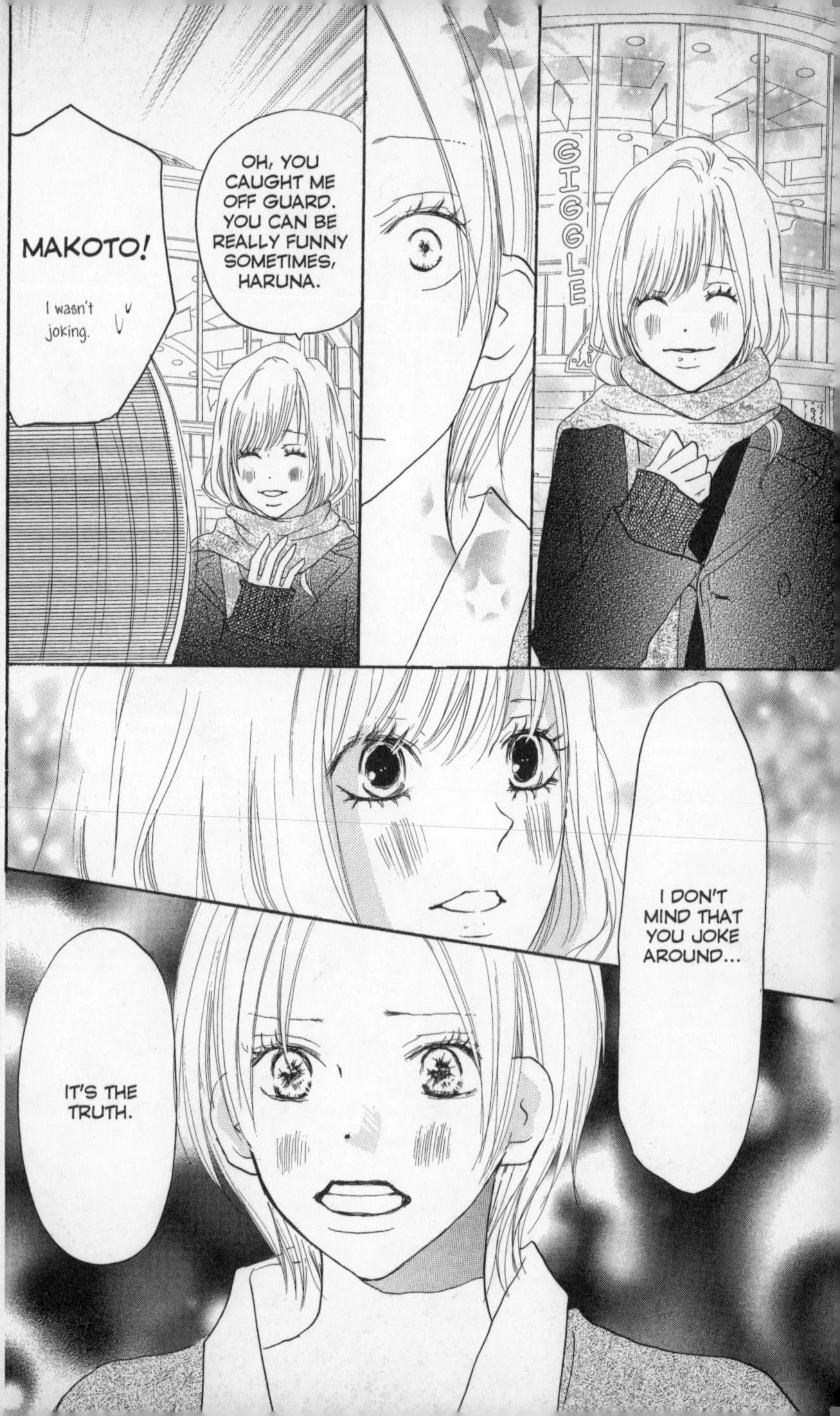
GIGGLE
OH, YOU CAUGHT ME OFF GUARD. YOU CAN BE REALLY FUNNY SOMETIMES, HARUNA.
MAKOTO!
I wasn't joking.
I DON'T MIND THAT YOU JOKE AROUND...
IT'S THE TRUTH.

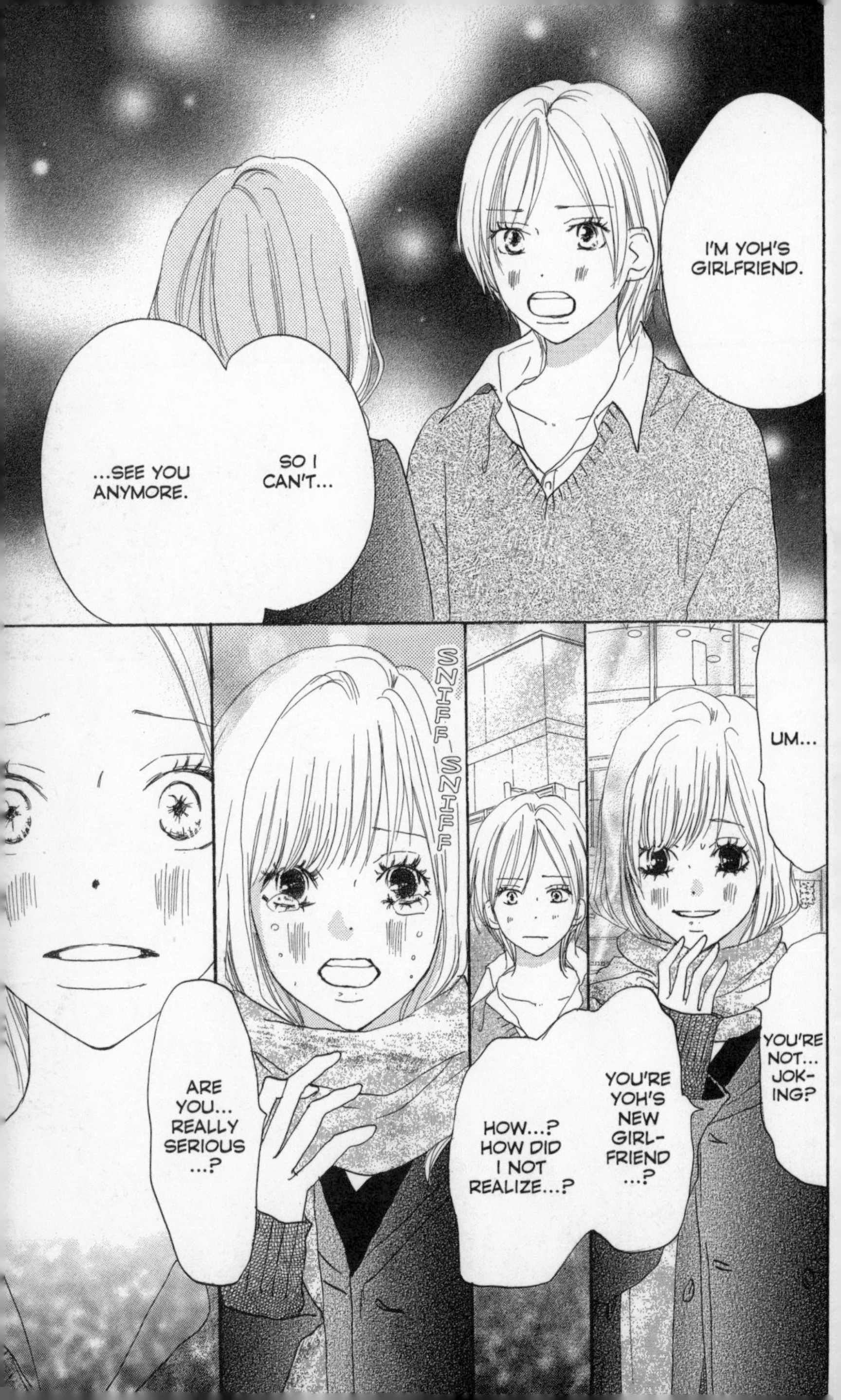
I'M YOH'S GIRLFRIEND.
SO I CAN'T...
...SEE YOU ANYMORE.
UM...
YOU'RE NOT... JOK-ING?
YOU'RE YOH'S NEW GIRL-FRIEND ...?
HOW...? HOW DID I NOT REALIZE...?
SNIFF SNIFF
ARE YOU... REALLY SERIOUS ...?

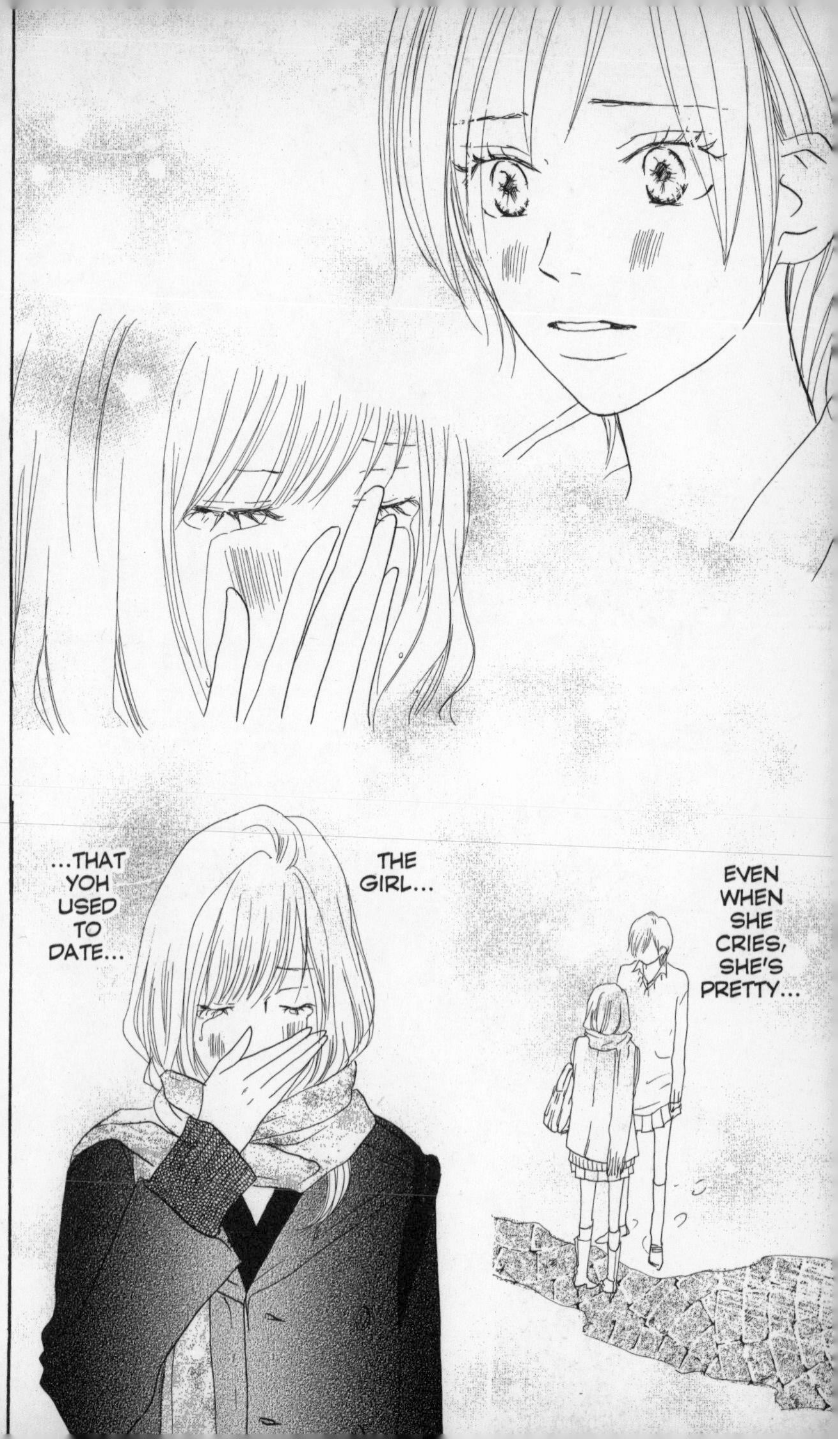
EVEN WHEN SHE CRIES, SHE'S PRETTY...
THE GIRL...
...THAT YOH USED TO DATE...

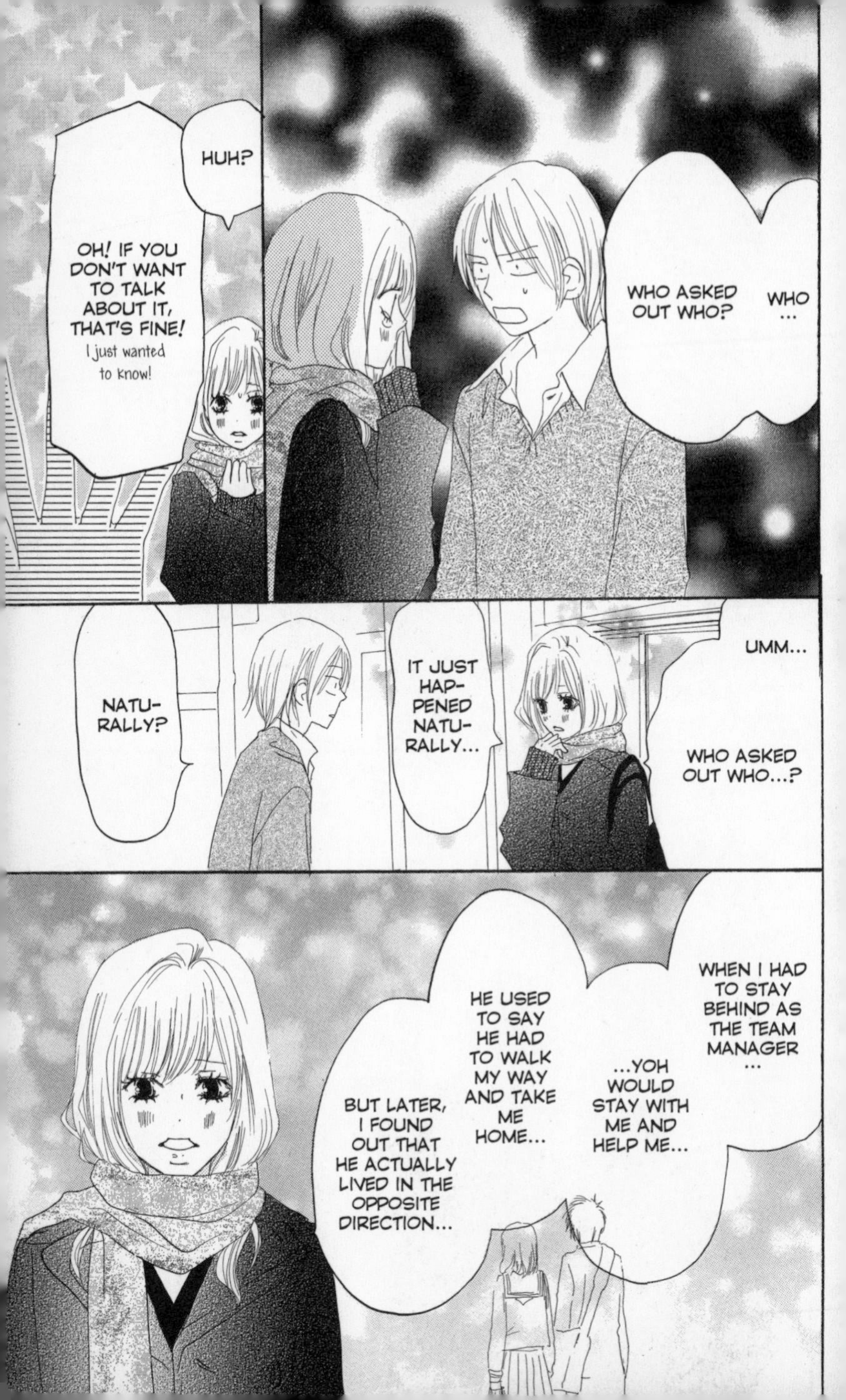
WHO … WHO ASKED OUT WHO?
HUH?
OH! IF YOU DON'T WANT TO TALK ABOUT IT, THAT'S FINE! I just wanted to know!
UMM...
WHO ASKED OUT WHO...?
IT JUST HAP-PENED NATU-RALLY...
NATU-RALLY?
WHEN I HAD TO STAY BEHIND AS THE TEAM MANAGER ...
...YOH WOULD STAY WITH ME AND HELP ME...
HE USED TO SAY HE HAD TO WALK MY WAY AND TAKE ME HOME...
BUT LATER, I FOUND OUT THAT HE ACTUALLY LIVED IN THE OPPOSITE DIRECTION...

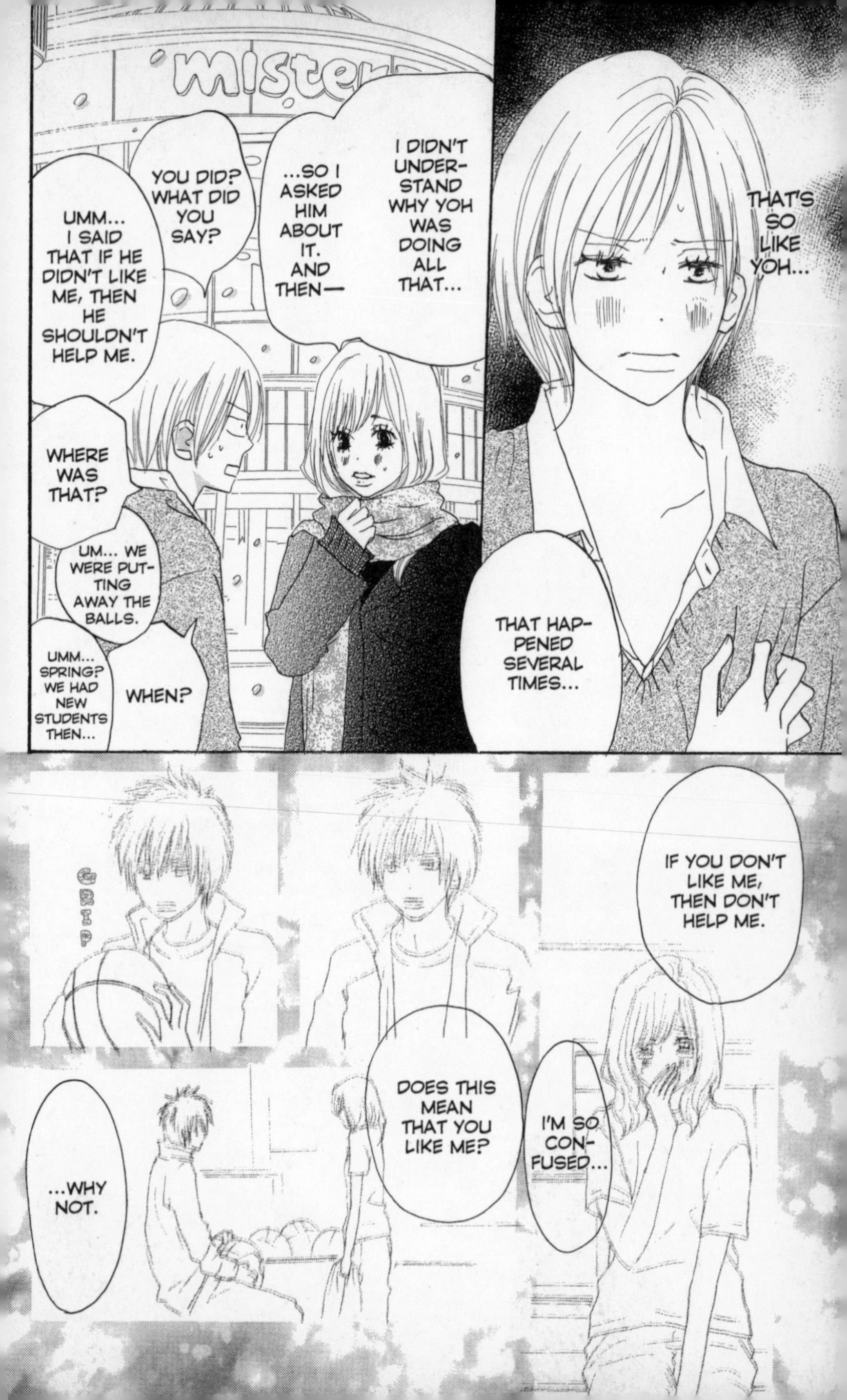
THAT'S SO LIKE YOH...
THAT HAPPENED SEVERAL TIMES...
I DIDN'T UNDERSTAND WHY YOH WAS DOING ALL THAT...
...SO I ASKED HIM ABOUT IT. AND THEN—
YOU DID? WHAT DID YOU SAY?
UMM... I SAID THAT IF HE DIDN'T LIKE ME, THEN HE SHOULDN'T HELP ME.
WHERE WAS THAT?
UM... WE WERE PUTTING AWAY THE BALLS.
WHEN?
UMM... SPRING? WE HAD NEW STUDENTS THEN...
IF YOU DON'T LIKE ME, THEN DON'T HELP ME.
I'M SO CONFUSED...
DOES THIS MEAN THAT YOU LIKE ME?
GRIP
...WHY NOT.

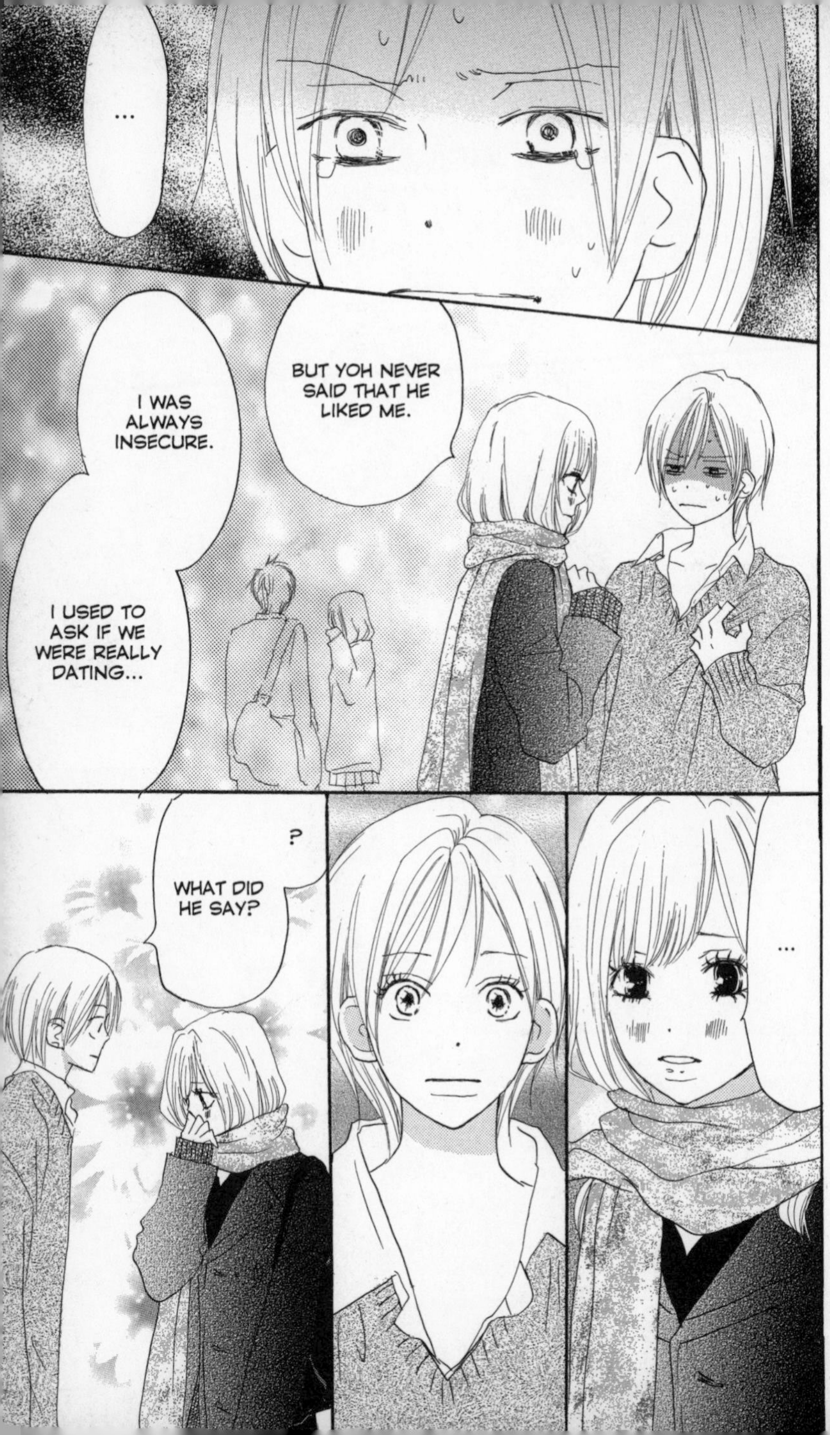
...
BUT YOH NEVER SAID THAT HE LIKED ME.
I WAS ALWAYS INSECURE.
I USED TO ASK IF WE WERE REALLY DATING...
...
? WHAT DID HE SAY?

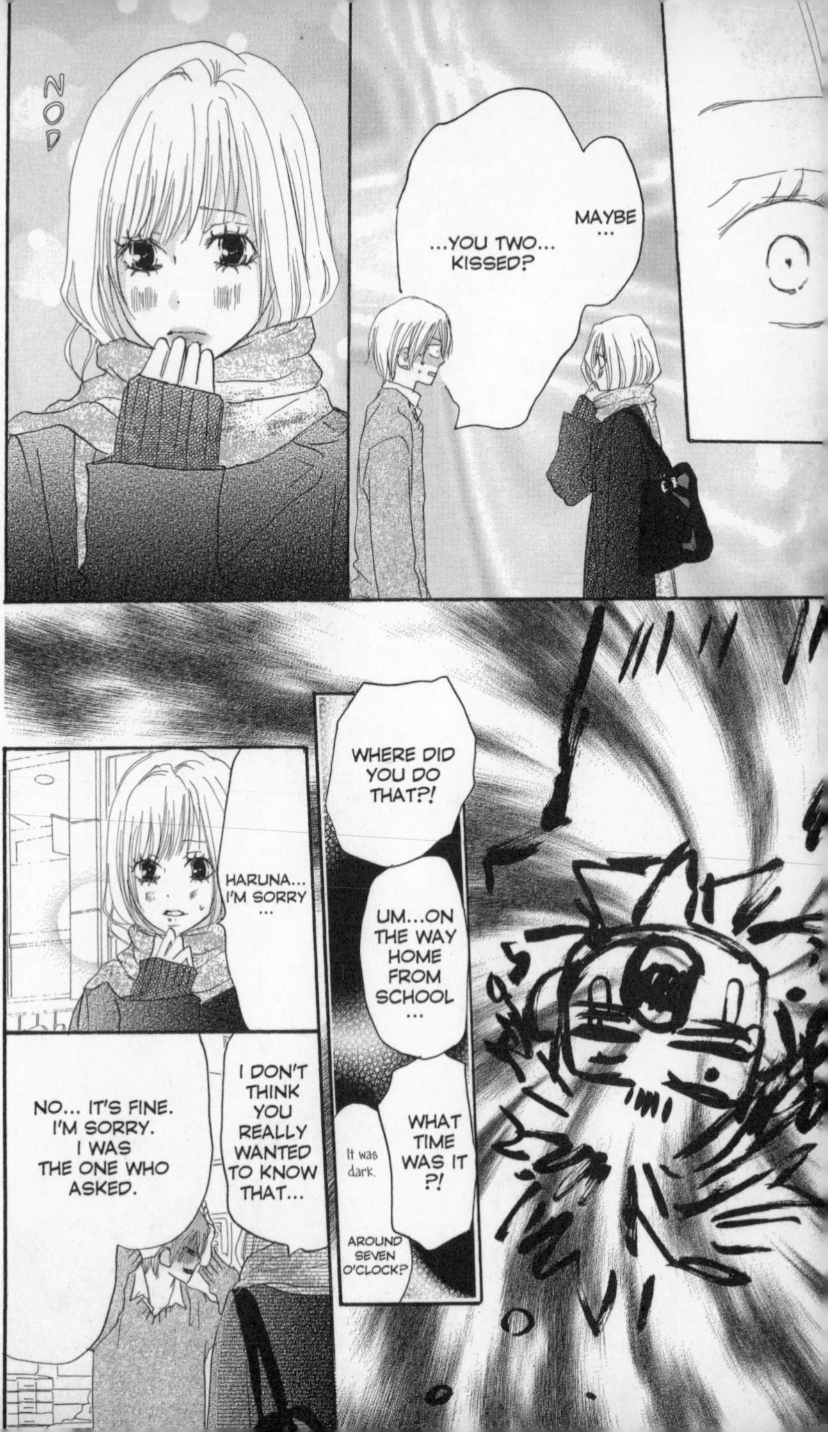
MAYBE ...
...YOU TWO... KISSED?
NOD
WHERE DID YOU DO THAT?!
UM...ON THE WAY HOME FROM SCHOOL ...
WHAT TIME WAS IT ?!
It was dark.
AROUND SEVEN O'CLOCK?
HARUNA... I'M SORRY ...
I DON'T THINK YOU REALLY WANTED TO KNOW THAT...
NO... IT'S FINE. I'M SORRY. I WAS THE ONE WHO ASKED.

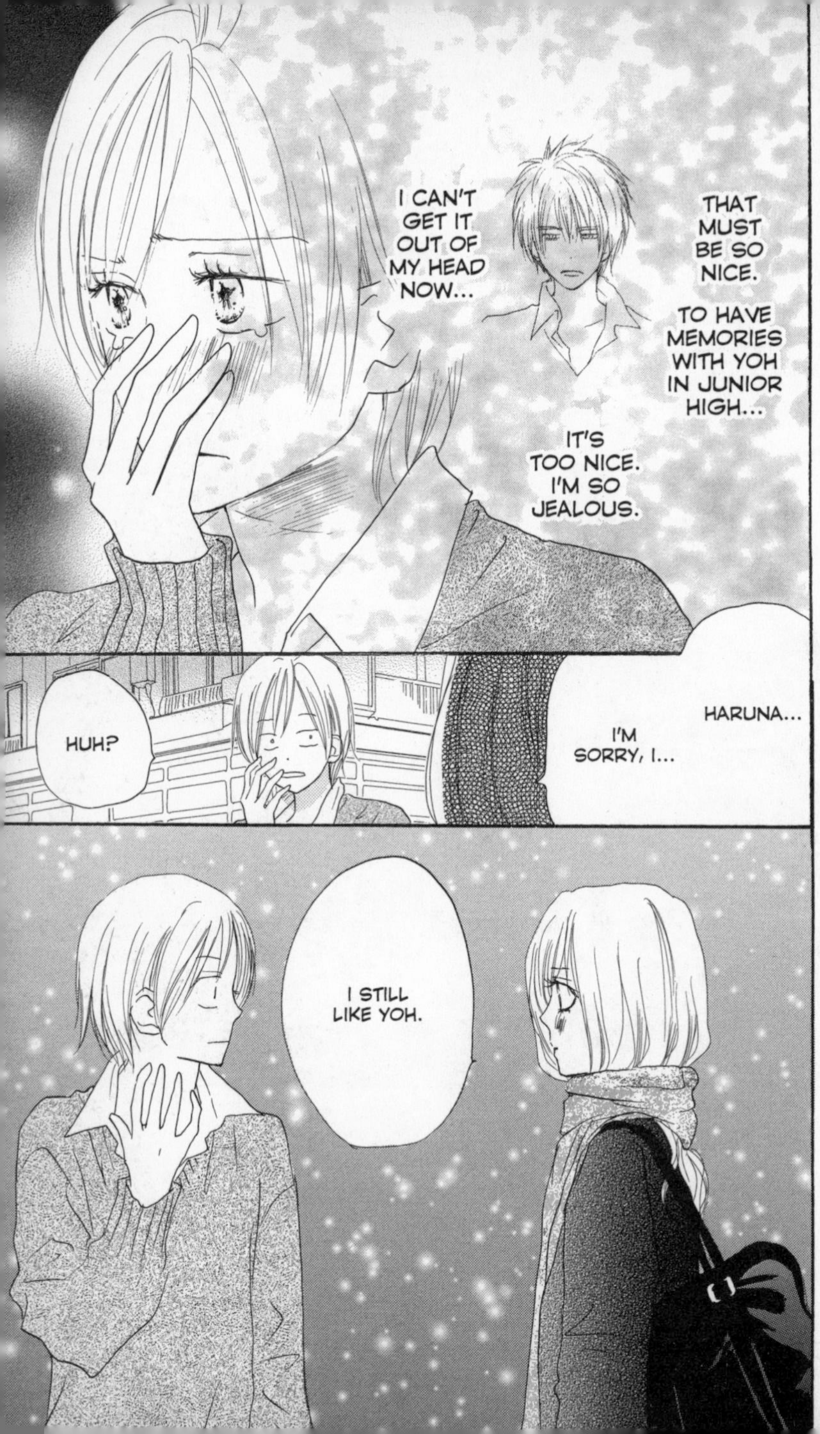
THAT MUST BE SO NICE.
TO HAVE MEMORIES WITH YOH IN JUNIOR HIGH...
I CAN'T GET IT OUT OF MY HEAD NOW...
IT'S TOO NICE. I'M SO JEALOUS.
HARUNA...
I'M SORRY, I...
HUH?
I STILL LIKE YOH.

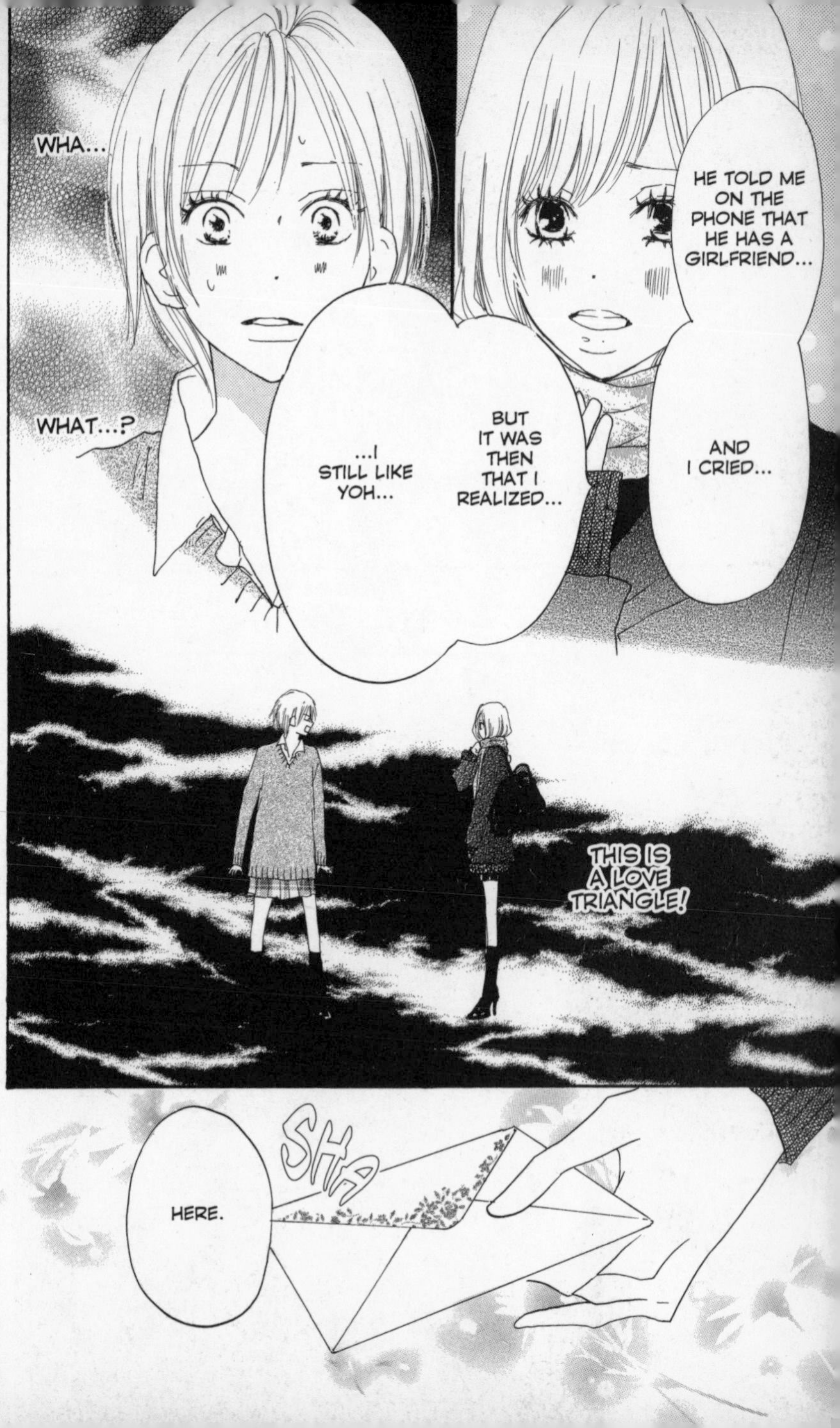

HE TOLD ME ON THE PHONE THAT HE HAS A GIRLFRIEND...
AND I CRIED...
BUT IT WAS THEN THAT I REALIZED...
...I STILL LIKE YOH...
WHA...
WHAT...?
THIS IS A LOVE TRIANGLE!
SHA
HERE.

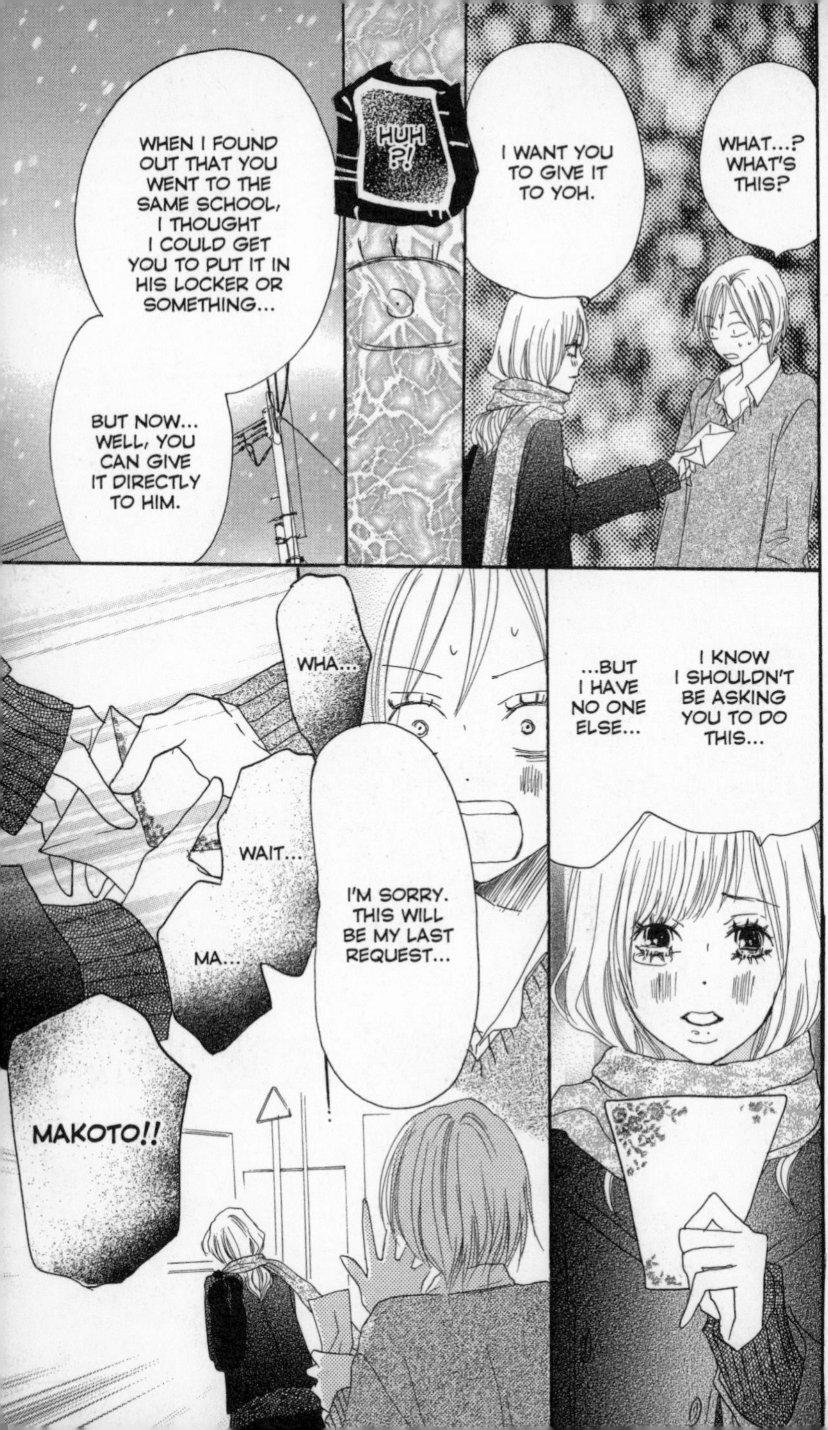
WHAT...? WHAT'S THIS?
I WANT YOU TO GIVE IT TO YOH.
HUH?!
WHEN I FOUND OUT THAT YOU WENT TO THE SAME SCHOOL, I THOUGHT I COULD GET YOU TO PUT IT IN HIS LOCKER OR SOMETHING...
BUT NOW... WELL, YOU CAN GIVE IT DIRECTLY TO HIM.
I KNOW I SHOULDN'T BE ASKING YOU TO DO THIS...
...BUT I HAVE NO ONE ELSE...
WHA...
I'M SORRY. THIS WILL BE MY LAST REQUEST...
WAIT...
MA...
MAKOTO!!

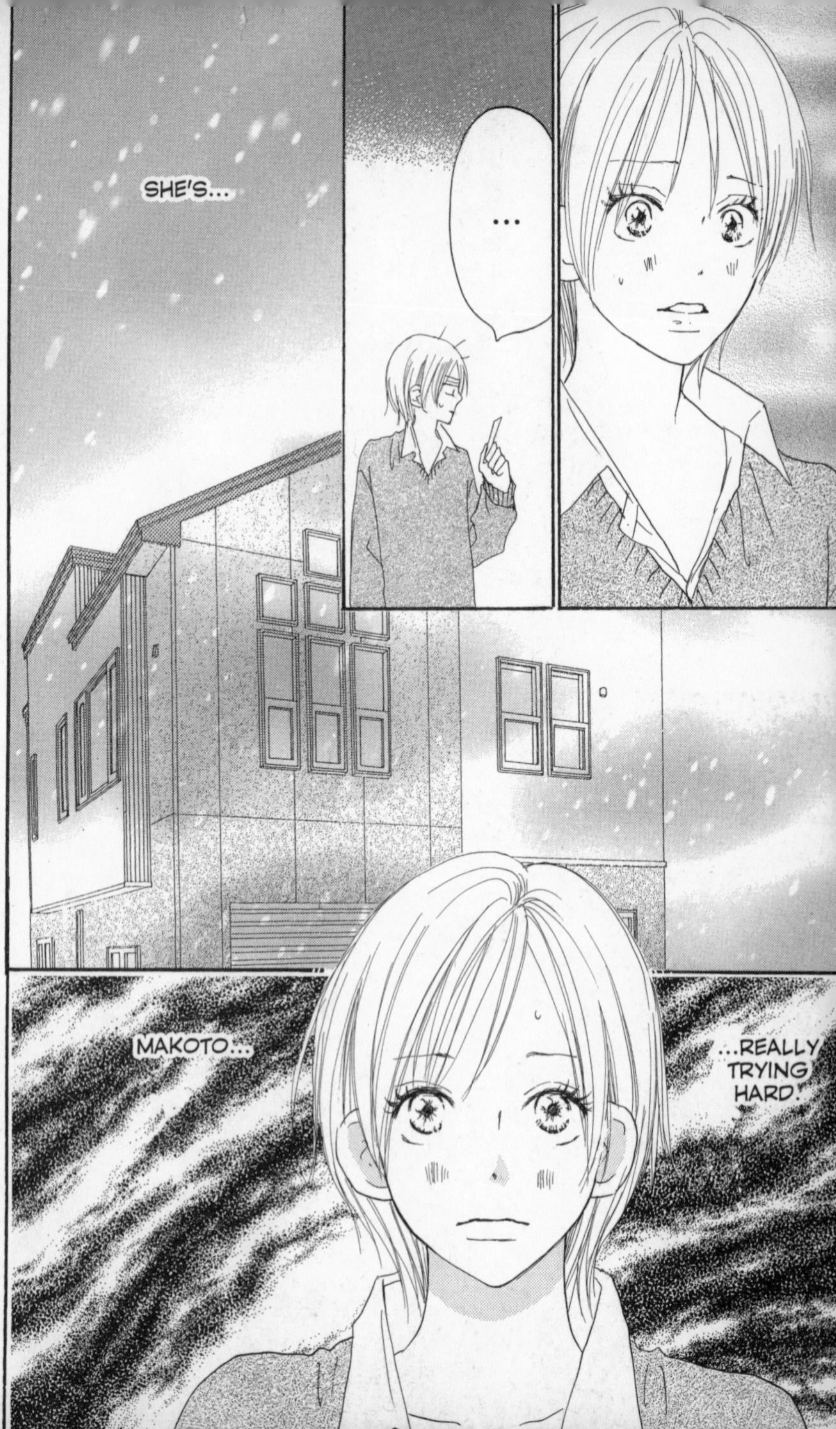
...
SHE'S...
MAKOTO...
...REALLY TRYING HARD!

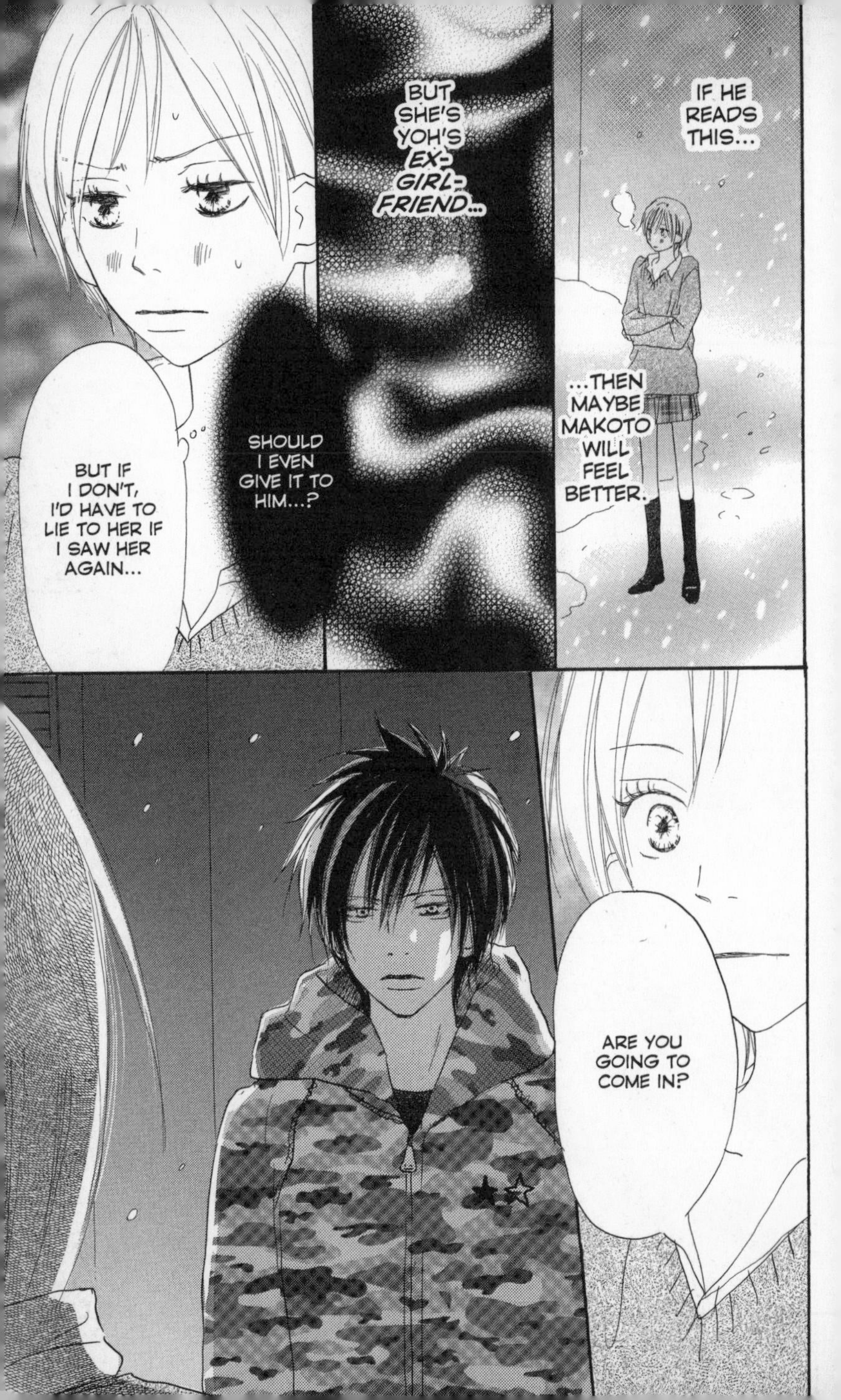
IF HE READS THIS...
...THEN MAYBE MAKOTO WILL FEEL BETTER.
BUT SHE'S YOH'S EX-GIRL-FRIEND...
SHOULD I EVEN GIVE IT TO HIM...?
BUT IF I DON'T, I'D HAVE TO LIE TO HER IF I SAW HER AGAIN...
ARE YOU GOING TO COME IN?

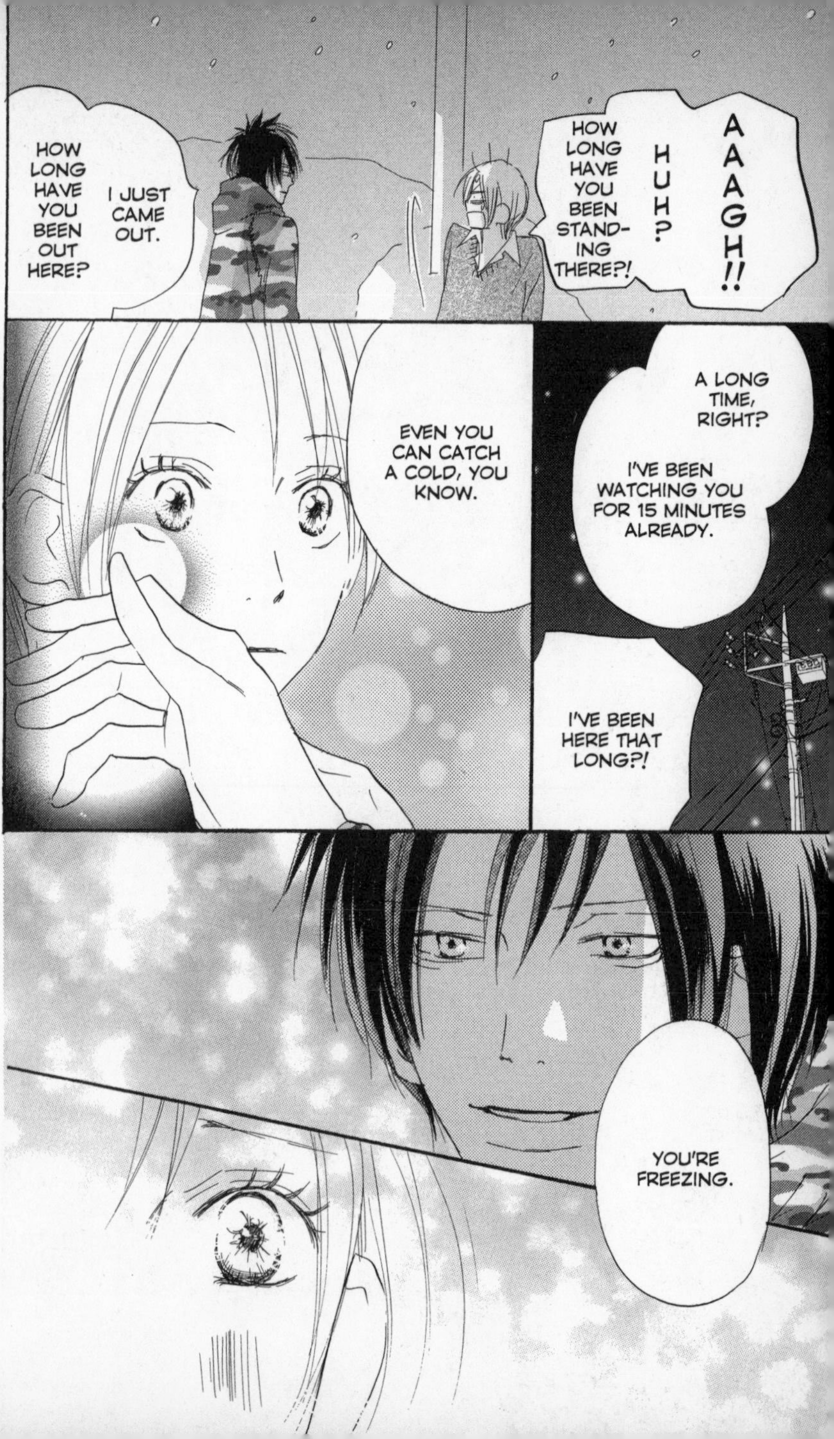
AAAGH!!
HUH?
HOW LONG HAVE YOU BEEN STAND-ING THERE?!
I JUST CAME OUT.
HOW LONG HAVE YOU BEEN OUT HERE?
A LONG TIME, RIGHT?
I'VE BEEN WATCHING YOU FOR 15 MINUTES ALREADY.
I'VE BEEN HERE THAT LONG?!
EVEN YOU CAN CATCH A COLD, YOU KNOW.
YOU'RE FREEZING.

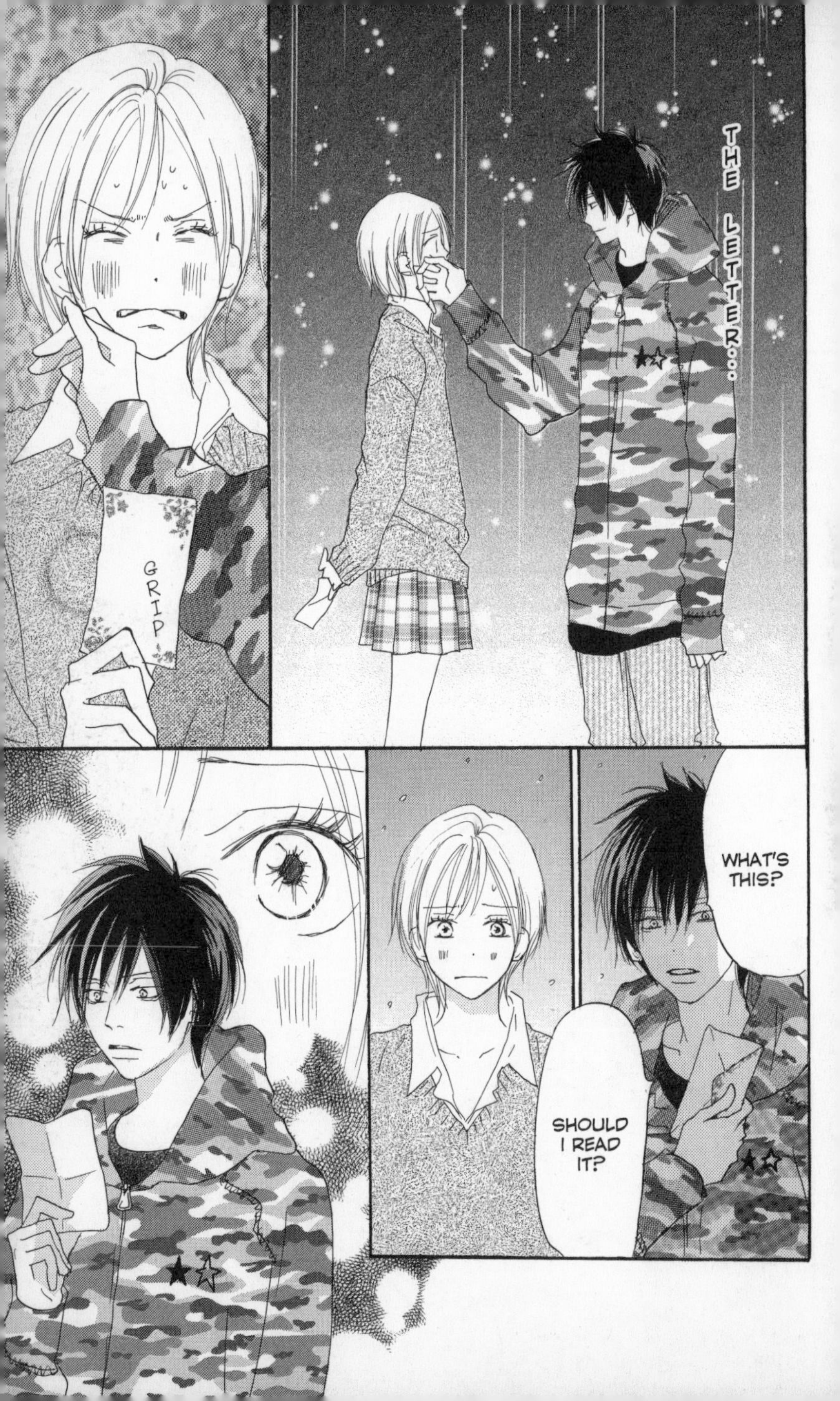
THE LETTER...
GRIP
WHAT'S THIS?
SHOULD I READ IT?

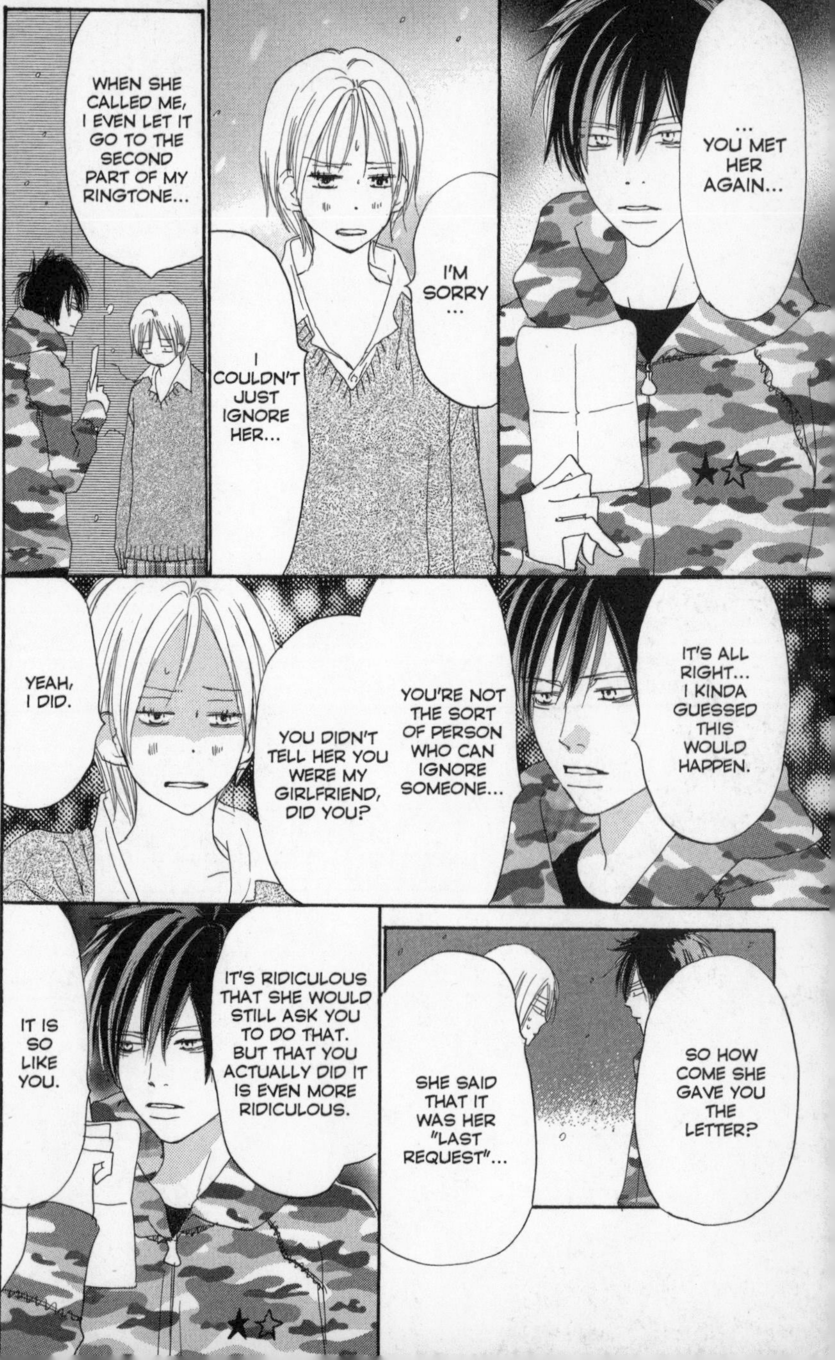
... YOU MET HER AGAIN...
I'M SORRY ...
I COULDN'T JUST IGNORE HER...
WHEN SHE CALLED ME, I EVEN LET IT GO TO THE SECOND PART OF MY RINGTONE...
IT'S ALL RIGHT... I KINDA GUESSED THIS WOULD HAPPEN.
YOU'RE NOT THE SORT OF PERSON WHO CAN IGNORE SOMEONE...
YOU DIDN'T TELL HER YOU WERE MY GIRLFRIEND, DID YOU?
YEAH, I DID.
SO HOW COME SHE GAVE YOU THE LETTER?
SHE SAID THAT IT WAS HER "LAST REQUEST"...
IT'S RIDICULOUS THAT SHE WOULD STILL ASK YOU TO DO THAT. BUT THAT YOU ACTUALLY DID IT IS EVEN MORE RIDICULOUS.
IT IS SO LIKE YOU.

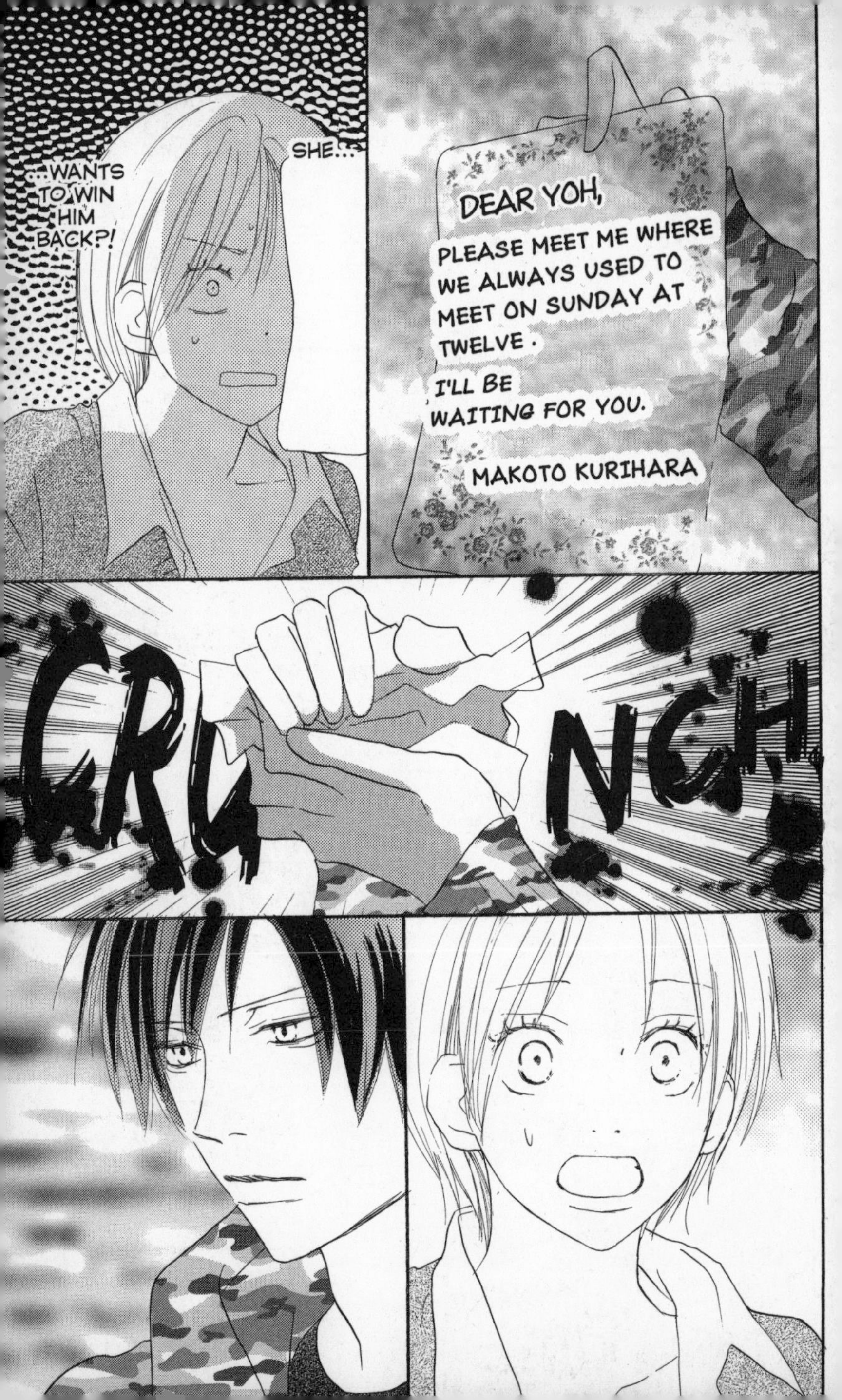
DEAR YOH,
PLEASE MEET ME WHERE WE ALWAYS USED TO MEET ON SUNDAY AT TWELVE.
I'LL BE WAITING FOR YOU.
MAKOTO KURIHARA
SHE...
...WANTS TO WIN HIM BACK?!
CRUNCH

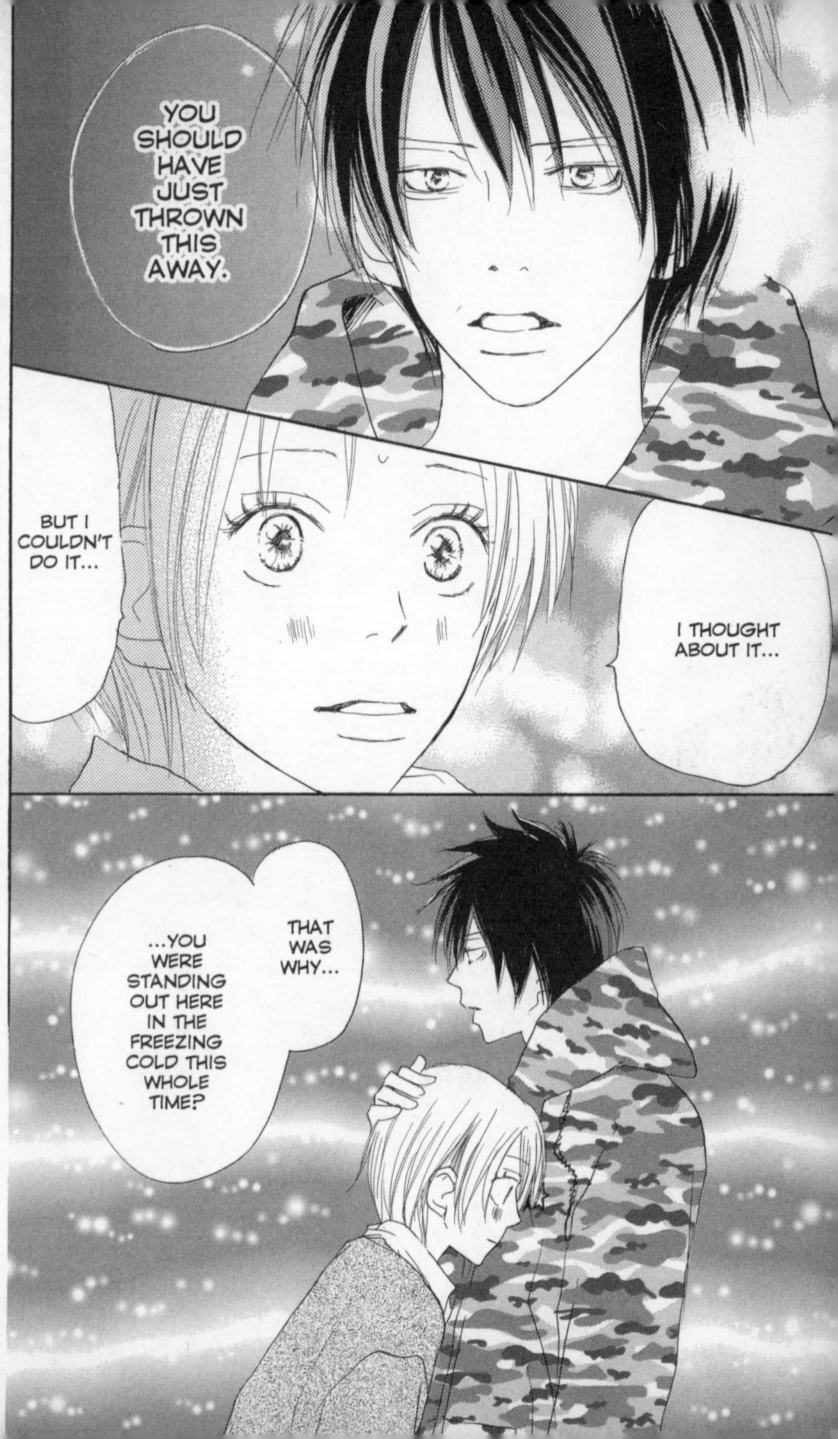
YOU SHOULD HAVE JUST THROWN THIS AWAY.
I THOUGHT ABOUT IT...
BUT I COULDN'T DO IT...
THAT WAS WHY...
...YOU WERE STANDING OUT HERE IN THE FREEZING COLD THIS WHOLE TIME?

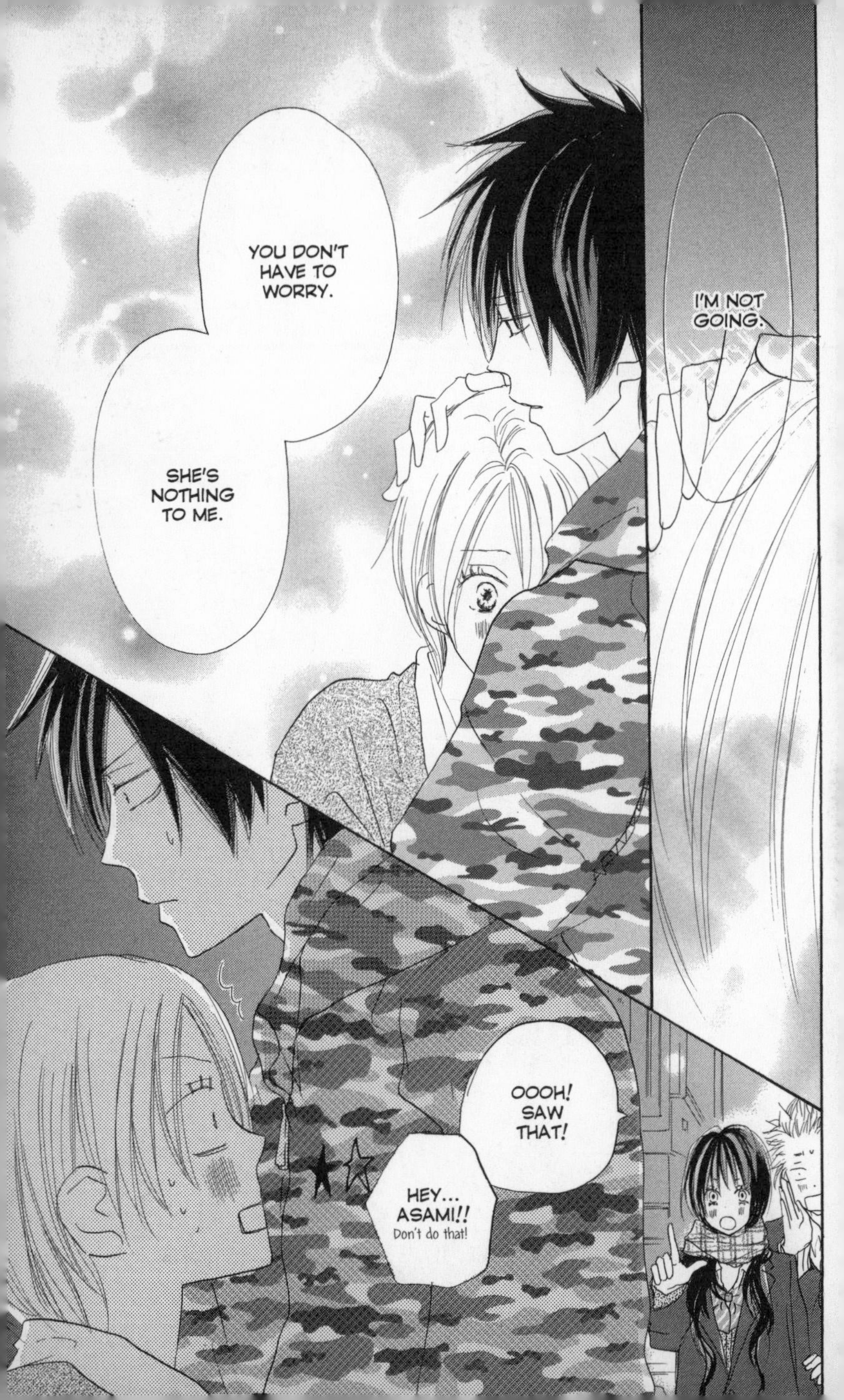
I'M NOT GOING.
YOU DON'T HAVE TO WORRY.
SHE'S NOTHING TO ME.
OOOH! SAW THAT!
HEY... ASAMI!! Don't do that!

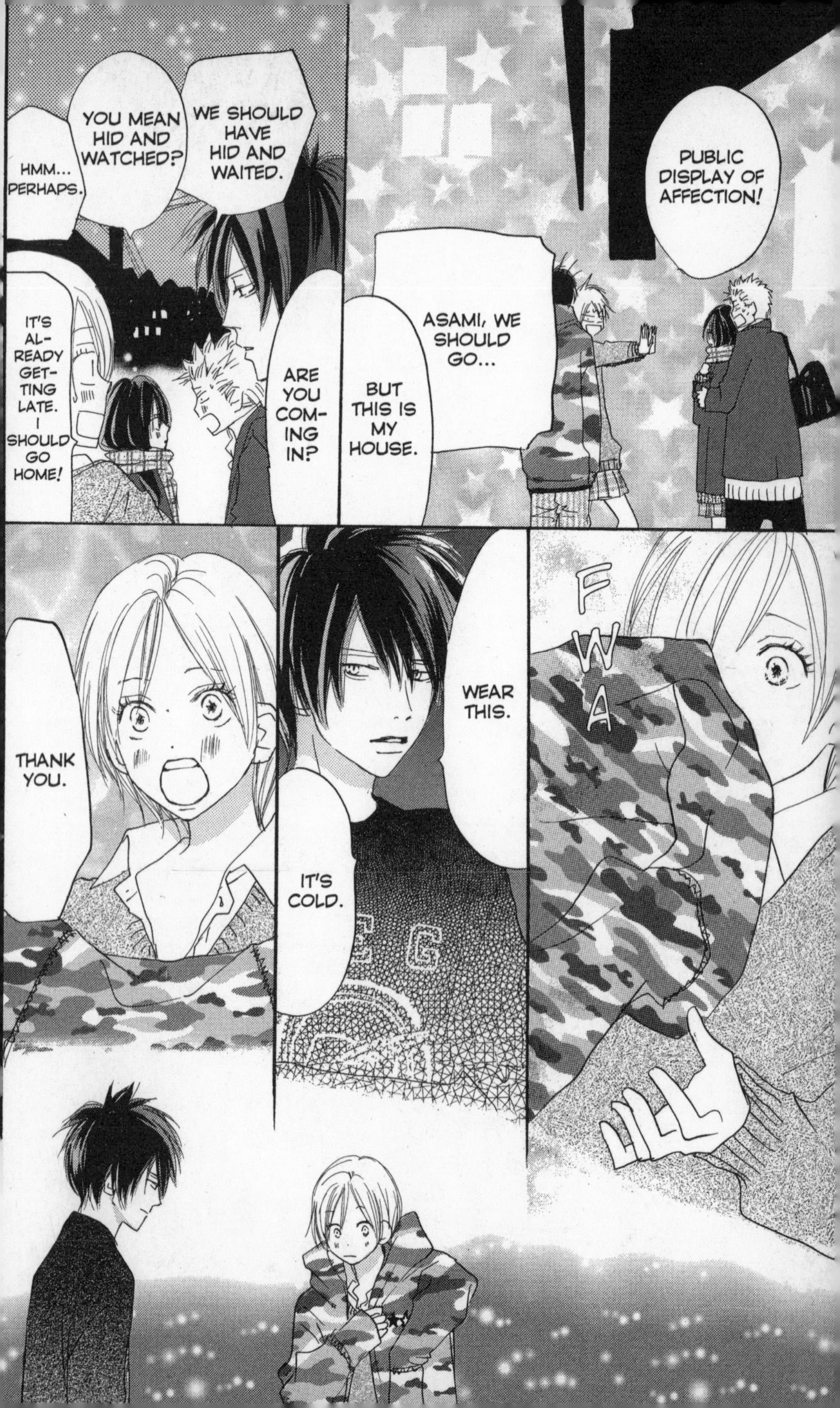
PUBLIC DISPLAY OF AFFECTION!
ASAMI, WE SHOULD GO...
WE SHOULD HAVE HID AND WAITED.
YOU MEAN HID AND WATCHED?
HMM... PERHAPS.
BUT THIS IS MY HOUSE.
ARE YOU COMING-IN?
IT'S AL-READY GET-TING LATE. I SHOULD GO HOME!
FWA
WEAR THIS.
IT'S COLD.
THANK YOU.

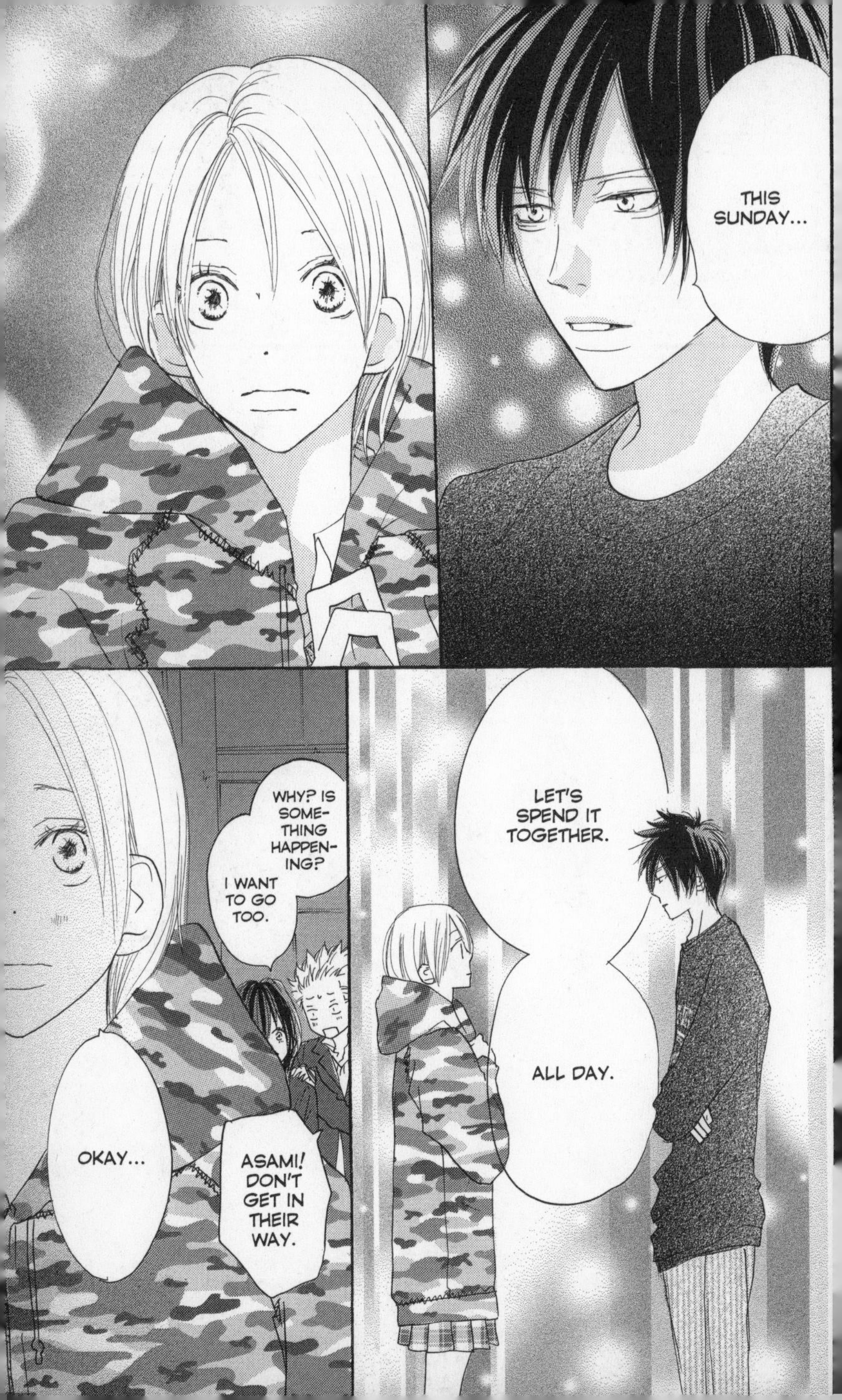
THIS SUNDAY...
LET'S SPEND IT TOGETHER.
ALL DAY.
WHY? IS SOME-THING HAPPEN-ING?
I WANT TO GO TOO.
ASAMI! DON'T GET IN THEIR WAY.
OKAY...

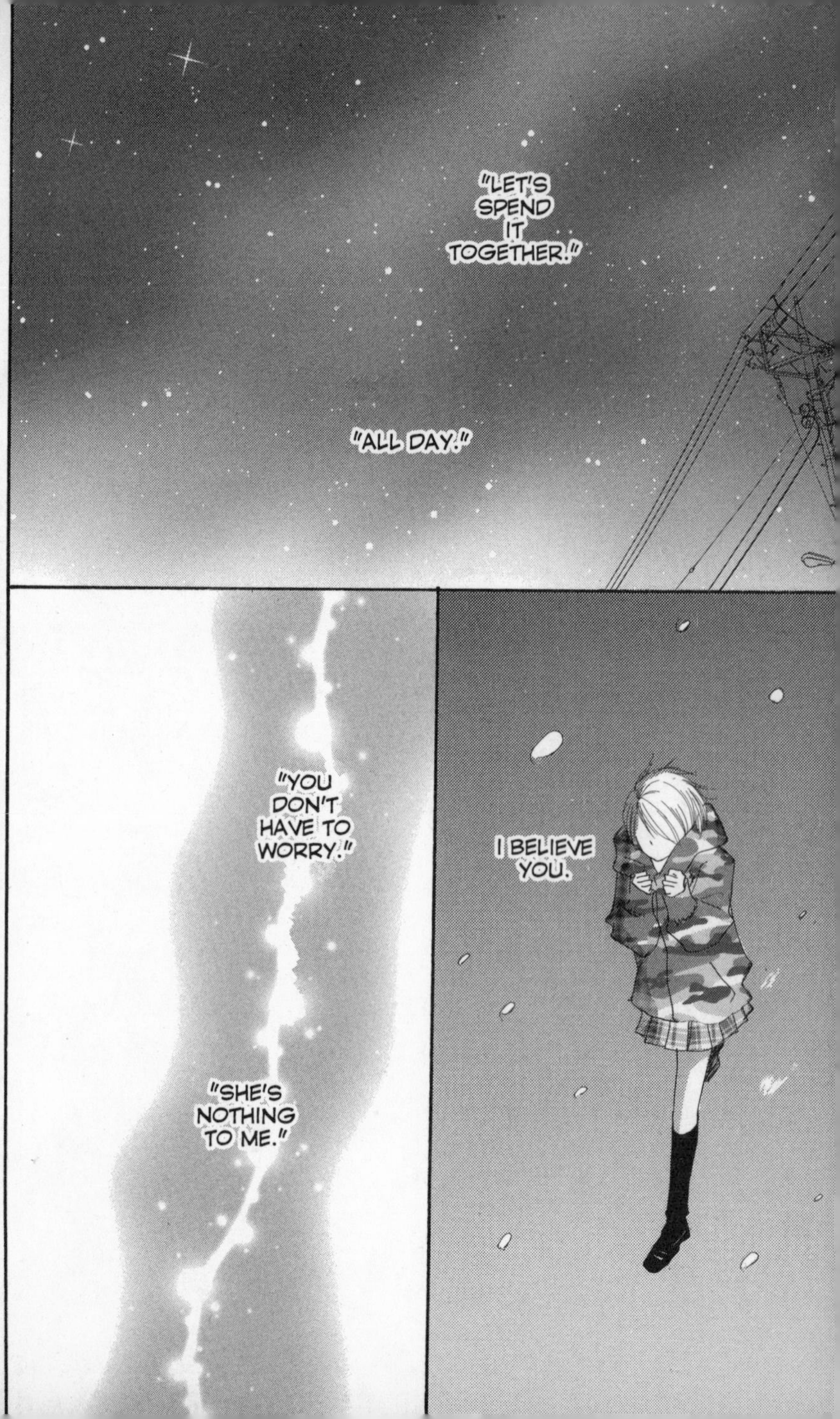
"LET'S SPEND IT TOGETHER."
"ALL DAY."
I BELIEVE YOU.
"YOU DON'T HAVE TO WORRY."
"SHE'S NOTHING TO ME."

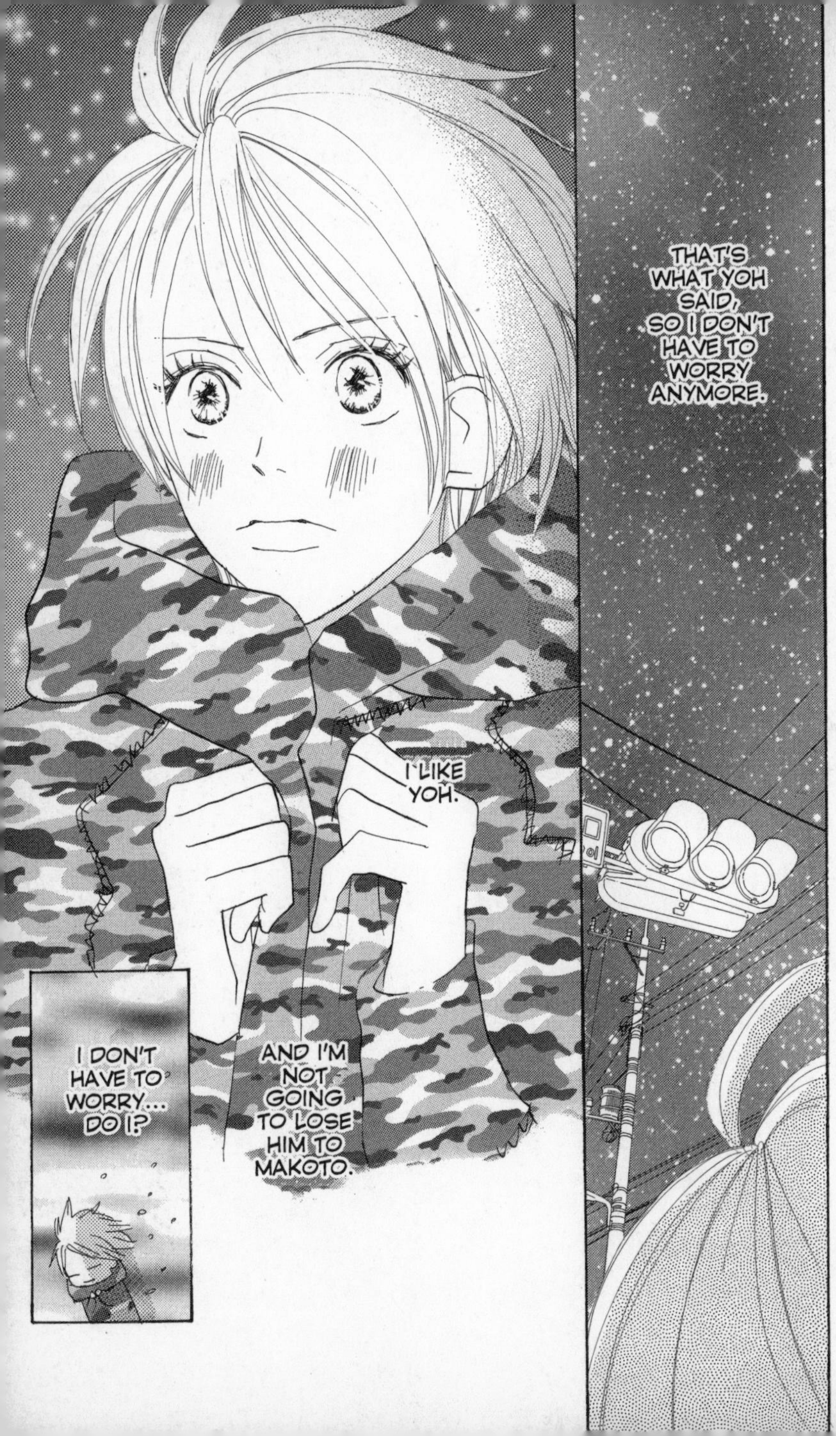
THAT'S WHAT YOH SAID, SO I DON'T HAVE TO WORRY ANYMORE.
I LIKE YOH.
AND I'M NOT GOING TO LOSE HIM TO MAKOTO.
I DON'T HAVE TO WORRY... DO I?

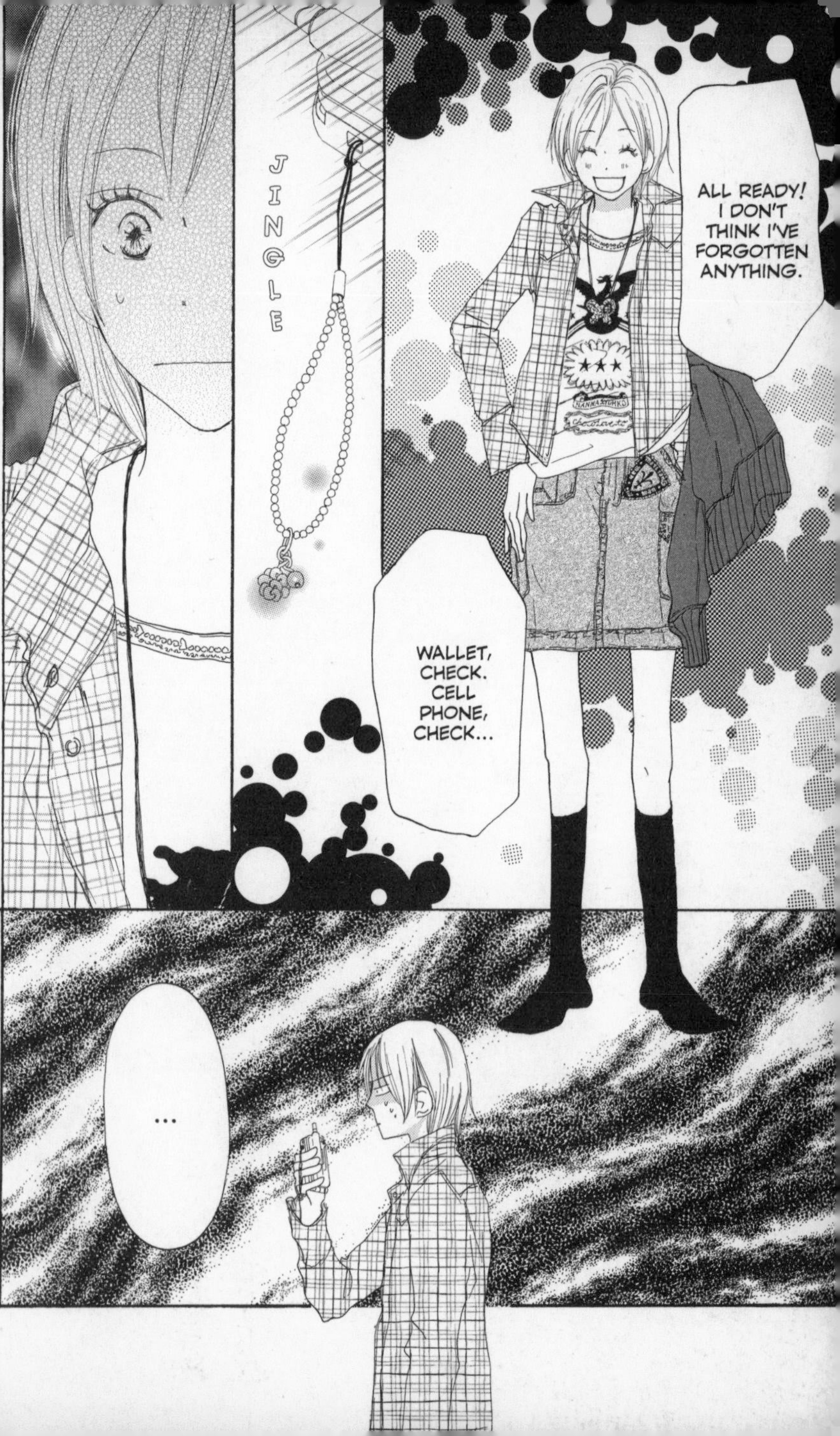
ALL READY! I DON'T THINK I'VE FORGOTTEN ANYTHING.
WALLET, CHECK. CELL PHONE, CHECK...
JINGLE
...

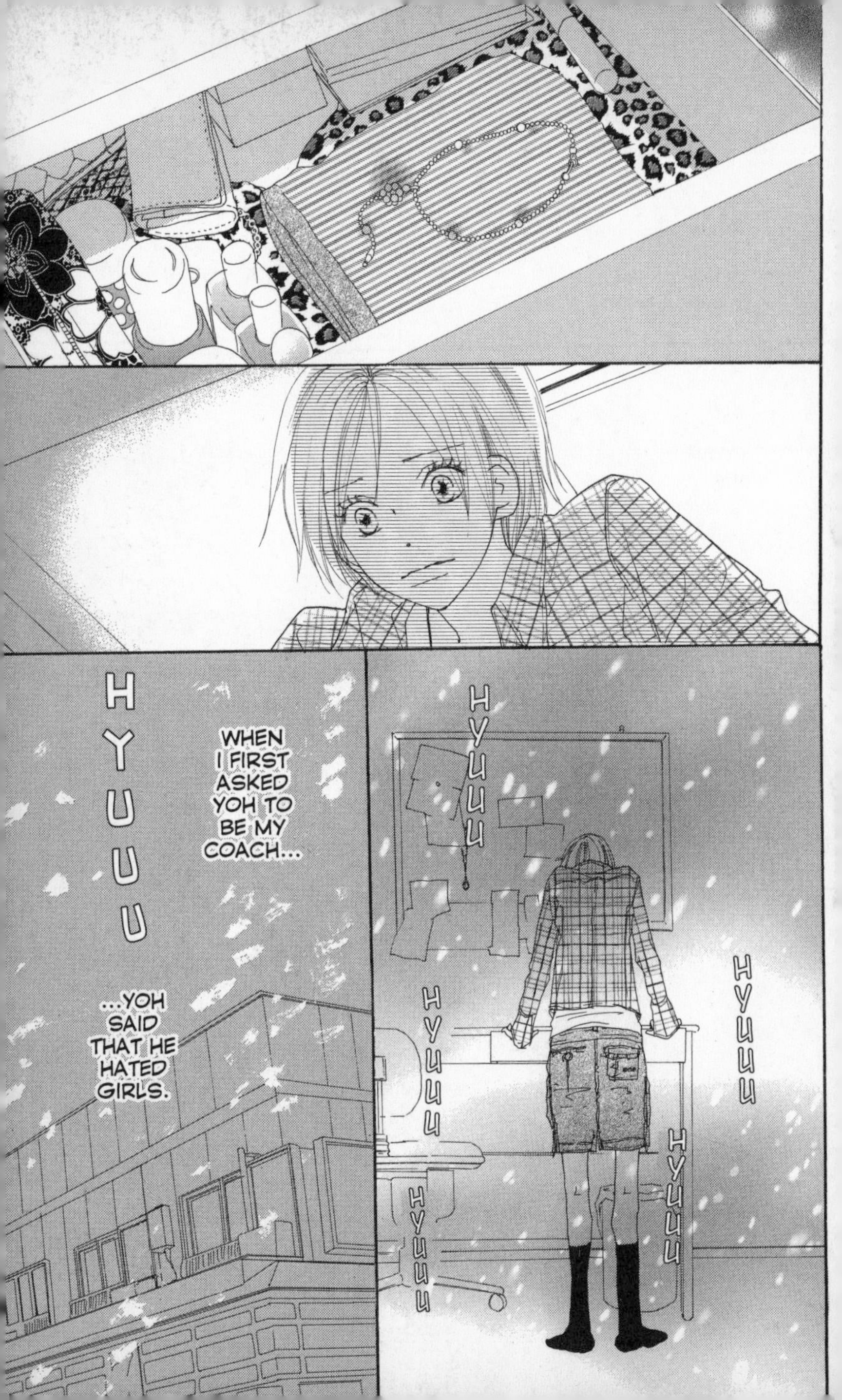
HYUUUU
HYUUUU
HYUUUU
HYUUUU
HYUUUU
HYUUU
WHEN I FIRST ASKED YOH TO BE MY COACH...
...YOH SAID THAT HE HATED GIRLS.

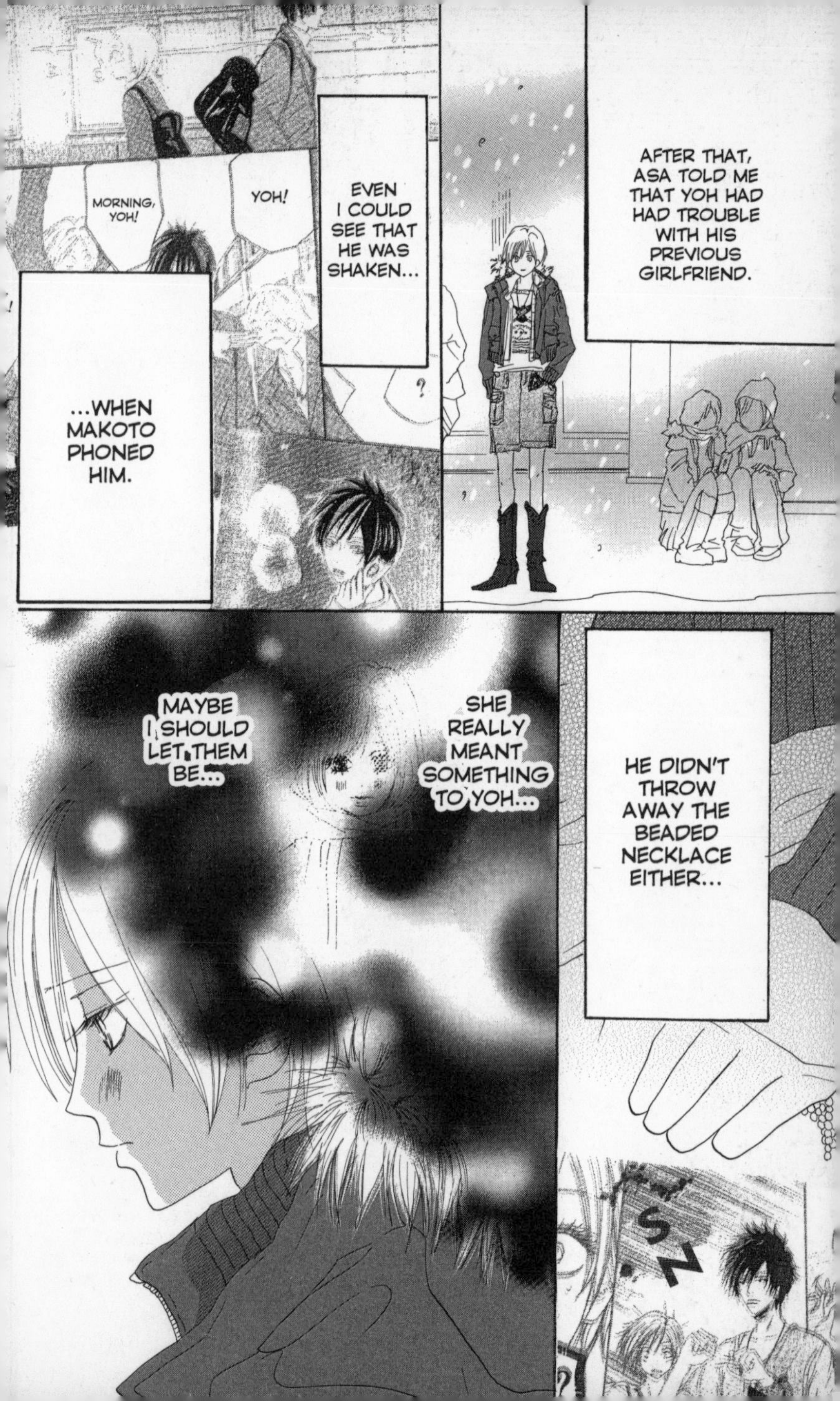
AFTER THAT, ASA TOLD ME THAT YOH HAD HAD TROUBLE WITH HIS PREVIOUS GIRLFRIEND.
YOH!
MORNING, YOH!
EVEN I COULD SEE THAT HE WAS SHAKEN...
...WHEN MAKOTO PHONED HIM.
HE DIDN'T THROW AWAY THE BEADED NECKLACE EITHER...
SHE REALLY MEANT SOMETHING TO YOH...
MAYBE I SHOULD LET THEM BE...

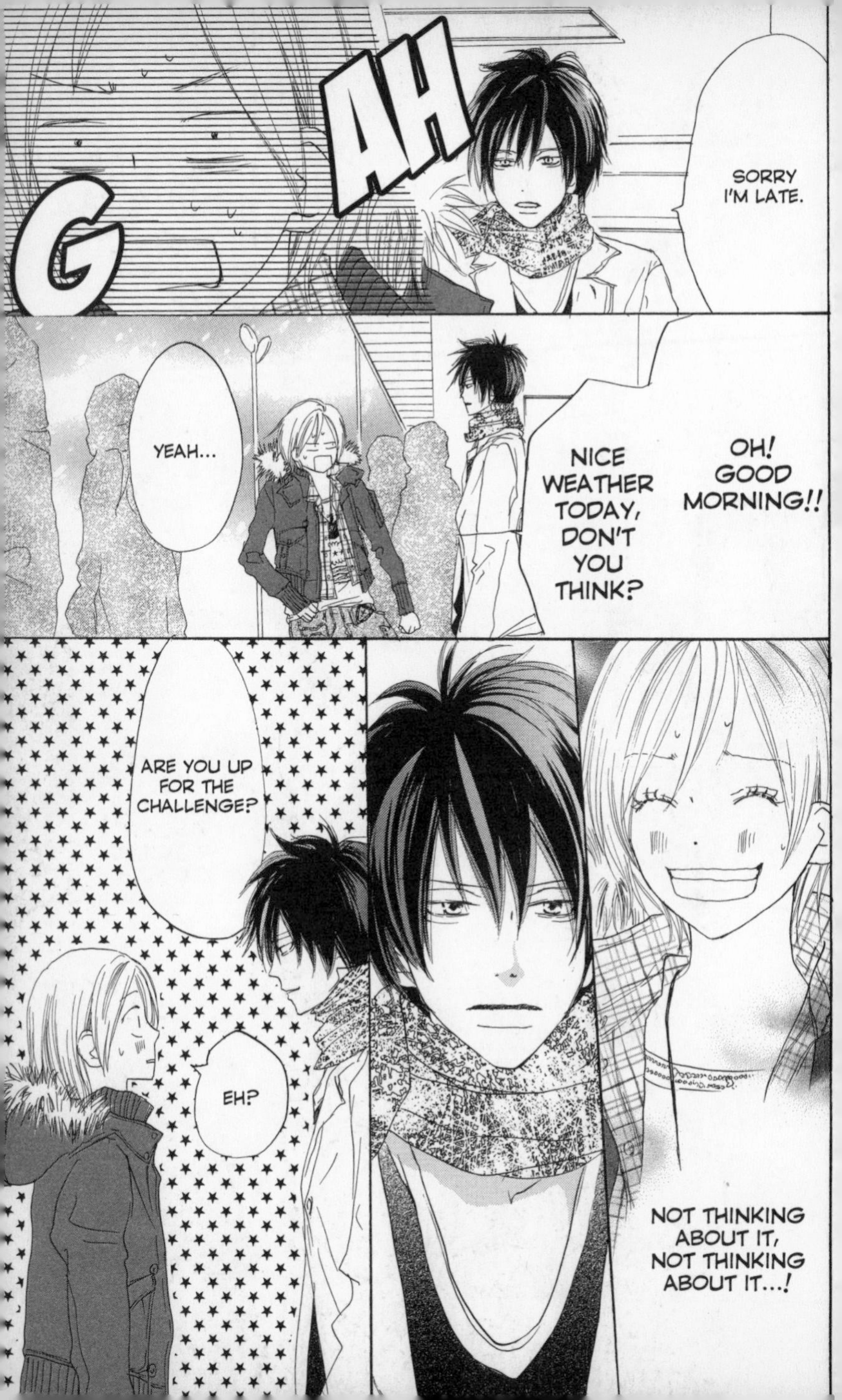
SORRY I'M LATE.
G
AH
OH! GOOD MORNING!!
NICE WEATHER TODAY, DON'T YOU THINK?
YEAH...
NOT THINKING ABOUT IT, NOT THINKING ABOUT IT...!
ARE YOU UP FOR THE CHALLENGE?
EH?

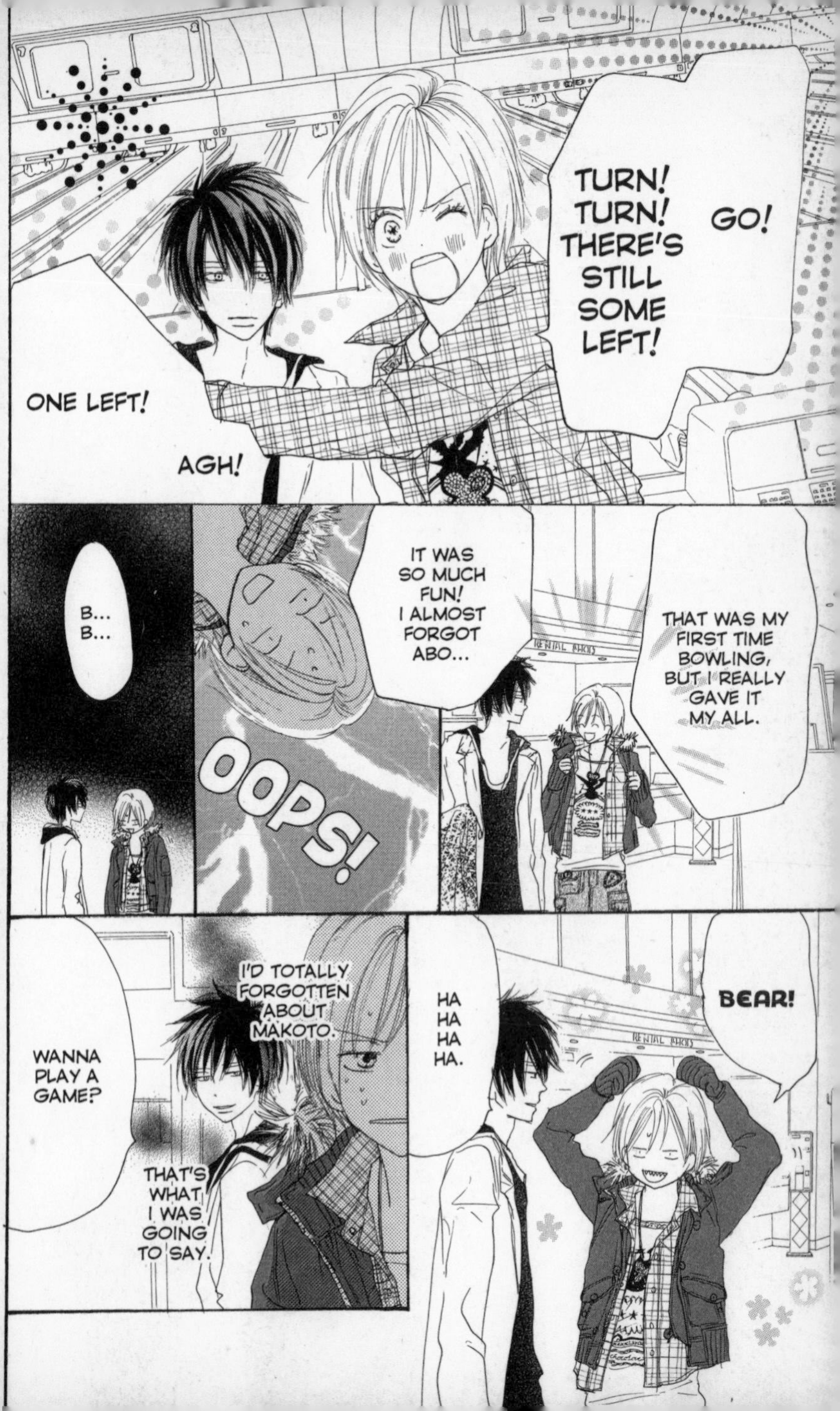
GO!
TURN! TURN! THERE'S STILL SOME LEFT!
ONE LEFT!
AGH!
THAT WAS MY FIRST TIME BOWLING, BUT I REALLY GAVE IT MY ALL.
IT WAS SO MUCH FUN! I ALMOST FORGOT ABO...
OOPS!
B... B...
BEAR!
HA HA HA HA.
I'D TOTALLY FORGOTTEN ABOUT MAKOTO.
WANNA PLAY A GAME?
THAT'S WHAT I WAS GOING TO SAY.

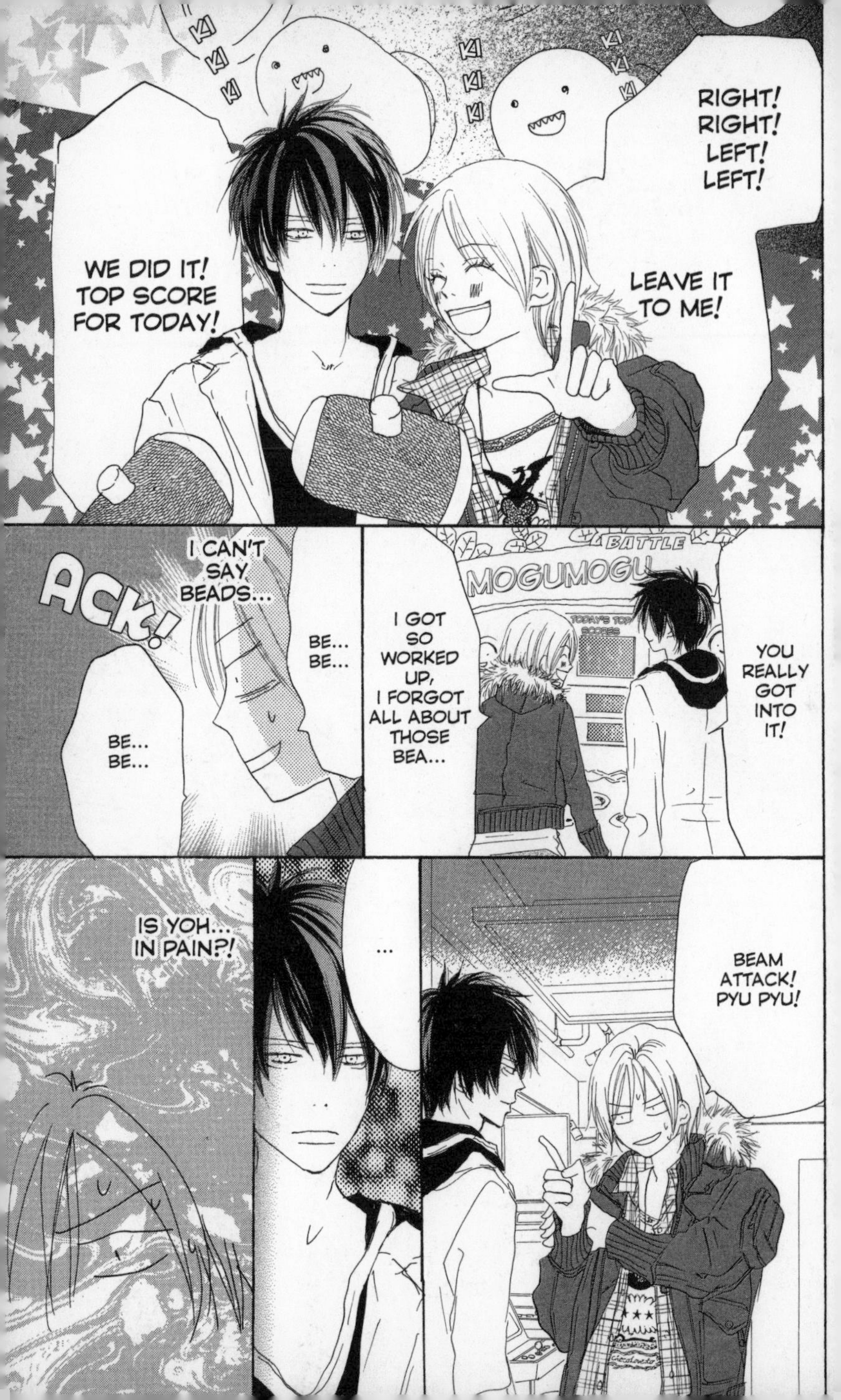
KI KI KI
RIGHT! RIGHT! LEFT! LEFT!
KI KI KI
KI KI KI
LEAVE IT TO ME!
WE DID IT! TOP SCORE FOR TODAY!
BATTLE
MOGUMOGU
TODAY'S TOP SCORES
YOU REALLY GOT INTO IT!
I GOT SO WORKED UP, I FORGOT ALL ABOUT THOSE BEA...
I CAN'T SAY BEADS...
ACK!
BE... BE...
BE... BE...
BEAM ATTACK! PYU PYU!
...
IS YOH... IN PAIN?!

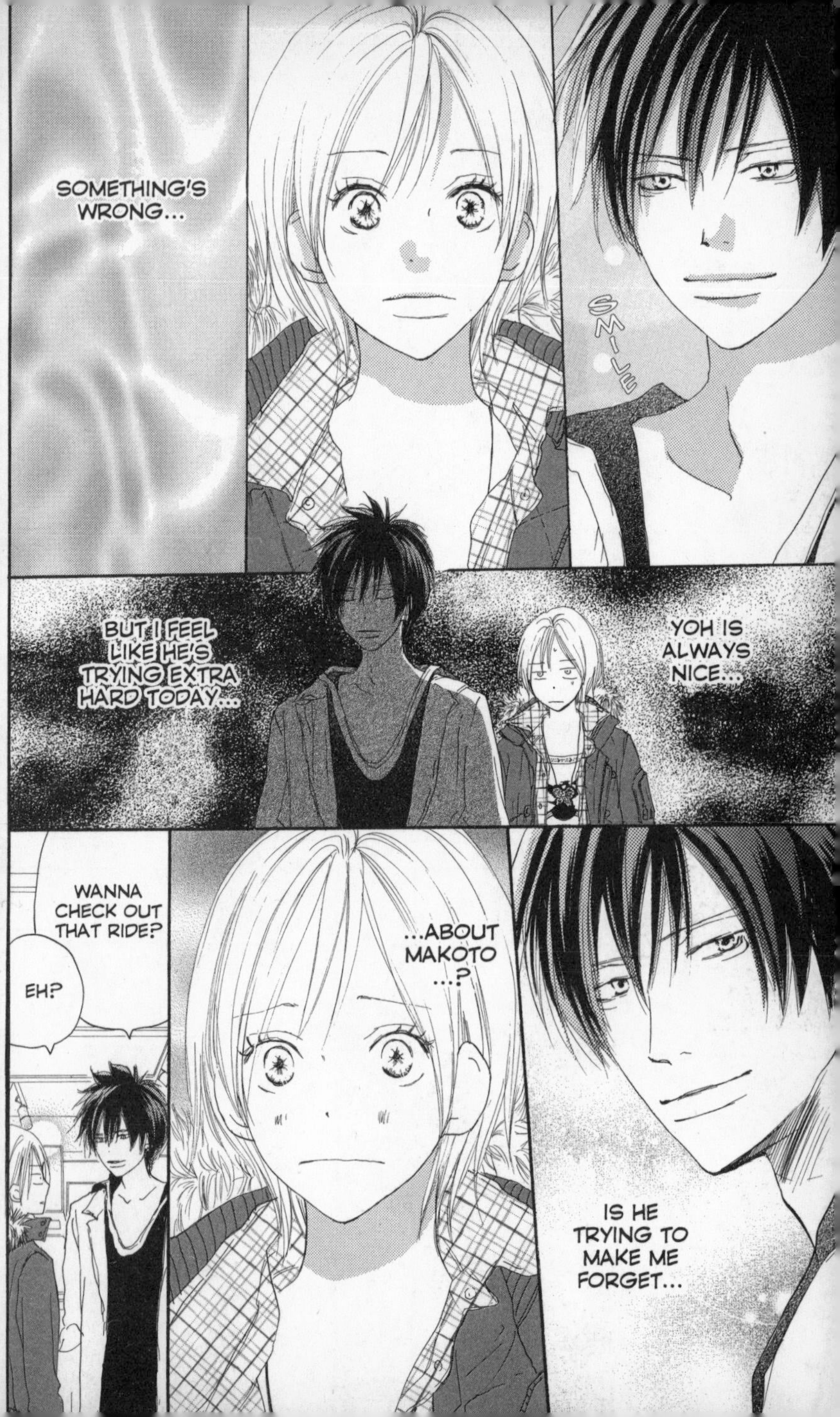
SMILE
SOMETHING'S WRONG...
YOH IS ALWAYS NICE...
BUT I FEEL LIKE HE'S TRYING EXTRA HARD TODAY...
IS HE TRYING TO MAKE ME FORGET...
...ABOUT MAKOTO...?
WANNA CHECK OUT THAT RIDE?
EH?

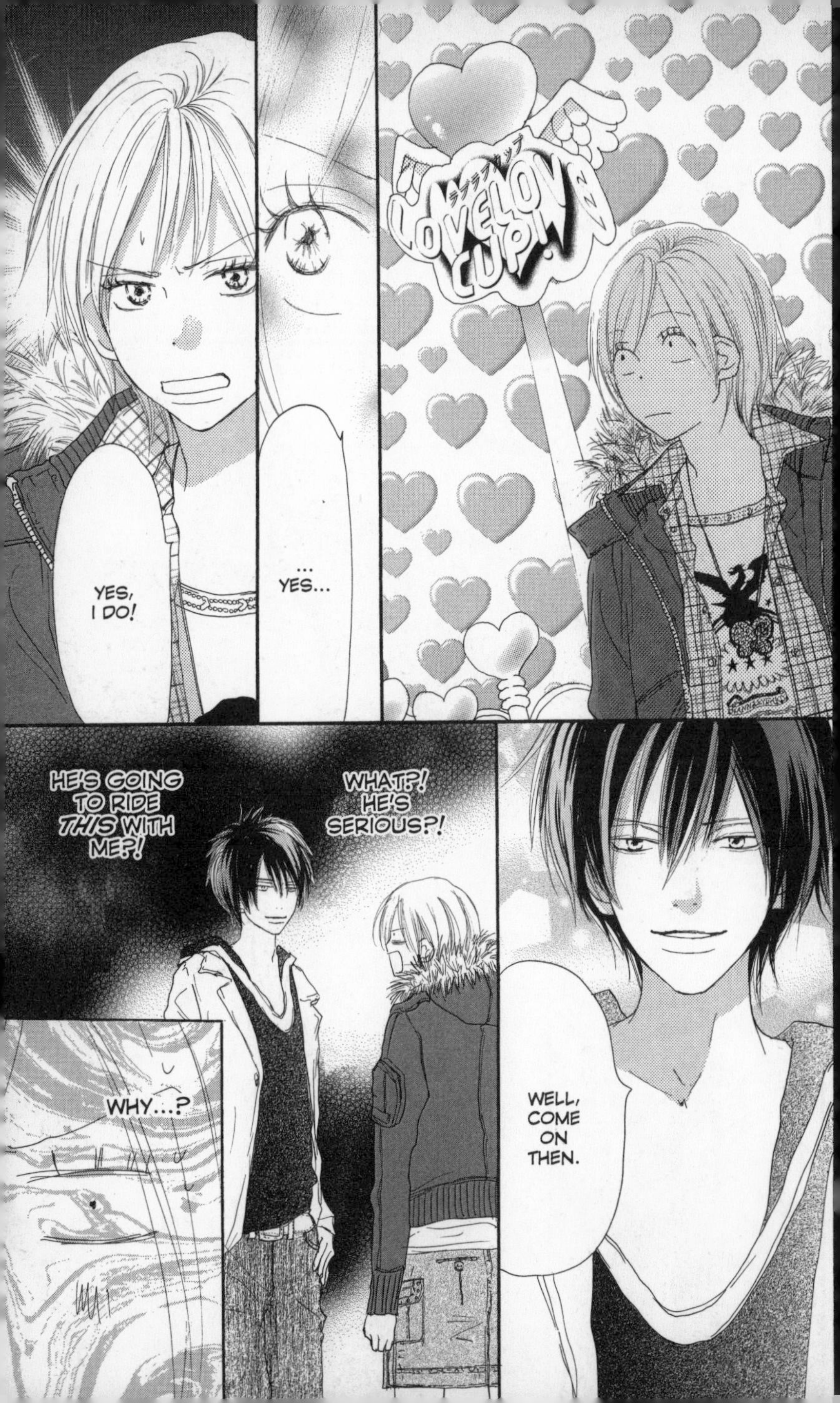

ラブラブカップ
LOVELOVE CUP!
... YES...
YES, I DO!
WELL, COME ON THEN.
WHAT?! HE'S SERIOUS?!
HE'S GOING TO RIDE *THIS* WITH ME?!
WHY...?

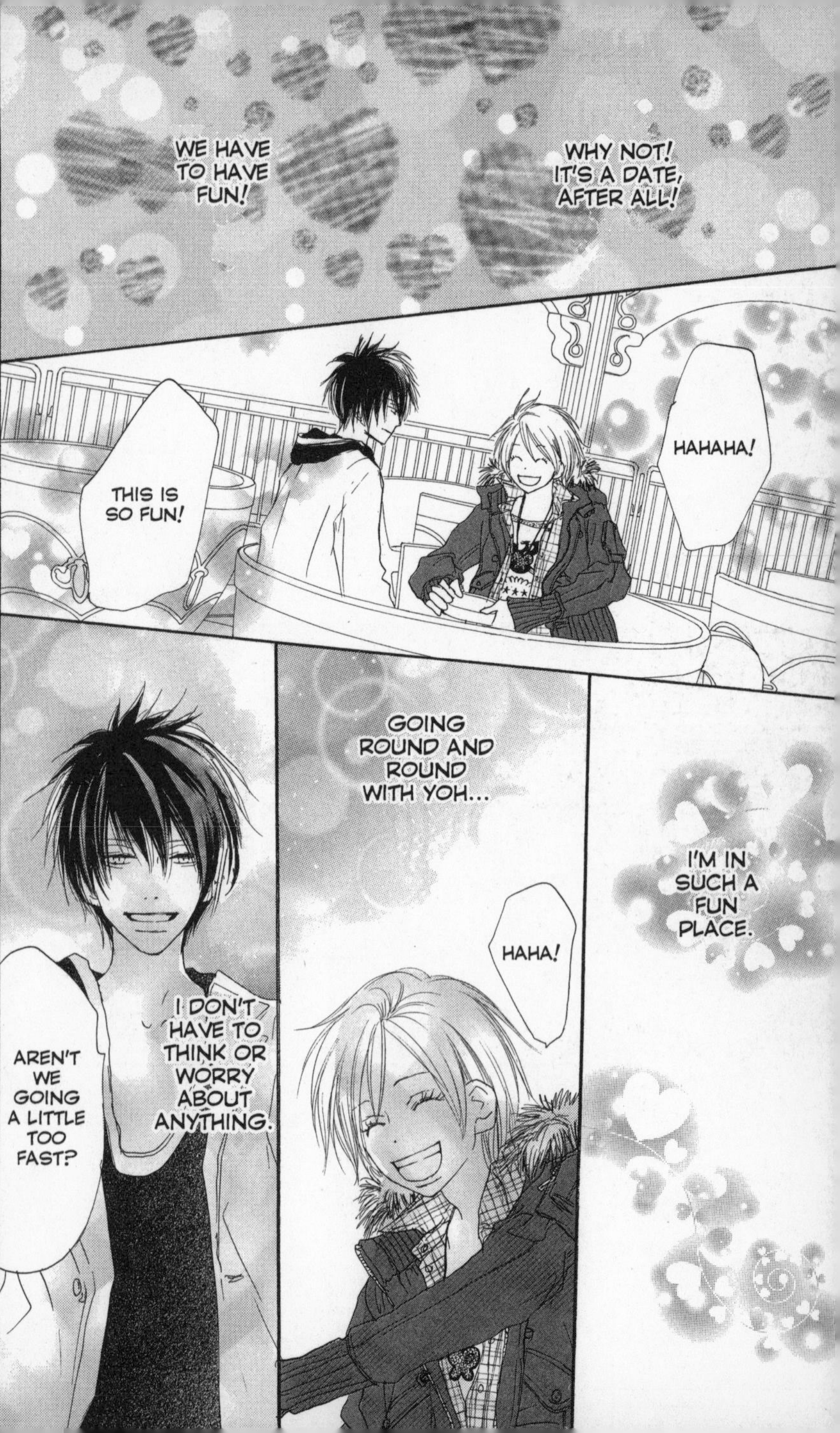
WHY NOT! IT'S A DATE, AFTER ALL!
WE HAVE TO HAVE FUN!
HAHAHA!
THIS IS SO FUN!
I'M IN SUCH A FUN PLACE.
GOING ROUND AND ROUND WITH YOH...
HAHA!
I DON'T HAVE TO THINK OR WORRY ABOUT ANYTHING.
AREN'T WE GOING A LITTLE TOO FAST?

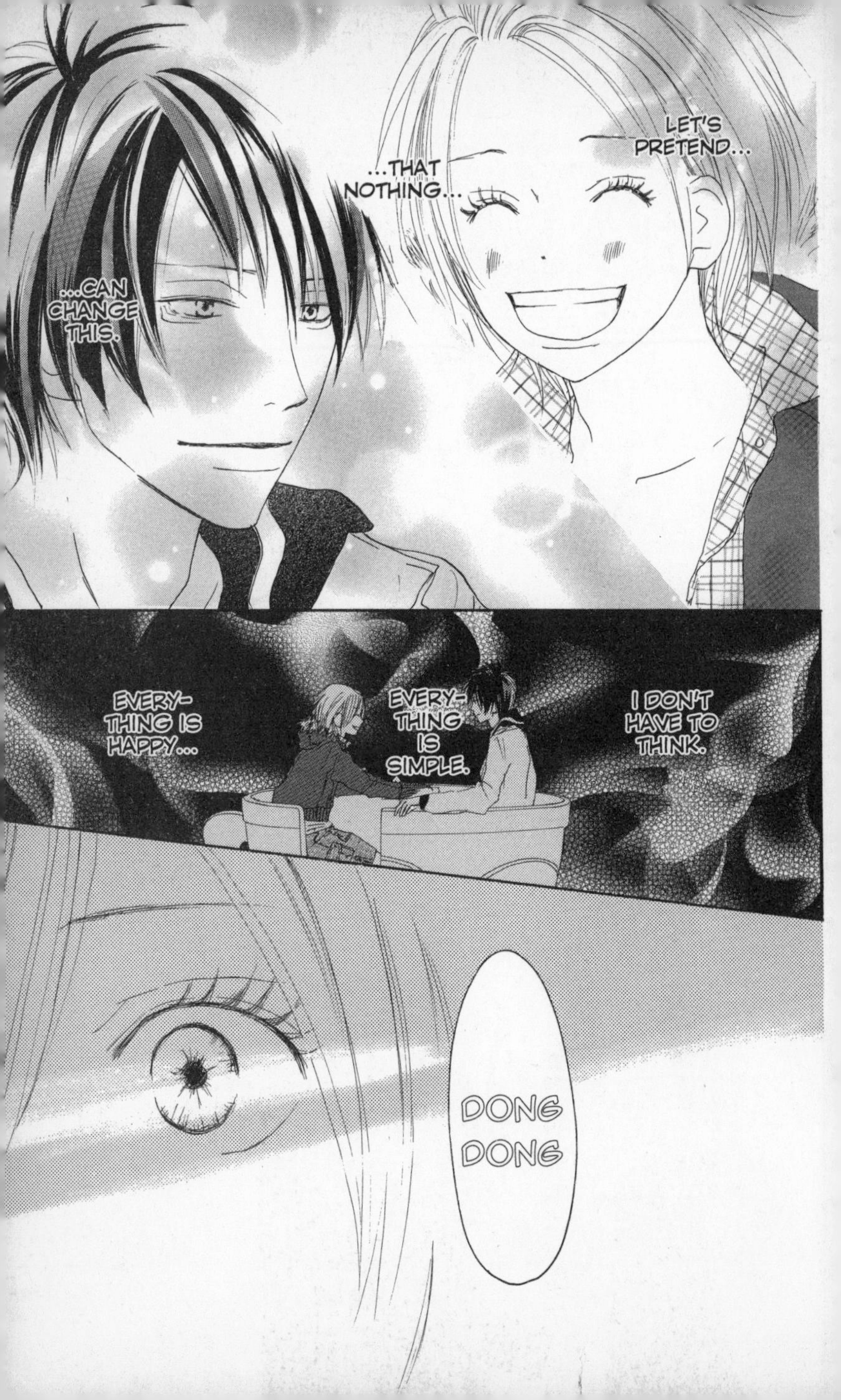
LET'S PRETEND...
...THAT NOTHING...
...CAN CHANGE THIS.
I DON'T HAVE TO THINK.
EVERY-THING IS SIMPLE.
EVERY-THING IS HAPPY...
DONG DONG

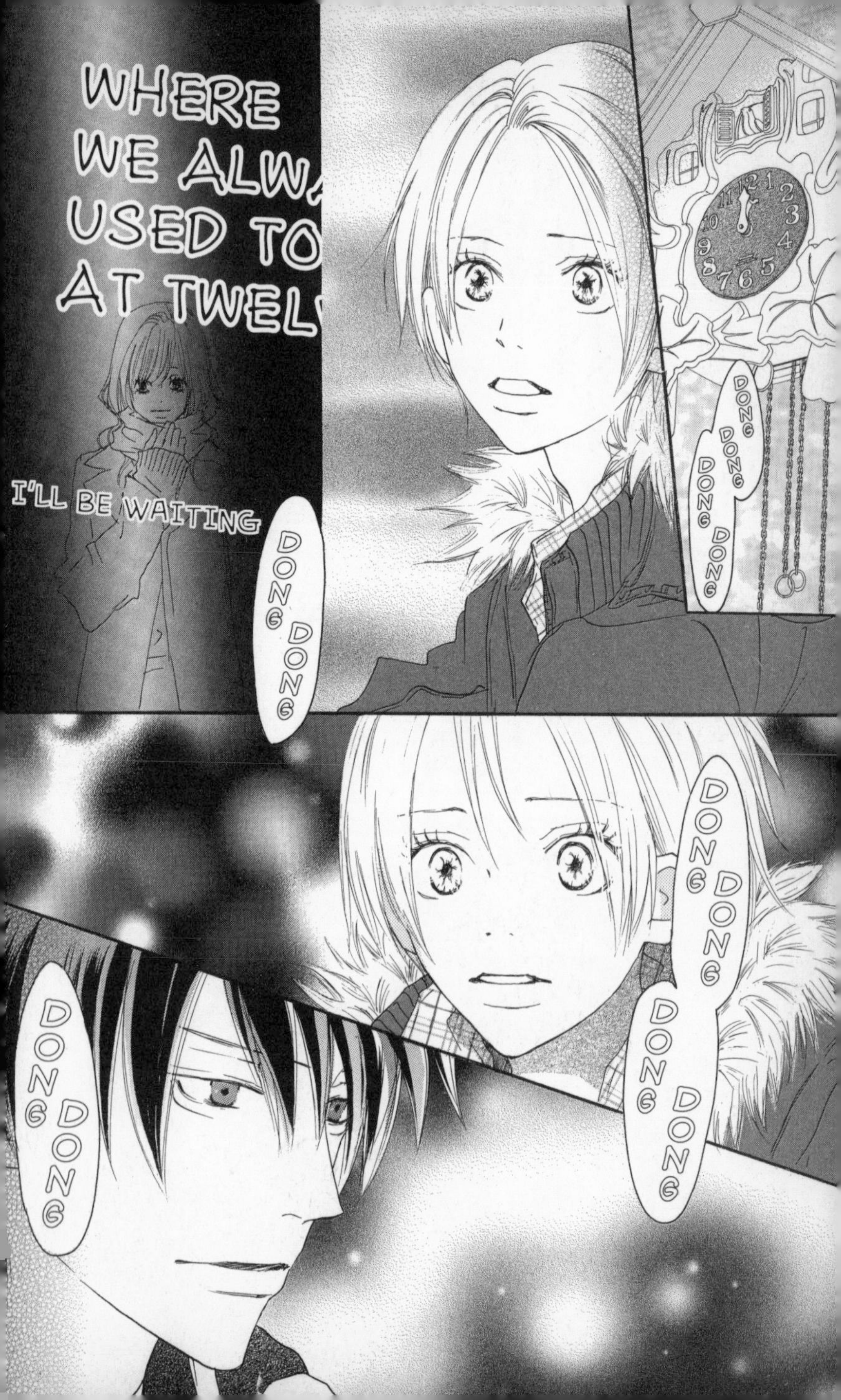
DONG DONG DONG DONG DONG
WHERE WE ALWA USED TO AT TWEL
I'LL BE WAITING
DONG DONG DONG
DONG DONG DONG
DONG DONG
DONG DONG

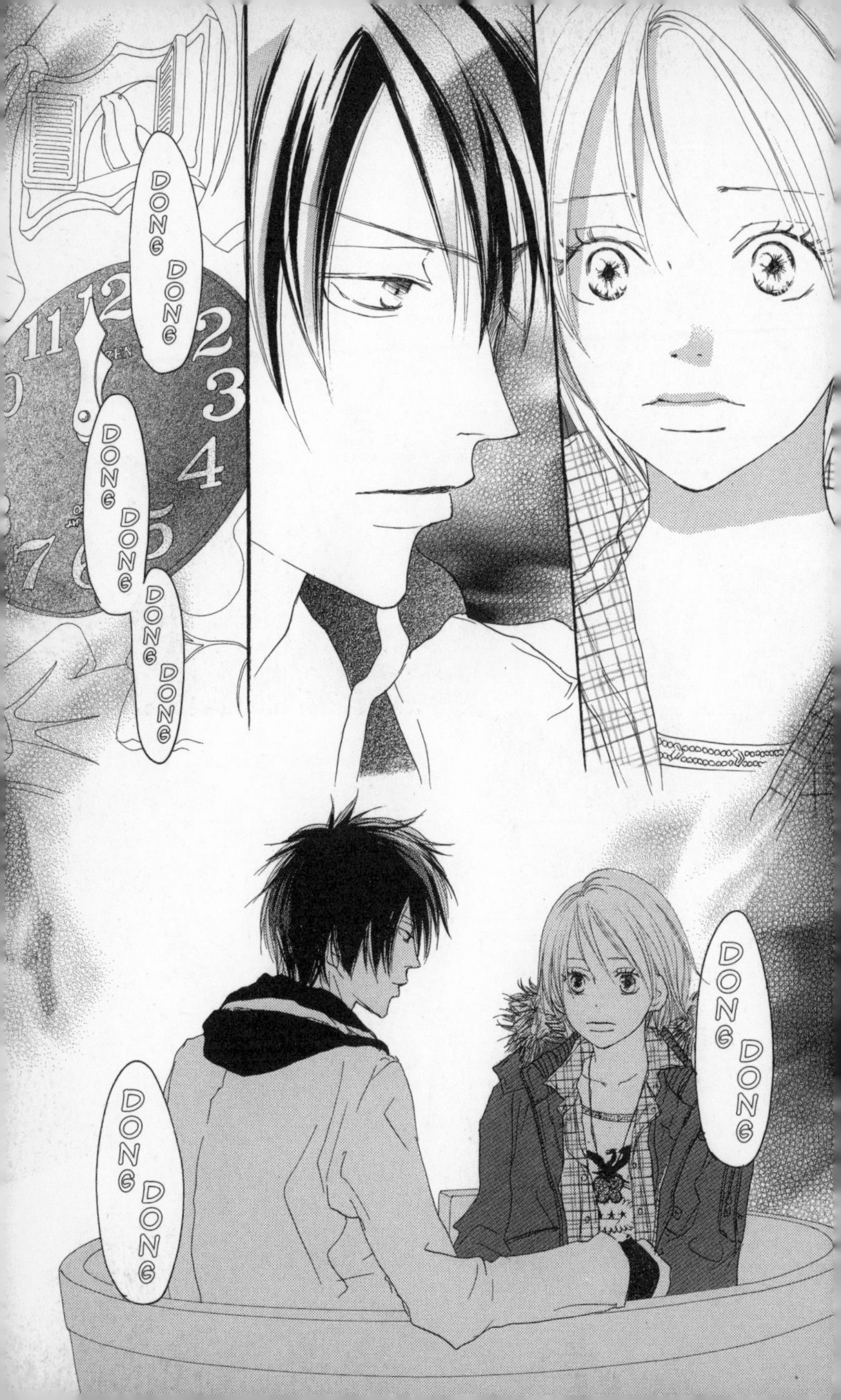
DONG DONG
DONG DONG
DONG DONG
DONG DONG
DONG DONG

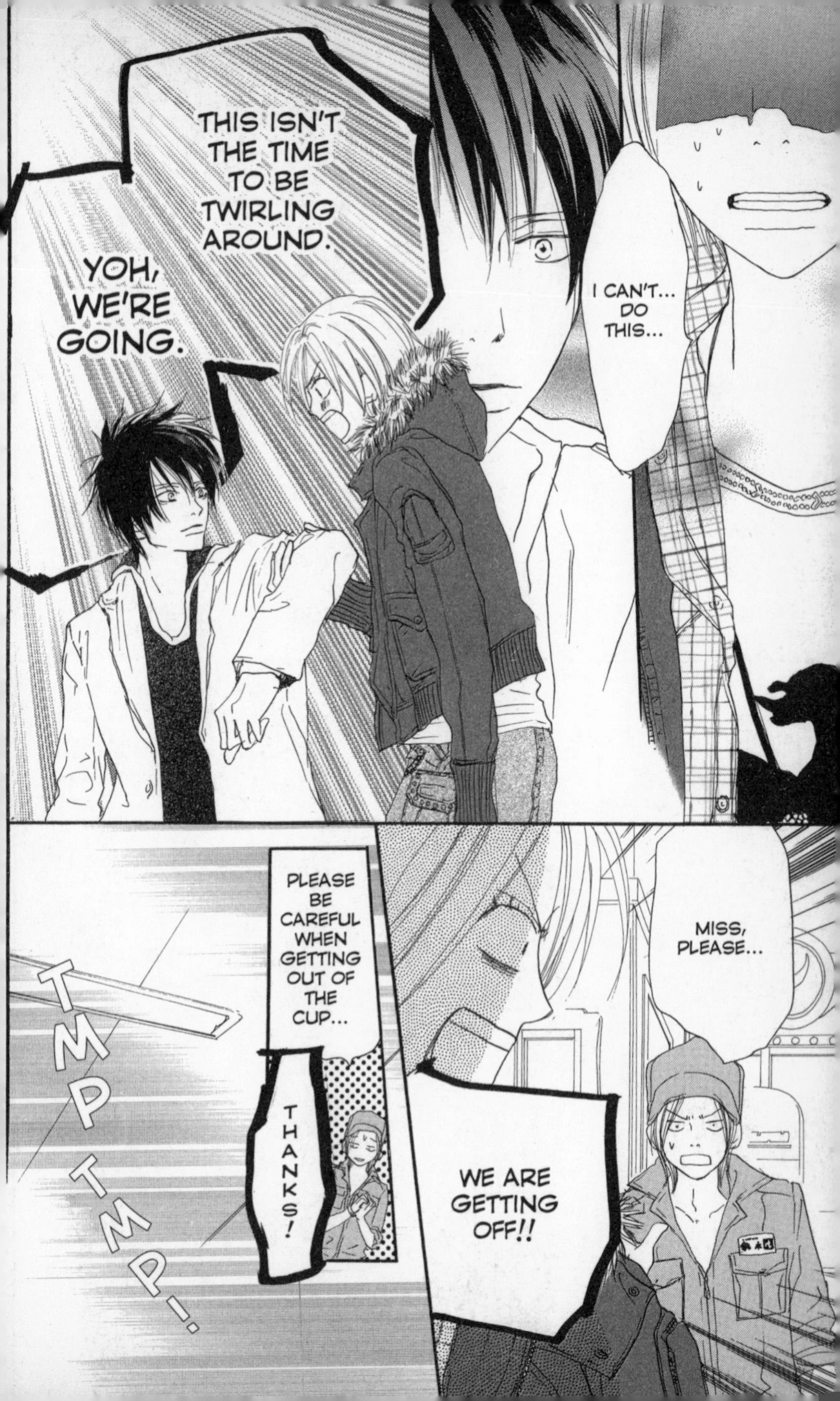
I CAN'T... DO THIS...
THIS ISN'T THE TIME TO BE TWIRLING AROUND.
YOH, WE'RE GOING.
MISS, PLEASE...
WE ARE GETTING OFF!!
PLEASE BE CAREFUL WHEN GETTING OUT OF THE CUP...
THANKS!
TMP TMP!!

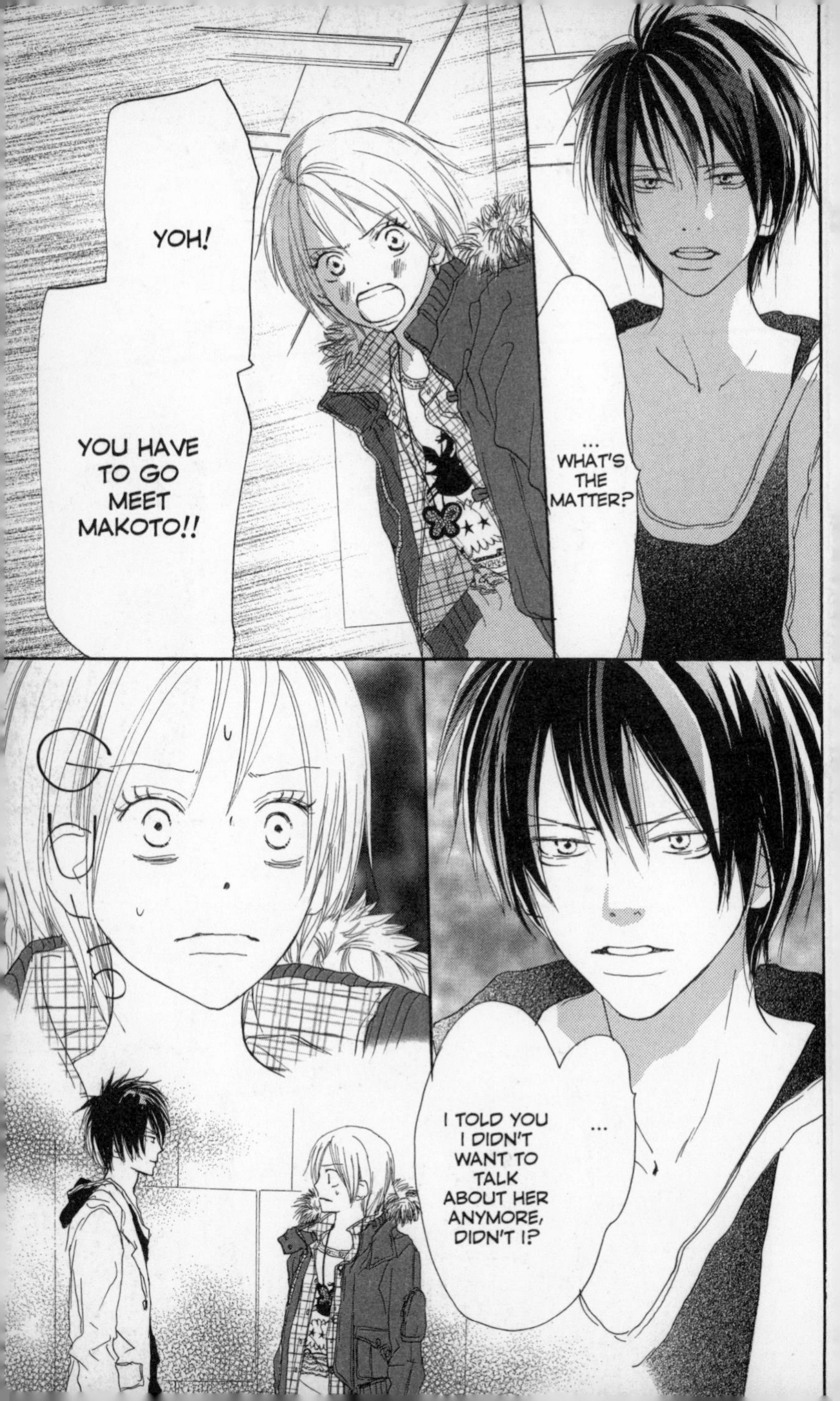

... WHAT'S THE MATTER?
YOH!
YOU HAVE TO GO MEET MAKOTO!!
...
I TOLD YOU I DIDN'T WANT TO TALK ABOUT HER ANYMORE, DIDN'T I?

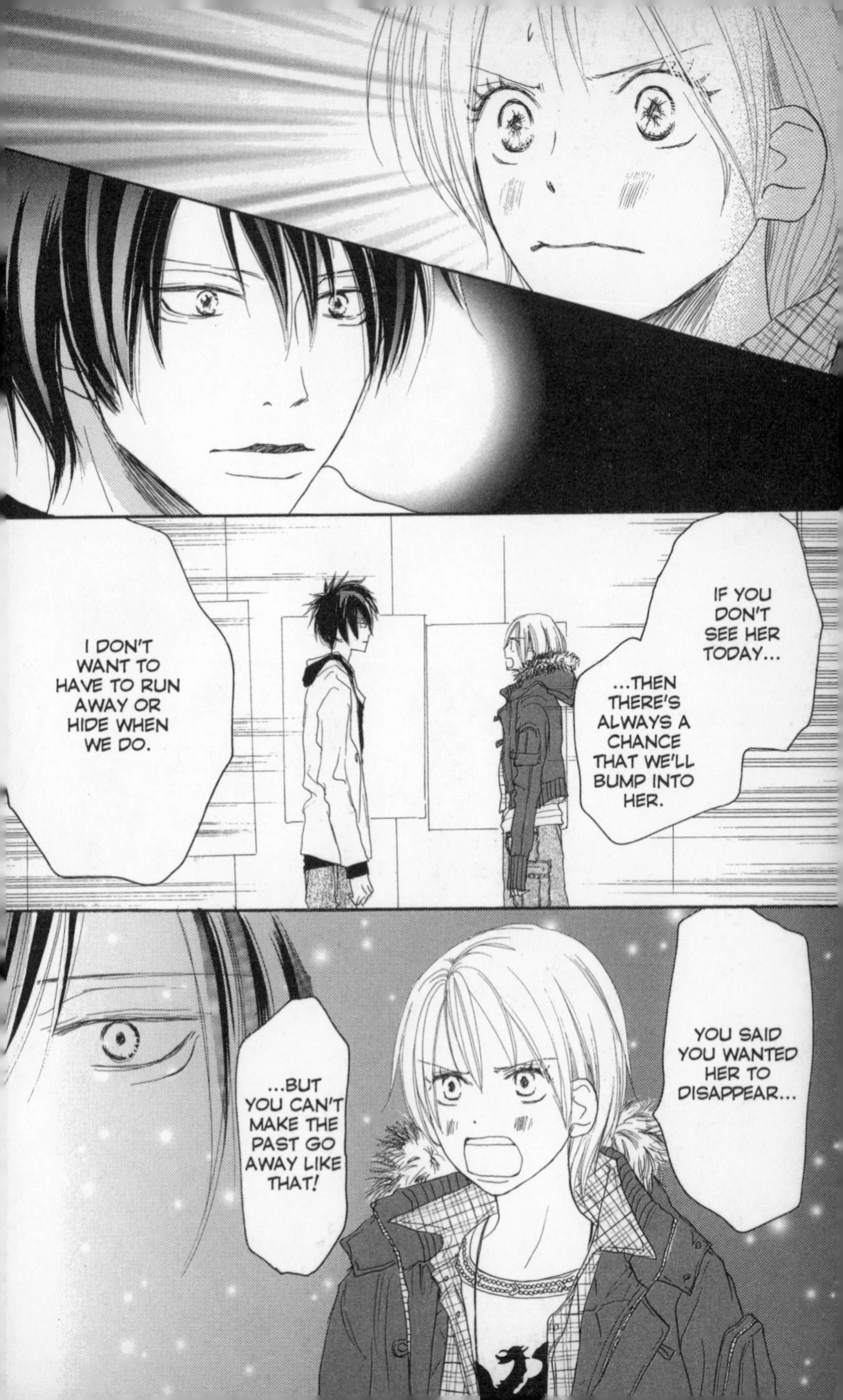
IF YOU DON'T SEE HER TODAY...
...THEN THERE'S ALWAYS A CHANCE THAT WE'LL BUMP INTO HER.
I DON'T WANT TO HAVE TO RUN AWAY OR HIDE WHEN WE DO.
YOU SAID YOU WANTED HER TO DISAPPEAR...
...BUT YOU CAN'T MAKE THE PAST GO AWAY LIKE THAT!

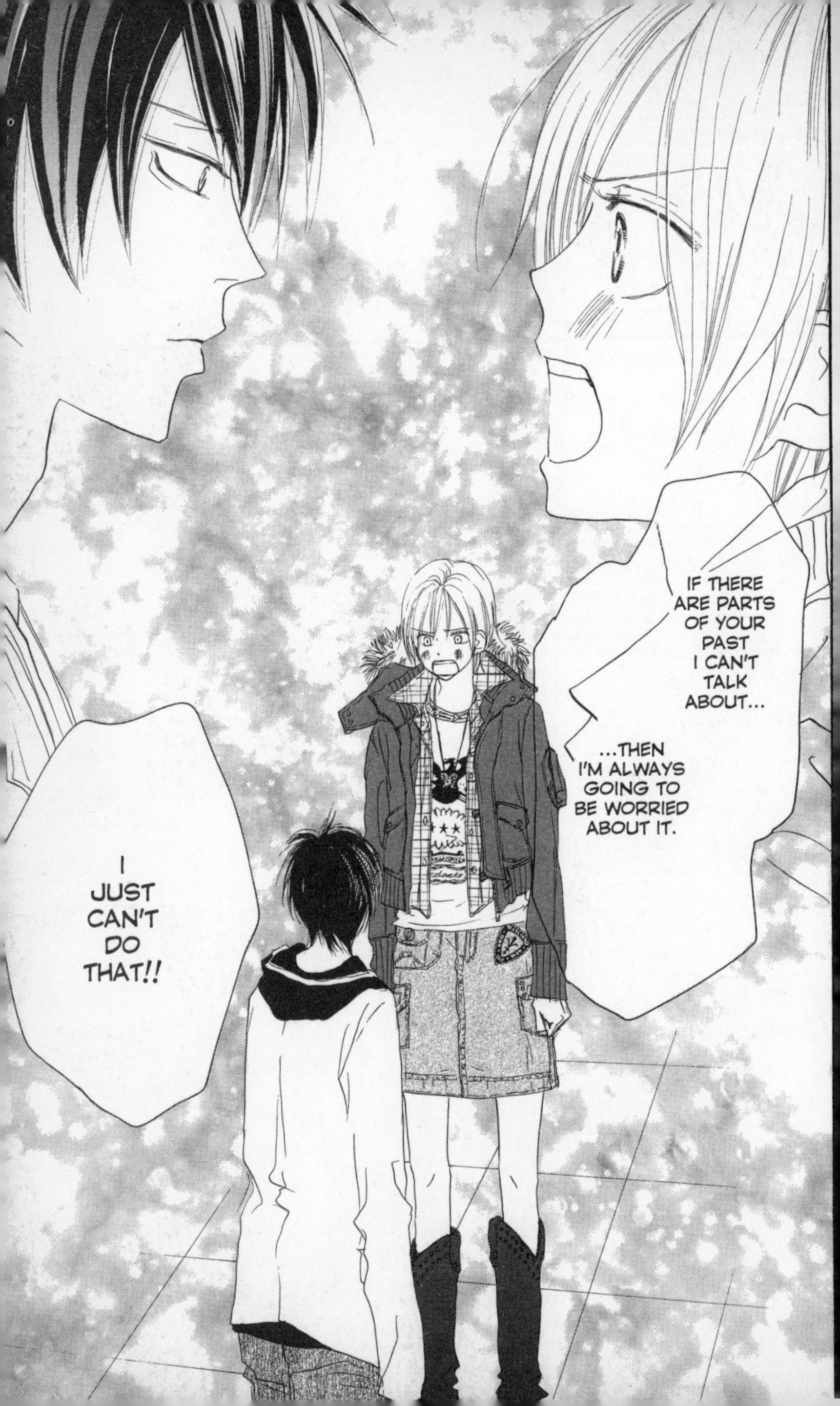
IF THERE ARE PARTS OF YOUR PAST I CAN'T TALK ABOUT...
...THEN I'M ALWAYS GOING TO BE WORRIED ABOUT IT.
I JUST CAN'T DO THAT!!

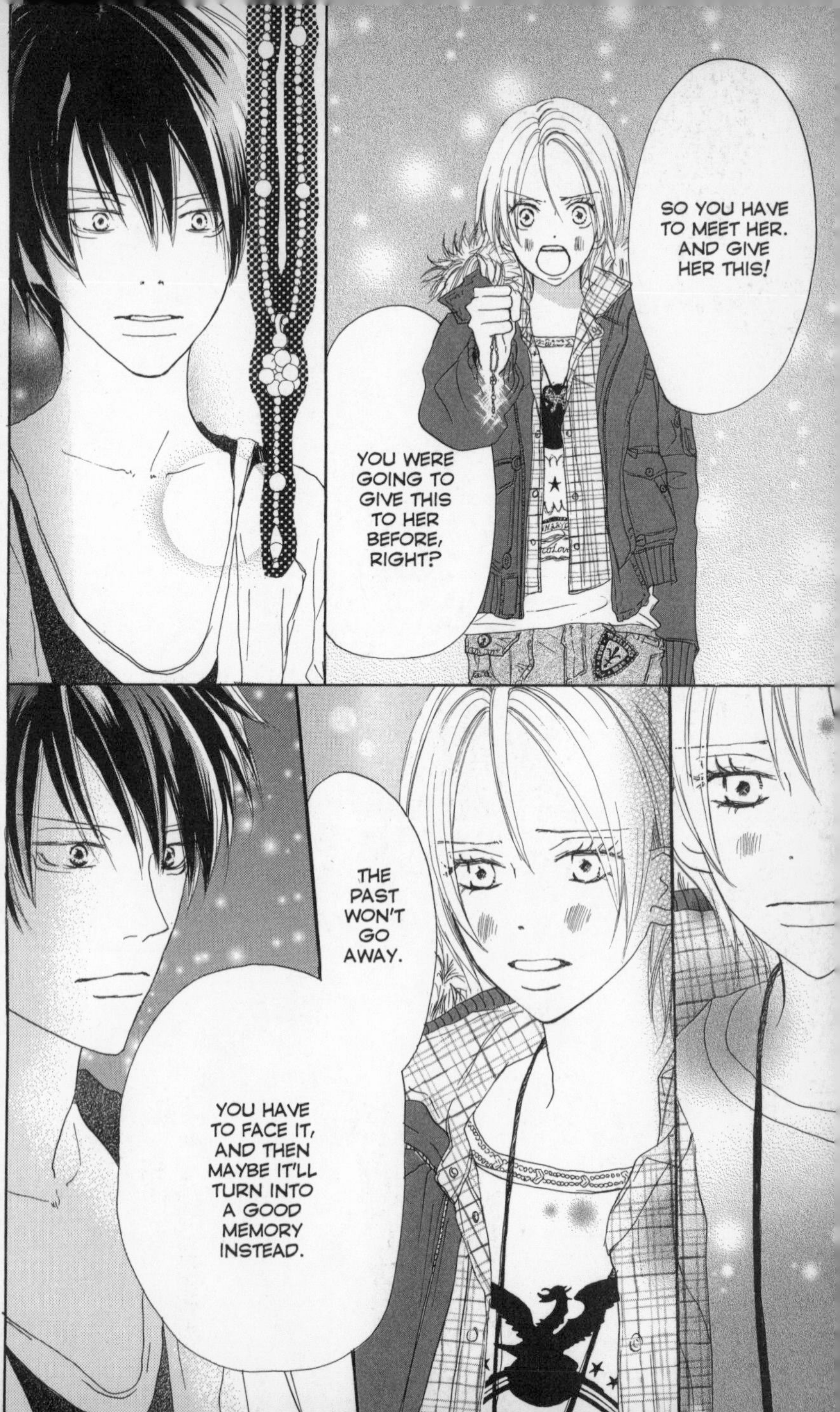
SO YOU HAVE TO MEET HER. AND GIVE HER THIS!
YOU WERE GOING TO GIVE THIS TO HER BEFORE, RIGHT?
THE PAST WON'T GO AWAY.
YOU HAVE TO FACE IT, AND THEN MAYBE IT'LL TURN INTO A GOOD MEMORY INSTEAD.

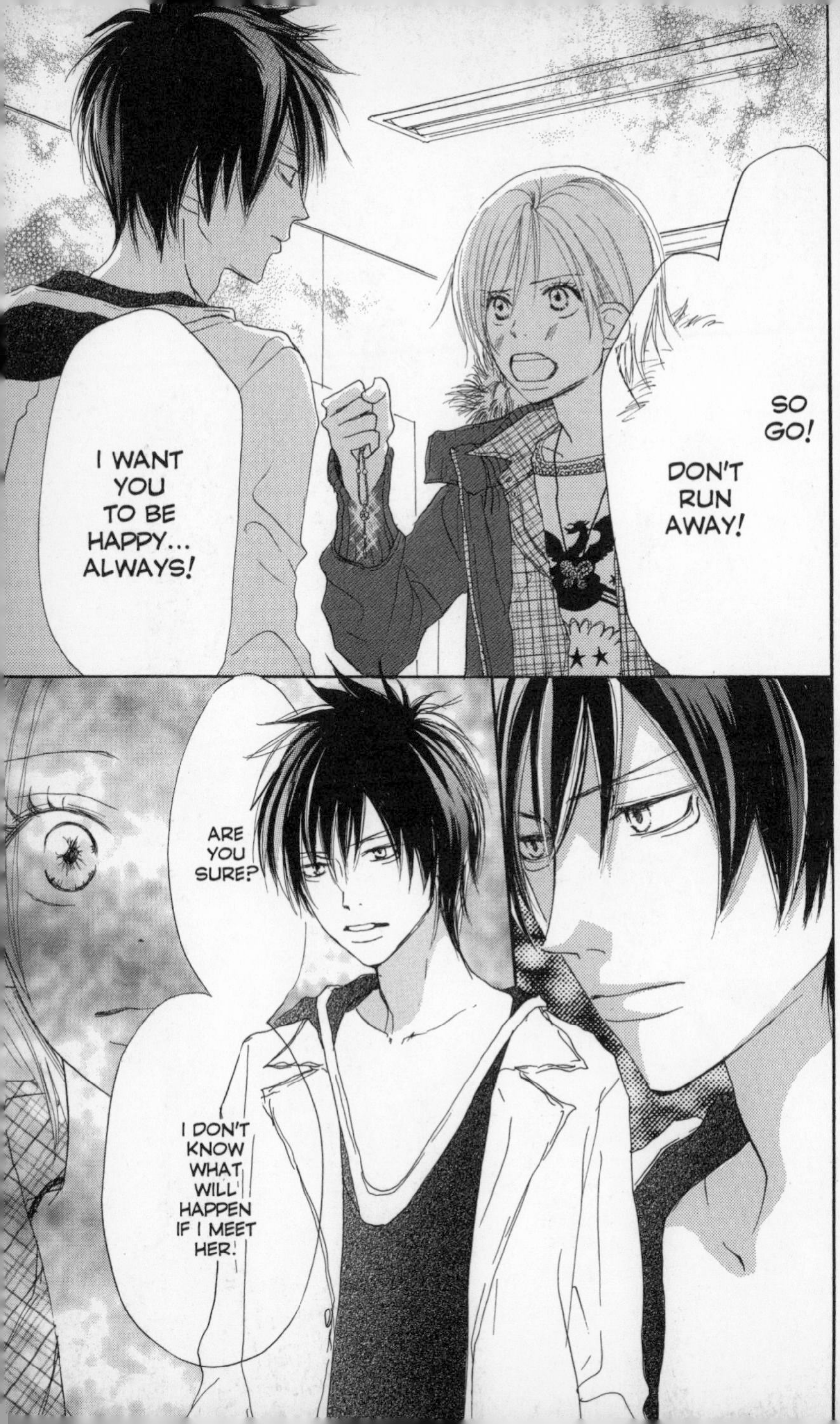
SO GO!
DON'T RUN AWAY!
I WANT YOU TO BE HAPPY... ALWAYS!
ARE YOU SURE?
I DON'T KNOW WHAT WILL HAPPEN IF I MEET HER.

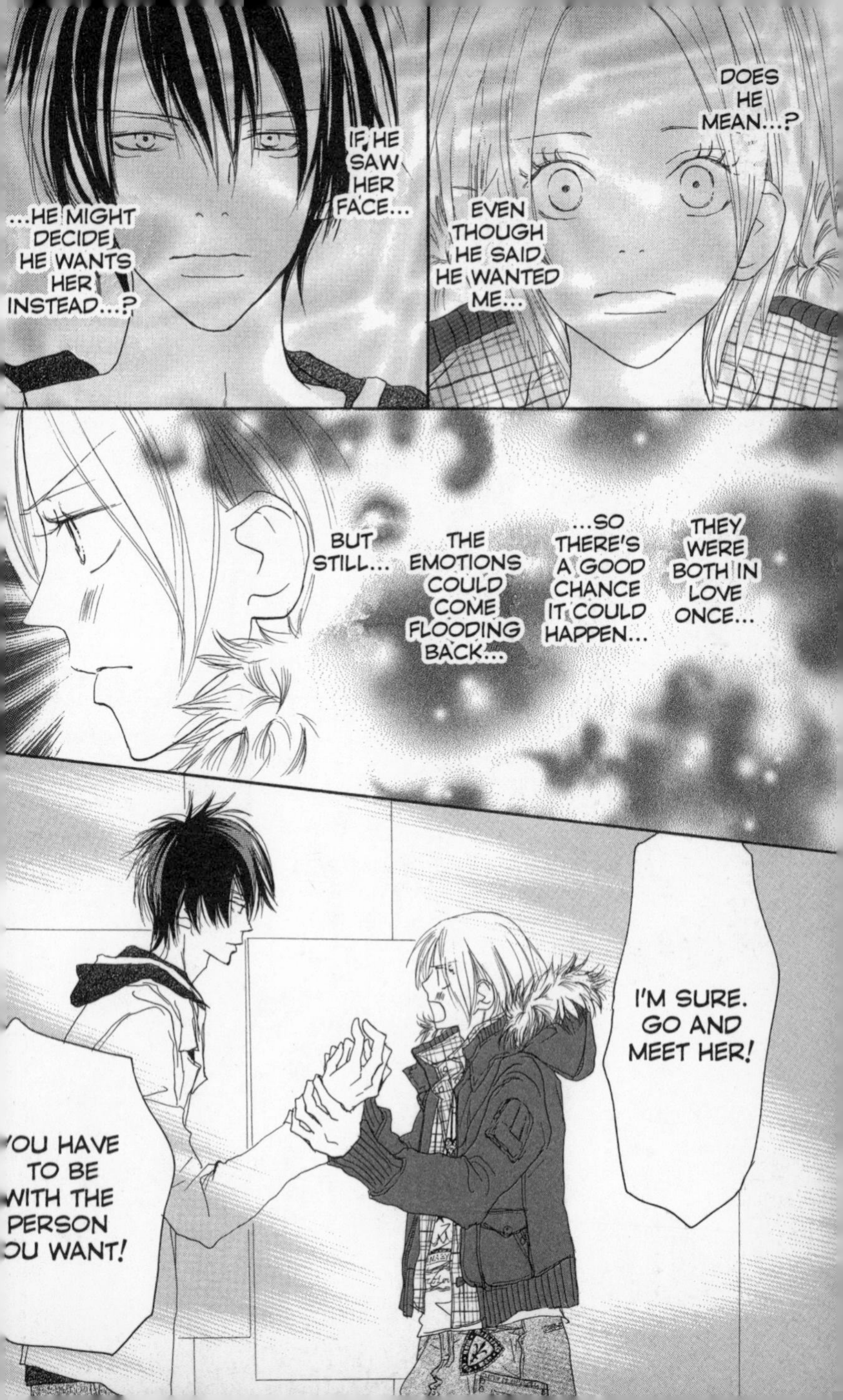
DOES HE MEAN...?
EVEN THOUGH HE SAID HE WANTED ME...
IF HE SAW HER FACE...
...HE MIGHT DECIDE HE WANTS HER INSTEAD...?
THEY WERE BOTH IN LOVE ONCE...
...SO THERE'S A GOOD CHANCE IT COULD HAPPEN...
THE EMOTIONS COULD COME FLOODING BACK...
BUT STILL...
I'M SURE. GO AND MEET HER!
OU HAVE TO BE WITH THE PERSON OU WANT!

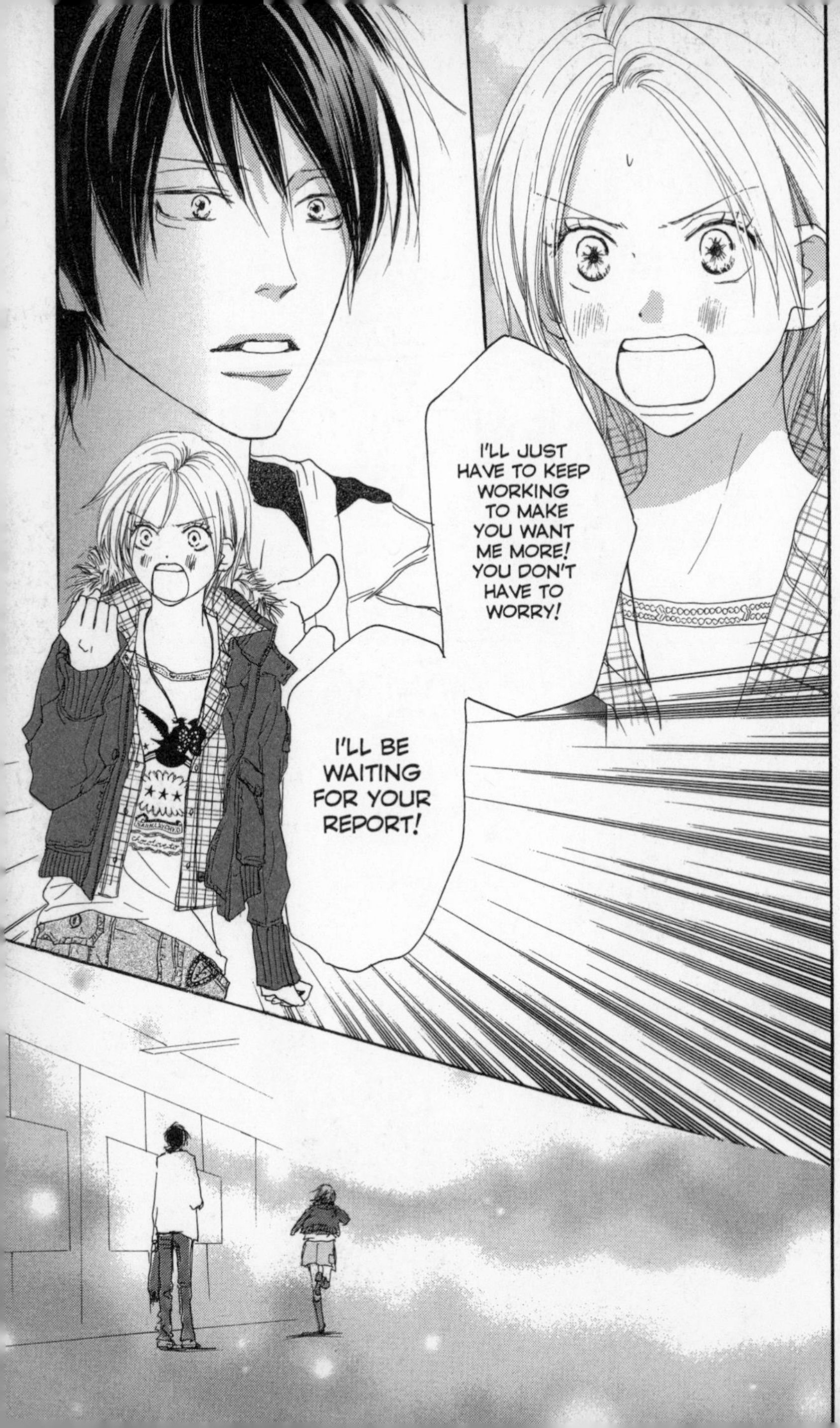
I'LL JUST HAVE TO KEEP WORKING TO MAKE YOU WANT ME MORE! YOU DON'T HAVE TO WORRY!
I'LL BE WAITING FOR YOUR REPORT!

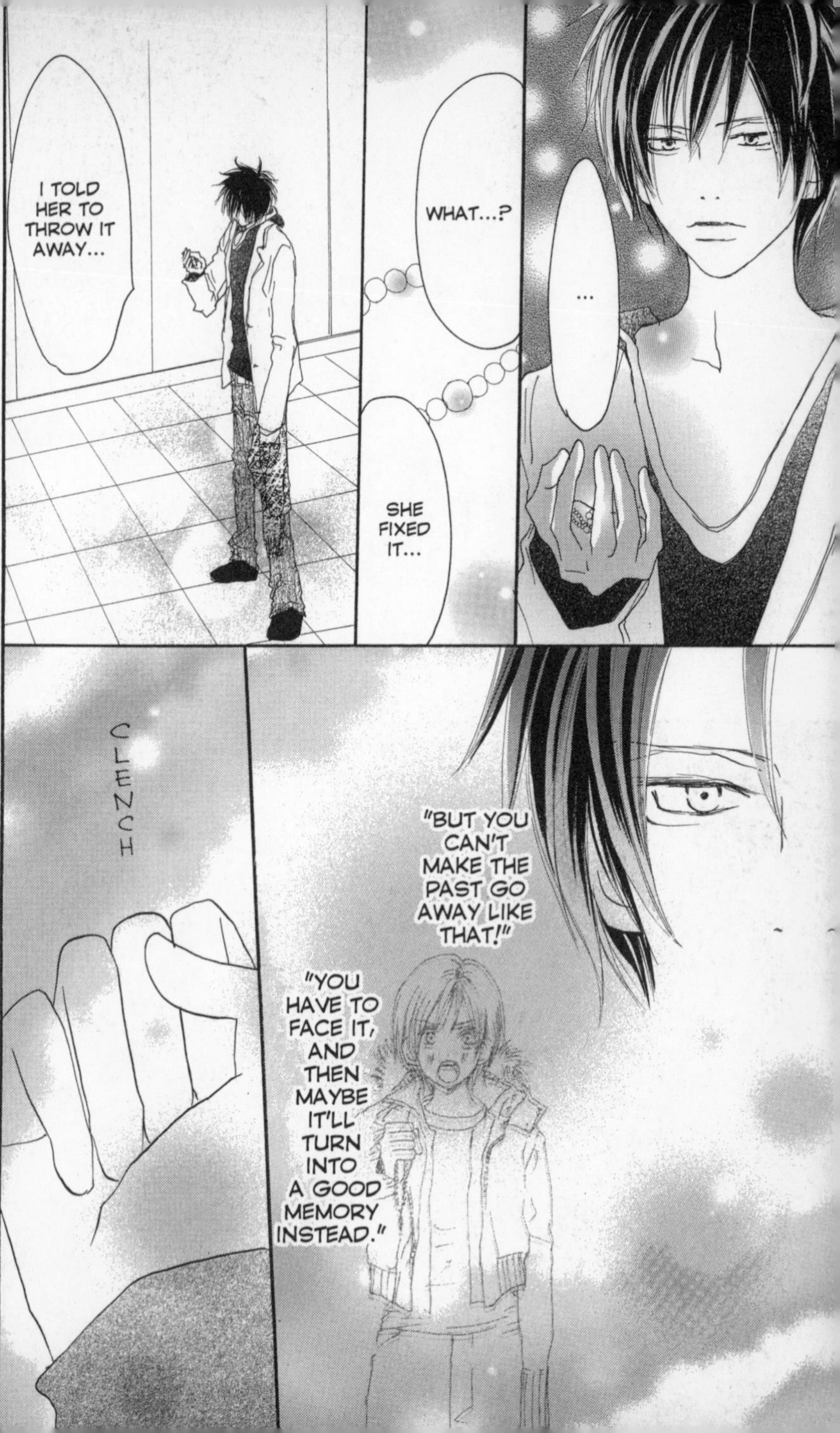
...
WHAT...?
SHE FIXED IT...
I TOLD HER TO THROW IT AWAY...
"BUT YOU CAN'T MAKE THE PAST GO AWAY LIKE THAT!"
"YOU HAVE TO FACE IT, AND THEN MAYBE IT'LL TURN INTO A GOOD MEMORY INSTEAD."
CLENCH

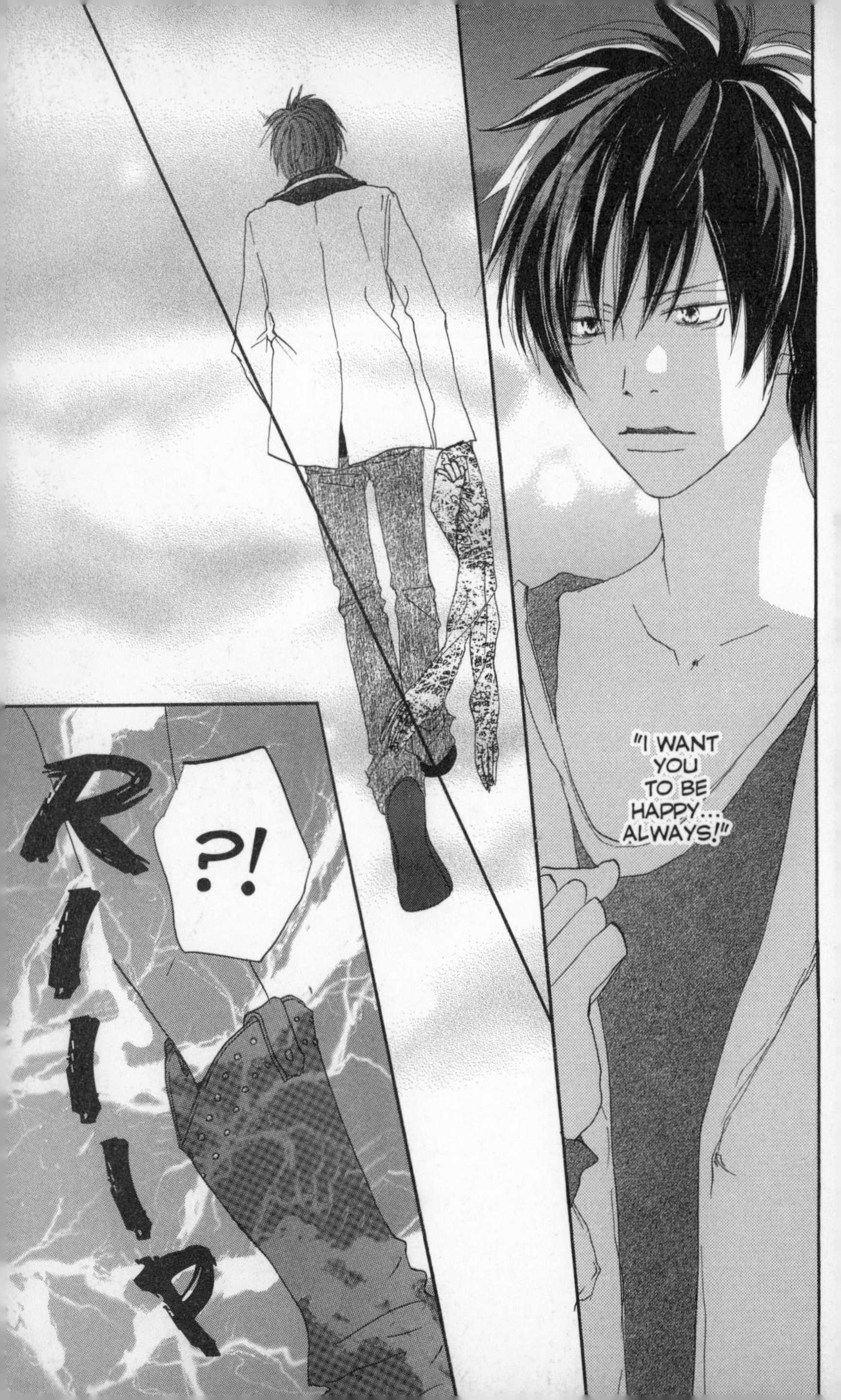
"I WANT YOU TO BE HAPPY... ALWAYS!"
?!
RIIIP

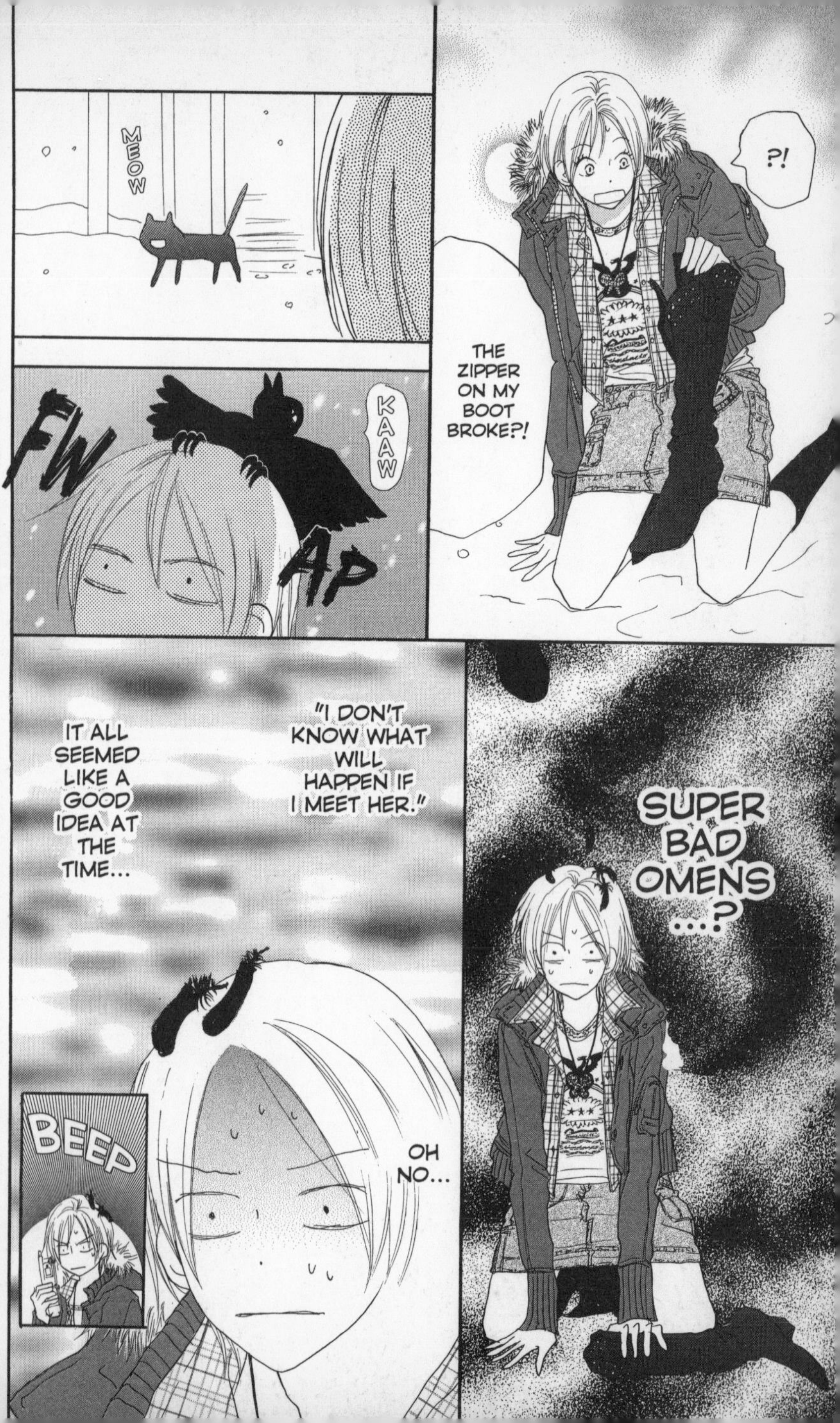
?!
THE ZIPPER ON MY BOOT BROKE?!
MEOW
KAAAW
FWAP
SUPER BAD OMENS ...?
"I DON'T KNOW WHAT WILL HAPPEN IF I MEET HER."
IT ALL SEEMED LIKE A GOOD IDEA AT THE TIME...
OH NO...
BEEP

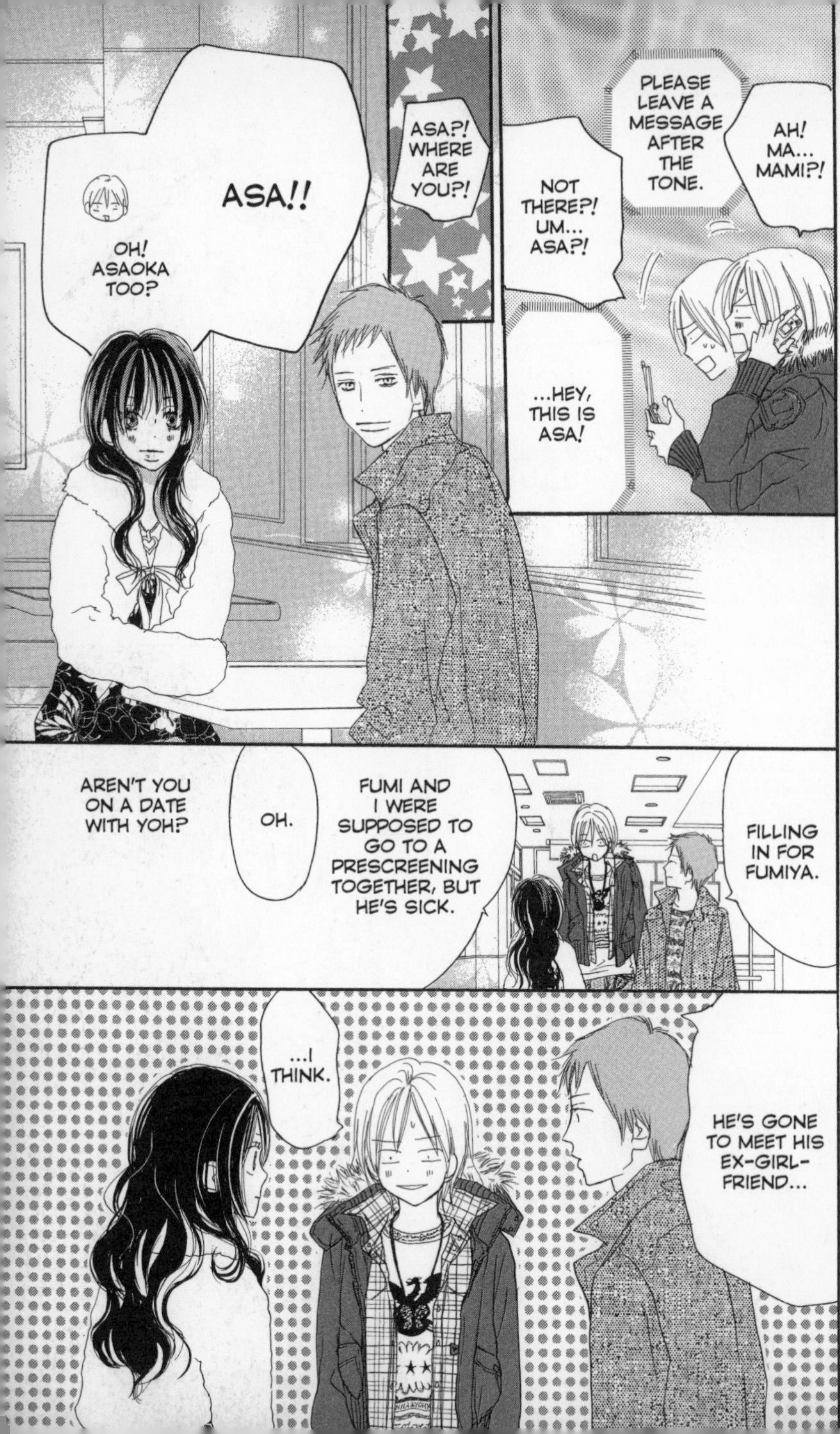
AH! MA... MAMI?!
...HEY, THIS IS ASA!
PLEASE LEAVE A MESSAGE AFTER THE TONE.
NOT THERE?! UM... ASA?!
ASA?! WHERE ARE YOU?!
ASA!!
OH! ASAOKA TOO?
FILLING IN FOR FUMIYA.
FUMI AND I WERE SUPPOSED TO GO TO A PRESCREENING TOGETHER, BUT HE'S SICK.
OH.
AREN'T YOU ON A DATE WITH YOH?
HE'S GONE TO MEET HIS EX-GIRL-FRIEND...
...I THINK.

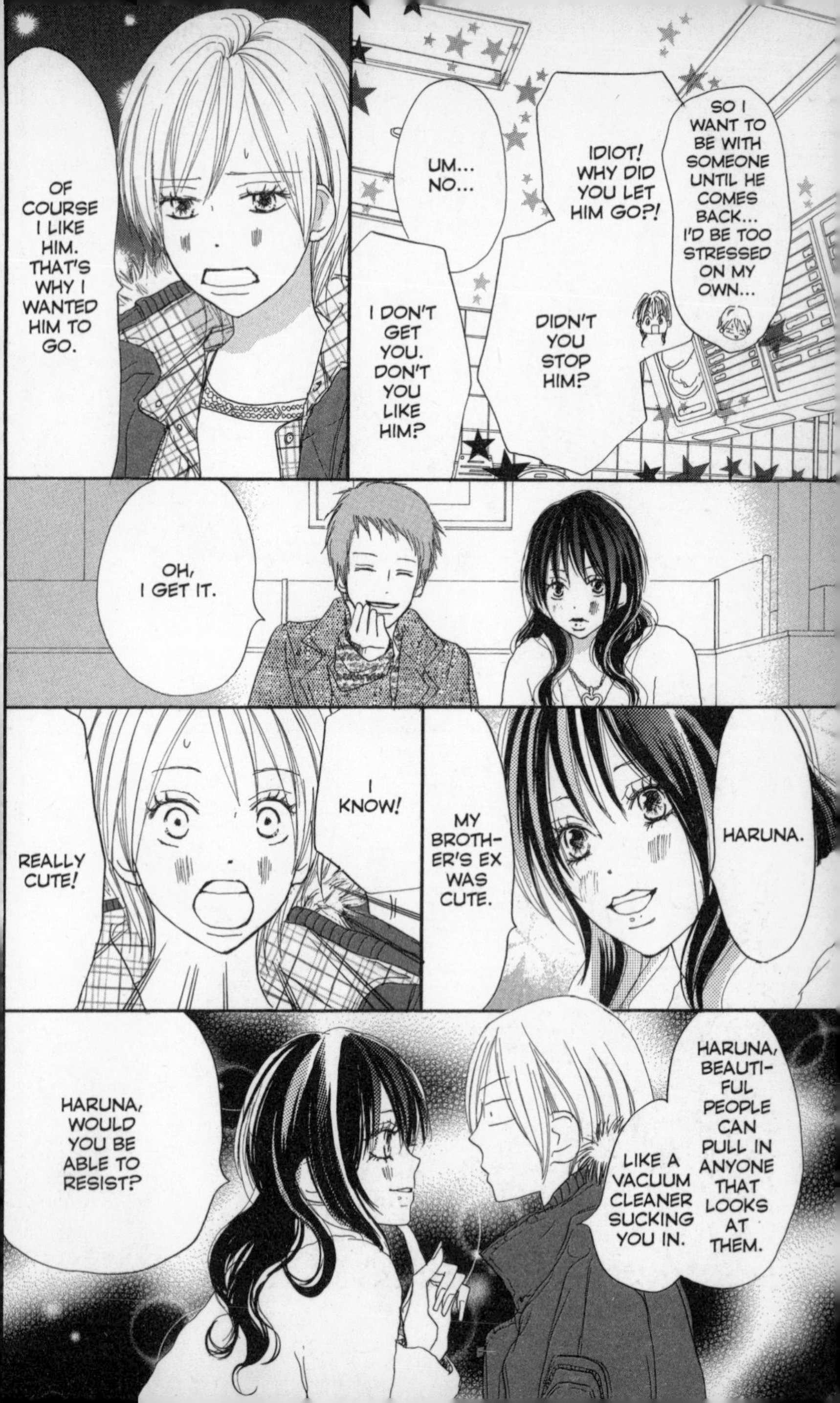
SO I WANT TO BE WITH SOMEONE UNTIL HE COMES BACK... I'D BE TOO STRESSED ON MY OWN...
IDIOT! WHY DID YOU LET HIM GO?!
UM... NO...
DIDN'T YOU STOP HIM?
I DON'T GET YOU. DON'T YOU LIKE HIM?
OF COURSE I LIKE HIM. THAT'S WHY I WANTED HIM TO GO.
OH, I GET IT.
HARUNA.
MY BROTHER'S EX WAS CUTE.
I KNOW!
REALLY CUTE!
HARUNA, BEAUTIFUL PEOPLE CAN PULL IN ANYONE THAT LOOKS AT THEM.
LIKE A VACUUM CLEANER SUCKING YOU IN.
HARUNA, WOULD YOU BE ABLE TO RESIST?

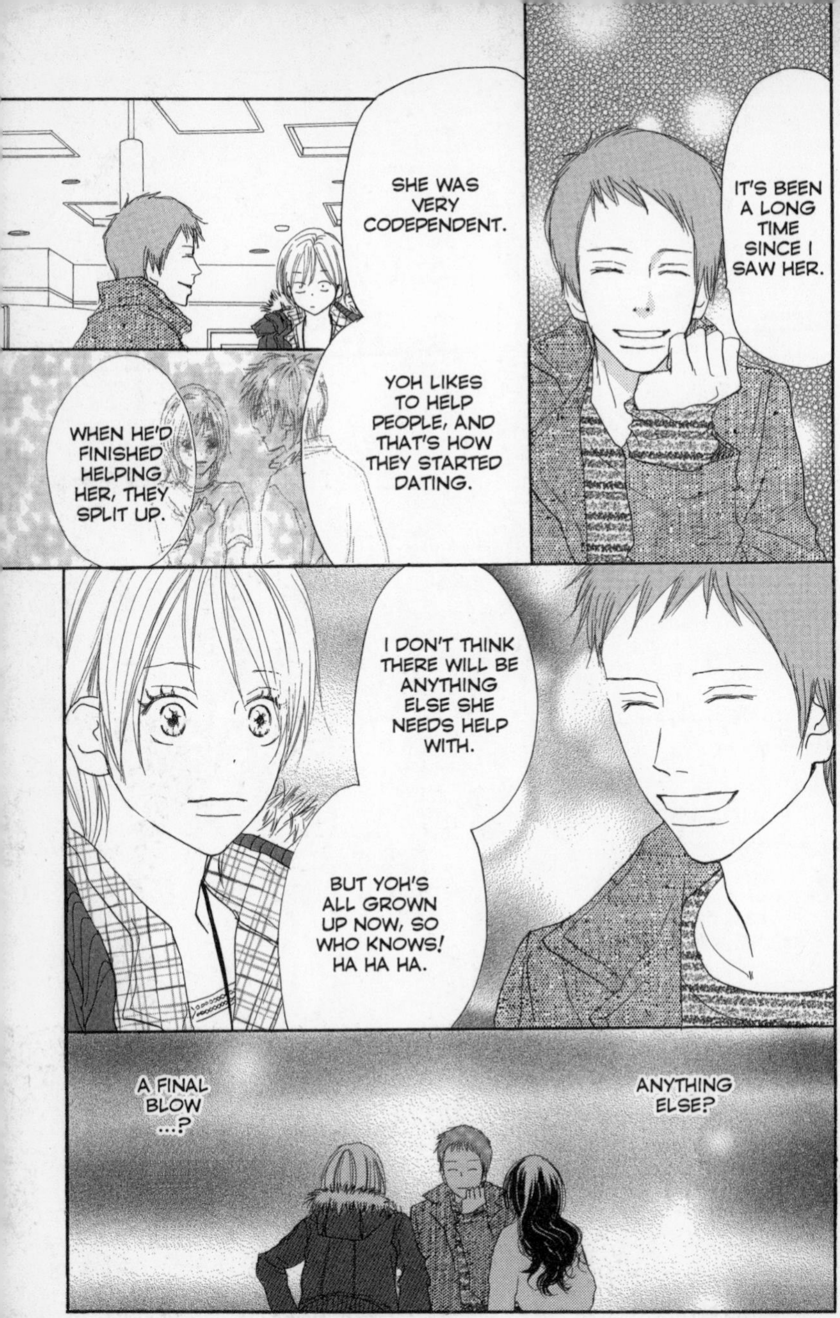
IT'S BEEN A LONG TIME SINCE I SAW HER.
SHE WAS VERY CODEPENDENT.
YOH LIKES TO HELP PEOPLE, AND THAT'S HOW THEY STARTED DATING.
WHEN HE'D FINISHED HELPING HER, THEY SPLIT UP.
I DON'T THINK THERE WILL BE ANYTHING ELSE SHE NEEDS HELP WITH.
BUT YOH'S ALL GROWN UP NOW, SO WHO KNOWS! HA HA HA.
ANYTHING ELSE?
A FINAL BLOW ...?

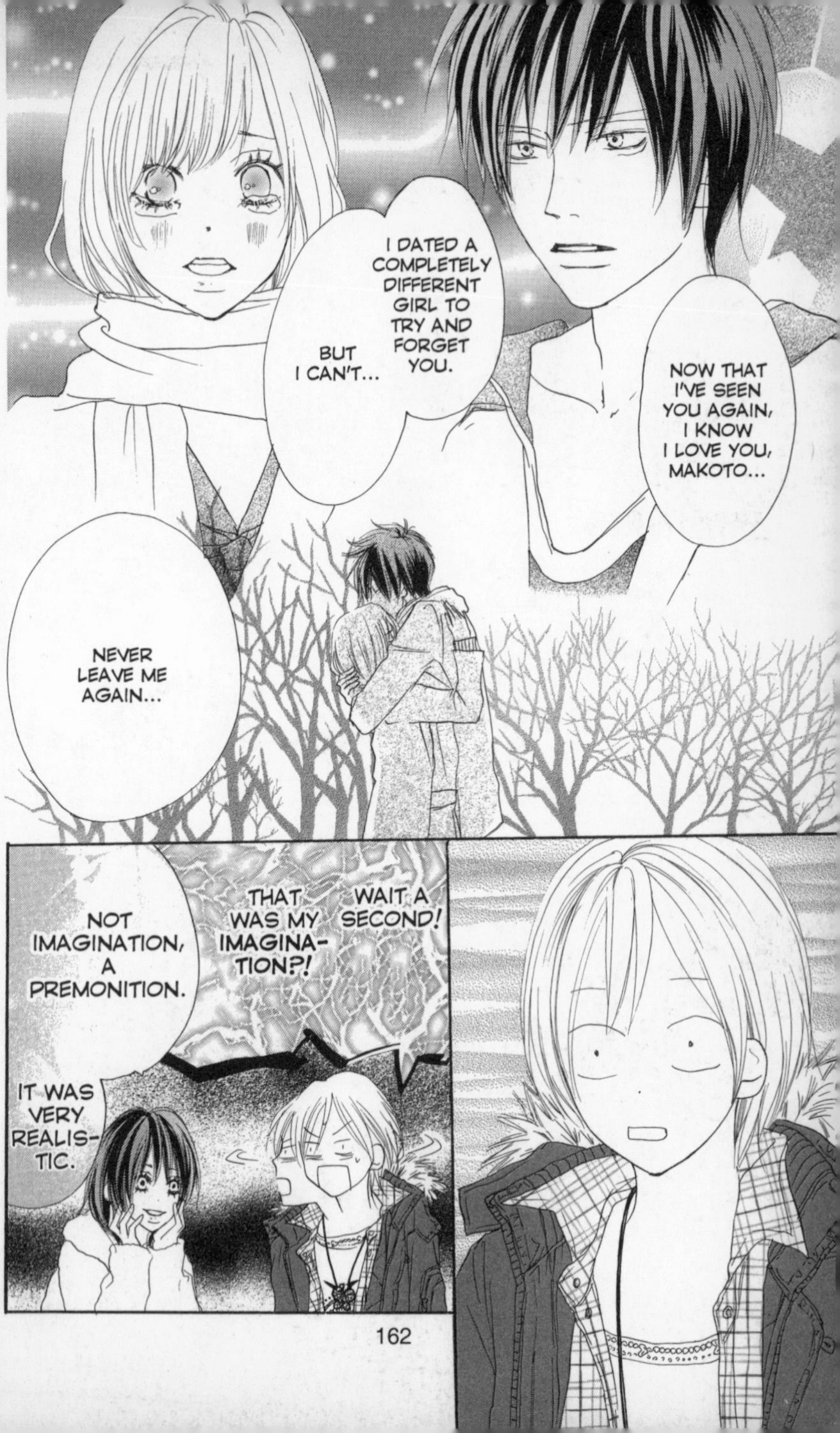
I DATED A COMPLETELY DIFFERENT GIRL TO TRY AND FORGET YOU.
BUT I CAN'T...
NOW THAT I'VE SEEN YOU AGAIN, I KNOW I LOVE YOU, MAKOTO...
NEVER LEAVE ME AGAIN...
WAIT A SECOND!
THAT WAS MY IMAGINA-TION?!
NOT IMAGINATION, A PREMONITION.
IT WAS VERY REALIS-TIC.

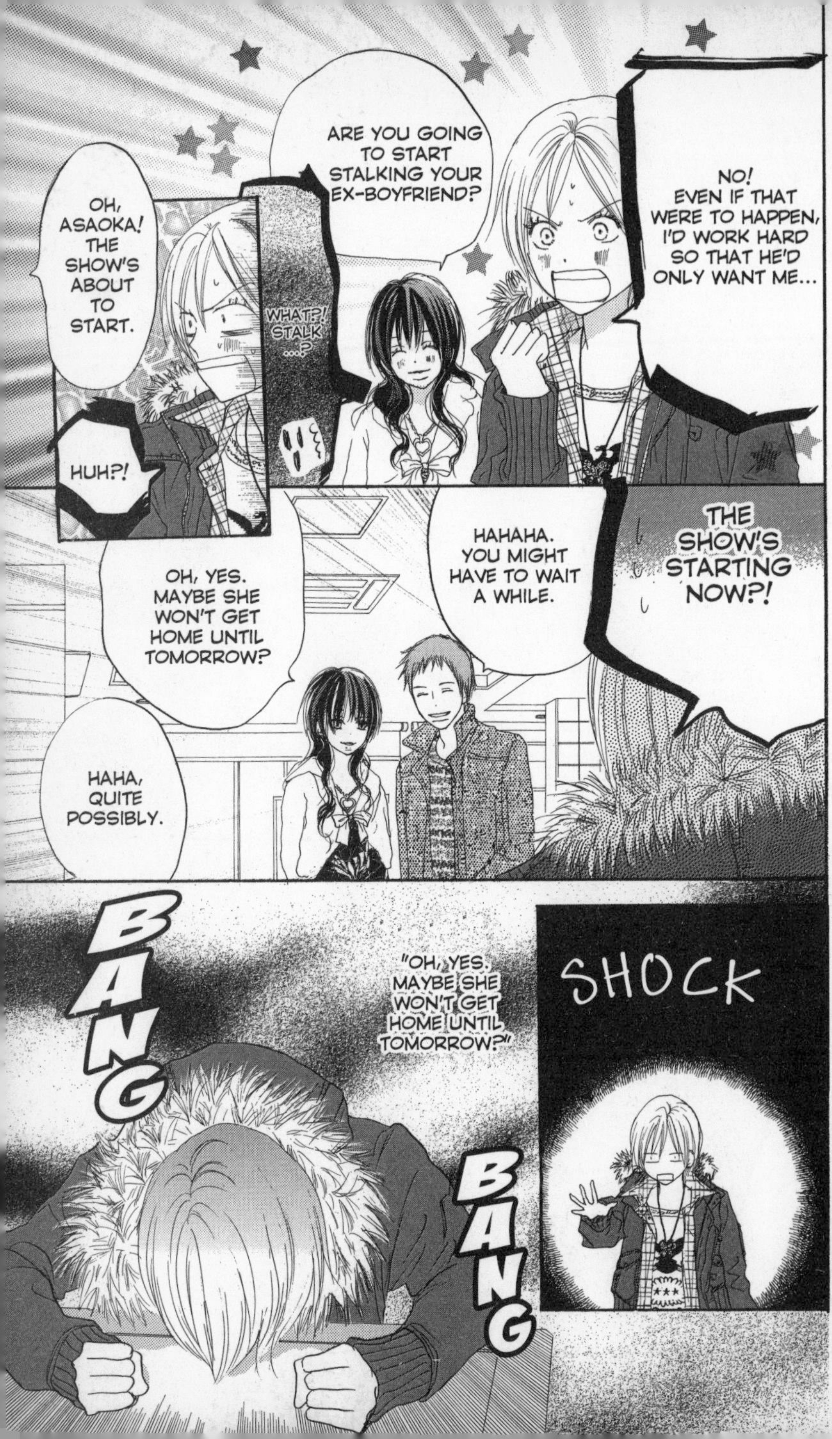
ARE YOU GOING TO START STALKING YOUR EX-BOYFRIEND?
NO! EVEN IF THAT WERE TO HAPPEN, I'D WORK HARD SO THAT HE'D ONLY WANT ME...
WHAT?! STALK ...?
OH, ASAOKA! THE SHOW'S ABOUT TO START.
HUH?!
THE SHOW'S STARTING NOW?!
HAHAHA. YOU MIGHT HAVE TO WAIT A WHILE.
OH, YES. MAYBE SHE WON'T GET HOME UNTIL TOMORROW?
HAHA, QUITE POSSIBLY.
SHOCK
"OH, YES. MAYBE SHE WON'T GET HOME UNTIL TOMORROW?"
BANG
BANG

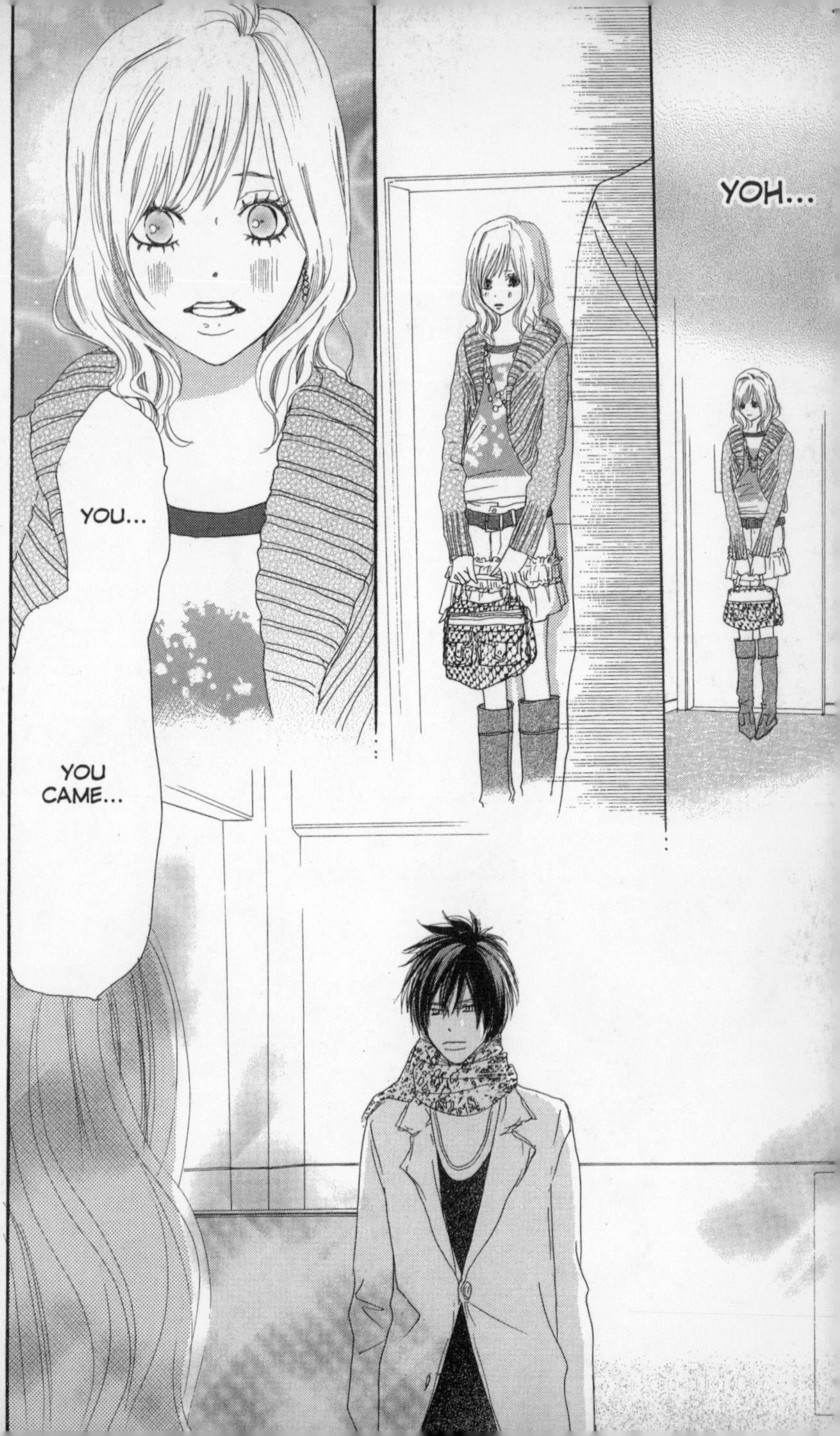
YOH...
YOU...
YOU CAME...

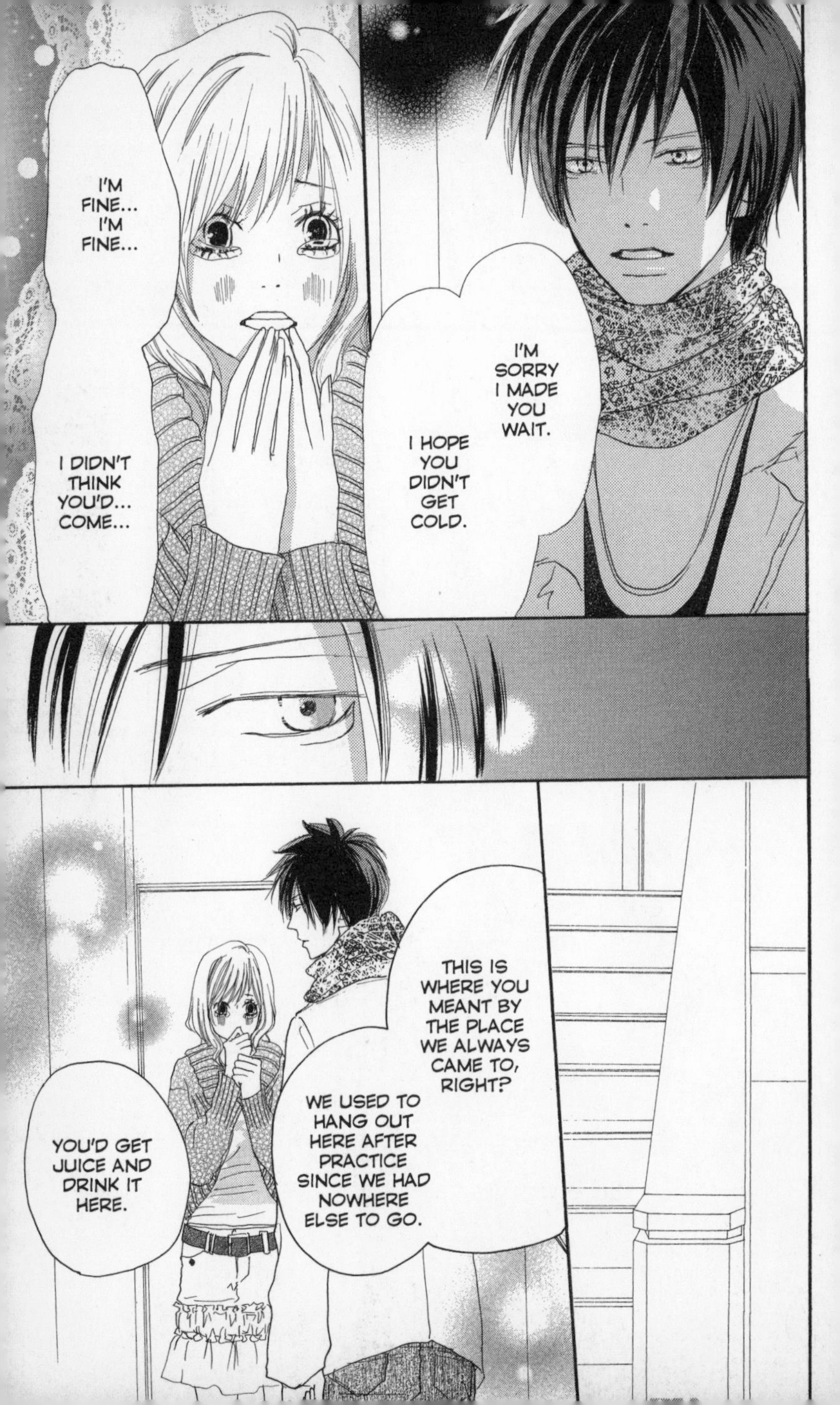
I'M SORRY I MADE YOU WAIT.
I HOPE YOU DIDN'T GET COLD.
I'M FINE... I'M FINE...
I DIDN'T THINK YOU'D... COME...
THIS IS WHERE YOU MEANT BY THE PLACE WE ALWAYS CAME TO, RIGHT?
WE USED TO HANG OUT HERE AFTER PRACTICE SINCE WE HAD NOWHERE ELSE TO GO.
YOU'D GET JUICE AND DRINK IT HERE.

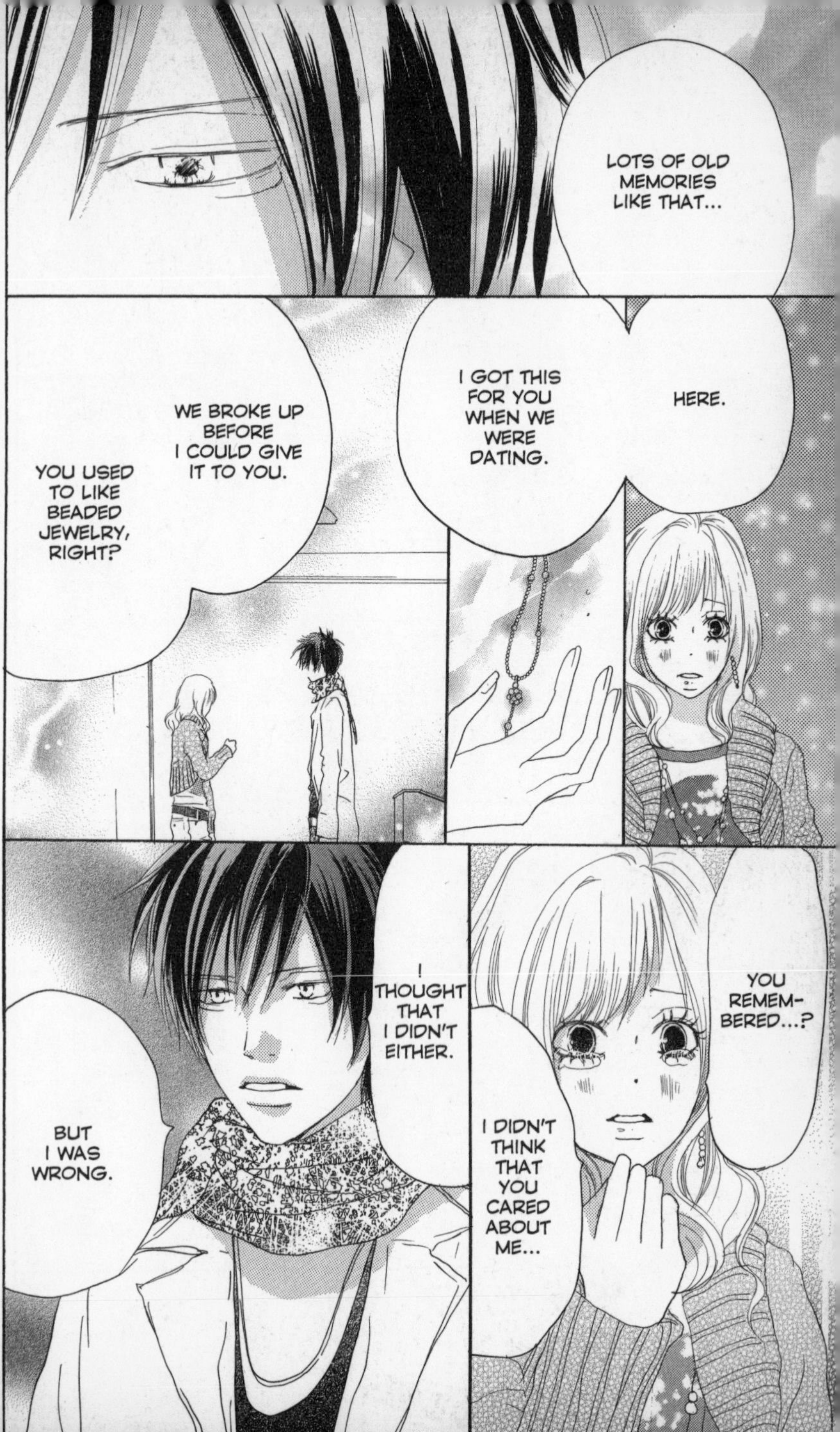
LOTS OF OLD MEMORIES LIKE THAT...
HERE.
I GOT THIS FOR YOU WHEN WE WERE DATING.
WE BROKE UP BEFORE I COULD GIVE IT TO YOU.
YOU USED TO LIKE BEADED JEWELRY, RIGHT?
YOU REMEM-BERED...?
I DIDN'T THINK THAT YOU CARED ABOUT ME...
I THOUGHT THAT I DIDN'T EITHER.
BUT I WAS WRONG.

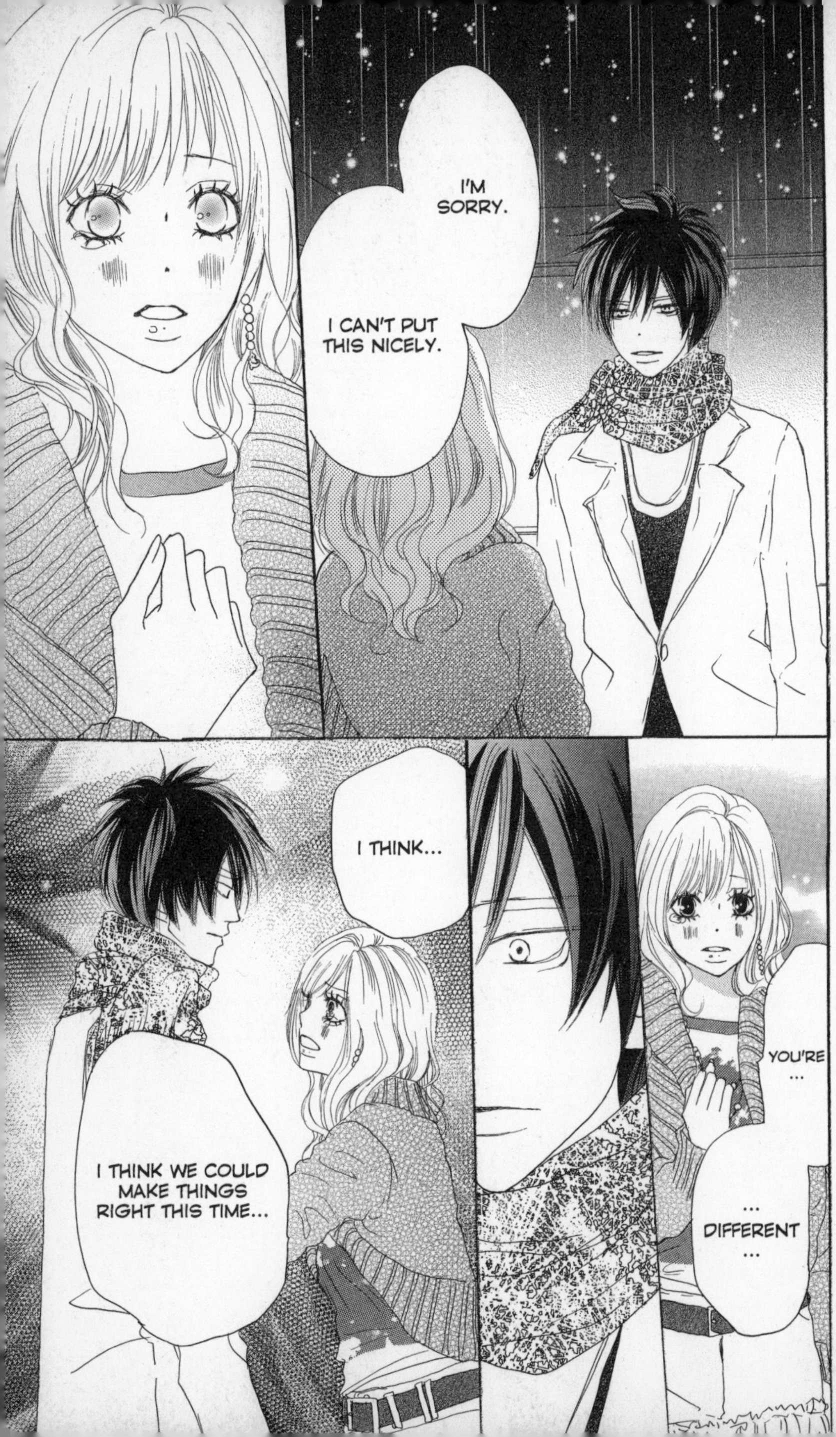
I'M SORRY.
I CAN'T PUT THIS NICELY.
YOU'RE ...
... DIFFERENT ...
I THINK...
I THINK WE COULD MAKE THINGS RIGHT THIS TIME...

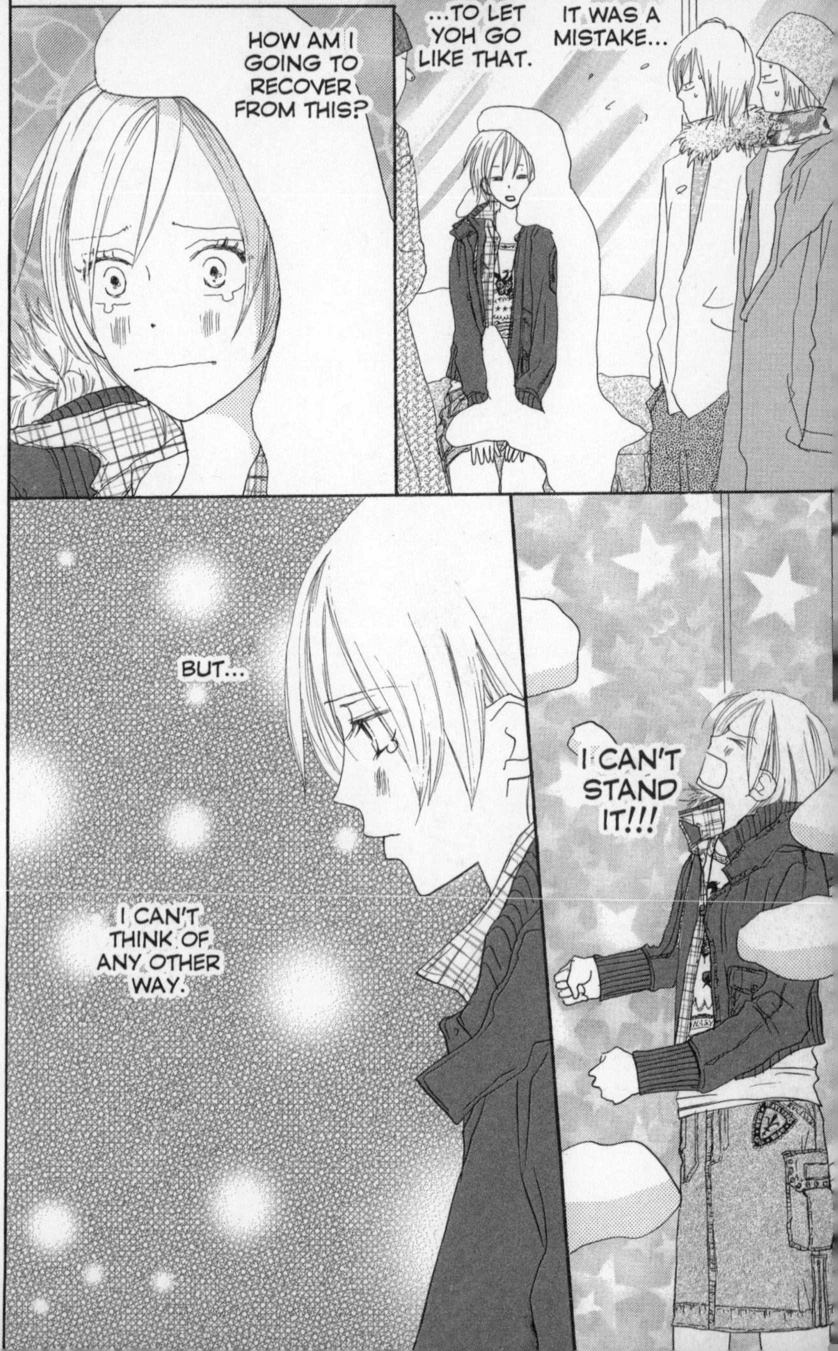
IT WAS A MISTAKE...
...TO LET YOH GO LIKE THAT.
HOW AM I GOING TO RECOVER FROM THIS?
I CAN'T STAND IT!!!
BUT...
I CAN'T THINK OF ANY OTHER WAY.

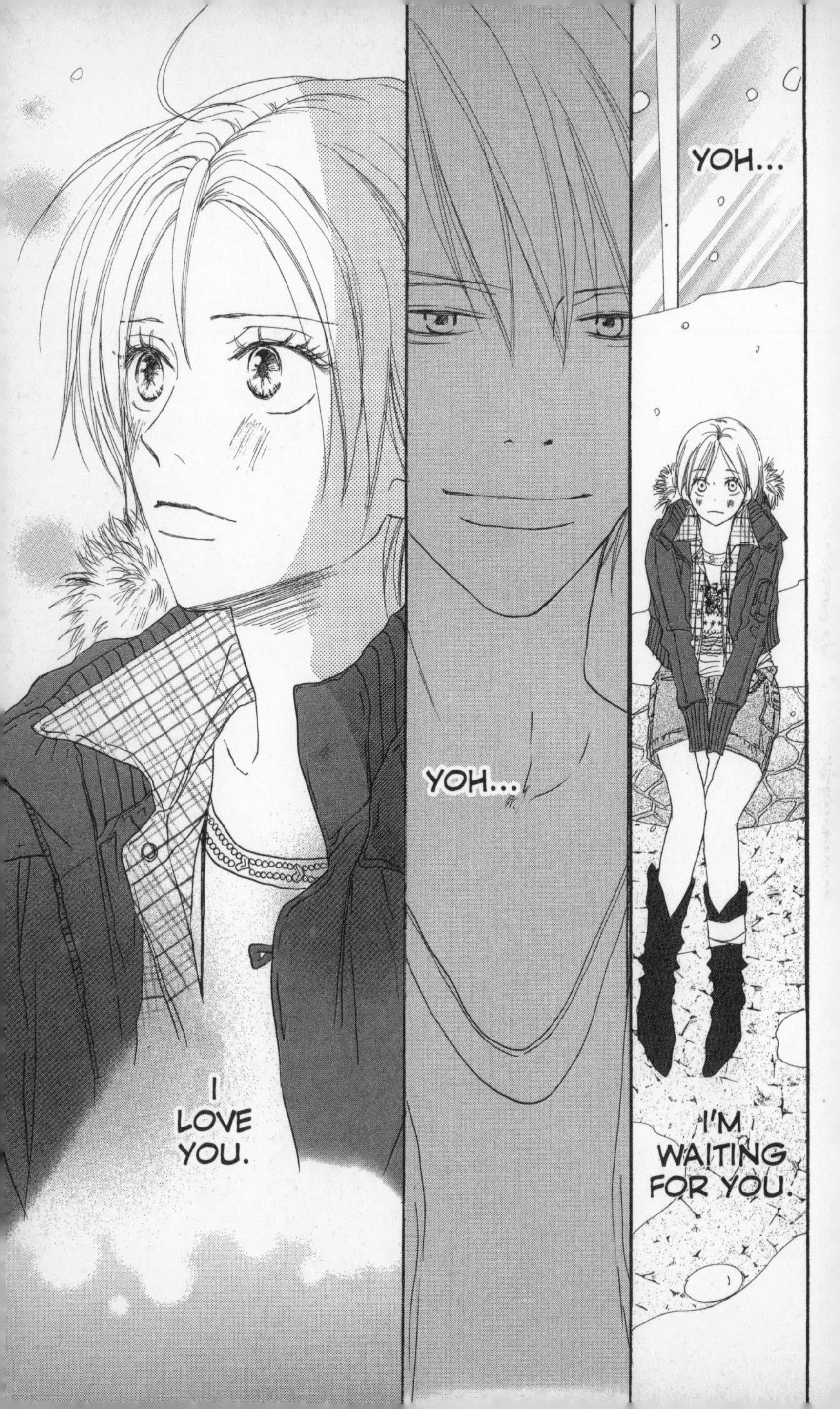
YOH...
I'M WAITING FOR YOU.
YOH...
I LOVE YOU.

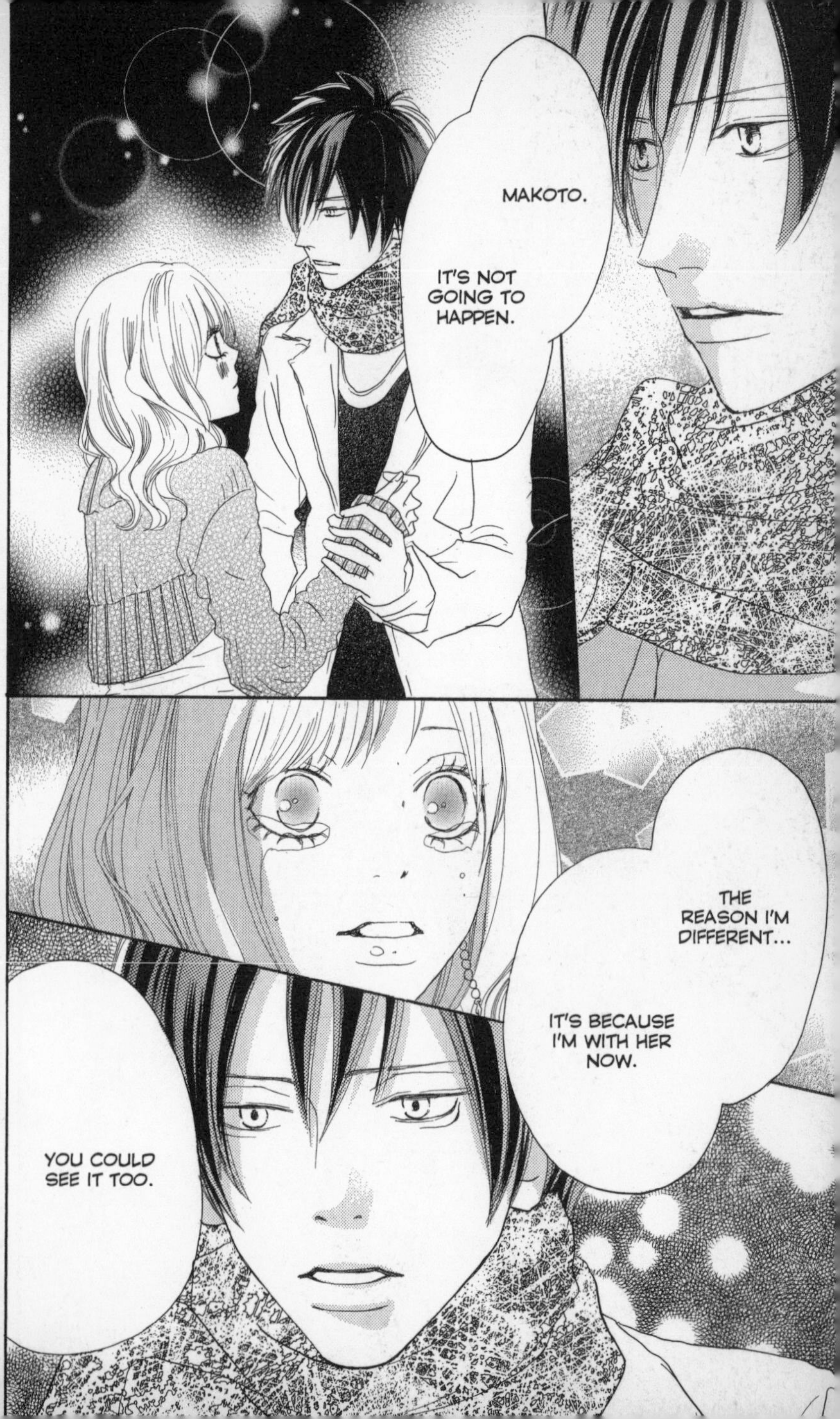
MAKOTO.
IT'S NOT GOING TO HAPPEN.
THE REASON I'M DIFFERENT...
IT'S BECAUSE I'M WITH HER NOW.
YOU COULD SEE IT TOO.

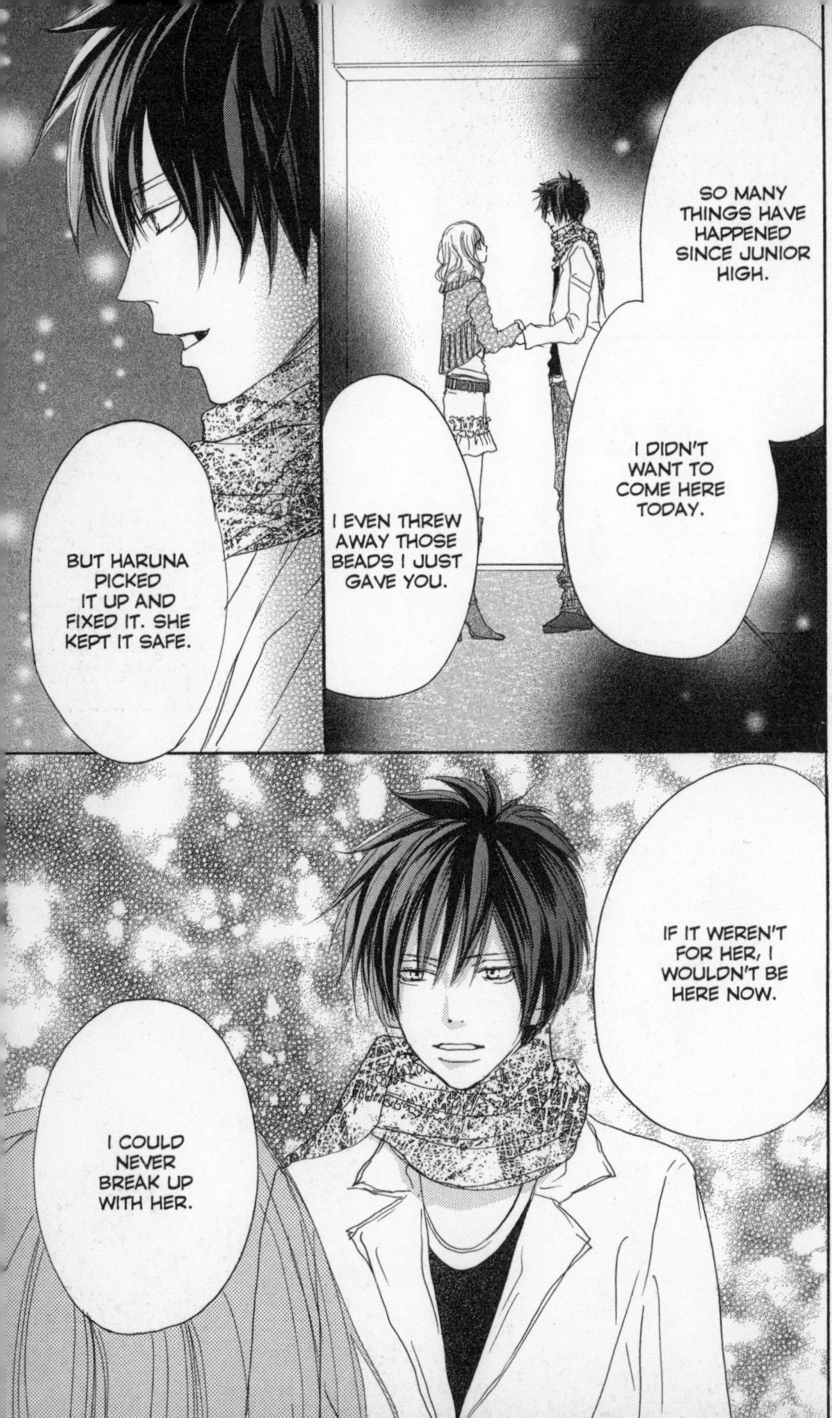
SO MANY THINGS HAVE HAPPENED SINCE JUNIOR HIGH.
I DIDN'T WANT TO COME HERE TODAY.
I EVEN THREW AWAY THOSE BEADS I JUST GAVE YOU.
BUT HARUNA PICKED IT UP AND FIXED IT. SHE KEPT IT SAFE.
IF IT WEREN'T FOR HER, I WOULDN'T BE HERE NOW.
I COULD NEVER BREAK UP WITH HER.

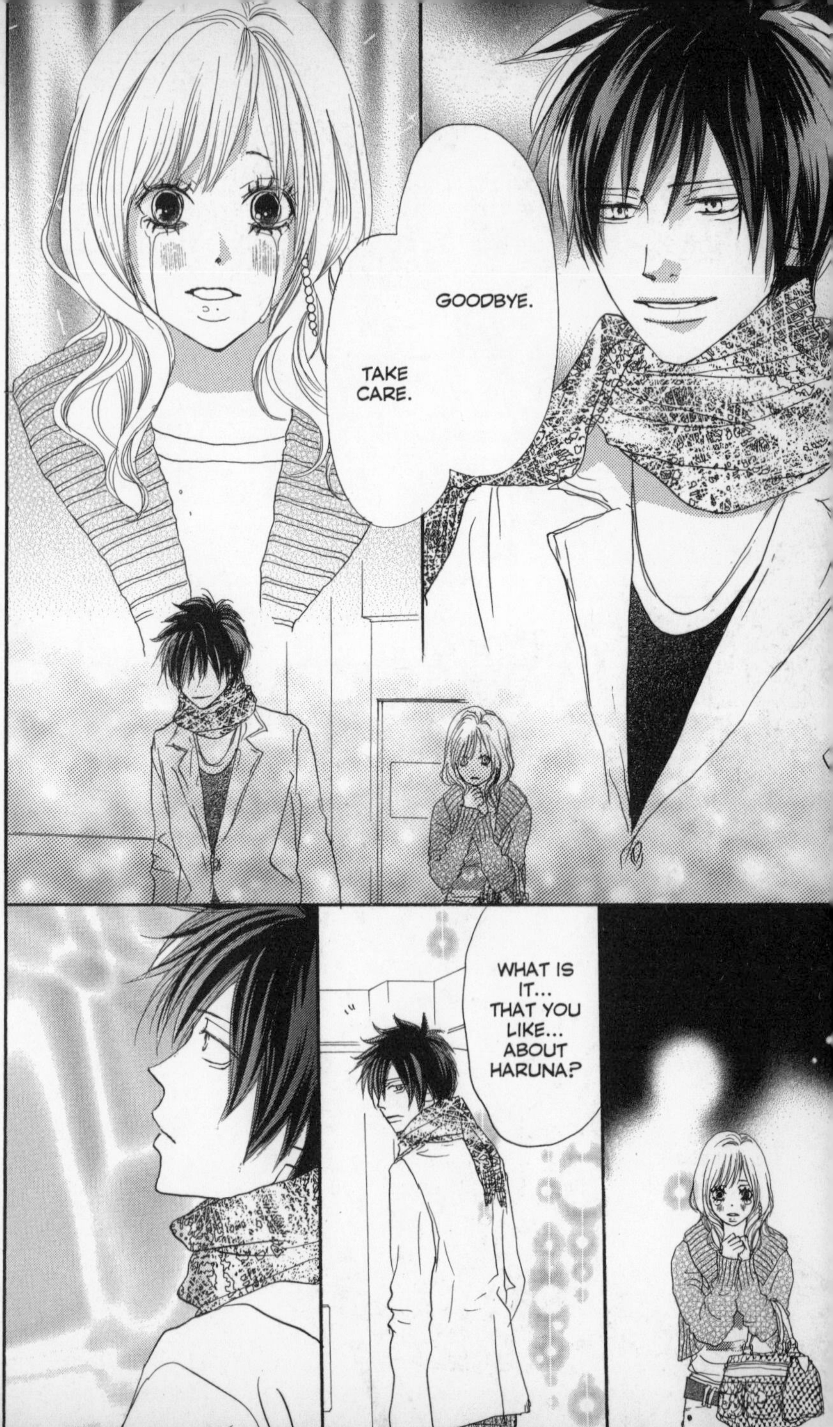
GOODBYE.
TAKE CARE.
WHAT IS IT... THAT YOU LIKE... ABOUT HARUNA?

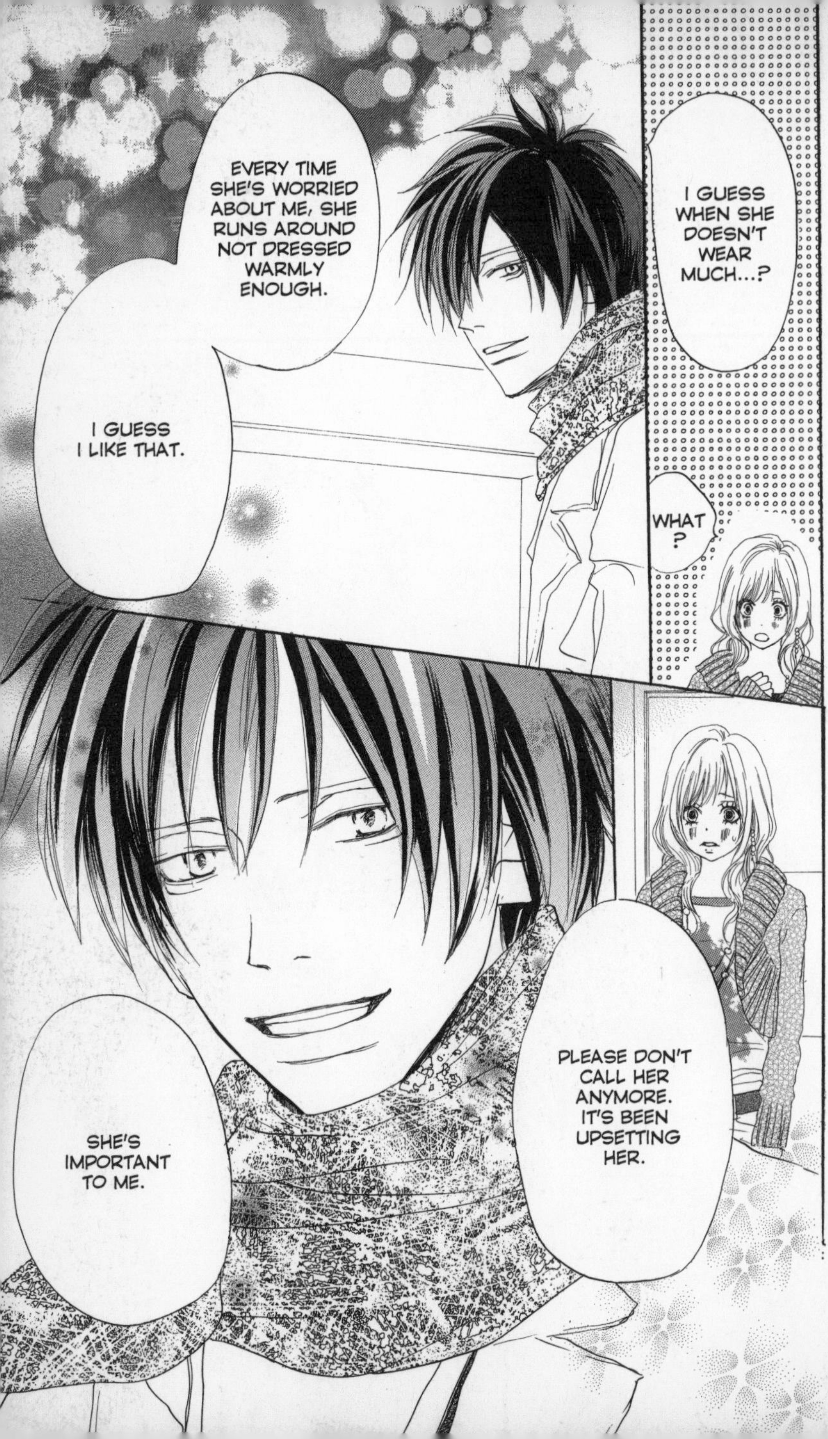
I GUESS WHEN SHE DOESN'T WEAR MUCH...?
WHAT?
EVERY TIME SHE'S WORRIED ABOUT ME, SHE RUNS AROUND NOT DRESSED WARMLY ENOUGH.
I GUESS I LIKE THAT.
PLEASE DON'T CALL HER ANYMORE. IT'S BEEN UPSETTING HER.
SHE'S IMPORTANT TO ME.

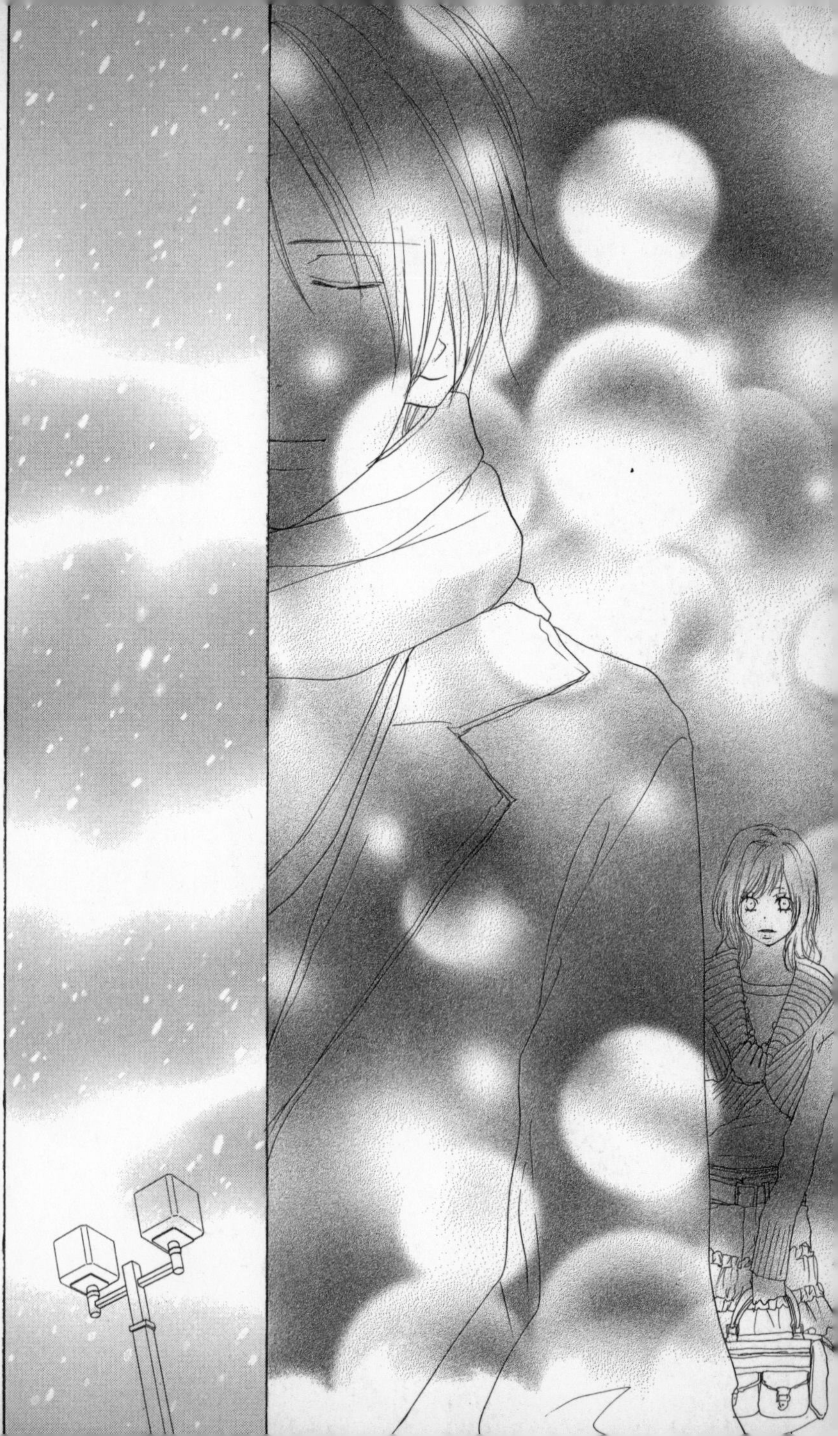

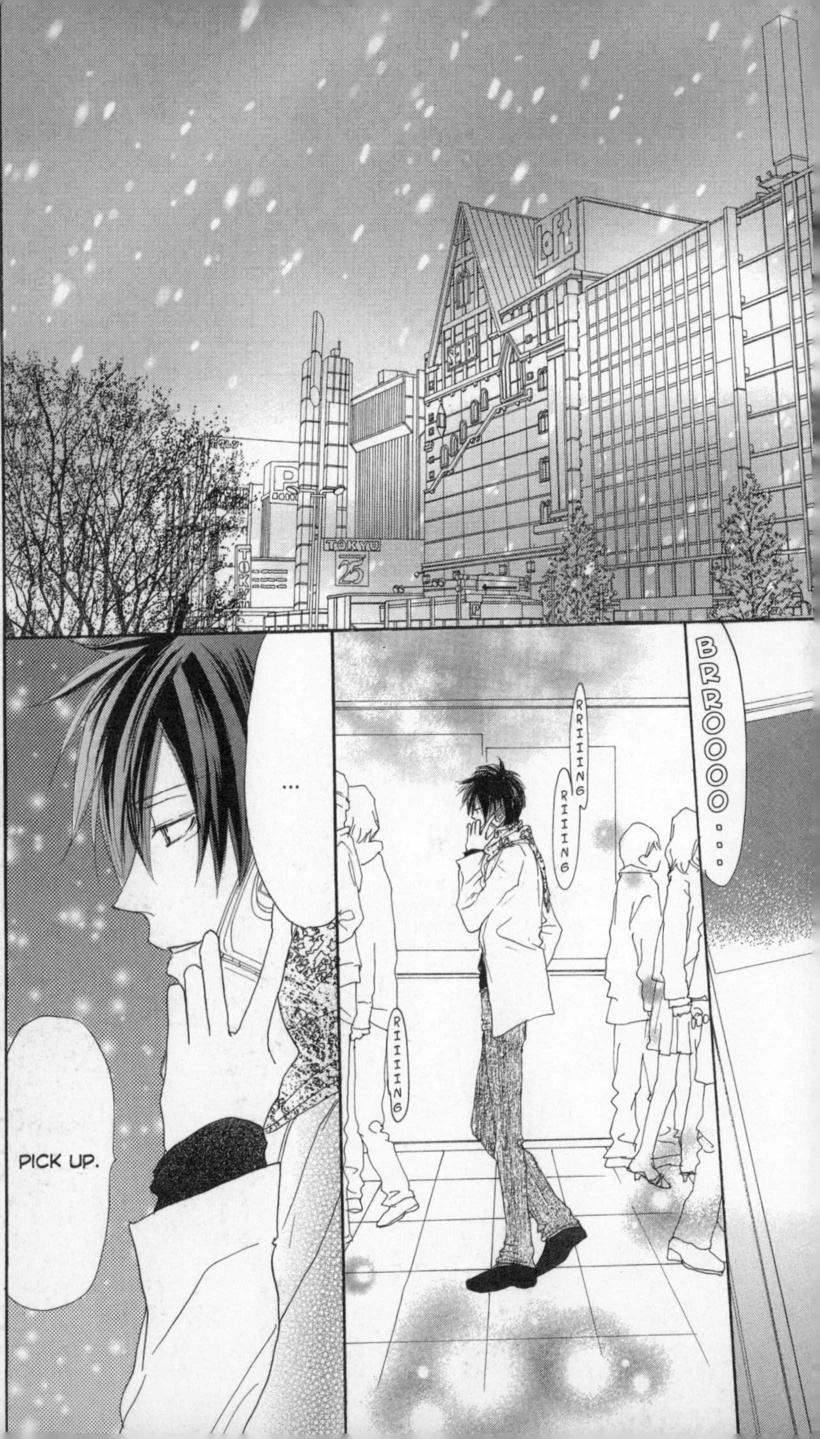
Loft
TOKYU
BRROOOO...
RIIIING
RIIIING
RIIIING
...
PICK UP.

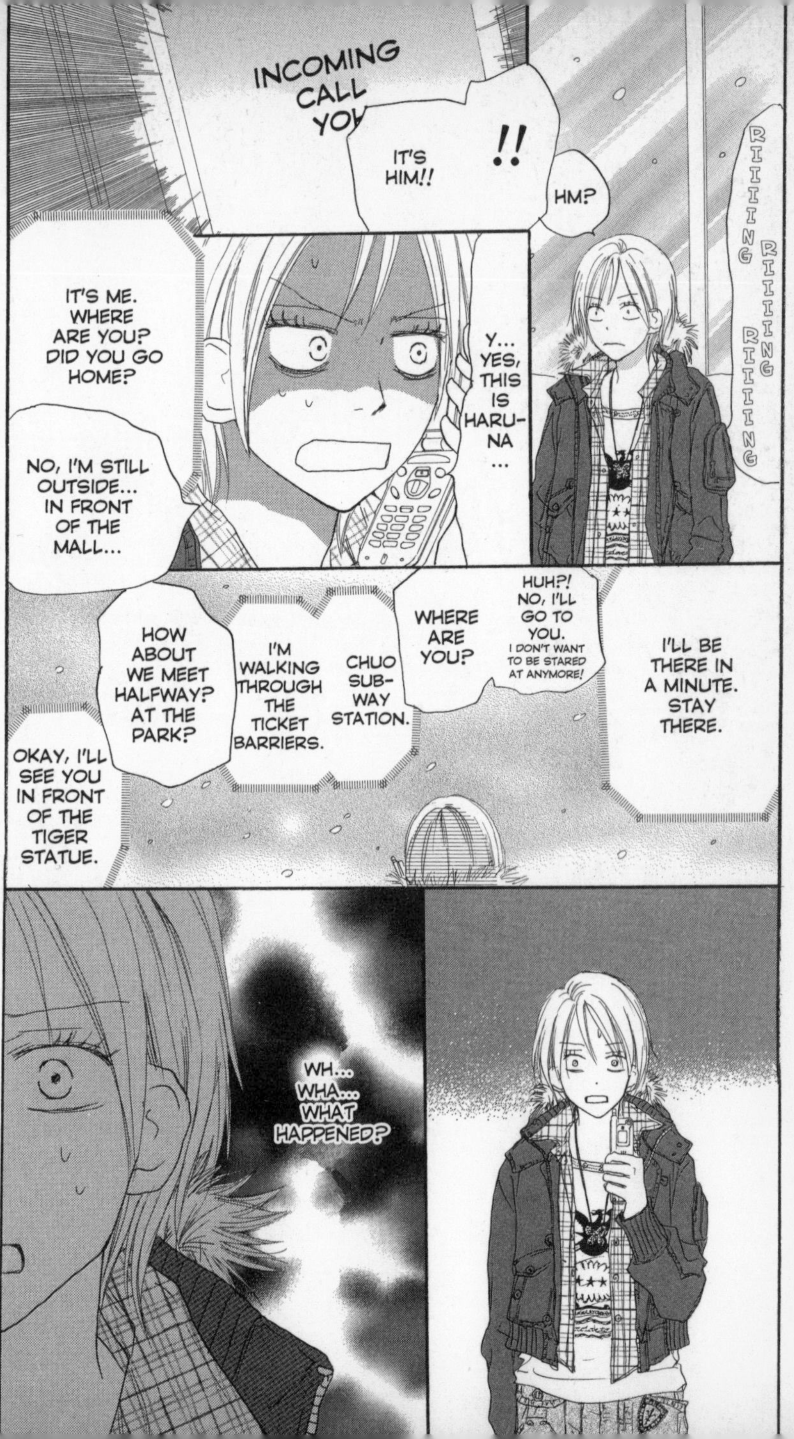
RIIIING
RIIIING
RIIIING
HM?
INCOMING CALL YO
!!
IT'S HIM!!
Y... YES, THIS IS HARUNA...
IT'S ME. WHERE ARE YOU? DID YOU GO HOME?
NO, I'M STILL OUTSIDE... IN FRONT OF THE MALL...
I'LL BE THERE IN A MINUTE. STAY THERE.
HUH?! NO, I'LL GO TO YOU. I DON'T WANT TO BE STARED AT ANYMORE!
WHERE ARE YOU?
CHUO SUBWAY STATION.
I'M WALKING THROUGH THE TICKET BARRIERS.
HOW ABOUT WE MEET HALFWAY? AT THE PARK?
OKAY, I'LL SEE YOU IN FRONT OF THE TIGER STATUE.
WH... WHA... WHAT HAPPENED?

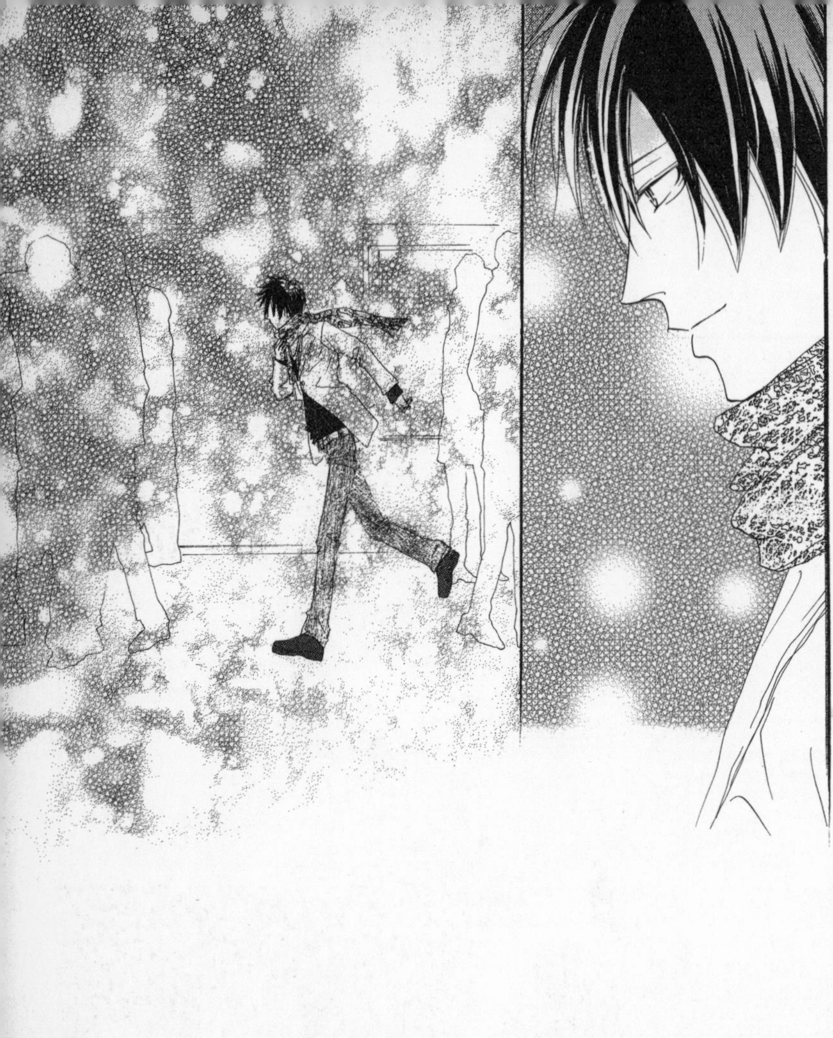

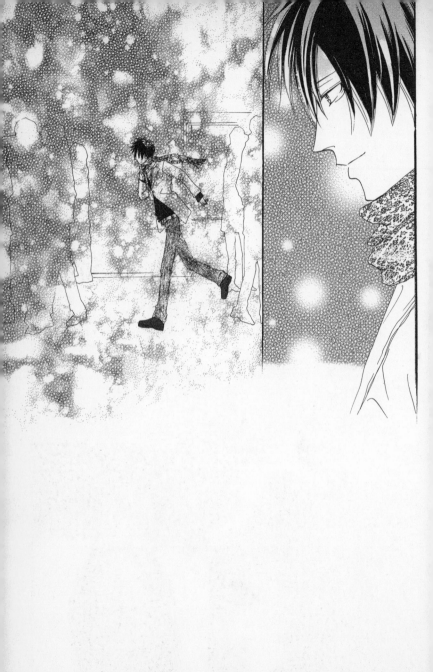

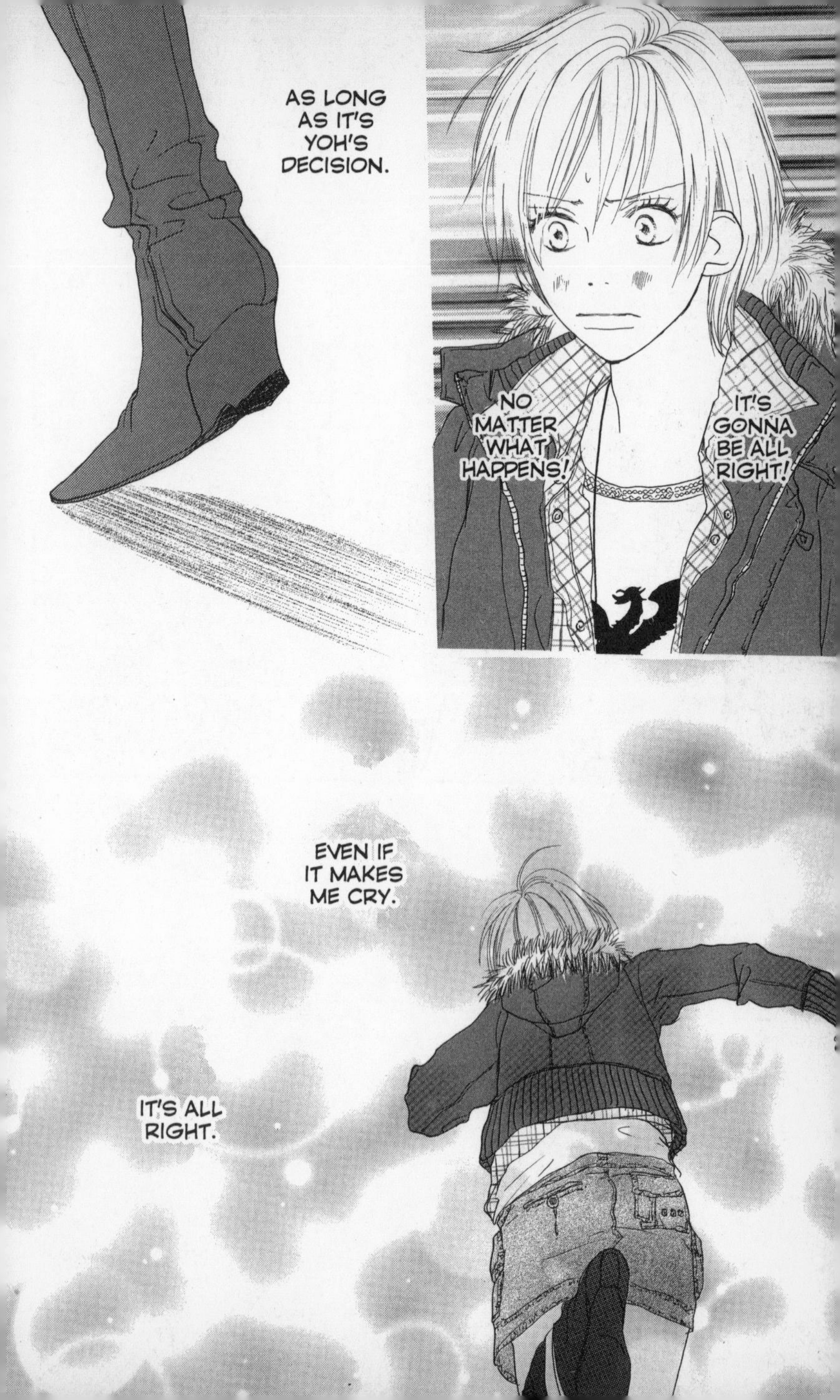
IT'S GONNA BE ALL RIGHT!
NO MATTER WHAT HAPPENS!
AS LONG AS IT'S YOH'S DECISION.
EVEN IF IT MAKES ME CRY.
IT'S ALL RIGHT.

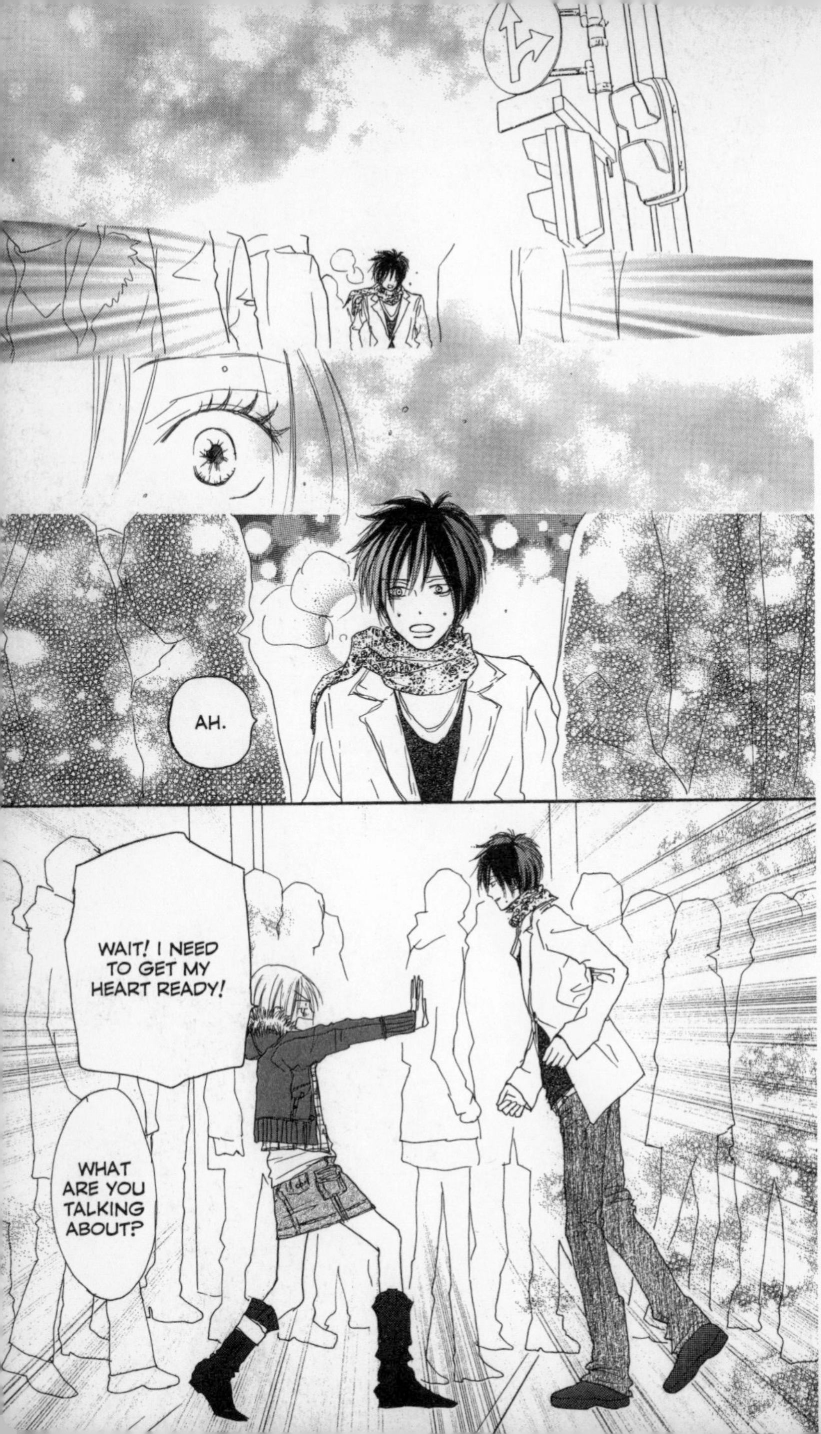
AH.
WAIT! I NEED TO GET MY HEART READY!
WHAT ARE YOU TALKING ABOUT?

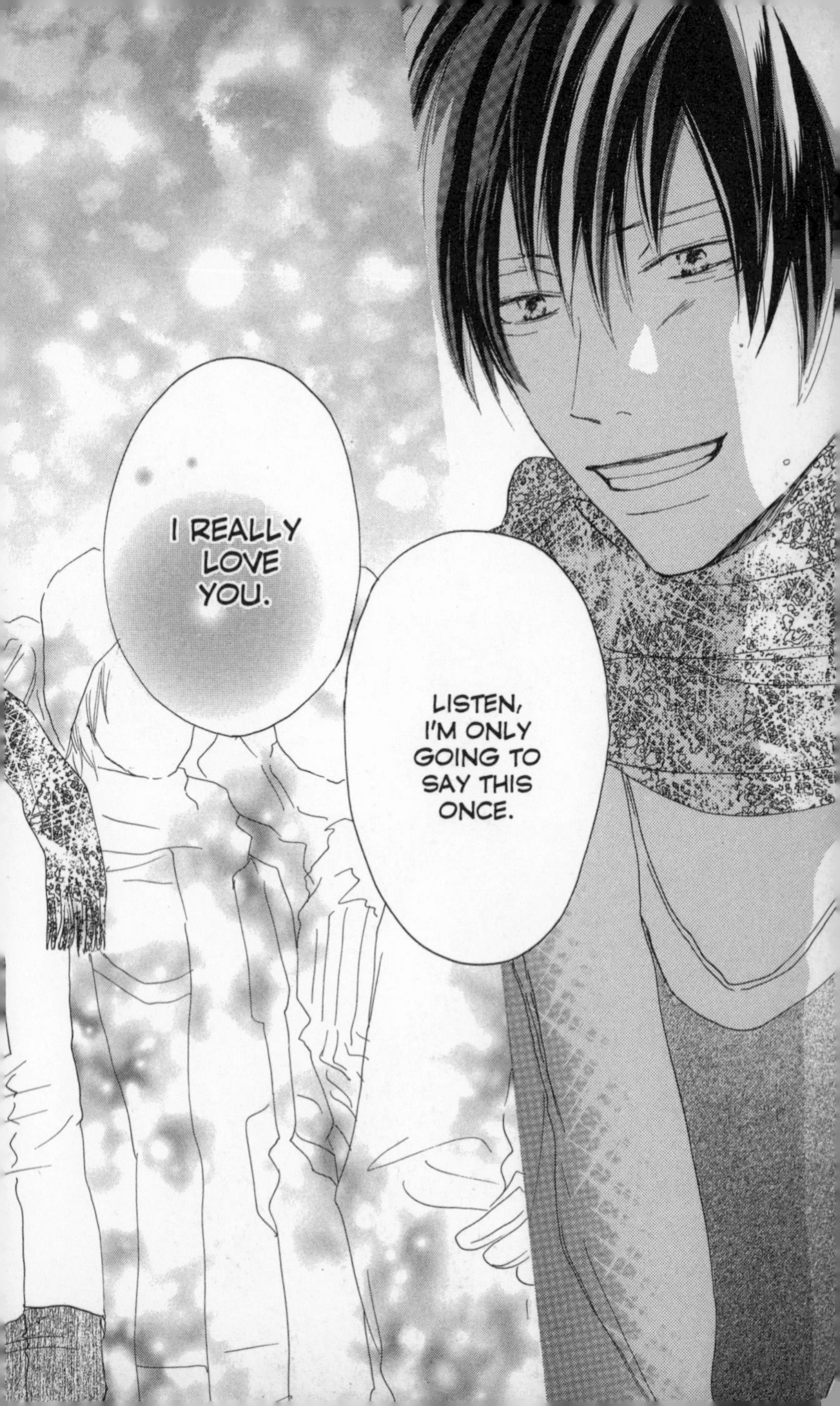
LISTEN, I'M ONLY GOING TO SAY THIS ONCE.
I REALLY LOVE YOU.

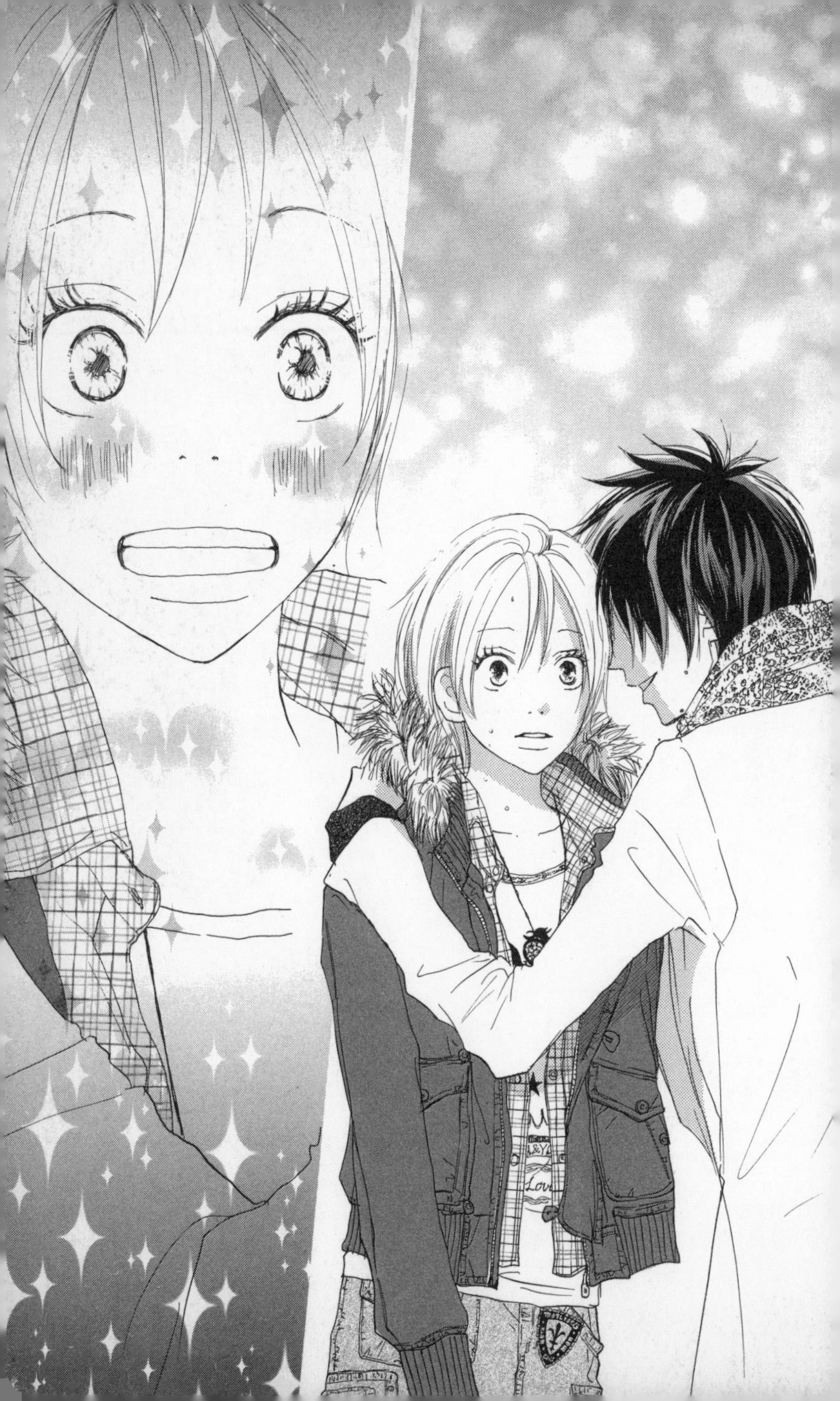

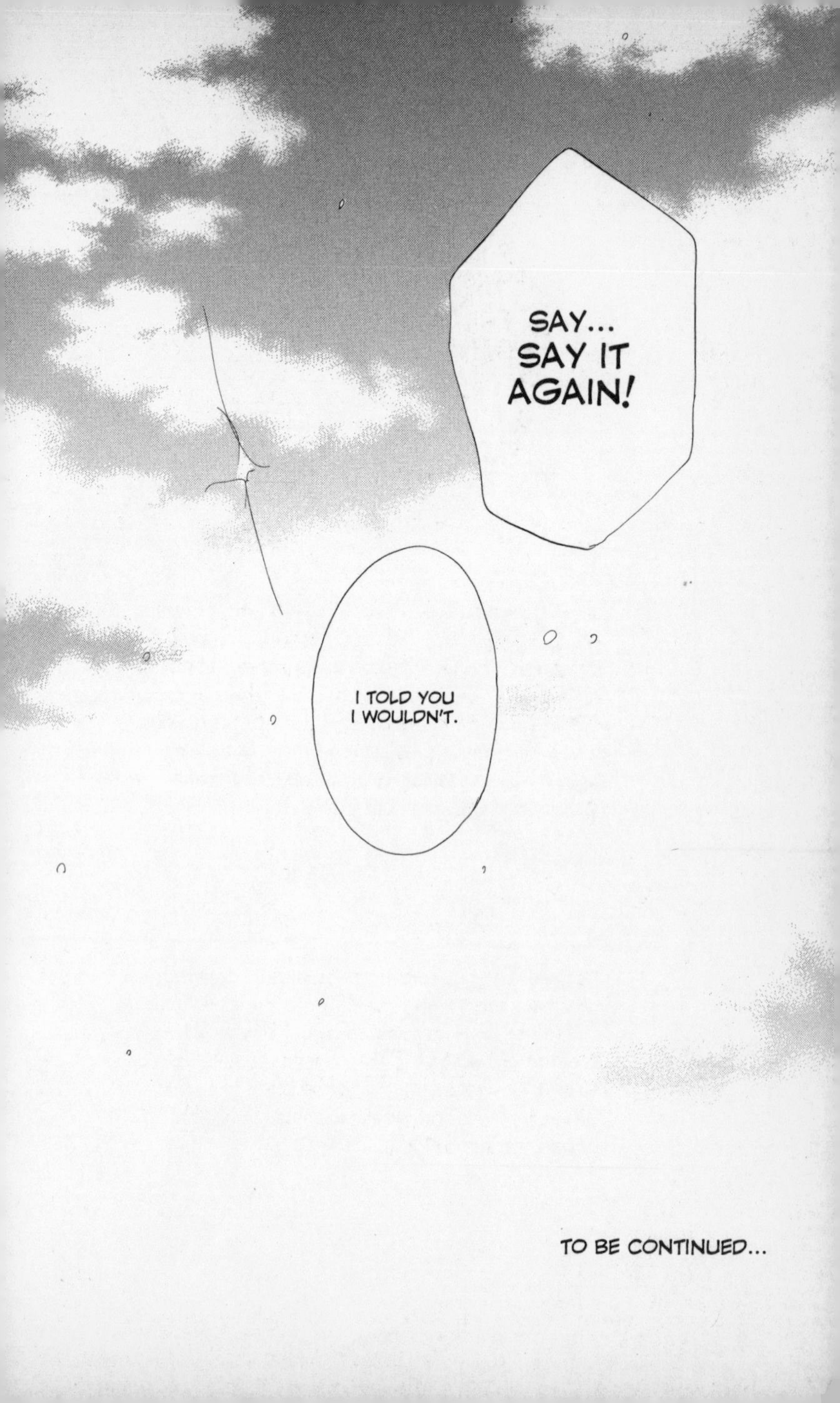
SAY... SAY IT AGAIN!
I TOLD YOU I WOULDN'T.
TO BE CONTINUED...

My CD player keeps breaking without warning.
My CD player, my videogame console, my
computer—none of them work properly. I do
my work on the computer and then burn it on a
CD to send to my editor, so I get really nervous
when my computer is acting funny. But every
time I think of buying a new one, it suddenly
starts working fine again. Odd.

– Kazune Kawahara

Kazune Kawahara is from Hokkaido prefecture
and was born on March 11th (a Pisces!). She
made her manga debut at age 18 with *Kare no
Ichiban Sukina Hito* (His Most Favorite Person).
Her other works include *Sensei!*, serialized in
Bessatsu Margaret magazine. Her hobby is
interior redecorating.

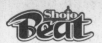

HIGH SCHOOL DEBUT
VOL. 6
The Shojo Beat Manga Edition

STORY & ART BY
KAZUNE KAWAHARA

Translation & Adaptation/Gemma Collinge
Touch-up Art & Lettering/HudsonYards
Design/Izumi Hirayama
Editor/Amy Yu

Editor in Chief, Books/Alvin Lu
Editor in Chief, Magazines/Marc Weidenbaum
VP of Publishing Licensing/Rika Inouye
VP of Sales/Gonzalo Ferreyra
Sr. VP of Marketing/Liza Coppola
Publisher/Hyoe Narita

Printed in Canada

Published by VIZ Media, LLC
P.O. Box 77010
San Francisco, CA 94107

Shojo Beat Manga Edition
10 9 8 7 6 5 4 3 2 1
First printing, November 2008

www.viz.com

store.viz.com

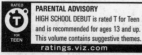

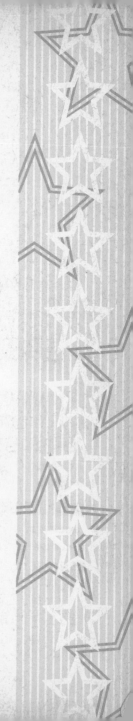

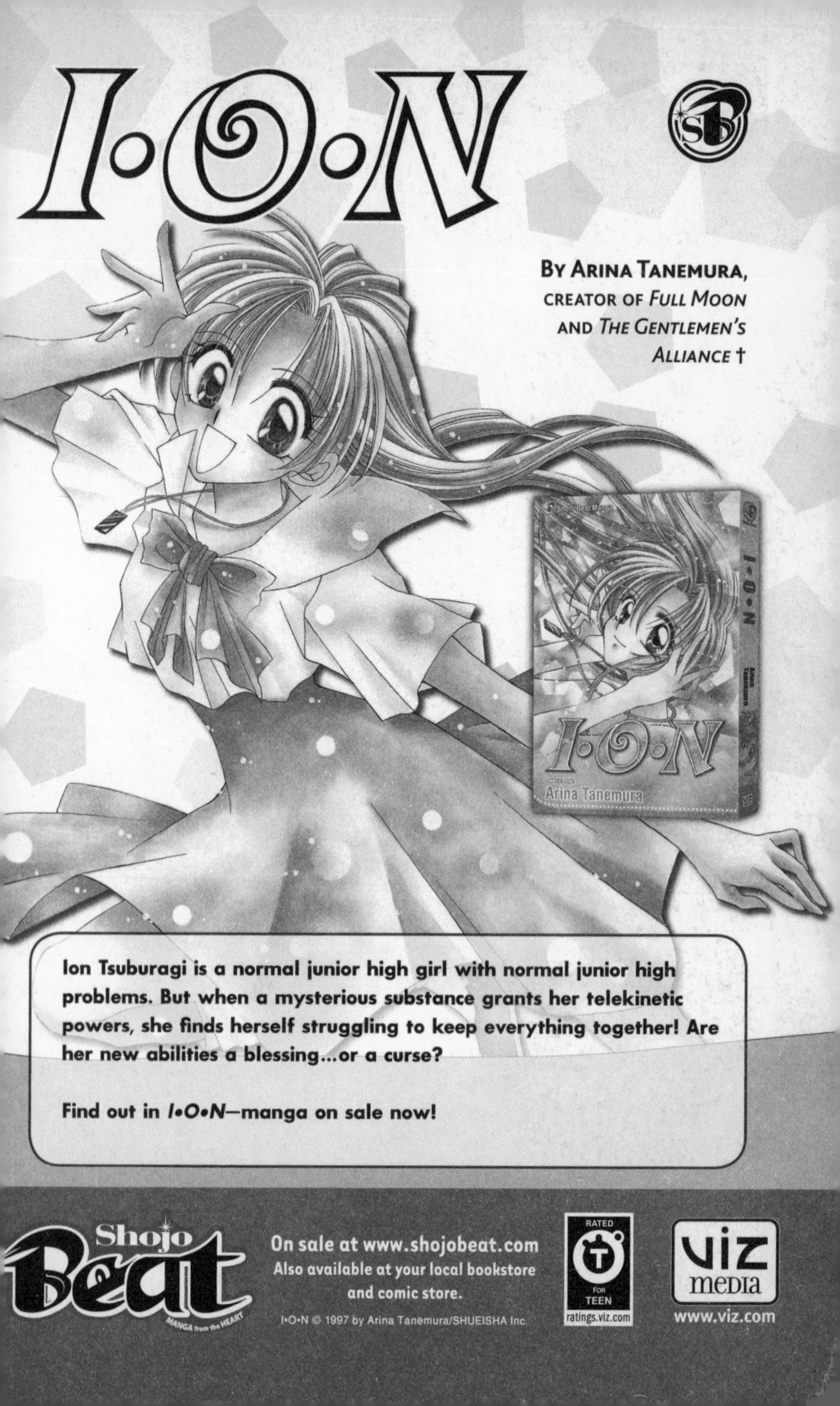
I•O•N
By Arina Tanemura, creator of *Full Moon* and *The Gentlemen's Alliance* †
Shojo Beat Manga
I•O•N
Arina Tanemura
Ion Tsuburagi is a normal junior high girl with normal junior high problems. But when a mysterious substance grants her telekinetic powers, she finds herself struggling to keep everything together! Are her new abilities a blessing...or a curse?
Find out in *I•O•N*—manga on sale now!
Shojo Beat
MANGA from the HEART
On sale at www.shojobeat.com
Also available at your local bookstore and comic store.
I•O•N © 1997 by Arina Tanemura/SHUEISHA Inc.
RATED
T
FOR TEEN
ratings.viz.com
viz media
www.viz.com

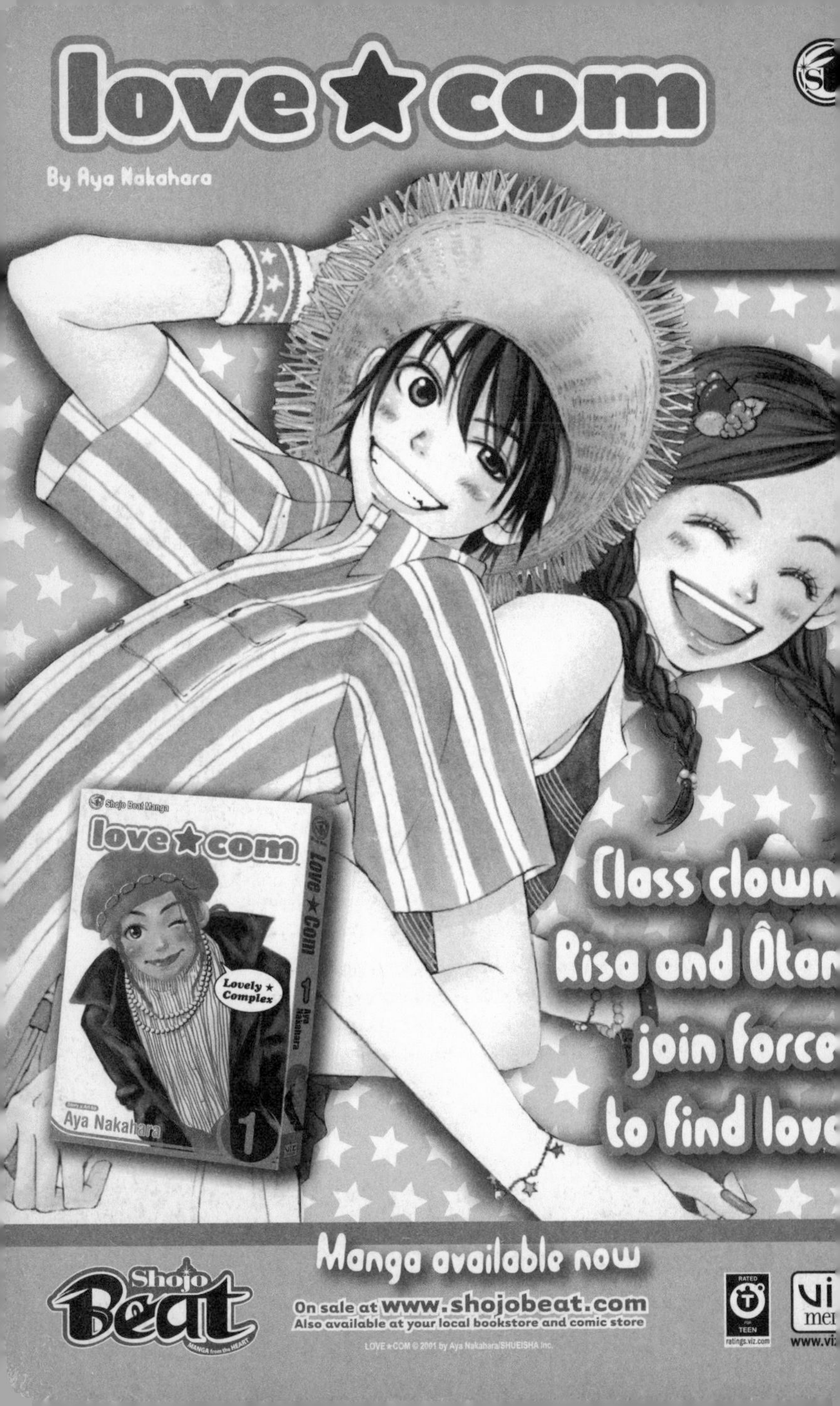
love★com
By Aya Nakahara
Shojo Beat Manga
love★com
Lovely ★ Complex
Aya Nakahara
Class clown
Risa and Ôtar
join force
to find love
Manga available now
Shojo Beat
On sale at www.shojobeat.com
Also available at your local bookstore and comic store
LOVE★COM © 2001 by Aya Nakahara/SHUEISHA Inc.
RATED T TEEN
ratings.viz.com

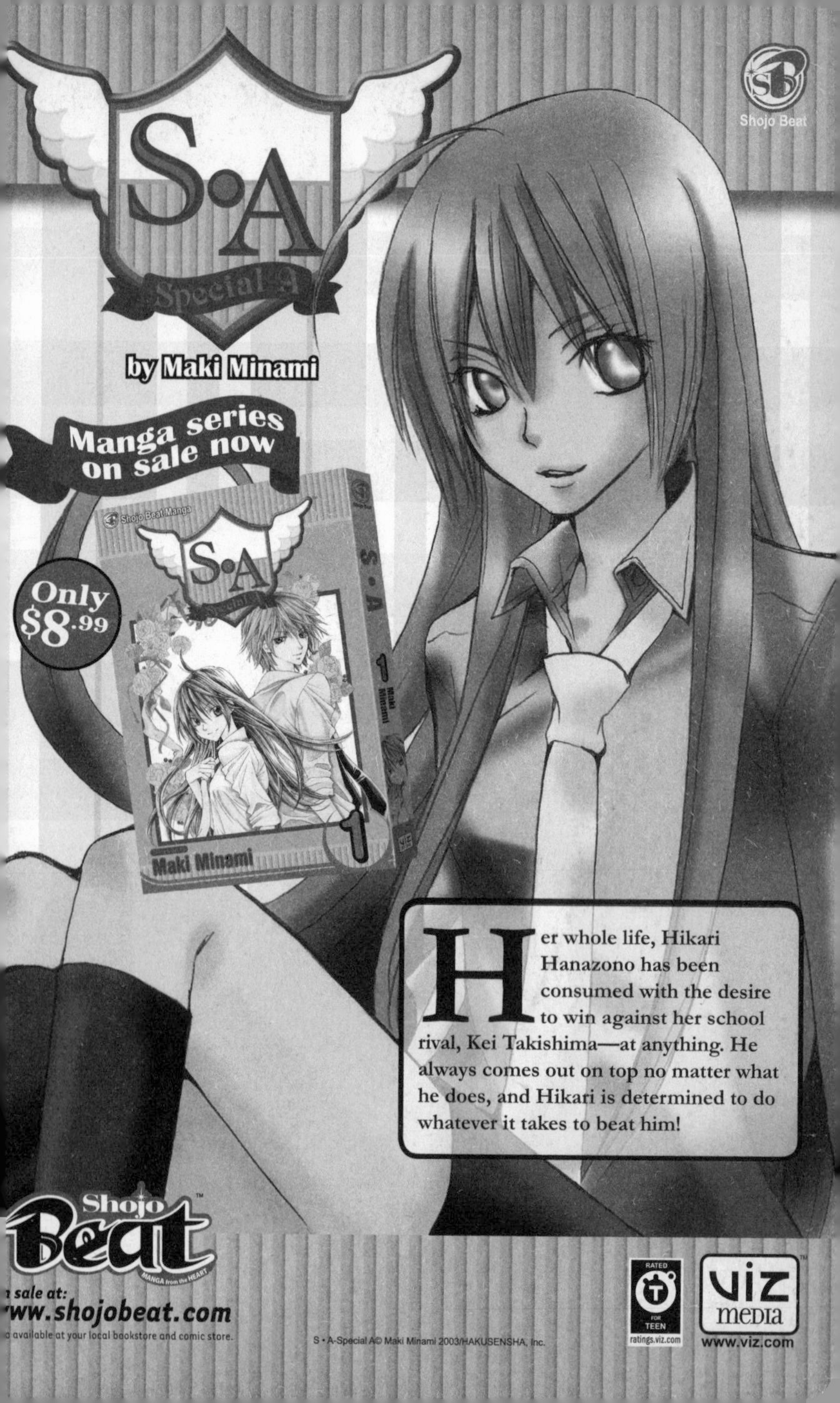

Shojo Beat
S•A
Special A
by Maki Minami
Manga series on sale now
Only $8.99
Shojo Beat Manga
S•A
1
Maki Minami
Her whole life, Hikari Hanazono has been consumed with the desire to win against her school rival, Kei Takishima—at anything. He always comes out on top no matter what he does, and Hikari is determined to do whatever it takes to beat him!
Shojo Beat™
MANGA from the HEART
n sale at:
ww.shojobeat.com
o available at your local bookstore and comic store.
S • A-Special A © Maki Minami 2003/HAKUSENSHA, Inc.
RATED T FOR TEEN
ratings.viz.com
VIZ MEDIA
www.viz.com

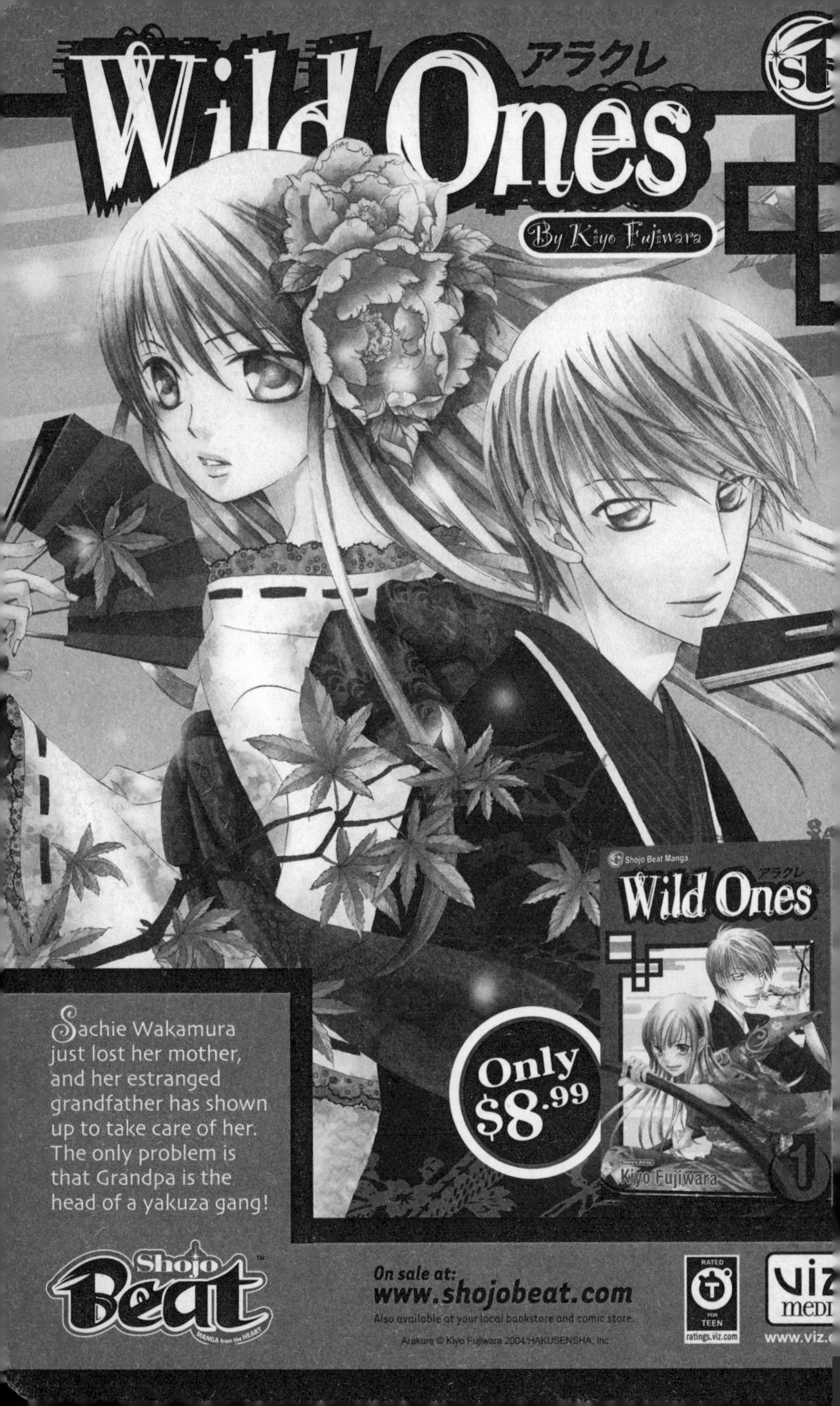

Wild Ones
アラクレ
By Kiyo Fujiwara
Sachie Wakamura just lost her mother, and her estranged grandfather has shown up to take care of her. The only problem is that Grandpa is the head of a yakuza gang!
Only $8.99
Shojo Beat Manga
Wild Ones
アラクレ
Kiyo Fujiwara
1
Shojo Beat
MANGA from the HEART
On sale at:
www.shojobeat.com
Also available at your local bookstore and comic store.
Arakure © Kiyo Fujiwara 2004/HAKUSENSHA, Inc.
RATED
T
FOR TEEN
ratings.viz.com